RAGS make paper,
PAPER makes money,
MONEY makes banks,
BANKS make loans,
LOANS make beggars,
BEGGARS make rags.
(unknown 18th century author)

The
Comprehensive Catalog
of

U.S.
PAPER MONEY

All United States Federal Currency
Since 1812

Sixth Edition

Gene Hessler

Library of Congress Cataloging in Publication Data

Hessler, Gene, 1928–

The comprehensive catalog of U.S. paper money.
Bibliography: p.
Includes index.
1. Paper Money United States. 2. Paper Money Catalogs. I. Title.
Copyright © 1974, 1977, 1980, 1983, 1992, 1997
All rights reserved
Published by BNR Press
132 East Second Street, Port Clinton, Ohio 43452,(419)734-6683,
(800) 793-0683, FAX (419)732-6683, (800) 793-0683
Manufactured in the United States
Library of Congress Catalog Number: 82-72745
International Standard Book Number: soft bound 0-931960-50-9
hard bound 0-931960-51-7
American Numismatic Association Library Catalog Number: US40.H4 1983

Books by Gene Hessler:

An Illustrated History of U.S. Loans
The Comprehensive Catalog of U.S. Paper Money
The Engraver's Line, an Encyclopedia of Paper Money and Postage Stamps
U.S. Essay, Proof and Specimen Notes

Contents

Foreword

Gene Hessler and I were first introduced at the Bureau of Engraving and Printing (BEP) in the early 1970s. I was struggling at the beginning of a ten-year apprenticeship in bank note and postage stamp engraving techniques. Gene and his colleague, the late Dr. Glenn Jackson, were trying to make sense of the then scattered materials in our archives. Gene's interest and extensive knowledge of the history and lineage of engravers in the United States bank note industry far exceeded that of the men in the industry who were training me. Now, nearly a quarter-of-a-century later, his book, *The Engraver's Line*, is the essential reference on that subject.

I am now in the position of training new apprentices at the BEP. We have a Historical Resource Center with a trained staff to aid researchers. The fifth edition of Gene's *Comprehensive Catalog of U.S. Paper Money* is housed in the Center and is packed full of bookmarks, adhesive note pads and slips of paper. It sits not on a bookshelf, but on the curator's desk, serving as a quick first-reference for answers to numismatic inquiries from both staff and the general public. More than simply detailing lists of objects, Gene's writing reflects his life-long interest and insight into the craft of producing engraved securities and the people involved.

The major aspect of my own involvment in the craft that has garnered public recognition to this point has been engraving postage stamps. Now a portrait of Benjamin Franklin that I engraved has been selected for use on the face of the new $100 Federal Reserve note, and I, at long last, have become intimately involved in a "New Currency Design Program." I was surprised to learn that a larger size, asymmetrically-positioned portrait, so common in worldwide currency design, is considered to be a radical change here in the U.S. Every aspect of a design is questioned, and any aesthetic change without a corresponding security rationale is summarily rejected. Generations of engravers, chronicled by Gene in *The Engraver's Line*, have worked their entire careers and retired since Charles Burt, Alfred Sealey, John Eissler and G.F.C. Smillie engraved the portraits that became the definitive *icons* on our paper money. Generations of Americans have grown up looking at and living with these familiar images. If this constant utility in billions of repetitions were not enough, they are incorporated everywhere in art and advertising. This universal recognition factor is not lightly dismissed. Marketing analysis of proposed changes in the past always generated the same comment--any new of different design looks like "Monopoly Money."

Nevertheless, 1996 marks the beginning of production in the first contemplated overall change in U.S. currency in 60 years. In a process dominated by politics, bureaucracy and focus groups, a decision to effect change has been made and the first steps have been taken. The public seems to accept the idea. This is good news for all of us.

Gene's catalog reflects this initial currency change, and with more to come, it might be necessary to update this publication more often to remain "comprehensive."

Thomas R. Hipschen
Chief Engraver
The U.S. Bureau of Engraving and Printing

Foreword to the Fifth Edition

The American Numismatic Association's Library copy of *The Comprehensive Catalog of U.S. Paper Money*, fourth edition, 1983, is worn and tattered. This condition is not from age, but rather because it is one of the most popular reference works on U.S. currency in the ANA's Resource Center. There is a copy of the same edition of the *Catalog* in the ANA library stacks immediately behind the librarian's desk. I know, as I often go to the library either to use it as a reference or to borrow it.

Indeed, Gene's *Catalog* is comprehensive. It begins with an extensive history of paper money, offers descriptions and illustrations of types of U.S. paper money, and ultimately examines, in-depth and by denomination, all types of U.S. federal paper money since 1812. It is a veritable treasure. I referred the producers of "Making a Dishonest Buck," a March 1992 NOVA Public Broadcasting System television documentary on counterfeiting, to *The Comprehensive Catalog of U.S. Paper Money* as the most concise and best presentation for reference and background purposes.

This new edition of *The Comprehensive Catalog of U.S. Paper Money* is again designed for easy use by the experienced syngraphist (a collector of paper money), the emerging collector and anyone in need of a great resource. In fact, any researcher will be caught by the layout and interesting facts and be led to study or peruse the *Catalog*'s other sections.

Gene Hessler is well-known to readers of *The Numismatist*, both as a columnist and a contributing editor. Gene received the 1991 first place award for Foreign Paper Money and the prestigious Howland Wood Award at the Centennial Convention of the American Numismatic Association held in Chicago for his Best of Show Exhibit, "Max Svabinsky Czechoslovak Designer, His Complete Works."

It is my expectation that the fifth edition of *The Comprehensive Catalog of U.S. Paper Money*, now in its 18th year of publication, will be received as warmly, and more extensively used, as its predecessors. I look forward to many well-worn copies, not only in the ANA Resource Center, but among the reference sets of currency collectors. This is a most welcome new edition.

Robert J. Leuver
Executive Director, American Numismatic Association
Former Director, Bureau of Engraving and Printing,
    U.S. Department of the Treasury.

Preface

This, the sixth edition, reflects the first major change in U.S. paper money since 1928, when the size of all notes was reduced. In 1996 about 9.6 billion notes will be produced by the Bureau of Engraving and Printing. Only a fraction of this amount will be newly-designed $100 notes. Additional newly-designed denominations, i.e., $50, $20, $10 and $5, will be issued in intervals of about six to nine months. An abundance of counterfeits, engraved and photocopied, convinced the U.S. Treasury Department to redesign our paper money and included more anti-counterfeiting devices. New notes usually stimulate collecting. Therefore, there could be a renaissance in paper money collecting in the U.S. There are many who have yet to discover the joy of holding a beautiful piece of history in their hand.

Since the first edition of *The Comprehensive Catalog of U.S. Paper Money* every effort has been made to present a work worthy of the title.

In the previous edition all federal paper money issued since 1812 is listed for the first time; therefore the title was fulfilled. It is the only paper money catalog to meet the comprehensive criterion. Over the course of the past 20 plus years I have undertaken extensive, intensive, research into the history of the paper money of the United States. The research continues, but I am pleased to share the knowledge that I have gained to date. The study has been time-consuming but fascinating. It has truly been a journey into the past and I am delighted to have you join me on the journey!

Some might ask why these early federal notes, most of which are uncollectible, are listed. They are part of our monetary history, and I would be guilty of omission if they were not included.

Some extremely rare notes were documented in the previous edition. While gathering information for *An Illustrated History of U.S. Loans, 1775-1898*, I uncovered at least six notes at the Bureau of the Public Debt; none of these had heretofore been illustrated in any catalog. Series 1863, 1870 and 1875 large denomination gold certificates were thrilling to discover and I was delighted to present them here.

To attribute the art and engraving that appears on bank notes to the artists who were responsible for these pieces of history is a continuing quest in order to satisfy my interest in, and respect for, the art of engraving. In this edition you will find additional attributions. And, the index will facilitate locating specific information of this type.

The 5th edition included a foreword by Robert J. Leuver, Executive Director of the American Numismatic Association and Thomas R. Hipschen, Chief Engraver at the U.S. Bureau of Engraving and Printing introduces this edition. For their kind words I am truly grateful.

I sincerely hope the information presented in this sixth edition of *The Comprehensive Catalog of U.S. Paper Money* will help both collectors and non-collectors to understand and appreciate our monetary history.

Acknowledgments

The information presented here was compiled with the assistance of others. I wish to thank those who helped and sincerely hope that none have been omitted from the following listing: Walter T. Allan, William T. Anton, Jr., Richard J. Balbaton, Dr. Frederick J. Bart, John Breen, Walter Breen (deceased), Amon Carter, Jr. (deceased), Frank Clark, Robert Cochran, Tom Conklin, Mark Davison, Charles A. Dean, Martin Delger, Tom Denly, William P. Donlon (deceased), William Doovas, Jack H. Fisher, Dennis Forgue, Martin Gengerke, who has documented many notes, Len Glazer, James Grebinger, John Hickman (deceased), Robert Hield, Richard Hoenig, Ronald Horstman, Mark B. Hotz, Peter Huntoon, John Isted, Glenn E. Jackson, D.D.S. (deceased), Harry E. Jones, Lyn F. Knight, Abe Kosoff (deceased), Chester L. Krause, Phil Lampkin (deceased), Bob F. Lemke, Lester Merkin (deceased), Robert R. Moon, Barbara Mueller, Doug Murray, Ed Neuce, James E. Noll, Dean Oakes, Chuck O'Donnell (deceased), Douglas Oswell, J. Roy Pennell, Morey Perlmutter, W.A. Philpott, Jr. (deceased), W.K. Raymond, Fred L. Reed III, Bruno S. Rzepka, Bernard Schaaf, M.D., C.F. Schwan, Dexter Seymour, PhD (deceased), Neil Shafer, Gary F. Snover, Mary Lou Stubbolo, Charles Surasky, R.L. Vandevender, II, Doug Walcutt, M.O. Warns (deceased), and L. Werner (deceased).

In addition I wish to thank the American Numismatic Association; the American Numismatic Society; *Coin World*, especially Beth Deisher and Margo Russell (retired); Krause Publications; Stack's; The Bureau of Engraving and Printing, especially Director Larry Rolufs, and former Directors Harry R. Clements, James Conlon, Peter H. Daly and Robert J. Leuver, also Ira Polikoff, Leah Akbar, Mary Halsall, Cecilia Wertheimer, Jane Soderquist, Claudia Dickens, Harriet R. Duckett (deceased), H.T. Krisak (retired), Michael L. Plant (retired), and Mary Workman (retired); The Bureau of the Public Debt, especially Peggy Diamond; The Comptroller of the Currency; The U.S. Secret Service; The National Archives; The Essay-Proof Society; the Federal Reserve Banks of New York and San Francisco; the Higgins Foundation; R.M. Smythe & Co.; and the Society of Paper Money Collectors.

Paper money photographs are by William Devine and Gene Hessler; printing operation and COPE-PAK courtesy of J.M. Johnson and the Bureau of Engraving and Printing.

◄━━ ❧❦❧ ━►

The author has received eight awards for this *Comprehensive Catalog*, his three other books and column, "Notes on Paper" in *The Numismatist. PAPER MONEY*, the journal of the Society of Paper Money Collectors, edited by Mr. Hessler, has been recognized by the American Numismatic Association as the premiere organizational numismatic publication. As part of "Money Talks," a daily series broadcast over 600 National Public Radio stations, one of his scripts was nominated for a Peabody Broadcasting Award in 1993.

Syngraphics

A new word was born in 1974 with the publication of the first edition of this catalog in 1974. Syngraphics, denoting the study and collecting of paper money, will now take its place beside numismatics and philatelics.

The Reverend Richard Doyle, Chairman of the Department of Classical Languages at Fordham University in New York, coined the long-needed word at the request of the author. The word comes from the Greek *syn*, meaning with or together (as in synagogue—a place where people come together), and *graphikos*, which means to write. In Latin, *syngrapha* means a written agreement to pay, a promissory note, a bond. The *Oxford Dictionary* defines paper money as "a written promise to pay". In the same source *syngraph* is defined "as a written contract or bond signed by both or all parties, an obligation or bond between two or more." The first paper money in the western world was a handwritten goldsmith receipt.

The art of engraving, etching and other methods by which copies of an original design are printed from a plate, block or the like is referred to as graphic art. Modern bank notes are no longer handwritten but are made from engraved plates. Therefore, *syngraphics* is interpreted as the collecting of paper money, and since a serious collector studies what is collected, he or she is a syngraphist. The definition holds up with the original and the current definition of paper money. The science of paper money collecting and study thereof is on a level equal with the study of coins and stamps.

Soon after the first edition of this catalog was published the word *syngraphics* was added to the editorial vocabulary for the *Bank Note Reporter, Coin World, The Essay-Proof Journal, The Numismatist, Paper Money*, and other publications.

Paper Money Terms

For most Federal Reserve notes prior to 1996

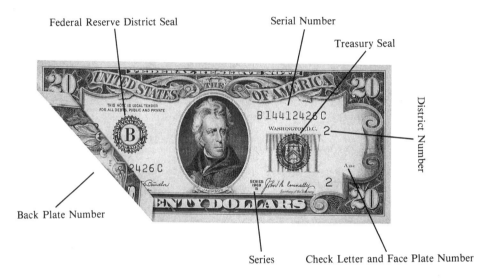

Federal Reserve District Seal

Serial Number

Treasury Seal

District Number

Back Plate Number

Series

Check Letter and Face Plate Number

Abbreviations

ABNCo	American Bank Note Co.	L-H	Lehman-Haupt
ANS	American Numismatic Society	MDF&Co	Murray, Draper, Fairman & Co.
BEP	Bureau of Engraving and Printing	NBNCo	National Bank Note Co.
		PBS	Public Broadcasting System
CCA	Currency Auctions of America, Inc.	R	Rarity
		RW&H	Rawdon, Wright & Hatch
ColBNCo	Columbian Bank Note Co.	RWH&E	Rawdon, Wright, Hatch & Edson
ContBNCo	Continental Bank Note Co.		
EPJ	The Essay-Proof Journal	TC	Toppan, Carpenter & Co.
IBNS	International Bank Note Society		

If you collect paper money, **you need** *PAPER MONEY*

the journal of
THE SOCIETY OF PAPER MONEY COLLECTORS
Organized in 1961

Bimonthly *PAPER MONEY* addresses all types of paper money and security documents, however, it specializes in its coverage of United States federal and obsolete notes, Confederate notes, and the artists and engravers of these historic pieces.

PAPER MONEY, is edited by Gene Hessler. This magazine has been recognized by the American Numismatic Association and the Numismatic Literary Guild as the best organizational journal. Hessler is one of the most respected authorities on paper money of all types. He is the author of standard catalogs, articles, and columns. He has received many awards for his writing and was honored with a nomination for a Peabody Broadcasting Award

The SPMC publishes books on obsolete notes and scrip from individual states. The number of books published, including one of the U. S. national banks notes, is approaching two dozen.

The ladies and gentlemen in the SPMC meet annually and hold regional meetings in conjunction with major numismatic conventions in the Untied States.

Annual dues in US funds: $24 in the U.S.; $29 for Canada and Mexico; $34 for other countries.

To join the SPMC send dues to SPMC, P. O. Box 117060, Carrollton, TX 75011. For a complimentary copy of *PAPER MONEY,* send $2 for postage and handling.

CHAPTER ONE

A History of Paper Money

A LL money, whether paper, metal, stone, or shell, is a symbol of value that can be exchanged as needed for goods purchased or services rendered. In the simplest economic arrangement it is easy enough to exchange my cow for your horse or my cabbage for your cantaloupe. But we would have trouble exchanging cows for cabbages if we did not have some common measure of value. So, in early Greece we find an iron spit (obol) or a handful of iron spits (drachma) serving as tokens of exchange. In early Rome, blocks of bronze were used as exchange symbols.

The earliest metal money had a face value equal to its intrinsic value. The first coins were those ingots and nuggets that were stamped by a sovereign authority in Lydia during the 7th century B.C. as being guaranteed full weight and quality. It was not long before the coins themselves became lighter, less pure, and more like present-day paper money. The coin became an instrument inscribed with a specific amount. For example, there were the coins minted by the Roman Empire during the inflation of the 4th century, coins made of the cheapest possible mixture of base metals. Even these coins took much valuable metal from a degenerating economy.

Although there are no surviving examples, some writers refer to paper money that was used during the Kao-tsung Dynasty (A.D. 650-683). Others say paper money, actually a banker's draft, was introduced during the T'ang Dynasty during the reign of Yan H'u (A.D. 806-820). These deposit receipts, called flying money, could be cashed in different cities and locations. In 1024 the government began to print Jiao Zi, receipts for metal currency. In 1160, during the Sung Dynasty, a circulating bill, not exchangeable for cash, was introduced. Better control and improvements followed, including currency printed on silk to instill confidence and deter counterfeiting. By 1277 Kublai Khan (1215-1294) had abolished coins. Only paper money circulated in his domain (Kranister 142-150). Today the latter are referred to as Ming notes, derived from the dynasty in power. The punishment for counterfeiters of these notes was decapitation.

THE DEVELOPMENT OF PAPER MONEY

The manufacture of paper money involves three elements: ink, the technique of engraving, and paper. Of these elements, ink was the first to be developed. Ink had been in use even before the use of papyrus in ancient Egypt. In both Egypt and China lampblack, a form of carbon, was suspended in gum or glue as early as 2,500 B.C. The invention of true ink took place in China in 400 A.D. Today, inks for printing are made of vegetable or mineral materials suspended in a vehicle, usually a type of linseed oil. Modern chemistry has developed a wide variety of printing inks for different conditions. Paper money requires ink that resists fading in sunlight, resists humidity and rubbing, and lacks odor.

The second element to be developed was paper. The history of paper begins with papyrus, which was made by laying strips of the stems of the papyrus plant crisscross and pressing the strips together. Next came parchment, the dried skin of sheep. Both papyrus and parchment were too variable in shape and quality for use as currency. True paper was invented in China ca. 105 A.D. by Ts'ai Lun, who made his paper from rags, bark, fish nets and hemp. A fragment of paper was found in a tomb in Shensi Province dating earlier than 105 A.D.

Later, paper was made by macerating a variety of cellulose fibers, cooking them in soda and lime, bleaching the result, and then pressing the mash into sheets for drying. In the 15th century rag pulp was bleached in sour milk and wood ash and then dried in the sun. On fine 18th century paper the pressing lines can be seen by holding the sheet to the light. Watermarks could be left in the paper during the pressing process, and many foreign governments used elaborate watermarks to further deter counterfeiting. One of the earliest watermarks can be traced to Fabriano, Italy in the year 1293.

It was the Arabs who brought fine paper to Europe; they had learned the secret of papermaking from the Chinese artisans ca. 751. Flax and its derivatives, such as linen cloth and linen rags, were used for the best papers. Linen papers in 18th century books are often as fresh and clean as the day they were made. Today, paper made from wood pulp browns and crumbles within a year or two and is used for ephemeral items, i.e., newspapers, for obvious reasons, non-scholarly journals and most paperback books. Governments, however, will use the best paper obtainable for paper money, often custom-made. "To the lay-mind, paper is paper, just as `pigs is pigs'" (Coudert 27). Different types of paper are required for specific needs, e.g., bonds, stock certificates, revenue stamps, etc. The first paper of quality made in the United States was produced by William Rittenhouse and Son in Germantown, Pennsylvania in 1690.

Engraving is the third element of a successful paper currency. Engraving differs from printing from woodcuts or stones in that an engraved imprint is made by incised lines rather than raised surfaces. The intaglio design is cut into the plate. (Here, intaglio refers to the deep, incised lines in a steel plate.) The surface of the plate is covered with ink and then wiped carefully so as to leave the incisions filled with ink. The advantage of engraving is that the plates are extremely durable since the whole face of the plate wears down slowly and evenly. If steel plates are chromium plated periodically they are virtually indestructible. The print from an engraved plate cannot be successfully reproduced photographically.

Printing was certainly within the capabilities of the Romans; they used seal stamps and stencils extensively. Perhaps the lack of an abundant medium on which to print made printing impractical for them. The earliest example of text printing on paper can be traced to Japan in 770 A.D.

Johann Gutenberg is credited as the first to print from movable type in Europe ca. 1452. However, movable type made of hardened clay was invented in China by Pi Sheng ca. 1045. (Wang Chen hand carved movable characters in wood in the late 13th century.) Eight years later the invention was abandoned; the numerous language characters did not lend themselves to this printing improvement. By 1403 movable type was produced in a type foundry in Korea; examples are in the National Museum in Seoul.

The first examples of intaglio engraving were done as plates for playing cards in the 1430s. Costumes worn by the human figures on the cards helped Lehrs, Geisberg and others to arrive at this date (VB 13); an anonymous artist, the Master of the Playing Cards, engraved these figures. In the early 1450s, both the Master and Gutenberg were working in Mainz perhaps together.

Engravings of the Master "were not created *a priori* for a card game, but as technical steppingstones toward the multiple reproduction of [illuminated] miniatures" (L-H 3). Playing card motifs, probably from a model book, were later found in a variety of manuscripts and codices, e.g., the *Book of Hours of Catherine of Cleves* (completed ca. 1435) and Gutenberg Bibles, specifically the Giant Bible of Mainz (completed ca. 1452), in the Library of Congress.

It is almost certain that Gutenberg cast relief metal plates from engraved molds and engaged in typographic experiments as early as 1436. He was therefore was also fundamentally associated with the beginning of intaglio engraving. As governments began to apply the techniques of printing and engraving to paper money, they employed fine artists in order to foil counterfeiters and to enhance the prestige of the issuing authority. Great printing offices in major capitals took on the job of printing the currency of other nations, with the engraving done by the best *etaliers*. It is always the battle of the gun against armor, and as superior guns are invented better armor is developed. The counterfeiters were clever, and as soon as paper money was made more elaborate, the efforts of counterfeiting improved. The counterfeiters strove to duplicate the official printing process. Fine engravers made careful copies of the real note, and the paper used was close to the original. Of course the governments kept up the race with better paper and with more sophisticated engravings.

Today counterfeiters use photoengraving devices that eliminate the need for a master engraver. Color photocopiers also present an increasing threat. Bills of $20, $50 and $100 are the notes most often counterfeited. Of course there is the story of the very small-time New York City maker of "queer" (counterfeit notes), who made only $1 bills for daily needs and led the Secret Service on the longest case of its history. (This case was reenacted in the 1950 movie, "Mr 880" with Edmund Gwenn as the friendly felon.)

In time of war, governments have been known to counterfeit currencies to try to weaken their enemy's economy. Skilled prisoners of the Germans were recruited to counterfeit British bank notes as part of "Operation Bernhard". Japan tried to add to the troubles of Chiang Kai-shek during World War II by duplicating Chinese national currency that was printed in the United States by American Bank Note Company and flown over the "hump" to China.

EARLY PAPER MONEY IN EUROPE AND AMERICA

In 1255, after visiting Ghengis Khan, the French priest William of Rubruk returned to the court of Louis IX and reported that paper money circulated in Mongolia. Marco Polo, however, was the first to bring examples of Ming Dynasty paper money to Europe. A few European rulers were moderately impressed, but governments were not ready to take such a giant monetary step. Gold and silver were still the basis of monetary exchange, with bronze abundant enough to supply the token coinage of everyday small change.

Promissory notes, IOUs, contracts, and other promises to deliver goods or services had been imprinted on clay, papyrus, parchment, metal, or stone since the earliest forms of writing were in use. All of these promissory notes were private exchange between individuals. In the case of a monetary note, however, the promisor is individual, either a bank or a government, but the promisee is unspecified and general.

According to J.P. de la Riva (*IBNSJ*, March 1965, 10) King James I of Catalonia and Aragon issued paper money in 1250. In 1453 emergency paper money was used by the besieged during la Moorish siege of Spain. Examples of neither have survived.

The first European "bank note," under this definition, was issued in Sweden by the Stockholm Banco on July 16, 1661. The earliest surviving note from this bank is dated 1662. Under Johann Palmstruch this bank issued too many bank notes, payable on demand against reserves of precious metals, and closed in 1666. The bank was reorganized as the Swedish Riksbank in 1668, but did not issue paper money until 1701, eleven years after paper money was issued in Massachusetts Colony.

In 1685 a form of paper money was issued in Canada. The paymaster for the French army had been delayed at sea, and, since there is nothing more surly than an unpaid army, Jacques de Meulles, the Intendant of New France, prevented a mutiny by issuing promissory notes redeemable when the ship arrived. His desperate expedient was to gather up all of the locally available paper, which happened to be playing cards, and to imprint them with values to be redeemed and with seals and signatures. The notes were redeemed within three months.

The basic ills of this paper money policy soon appeared. The first problem was counterfeiting. The second was depreciation. Discouraged soldiers sold off their notes at a reduced rate before the ship appeared. The third ill to appear was inflation, which was caused by the issuer and not the receiver. The authorities soon discovered how easy it was to solve financial problems by issuing as much paper as was needed to cover expenses and worrying about redemption in metal later. The authorities tried to refrain from this practice, but the playing card money was revived periodically as wars and ship delays caused more payment problems. The three problems of counterfeiting, depreciation, and over issuance, they are still with us today. However, the usefulness of paper money outshone its drawbacks. Thus the Massachusetts General Court decided to imitate its northern neighbor and authorize the first notes. These "Old Charter" bills were printed from engraved copper plates; denominations were 5, 10 and 20 shillings, and 5 pounds. With the outbreak of hostilities with Canada in King William's War in 1689, large numbers of these bills were issued to meet the provincial payrolls. These Old Charter bills were not like our paper money that is legal tender for all private debts and transactions. The Massachusetts notes were valid for paying taxes, a clever way for a government to issue excessive paper and then recall it at will.

The real troubles with paper money that was not backed sufficiently by metal had not yet begun, however. In 1694 the Bank of England issued notes to cover war expenses. In November 1696 the world's first bank run reduced the true value of its notes by 20 percent, making it apparent that what counted was not the value printed on the note but what the holder believed the note to be worth.

Paper money became well established across Europe in the following century, although France went bankrupt under Louis XVI because of experiments by Finance Minister John Law, who tried to overprint notes with reinforced promises to pay. The assignats issued during the French Revolution were equally disastrous. Paper money was obviously a good invention, but without proper controls it had a poor future in any stable society.

PRIVATE BANK NOTES IN AMERICA

In 1714 a group of Boston merchants, headed by John Colman, applied for a bank charter; their land security proposal was rejected. The unchartered New London Society United for Trade and Commerce issued bank notes dated October 25, 1732; this emission was a fiasco. In 1740 Colman was briefly successful in having "manufactory bills" issued. Forty years later the issue of private bank notes was tried again. What began as a trickle became an avalanche that ended in 1866.

Later in the 18th century, during the American Revolution, the Continental Congress tried to finance the war with voluminous issues of Continental currency. By the end of the war the new government was in a state of financial chaos. Alexander Hamilton came to the rescue and proposed that the central government assume all war debts incurred by the individual states. He also proposed a tariff on imports to raise revenues.

The Bank of the United States

In 1781 the Continental Congress authorized the Bank of North America as the first incorporated bank; the bank received a perpetual charter. Three years later the Bank of New York and the Massachusetts Bank were formed. The Bank of New York, under the leadership of Alexander Hamilton, was granted a charter in 1791.

Soon after his appointment as Secretary of the Treasury, Hamilton proposed the establishment of a national bank. He would have favored the Bank of North America as a national bank, but the state charters that the bank had accepted disqualified it. Although both Jefferson and Madison opposed him, Hamilton succeeded in establishing the Bank of the United States as the first national bank.

The Bank of the United States received the first of its two charters in 1791; it was preceded only by the Bank of North America, the Bank of New York, and the Massachusetts Bank. (The latter three banks are still operating; the Massachusetts Bank is now the First National Bank of Boston.) The Bank of the United States could have continued to serve the needs of the new nation if it had not been for the question of the constitutionality of the Bank. The effect of the Bank was obviously beneficial. Not only did it render valuable financial assistance to the government, but it exerted a profitable influence on the general economy. In a period of tremendous and sometimes precarious expansion and speculation, the Bank of the United States acted as a moderating force. For example, it refrained from calling in its loans from state banks, when such a move would have led to financial panic.

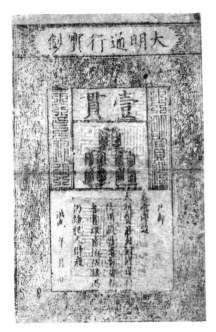

A Ming Dynasty note for one kwan (1,000 cash) issued during the reign of Emperor Hung Wu, similar to the type reported by Marco Polo. (Below) An early bank note from Sweden.

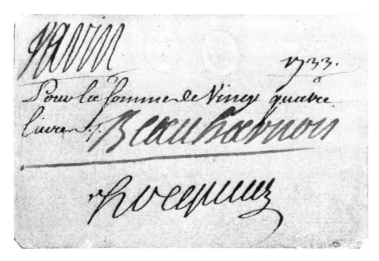

There are only about fifty acceptable examples of this type of Canadian playing card money; the Bank of Canada has half of them.

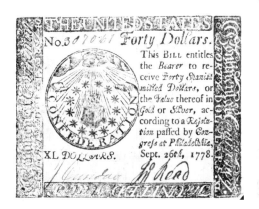

The face and back of a $40 Continental currency note dated September 26, 1778. (Below) A colonial Pennsylvania note printed by Benjamin Franklin.

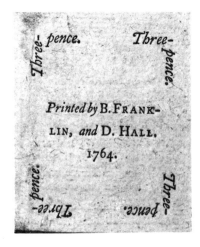

One of the earliest privately issued bank notes from New London, Connecticut.

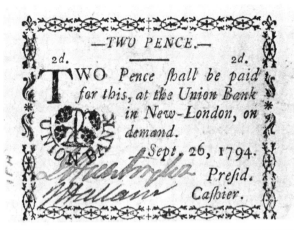

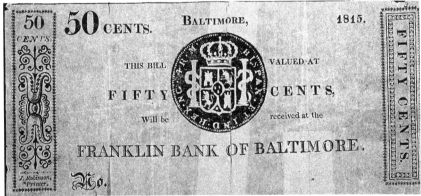

The first charter of the Bank was not renewed, and state banks proved inadequate when the War of 1812 forced the United States to borrow money. U.S. Treasury notes were issued in denominations of $5 to $100 amounting to $37 million, although up to $60.5 million had been authorized, to be receivable only in public dues and debts. These notes were not meant to circulate and were retired soon after the war. The Bank of the United States was rechartered in 1816, and it opened again for business on January 17, 1817.

In 1832, five years before the Bank's second charter was to expire, Andrew Jackson vetoed its recharter. Samuel D. Ingham, former Secretary of the Treasury, said, "The United States Bank has given us the best currency known among nations. It supplies a medium equal in value to gold and silver in every part of the Union....[The Bank] enables the government to transmit its funds from one extremity of the Union to another...with a dispatch which is more like magic than reality."

Despite Ingham's protests, the Bank's second charter was not renewed. The Bank of the United States continued to operate, but as a state bank under a charter from the state of Pennsylvania. With the demise of the Bank of the United States, state banks began to flourish, and soon caused a severe inflation. There was no uniformity in the laws under which the state banks operated. The banking system was up for grabs.

When the Civil War was imminent, Salmon P. Chase, then Secretary of the Treasury, devised a plan to stabilize the currency. His plan "included non-interest bearing notes payable on demand, interest-bearing notes for short terms, and bonds for long terms; the first to be convertible into the second and the second into the third form of obligation." Thus, he expected to avert the evil that many of his predecessors had experienced being compelled to receive, as payments to the Treasury, notes of state banks, most of which were fluctuating in value and might even have become valueless. On July 17, 1861 Congress adopted Chase's plan and authorized the borrowing of $250 million. The demand notes ("greenbacks") that soon followed saved the Union and were the beginning of our national paper money.

Varieties of United States Paper Money

United States paper money falls into five major categories: Continental, Bank of the United States, State and Private Banks (obsolete or broken banks), Confederate, and federal. Only the federal issues have survived into the twentieth century. Of these five categories, we have already discussed the Continental and Bank of the United States notes. The history of state bank and Confederate notes will be surveyed later in this chapter. The primary subject of the present work will be federal issues, which comprise most of this book. Before we proceed, however, it is appropriate to mention some of the literature on the five categories of United States paper money.

The Colonial and Confederate issues have been cataloged by Eric P. Newman and Grover Criswell respectively. What may be the largest series of all, obsolete, or broken, bank notes has been magnificently compiled by James Haxby (see bibliography).

These 30,000 varieties, issued by 3,000 different banks in 34 states between 1782 and 1866, are being cataloged by individual states. These individual catalogs will also include private scrip issued within the state. Individual members of the Society of Paper Money Collectors, the sponsor, have thus far cataloged obsolete notes and scrip for: Alabama, Arkansas, Florida, Illinois, Indian Territory/Oklahoma/Kansas, Iowa, Kentucky, Maine, Michigan, Minnesota, Mississippi, Nebraska, New Jersey, Pennsylvania, Rhode Island, Tennessee, Territorials, Texas, Vermont and Virginia.

With adequate catalogs for all of the states here or on the way, the collecting of obsolete bank notes has become a major part of our hobby. Collectors need these catalogs to guide them. They also need to know values and rarities so that they can buy and sell intelligently. Prices often rise rapidly as collecting popularity increases.

One interesting pattern for obsolete bank note collecting not available for other types of currency, is the collecting of odd denomination bills. Just about every cent and dollar figure was issued. A collection of $4 or $7 bills certainly would prove fascinating; or how about a collection of $1.25 and $1.75 notes? These bills are most often related to the Spanish milled dollar, "piece of 8", or "8 real" that was accepted in the United States as legal tender until 1857. This large silver coin was divided at times physically into bits equaling 12½ cents. The term two bits is derived from one quarter of one "piece of 8".

As for the cost of collecting these obsolete notes, numerous privately issued notes can be purchased for $25 or less, an inexpensive way to collect a tangible piece of history.

Frequently works of art were reproduced as engravings on these notes. The famous American painter, Gilbert Stuart, is frequently represented. Another is Felix O.C. Darley who illustrated *Scenes of Indian Life* in 1843, *Rip Van Winkle* in 1848 and *The Legend of Sleepy Hollow* in 1849. Darley is also responsible for more than five hundred drawings illustrating the novels of James Fenimore Cooper. James B. Longacre, United States Mint engraver from 1844-1869, prepared vignettes for Draper, Toppan, Longacre and Company, one of the historical printers of obsolete currency. More than one painting by Queen Victoria's favorite artist, Edwin Landseer, adorns obsolete state bank notes.

A History of Broken Bank Notes

As the name implies, a broken bank note (obsolete bank note) is one issued privately, often by a bank that went under, or went broke. The confusion in the strange episode represented by these notes can be laid to the long distrust of a central government and of a central economic authority. Some of the distrust can be traced to the Continental Congress. The voluminous amounts of Continental currency poured out to finance the Revolution originally was backed by Spanish milled dollars, but that backing was soon removed. The Continental currency gradually depreciated to a point where a $40 Continental note was worth only $1; ultimately it was worth nothing at all. In accordance with Gresham's Law bad money drives out good money gold and silver went out of circulation. Hoards of coins that have survived until today may be a boon to the coin collector, but they helped engender a deep distrust of any national currency, a distrust that lasted until the Civil War.

In 1789 the Constitution of the United States tried to prevent a repetition of the Continental currency fiasco by forbidding any state or federal authority to issue "bills of credit." However, an enormous loophole was discovered. The Constitution did not ban bills of credit issued by private or municipal authorities.

The first privately issued notes in colonial America were issued in New London, Connecticut in 1732, the year George Washington was born. The experiment failed then, but was reinstated and popular by the time Washington was on his way to the presidency in 1790. State and private note issues became a flood in the 1800s. The Constitution allowed state issues provided they were regulated by the state.

In his report to the Congress on December 9, 1861, Secretary of the Treasury Salmon P. Chase the said: "It has been questioned by the most eminent statesmen, whether a currency of bank notes, issued by local institutions under State laws, is not, in fact, prohibited by the national Constitution. Such emissions certainly fall within the spirit, if not within the letter, of the constitutional prohibition of the emission of bills of credit by the States..." (Knox 12).

The history of broken bank notes ranges from the hilarious to the tragic. Crooks and sharpies perceived at once that what governments could do with paper money, they could do as well. A printing press, an impressive design, and a con man's talent could bring riches overnight. An example from the earliest days of state bank notes is instructive. In 1806 Judge Augustus B. Woodward of the village of Detroit, Michigan (population 600), organized the Bank of Detroit. He announced its capital at $1 million, ordered at least $3 million from the printer in notes of $1 to $10, signed them, or had them signed for him, and shipped them East. Smart Easterners can always take advantage of country folk, so they bought up the issue at discounts of 10 to 25 percent. When they tried to redeem the notes at face value in 1808, they found that the Bank of Detroit had closed its doors. Judge Woodward, a Cheshire cat smile on his face, had in the meantime put quite a bit of money in the form of hard coin in another, honest bank. As late as 1824 outraged citizens were still trying to prevent Judge Woodward's continuing reappointment by the United States Senate to the local bench. Woodward's Bank of Detroit notes are today the most common of all broken bank notes.

The weak, Michigan General Banking Law of 1837 really opened the gates of the paper flood. Fifty-five banks were immediately organized, most of them for the sole purpose of issuing paper money. A year later, after the disaster had almost wrecked the state, the law was suspended. The 55 banks and many previously established banks, honest or not, had broken, adding notes for the modern collector and subtracting wealth from the Michigan citizenry.

A little caution might well have averted such a disaster. Supervision of bank operations seems obvious to our modern minds, and the bank examiner is a well-known contemporary official. What little inspection was done then was satisfied with false books, uncollectible collateral and mortgages, or cash borrowed for the day of the inspection. In light of what has happened with the Savings & Loan field since 1989, there is something bordering on *deja vu*.

To discourage inspectors, or note-holders, from paying a visit many banks had their "main office" far out in the woods. Some notes were postdated or had false bank addresses to hamper any attempts at redemption. The Bank of Battle Creek, Michigan (1838-1840) used the ruse of having its cashier, Tolman W. Hall, run out the back door whenever a note-holder came in the front. The "pigeon" found the bank deserted except for a singing janitor, who eventually drove the note-holder away by incessantly whistling or singing and answering all questions with gibberish. In Barry, Michigan the Farmers Bank of Sandstone (1837-1838) tried to be honest in that it offered to redeem its notes in merchandise of the locality. Since the principal natural resource of the area named Sandstone was exactly that, the bank would redeem a $10 note with one millstone, a $5 note with one grindstone, and $1 notes with one whetstone. As can be imagined, few note holders bent on redemption took advantage of the offer, especially if they had come by buggy from a great distance.

Bowen's *State Bank Notes of Michigan* has many such stories, some comic and some tragic. Many of the stories represent not only broken banks but broken hearts, homes, hopes, farms and families as well. The ultimate victims of these frauds were the local working people, the immigrants, the settlers.

There were also honest banks out in the sticks. After traveling by train and then horseback, Alexander L. Stimpson, an agent for Adams Express Company, finally reached what he was told was Morocco, Indiana, although he was in the middle of the prairie. It seems that the blacksmith, the only person around, was also the banker. When Stimpson presented $1,000 in notes issued by the Bank of America (Morocco, Indiana), the blacksmith, after removing pounds of potatoes from a large barrel, brought forth a bag from which he took five $20 gold pieces and gave them to his astonished visitor.

As if the broken bank problem was not enough it was compounded by counterfeiting! Notes that were aost worthless were nevertheless altered or counterfeited by other crooks trying to get in on the orgy. In order to combat these privately issued notes, dozens of counterfeit detectors were published to assist bankers and merchants in the detection of bogus bills. An Iowa banker, H. Price, said, "The two most important books that every businessman needed were a bible and a counterfeit detector. And of these two, the detector seemed to be the more important for at least six days out of seven."

The private bank note companies that prepared most of the notes issued by state banks employed the best engravers to engrave designs difficult to engrave without years of experience. After the camera was invented, counterfeits were photoengraved. Even the previously mentioned counterfeit detector could not always come to the rescue. The result of the intricate, geometric patterns, the lovely vignettes, and the colors that were introduced, was some exceptionally beautiful notes. Some, in many respects surpassed present-day currency.

Even during the worst period of the broken bank note era there were honest and far-seeing bankers who issued reliable money. They realized that the convenience of paper money was necessary if the nation was to develop and expand. These bankers were the ones who took the countermeasure of superb production to its limit. Seven engraving companies serving these bankers merged to form American Bank Note Company in 1858, which continues to produce currency and a variety of security paper for many nations.

The history of obsolete or broken bank notes came to an end after the Civil War. When the Confederacy was formed, paper money issued by the Richmond government and by the "sovereign states" supplanted private bank issues very quickly. In the beginning the Confederacy tried to back its paper money with cotton bales stored in Southern ports, but the Confederate notes went the way of Continental currency and ultimately became worthless paper. As part of the National Bank Act of 1863, a 10 percent tax was levied on all private bank note issues. The issue of scrip below $1 was also forbidden. By 1866 private and state banks had either joined the National Banking System or closed their doors. The colorful, fascinating, humorous and tragic broken bank note era came to an end.

The original image of *Standing Liberty* by Thomas Crawford appears in the frieze of the Senate wing of the U.S. Capitol. The central engraving is the *Young Students*.

A portrait of Henry Clay appears on this note printed by the National Bank Note Co.

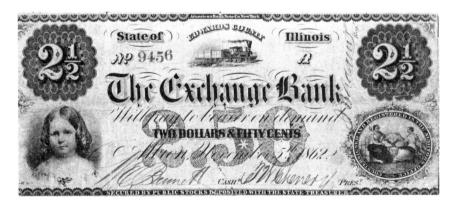

The little girl is named Mary Lamar. American Bank Note Co. printed this note.

State bank notes often pictured silver dollars in numbers equal to the denomination of the note.

The portrait of Peter Stuyvesant was originally painted by Hendrick Courturier. The engraving of *St. Nicholas* is based on a painting by R.W. Weir.

This note printed by Rawdon, Wright & Hatch bears a portrait of James Monroe.

The image of the young girl was engraved by James Bannister for American Bank Note Co.

This attractive proof $12 note was printed by Rawdon, Wright & Hatch.

This sheet of odd denominations was prepared by Casilear, Durand, Burton and Edmonds.

Rawdon, Wright and Hatch printed this ornate $13 note.

UNITED STATES PAPER MONEY SINCE THE CIVIL WAR

When Congress authorized the first demand notes on July 17, 1861, it was up to the executive branch of the government to see that the new notes were printed and distributed in a proper manner. The Secretary of the Treasury and the Office of the Treasurer of the United States thus became the vehicle for all financial and monetary functions of the federal government. Until the terms of U.S. Treasurer and Secretary of the Treasury Burke and McAdoo began, the signatures of the Register of the Treasury and the Treasurer appeared on United States bank notes.

Office of the Secretary of the Treasury

As a major policy advisor to the President, the Secretary of the Treasury and his office have primary responsibility for formulating and recommending tax policy; participate in formulating broad fiscal policies that have general significance for the economy; manage the public debt; and formulate policies for, and generally oversee, all operations of the Department. These duties are carried out by the ninety thousand department employees located in Washington, DC, and some 1,800 field offices in this country and abroad.

Office of the Treasurer of the United States

Both the Secretary of the Treasury and the Treasurer are appointed by the President, with the advice and consent of the Senate. In 1974 the position of Treasurer was transferred to the Office of the Secretary of the Treasury. The Bureau of Government Financial Operations was given the complementary operating functions of the Treasurer at this time. The Treasurer now acts as a Department spokesperson, reviews currency and redemptions, signs currency, and participates in the promotion of the selling and holding of United States Savings Bonds. The Office of the Treasurer now oversees the operations of the U.S. Mint and the Bureau of Engraving and Printing. This office has been held by a woman since the appointment of Georgia Neese Clark in 1949.

Initially Michael Hillegas and George Clymer jointly held the office of U.S. Treasurer, beginning September 6, 1777. Nevertheless, the office of Treasurer was not officially established by Congress until September 2, 1789.

The U.S. Bureau of Engraving and Printing

On August 29, 1862 four women and two men began to separate and trim $1 and $2 United States (legal tender) notes that had been printed by American Bank Note Company and the National Bank Note Company in New York City. Miss Jennie Douglas was the first woman to be hired to trim notes. In 1863 seventy additional women were employed to perform this operation. (Late in life, Treasurer Francis E. Spinner said, "I don't claim that I have done much good in the world; but my success in introducing women into government employment makes me feel that I have not lived in vain.") This manual chore was done practically in a state of siege

The U.S. Bureau of Engraving and Printing

in beleaguered Civil War Washington, with sandbags filling the windows of the old Treasury Building, still at 15th Street and Pennsylvania Avenue, N.W.

As the Civil War continued, the need for a truly national currency became more and more apparent. The currency-cutting operation as described, designated as the First Division of the National Currency Bureau in 1862 under the leadership of S.M. Clark, was the first step toward such a national currency. By the fall of 1863 the Bureau had printed its first notes. In 1864 Secretary of the Treasury Salmon P. Chase established a distinct entity in the Treasury Department to be called "The Engraving and Printing Bureau of the Treasury Department." The first reference to the Bureau of Engraving and Printing can be traced to 31 July 1868. With more important matters at hand, such as Gettysburg and Appomattox, it was not until March 3, 1869 that an appropriation act was signed by President Andrew Johnson to give recognition to this agency.

In succeeding years the Bureau became increasingly important. In 1877 an appropriation act authorized the Bureau to print all internal revenue stamps. On October 1, 1887 the printing of all United States paper money was entrusted to the Bureau. Seven years later postage stamps were added to the list of items to be produced.

From a basement room with six employees, the Bureau has grown to a modern industrial plant housed in two buildings in Washington, DC where where 1800 people are employed; this includes about 85 printers and about 20 designers and engravers. During fiscal year 1994, 6.4 billion Federal Reserve notes were produced at the Bureau of Engraving and Printing in Washington; 2.9 billion notes were printed in Ft. Worth. This 9.3 billion total was a 16 percent increase over 1993. The Ft. Worth plant, which began operation in 1991, will be at full capacity in 1996; a staff of 700 will produce 5 billion notes annually. Notes produced in Fort Worth bear the initials "FW." With 30 high-speed presses, the Washington facility operates 24 hours a day; with 10 high-speed presses, the Fort Worth plant functions for 16 hours a day, five days a week. The cost to print one piece of paper money is about four cents.

In addition to revenue stamps, United States paper money and postage stamps, treasury bonds and certificates, food coupons, certificates of award, permits, and other miscellaneous items emanate from the Bureau of Engraving and Printing. The Federal Reserve is responsible for 70 percent of the Bureau's business.

As previously stated, private bank note companies printed the first greenbacks for the Treasury Department in 1861. In 1862 Secretary Chase introduced a proposal in Congress that would authorize the Treasury Department to engrave and print notes. Approval of the proposal was granted in July of the same year, and work commenced one month later.

Printing Presses

In addition to nine COPE-PAK machines and one overprinting press (for overprinting uncut sheets) the Bureau uses four different Giori presses to print backs and faces of currency: twelve I-8s, four I-10s (at Fort Worth), two 98s and two 74s.

In February 1990 it was announced that the Hamilton Tool Co. in Hamilton, Ohio would produce a new web press that prints face and back of 32-subject sheets simultaneously. The estimated cost of this press is $10 million. Five of these systems will replace 16 sheet-fed presses, each of which produces about seven billion notes per year. Each new Hamilton press will considerably reduce the number of operators required. The first Hamilton press was to begin operating in 1992.

Web-Fed Press

In July 1992, some Series 1988A $1 notes for Boston, New York, Philadelphia, Richmond, Atlanta and Chicago were the first to be printed by the new (continuous sheet) web-fed press, which had been installed in 1991. There were 2.56 million Series 1993 $1 notes printed by the web-fed press. The first $1 notes produced on this press caused concern for some average Americans. Most of the engraved lines on the image of George Washington were light, some were missing. With this change the word "counterfeit" was mentioned in the daily press and on nightly news programs.

The depth of the engraved lines were reduced from 60 and 120 microns, to 40 and 80 microns. This change was made to accommodate the printing on the mechanically, water wiped presses. The presses were adjusted with minimum success, to improve the printed image. Compare any current note with one of the early small-size notes produced 50-65 years ago; the differences are astonishing. The earlier notes, printed on wet paper and by slower presses designed to print from plates with deeper-engraved lines, have darker, bolder images.

In July 1995, as part of H.R. 2020, it was announced that the use of the 120-foot Hamilton press, which cost 12.7 million and another $32 million to develop, would be discontinued. Some Series 1995 $1 notes were printed on this press. Notes produced on this press lack the face plate location number and face and back check letter. Notes printed by the web-fed press places the back plate number above the "E" in ONE. Only $1 notes were printed on the Hamilton press.

COPE-PAK

In 1976 seven Currency Operating and Process Equipment (COPE) machines were installed. In April 1985 the Bureau began replacing the COPE machines with the first of nine Currency Overprinting, Processing Equipment and Packaging (COPE-PAK) machines. This is the most modern and automated equipment of its type in the world. Prior to the installation of COPE, overprinting, note examination and packaging were accomplished in three separate areas of the Bureau; now all are performed in one area.

Currency that continues to be printed in 32-subject sheets first on the back, and the face on the following day, is trimmed and halved into 16-subject sheets and then examined mechanically and spot checked by examiners. The half sheets are then delivered to the COPE-PAK machines, where they are fed simultaneously in two 10,000-sheet stacks for overprinting, examination and packaging.

Blowers, suction, and grippers move the sheets into the printing cylinders where serial numbers, Federal Reserve and Treasury seals, and Federal Reserve letters are applied. When stacks of 100 accumulate, they receive multi-cuts from both angles, and stacks of individual notes are fed into a paper bander according to denomination. At this stage the new COPE-PAK demonstrates its superiority and efficiency over the original COPE.

Banded notes pass into an examination station where they are checked at random by examiners. The notes proceed to a rotating carousel with 32 compart-ments. When 10 packages of 100 notes are collated in the carousel compartments, they move to another bander where they are banded and shrink-wrapped before they continue on in 1,000-note packages. Labels identify the package by denomi-nation, bank and serial numbers. The last step, after two additional countings, is to shrink-wrap packages of four into a final 4,000-note brick weighing 8½ pounds.

The note production increase of COPE-PAK has increased note production over that of COPE is about 10 percent. A record number of over 41,000 notes has been processed in a nine-hour period. COPE-PAK is programmed to detect 700 different malfunctions, shut down automatically if a problem occurs, and identify the mal-function. Components for COPE-PAK are made in England, Switzerland and West Germany, where final assembly takes place.

Treasury Department Signatures

Bank notes are essentially promissory notes. Users do not feel secure if the notes do not have signatures that represent some authority. Handwritten signatures were also thought necessary on the Union side in those bleak days of 1861, when Confederate campfires could be seen across the Potomac from the Treasury Building. Nineteen days after the first paper money was issued, President Lincoln signed a bill that allowed the Secretary of the Treasury to delegate personnel to sign the first demand notes for the two Treasury officials. Seventy employees were assigned the task of signing their own names, with a handwritten "For the" before the appropriate title. Almost immediately it was found necessary to have these words engraved into the printing plates. These signers received an annual salary of $1,200 in the greenbacks that they signed.

Starting in 1863 facsimile signatures were printed directly on the bills. Most United States paper money bears two signatures. National bank notes bear four. Those of the bank president and the cashier are added. Federal Reserve Bank notes bear the signatures of the governor and the cashier or the deputy governor of the issuing bank. A complete list of Treasury officials' signatures is included here.

The signature of the Register of the Treasury appeared from 1862-1925. The Register of the Treasury is an official appointed by the President. Seventeen Registers held office during the period during which they were required to sign notes and other security instruments. It is not generally known that four of the Registers were African-Americans: Blanche K. Bruce, Judson W. Lyons, William T. Vernon and James C. Napier. A fifth African-American Register, Louis B. Toomer was appointed in 1953; however, he did not sign currency.

| | | Terms of Office | |
Register of the Treasury	Treasurer	Began	Ended
Lucius E. Chittenden	F.E. Spinner	4-17-1861	8-10-1864
S.B. Colby	F.E. Spinner	8-11-1864	9-21-1867
Noah L. Jeffries	F.E. Spinner	10-05-1867	3-15-1869
John Allison	F.E. Spinner	4-03-1869	6-30-1875
John Allison	John C. New	6-30-1875	7-01-1876
John Allison	A.U. Wyman	7-01-1876	6-30-1877
John Allison	James Gilfillan	7-01-1877	3-23-1878
Glenni W. Scofield	James Gilfillan	4-01-1878	5-20-1881
Blanche K. Bruce	James Gilfillan	5-21-1881	3-31-1883
Blanche K. Bruce	A.U. Wyman	4-01-1883	4-30-1885
Blanche K. Bruce	Conrad N. Jordan	5-01-1885	6-05-1885
William S. Rosecrans	Conrad N. Jordan	6-08-1885	5-23-1887
William S. Rosecrans	James W. Hyatt	5-24-1887	5-10-1889
William S. Rosecrans	J.N. Huston	5-11-1889	4-21-1891
William S. Rosecrans	Enos H. Nebeker	4-25-1891	5-31-1893
William S. Rosecrans	Daniel N. Morgan	6-01-1893	6-19-1893
James F. Tillman	Daniel N. Morgan	7-01-1893	6-30-1897

| | | Terms of Office | |
Register of the Treasury	Treasurer	Began	Ended
James F. Tillman	Elis H. Roberts	7-01-1897	12-02-1897
Blanche K. Bruce	Elis H. Roberts	12-03-1897	3-17-1898
Judson W. Lyons	Elis H. Roberts	4-07-1898	6-30-1905
Judson W. Lyons	Charles H. Treat	7-01-1905	4-01-1906
William T. Vernon	Charles H. Treat	6-12-1906	10-30-1909
William T. Vernon	Lee McClung	11-01-1909	3-14-1911
James C. Napier	Lee McClung	3-18-1911	11-21-1912
James C. Napier	Carmi A. Thompson	11-22-1912	3-31-1913
James C. Napier	John Burke	4-01-1913	9-30-1913
Gabe E. Parker	John Burke	10-01-1913	12-31-1914
Houston B. Teehee	John Burke	3-24-1915	11-20-1919
William S. Elliott	John Burke	11-21-1919	1-05-1921
William S. Elliott	Frank White	5-02-1921	1-24-1922
Harley V. Speelman	Frank White	1-25-1922	9-30-1927
Walter O. Woods	Frank White	10-01-1927	5-01-1928
Walter O. Woods	H.T. Tate	5-31-1928	1-17-1929
Edward E. Jones	Walter O. Woods	1-22-1929	5-31-1933

| | | Terms of Office | |
Secretary of the Treasury	Treasurer	Began	Ended
William G. McAdoo	John Burke	4-01-1913	12-15-1918
Carter Glass	John Burke	12-16-1918	2-01-1920
D.F. Houston	John Burke	2-02-1920	1-05-1921
A.W. Mellon	Frank White	5-02-1921	5-01-1928
A.W. Mellon	H.T. Tate	4-30-1928	1-17-1929
A.W. Mellon	Walter O. Woods	1-18-1929	2-12-1932
Ogden L. Mills	Walter O. Woods	2-13-1932	3-03-1933
W.H. Woodin	Walter O. Woods	3-04-1933	5-31-1933
W.H. Woodin	W.A. Julian	6-01-1933	12-31-1933
Henry Morgenthau, Jr	W.A. Julian	1-01-1934	7-22-1945
Fred M. Vinson	W.A. Julian	7-23-1945	7-23-1946
John W. Snyder	W.A. Julian	7-25-1946	5-29-1949
John W. Snyder	Georgia Neese Clark	6-21-1949	1-20-1953
George M. Humphrey	Ivy Baker Priest	1-28-1953	7-28-1957
Robert B. Anderson	Ivy Baker Priest	7-29-1957	1-21-1961
C. Douglas Dillon	Elizabeth Rudel Smith	1-30-1961	4-13-1962
C. Douglas Dillon	Kathryn O'Hay Granahan	1-03-1963	3-31-1965
Henry H. Fowler	Kathryn O'Hay Granahan	4-01-1965	10-13-1966
Joseph W. Barr	Kathryn O'Hay Granahan	12-21-1968	1-20-1969
David M. Kennedy	Dorothy Andrews Elston*	5-08-1969	9-16-1970
David M. Kennedy	Dorothy Andrews Kabis	9-17-1970	2-01-1971
John B. Connally	Dorothy Andrews Kabis	2-11-1971	7-03-1971
John B. Connally	Romana Acosta Banuelos	12-17-1971	5-16-1972
George P. Shultz	Romana Acosta Banuelos	6-12-1972	5-08-1974
William E. Simon	Francine I. Neff	6-21-1974	1-13-1977
W. Michael Blumenthal	Azie Taylor Morton	9-12-1977	8-04-1979
G. William Miller	Azie Taylor Morton	8-06-1979	1-19-1981

Secretary of the Treasury	Treasurer	Terms of Office Began	Ended
Donald T. Regan	Angela M. Buchanan	3-17-1981	7-01-1983
Donald T. Regan	Katherine Davalos Ortega	9-23-1983	1-29-1985
James A. Baker, III	Katherine Davalos Ortega	1-29-1985	8-17-1988
Nicholas Brady	Katherine Davalos Ortega	9-15-1988	6-30-1989
Nicholas Brady	Catalina V. Villalpando	12-11-1989	1-20-1993
Lloyd Bentsen	Mary Ellen Withrow	3-01-1994	12-23-1994
Robert Rubin	Mary Ellen Withrow	1-10-1995	

* During her term, Mrs. Elston married Walter L. Kabis. This is the firsttime the signature of a United States Treasurer was changed while in office.

Directors of the Bureau of Engraving and Printing

Directors	Term Began	Ended	Directors	Term Began	Ended
Spencer Morton Clark	8-22-1862	11-17-1868	James L. Wilmeth	12-10-1917	3-31-1922
George B. McCartee	3-18-1869	2-19-1876	Louis A. Hill	4-21-1922	2-14-1924
Henry C. Jewel	2-21-1876	4-30-1877	Wallace W. Kirby	6-16-1924	12-15-1924
Edward McPherson	5-01-1877	9-30-1878	Alvin W. Hall	12-22-1924	12-15-1954
O.H. Irish	10-01-1878	1-27-1883	Henry J. Holtzclaw	12-15-1954	10-08-1976
Truman N. Burrill	3-30-1883	5-31-1885	James A. Conlon	10-09-1967	7-01-1977
Edward O. Graves	6-10-1885	6-30-1889	Seymour Berry	7-02-1977	4-07-1979
Claude M. Johnson	7-01-1893	5-10-1900	Harry Clements	7-05-1979	1-03-1983
William M. Meredith	11-23-1900	6-30-1906	Robert J. Leuver	2-22-1983	4-01-1988
Thomas J. Sullivan	7-01-1906	5-04-1908	Peter H. Daly	8-26-1988	7-22-1995
Joseph E. Ralph	5-11-1908	10-31-1917	Larry Rolufs	7-24-1995	

Prior to July 1896 the head of the Bureau of Engraving and Printing was designated as "Chief."

The Treasury Seal

The U.S. Treasury Seal appears on all notes printed by the Bureau with the exception of the demand notes of 1861 and the first three issues of fractional currency.

Following the first issue of United States paper money in 1861, Spencer Clark, the Chief Engineer of the small National Currency Bureau, was requested by Secretary of the Treasury Chase to design a new seal for the Department.

The Department of the Treasury has had a variety of seals; the first, supposedly designed by Governeur Morris in 1778. Francis Hopkinson, who designed other departmental seals, could have had a hand in creating the seal that was adopted by the Continental Congress in 1789.

Spencer Clark had these words to say about his design, a variation of the 1789 version and still used today: "...its interior a facsimile of the seal adopted by the Treasury Department for its documents on a ground of geometric lathe work, the exterior being composed of thirty-four points, similarly executed. The points were designed to be typical of the thirty-four states, and to simulate the appearance of the seals ordinarily affixed to public documents." Clark preferred not to recognize the secession of eleven states the year before.

Until January 1968 the legend of the Seal appeared in Latin, THESAUR(I) AMER(ICAE) SEPTENT(RIONALIS) SIGIL(LUM); translated, "The Seal of the Treasury of North America." The new version of the Seal in English made its first appearance on the $100 United States note, Series 1966 printed in 1968. This new seal has the legend, "THE DEPARTMENT OF THE TREASURY 1789."

The Great Seal of the United States

Three designs for the Great Seal were submitted (1776, 1780 and May 1782), however it was the Charles Thomson's obverse design, adopted on June 20, 1782, that resembles the one we see in use today. The reverse is by William Barton, who had submitted obverse and reverse designs in May 1782.

The Great Seal symbolizes strength and victory and became the National Emblem in 1782. It first appeared on U.S. paper money as part of the back design of the 1907, $20 gold certificate. Since 1935 it has remained part of the back design of our $1 notes. Always desiring peace the American bald eagle faces the olive branch with 13 leaves, and holds arrows, the American Indian symbol of war, in its left talon. There are 13 stars above the eagle, one for each original colony. "E PLURIBUS UNUM," with 13 letters, means "ONE FROM MANY" and the 13-striped shield represents the Continental Congress.

The Latin motto on the reverse, "ANNUIT COEPTIS," with 13 letters means "HE (GOD) HAS SMILED ON OUR UNDERTAKINGS." Below the pyramid is a second motto, "NOVUS ORDO SECLORUM," or "A NEW ORDER OF THE AGES," signifying a new American age. The pyramid is a symbol of strength and permanence; it is incomplete, signifying that the United States continues to grow and build. The eye in the triangle suggests the all-seeing Deity, emphasizing spiritual welfare; it also indicates acknowledges education and freedom of knowledge. The date 1776 on the base of the pyramid with 13 steps refers to our Declaration of Independence.

The National Motto

The national motto, "In God We Trust," was added to the back of those $1 silver certificates that were printed on the Bureau of Engraving and Printing's new flatbed presses. The changeover to high-speed presses was completed in April 1868, and so Series 1935G of silver certificates printed in 1962 is found with and without the motto.

The suggestion to include "In God We Trust" was presented to Secretary of the Treasury George M. Humphrey in November 1953 by Matthew H. Rothert of Camden, Arkansas. Secretary Humphrey favored the idea but felt that Congressional sanction was required. In March 1955, through Mr. Rothert's efforts, bills to this effect were introduced into the Senate by Senator Fullbright of Arkansas and into the House of Representatives by Congressmen Bennet of Florida and Harris of Arkansas. The bill, which was approved by President Eisenhower on July 11, 1955, specified "that at such time as new dies for the printing of currency are adopted...by the Bureau of Engraving and Printing, the dies shall bear...the inscription "In God We Trust" and thereafter this inscription shall appear on all United States currency and coins."

In 1864 the motto had first appeared on a United States coin, the two-cent piece. It took 93 years and an act of Congress before the same motto was added to United States currency.

Dating, Size and Color of U.S. Paper Money

United States paper money includes at least one date, sometimes two. Large-size paper money most often included the date of issue, the date of the authorizing act, or a series date, and at times, two of the three. Coins bear an annual date; paper money does not. For some large-size notes a series did not change once it was established, even if United States Treasury signatures were changed. The note usually was given a different series date if the design was changed or altered.

With the exception of refunding certificates, compound interest and interest-bearing Treasury notes, all large-size notes are 7 3/8 x 3 1/8 inches in size.

Originally, small-size notes received a new series date or, most often, had a letter added to the original series date if either of the signatures changed. Today, a letter is added to the series date for one change of signature. However, if more than one year elapses from the original date, a date that corresponds to the year of issue is assigned.

A patent originated by Dr. Thomas Sterry Hunt and dated June 30, 1857 created an anti-photographic green ink. The primitive camera, a primary aid for counterfeiters, could not photograph this color. The 1857 interest-bearing treasury notes were the first United States federal currency to be printed with this ink. Green ink continues to be used for the back of current Federal Reserve notes.

Anti-counterfeiting Additions/Series 1990, 1993, 1995

Some predict a future cashless society. Cash now exceeds credit card payments in the amount of 300%. "By the year 2000 cash will account for 35% of consumer spending compared to only 14% of credit cards.... Cash in the U.S. is 7% coin and 93% bank notes..." (*The Nihlson Report*, February 1991).

Between 1985 and 1990 the loss to the public from counterfeit bank notes has doubled from $7 million to $14 million. "Counterfeiting originates from three categories: (1) individuals who are eccentric, mischievous, or criminal, (2) organized criminal groups, domestic and foreign, and (3) extremist groups sponsored or supported by unfriendly governments (*The Nihlson Report*, March 1991).

As much as 70% of U.S. paper money circulates outside the U.S. Approximately 37% of all counterfeit U.S. bank notes come from abroad. During each of fiscal years 1990 and 1991 the U.S. Secret Service seized $131.8 million. For the latter year, $50.8 million was seized abroad. (The U.S. Secret Service now has offices abroad.) The $131.8 million is an increase over $121.1 million for fiscal year 1898.

After seven years of research and development, two, visible anti-counterfeiting devices have been added to U.S. Federal Reserve notes, the only circulating notes. Advanced, color photocopiers posed a threat to all currencies. In an attempt to eradicate this threat, micro-printing and a plastic strip was added to the paper on which series 1990 was printed.

The first notes to be issued with these changes were the $100 and $50 denominations; eventually all but the $1 note included these same features.

"United States of America" is repeated in micro letters around each portrait. There is also a vertical plastic strip that bears the repeated denomination. The strip is visible when the note is held against a light; a magnifying glass might be necessary to see the micro-printing. It is difficult for photocopiers cannot copy either feature. Nevertheless, any document can be counterfeited given both technology and time.

A Counterfeit Supernote?

Extremely good counterfeit U.S. $100 notes appeared in Europe in the early 1990s. These bogus notes were so deceiving that many European banks began to refuse all U.S. $100 notes, fearful that some might be examples of what are the best counterfeits ever seen. Americans, including Vermont Senator Patrick Leahy, a member of the Banking Committee, discovered that while on vacation in Europe, traveler's checks were preferred to U.S. $100 notes. According to Dannen and Silverman, the trail led to three official security printing facilities in the Syrian-controlled Bekka Valley of Lebanon. The notes are transported over drug routes through Turkey to Europe by truck and by ship from Lebanon to Cyprus (Dannen and Silverman 52). The authors of "The Supernote" said there could have been between two and three billion dollars in $100 notes printed in just two years.

During his last days, the Shah of Iran requested and received two De La Rue Giori presses from the U.S. Since then, one press, to print "supernotes," was moved to a city closer to the Turkish border, from where these counterfeits could be shipped through Syria (Nathan Adams, TechnoPolitics, PBS Feb. 4, 1996).

To reproduce the notes, the counterfeiters probably scanned an image of a U.S. $100 note into a computer system. Then the image was projected onto a plate, which was then photoengraved and ultimately retouched by "conscripted skilled Armenian engravers" (Dannen and Silverman 52). Formulated inks, which contain ferrous oxide magnetic particles were simulated. Bleached $1 notes or paper that was indistinguishable helped to make counterfeits that not only look like authentic notes but also feel like them. The press has also reported that automatic counting devices, which would normally reject counterfeit notes, accepted many of these so called supernotes as genuine.

U.S. Series 1990 Federal Reserve notes were the first American notes to include modern anti-counterfeiting devices: micro-printing and a plastic strip. These two devices were introduced primarily to frustrate those who previously took the chance of passing photocopied images of U.S. paper money. These moderate changes were, unfortunately, too little and much too late. Robert Leuver, former Director of the BEP reported that Donald Regan, Treasury Secretary, had rejected more sophisticated devices in 1984.

The U.S. Secret Service has about 2000 agents; only a fraction were stationed outside the U.S. Reports of the $100 supernotes changed this proportion. In 1992 the first permanent Secret Service office in the Mid-East was set up in Cyprus in an attempt to monitor the counterfeiting activity in Lebanon. There are now at least

20 Secret Service agents outside the U.S. Dannen and Silverman reported that in May 1994 Secretary of State Warren Christopher met with Syrian President, Hafiz al-Assad; one of the topics of discussion was the $100 counterfeits. Then, to assist the Russian Federation with increasing mob dominance in business and banking, the U.S. F.B.I. set up an office in Moscow. Now the F.B.I. and the Secret Service are working together because of the large number of counterfeit $100 notes in Russia Russians hold more U.S. dollars then rubles, about $20 billion dollars, primarily in American $100 notes: 75% are probably counterfeits, many from the Mid-East.

On September 13, 1995, according to Dannen and Silverman, Viktor Melnikov from the Russian Central Bank described the supernote as an epidemic. If the production of the so-called supernotes came to an end, many could continue to circulate along with the new Series of 1996 notes. If the counterfeiters are not stopped, and since the two types of $100 notes will circulate together for years, the counterfeiters could continue to produce the same note while they work on creating imitations of Series 1996.

About $400 billion in U.S. paper money is in circulation; more than $250 billion is held outside the U.S. Counterfeits have always been part of this figure; however, high grade counterfeits could cause serious damage and confidence throughout the world. In the mid-1990s there were other serious sources for confiscated U.S. counterfeits, e.g., Bogota, Colombia and Saint Constant, Quebec. However, these are not the same quality as the bogus notes from Mid-East.

Series 1996

The use of advanced full color copiers and digital electronic scanners do not require extensive expertise. With this equipment anyone can counterfeit paper money. Consequently, the U.S. Treasury decided it was necessary to alter the appearance of our paper money.

The design of the American *greenback* is an international financial icon, one that the U.S. Treasury Department has hesitated to change since 1928. Although the new notes look different, one can easily recognize the resemblance to the previous design. This will make acceptance easier throughout the world. When all denominations for Series 1996 have been issued, we will most certainly follow the custom of other countries and change our currency designs about every eight to ten years. Counterfeiters are fast learners.

Concentric Fine-Line Printing: These fine lines behind the portrait are difficult to reproduce with color copiers and computer scanners. The same fine lines are used on the back.

Portrait and Watermark: The larger portrait, now moved to the left, allows space for a watermark of Franklin. Watermarks on future denominations will be the same as the engraved portrait on the individual note   This feature is visible when the note is held to the light.

Serial Numbers: The serial number now has a combination of eleven letters and numbers. An additional numeral and letter identifies an individual Federal Reserve District.

Federal Reserve Seal: A new seal replaces the older one that had included letters for individual Federal Reserve districts. The letter and numeral below the serial number identifies the Federal Reserve district, e.g., A1= Boston; B2=New York, etc.

Micro Printing: Within the "100" at the lower left, "USA 100" appears in microletters. Just below Franklin's collar there is "United States of America." These are visible when magnified, however, they are too small to be reproduced by photocopiers, or to be read by scanners.

Security Thread: A polymer thread, which identifies each denomination, is embedded in the paper. The words on the thread are visible when held to the light; however, they cannot be duplicated by copiers. This thread will be positioned according to the denomination, and will glow red if held under an ultraviolet light source. Security threads on Series 1990 notes were in the same position for all denominations.

Color Shifting Ink: The numeral "100" at the lower right is printed in green; however, it changes to black if you hold the note at an angle.

Engraving and Plate Making

In the past, steel bank note plates were created by the transfer process. Plates for Series of 1996 notes are photoengraved from copper plates.

After a hand-engraved plate is finished in soft steel, all in reverse, the plate is hardened by immersion. Then, under tons of pressure, a soft steel roll is moved back and forth to pick up the incised lines. This process, called siderography, now has created a roll with raised images. Once the roll is hardened, it can be used to make multiple plates that are precisely the same. After a plate with multiple images is complete, the soft steel is hardened and chrome- or nickel-plated to extend the life of the plate. When a worn plate must be replaced, the siderographer's roll is used to make a new plate.

Photoengraving is less expensive, and the method has been adopted by most security companies and, to produce Series 1996, the BEP. After the portrait, picture, letter and script engravers complete their work, and the lathe work is in place on a copper plate, the plate is photographed. The images for separate face and back plates are projected on light-sensitive copper plates, covered with a substance that will make the plate sensitive only to the projected images. The finished plate is a combination of hand-engraving and photo etching. Iron chloride is used as the agent to etch the images in the photo etching process at the Bureau of Engraving and Printing.

To make multiple plates, a plastic mold of the master die, or *basso*, is made using heat and hydraulic pressure. The multiple plates are welded together into a 32-subject plastic *alto* to be used in the nickel plate-making process. The finished 32-subject nickel basso plates are chrome-plated to extend the life of the plate and resist damage from handling.

Counterfeiting Statistics

With the appearance of the Mid-East counterfeits, and technology that is available to criminals, more advanced anti-counterfeiting devices were necessary. In 1993 the National Research Council predicted that by the year 2000, unless sophisticated devices were introduced, $2 billion in U.S. counterfeit notes would enter circulation annually.

The color photocopier has become a convenient tool for the dishonest mind. Though minimal, the ink on the reproduced engraved lines from some color copiers can be felt, but not to the degree that the ink on an engraved note is noticeable. The ink on an engraved note actually rests *above* the paper. During the printing operation, the paper, under tons of pressure, is forced into the engraved lines of the plate, lines that holds the thick colored inks.

By September 30, 1995, the end of the fiscal year, 1995, $30.7 million in counterfeit bills were passed in the United States, an increase of $5.7 million from 1994. An additional $72 million in counterfeit notes were seized before they entered circulation. Abroad, $260 million in counterfeit notes were seized; this includes those confiscated before entering circulation (U.S. Secret Service).

In 1994, $990,138 counterfeit notes made by color photocopiers was passed. In the middle of fiscal year 1995, $448,168 in photocopied notes were passed; only 75% was seized before it was passed. In mid-1995 calendar year, $13,312 in photocopied notes were passed. During this same period $4 million of these counterfeits were created overseas; $54,400 was seized before it was passed (Schafrick & Church).

CHAPTER TWO

Types of United States Paper Money

NUMBERING SYSTEMS OF UNITED STATES PAPER MONEY

ONE of the chief functions of the numbering systems used on United States currency has been to foil counterfeiters. At first the Treasury Department kept the details of the numbering systems secret so that forgers could not find the correct combinations of serial numbers and plate position letters and numbers. More recently, the Treasury's "Know Your Money" campaign has stressed maximum publicity of all details of the currency so that the general public can be well-prepared to detect counterfeits. Thus the details of the numbering systems have become better known, though, as will be demonstrated, gaps still exist.

No serial number prefix or suffix was added to United States currency prior to April 1869.

Repeat Numbering

The earliest numbering system used on United States paper money was repeat numbering. All notes from a given sheet would have the same serial number, including prefix and suffix letters and ornaments, if any. These notes are differentiated only by plate position letters, usually A, B, C and D or E. F, G and H on a 4-subject plate. A national bank note plate of $1-1-1-2 would have plate letters A-B-C-A. Sheets of other mixed denominations would use letters similarly. Repeat numbering is found on all classes of interest-bearing notes except the refunding certificates of 1879, and on large-size national bank notes of all charter periods. Repeat numbering was originally a device to avoid impossibly large serial numbers.

Consecutive Numbering

In consecutive numbering all notes on a sheet have consecutive numbers. The bottom note of a 4-subject sheet has a serial number divisible by 4 and a plate letter "D", or occasionally an "H". Consecutive numbering is found on all large-size notes except compound interest treasury notes, interest-bearing notes and national bank notes. This numbering system was continued on all 12-subject small-size notes (1929-1953) except for the special uncut sheets issued for use in Hawaii and North Africa during World War II. The relationship on these small-size notes between a serial number divisible by 12 and a plate position letter is an anti-counterfeiting device.

Consecutive numbering enabled many early sheets to be reconstructed for display, affording an idea of the original appearance of plates even though no uncut sheets survived. This is generally not possible with skip numbering. The earliest bills demand notes, United States notes, and gold certificates bear serial numbers 1 to 1,000,000. The numbering system was then repeated with the addition of "series 1", "series 2", etc. United States notes of 1862 and 1863 are known with series as high as 284. Interest-bearing Treasury notes were not issued in large enough quantities to require this practice; repeat numbering to six digits was sufficient.

Skip Numbering

Beginning in November 1952, 18-subject sheets show skip numbering, the first sheet bearing numbers 1, 8001, 16001, and so forth to 136001. The next sheet would commence with 2, 8002, 16002, through a run of 8,000 sheets. A similar system is now in use for 32-subject sheets.

Block Numbering

A new system, block numbering, began with the 1869 United States notes. Serial numbers were prefixed with "A" (1 to 10,000,000), then B, K, V and Z advancing to the same figure. Other letters used with a star suffix (these are not replacement notes) appeared on higher denominations. On the United States notes of 1880, prefix letters and ornament suffixes continued, but a complete block was 10,000,000; many blocks are incomplete because prefix letters were changed when different seals were introduced. United States notes in 1917 introduce letter suffixes as well. Blocks A-A, B-A, D-A, E-A, H-A, K-A, M-A, N-A, R-A and T-A are found on $1 notes.

Silver certificates of 1878 are from block A-X, those of 1880 are from block "B" with ornament, those of 1866 are from block "B" with a different ornament, those of 1891 are from block "E" with yet another ornament, and the issues of 1896 (and the 1899 issue bearing signatures of Lyons and Roberts) have two pheons. Subsequent blocks are B, D, E, H, K, M, and so forth with an ornament as a suffix. In 1912 identical prefix and suffix letters were introduced, producing A-A, B-B, D-D, E-E and H-H.

From about 1917 the suffix "A" is constant: B-A, D-A, E-A, H-A...X-A. On small-size currency the block system is continued with the entire alphabet used except for "O;" after 100,000,000 (today a star note) in block Z-A, the numbering starts again with A-B. The exception to this is Federal Reserve notes A through L on which the letter is always that of the Federal Reserve District.

Before August 22, 1925 all national bank notes bore both a Treasury serial number and a bank sheet number; after 1925 the bank sheet number was printed twice. The bank sheet number generally not prefixed and never suffixed is the cumulative total of notes of that denomination and type issued for that bank. Prefix "A" is rarely found on national bank notes issued between 1925 and 1929. Apparently, "A" signifies the second million sheets of that denomination and type. The Treasury number to six digits, at first plain, then in parenthesis, suffix, and letter prefix were cumulative for sheets of the denomination and type over all of the banks for which they were issued. Later, blocks in Treasury numbers were generally similar to those in other classes of notes. Double letters (A-A, B-B, D-D) were in use between 1899 and 1908; letters B-A, D-A and E-A began on May 5, 1911. Information allowing the accurate dating of a national bank note from the Treasury number is not available since certain archival records of 1916-1922 are incomplete.

Small-size national bank notes of type I, issued between 1919-1933, used repeat numbering with six subjects prefixed A to F and suffixed "A". The millionth sheet was then numbered A to F with suffix "B". The "B" suffix is known on $5 notes issued by The Chase National Bank of New York. Type II notes, issued from May 1933 through May 1935, were consecutively numbered with the bank's charter number in brown beside the bank serial number. The complete "A" block totals 699,996 notes from 166,666 sheets; the next sheet was numbered B1 to 6. Five dollar notes of block "B" are known from the Bank of America, San Francisco, California.

Star or Replacement Notes

Defective notes printed at the Bureau of Engraving and Printing before June 1910 were replaced with hand-stamped notes with the same serial number as the imperfect note. As the production of notes increased this became impractical. Star notes with different serial numbers were the answer.

The use of a star as a prefix, on notes that replaced defective notes discovered at the Bureau of Engraving and Printing during inspection, began in 1910 with block ☆-B on United States notes and silver certificates; later, suffix "D" was used. The system continued with the use of a solid star (★), which was applied to small-size notes. Federal Reserve Bank notes and Federal Reserve notes employ the star as the suffix. No star notes were issued for national bank notes, although a replacement system was used. Defective national bank notes were replaced with individually prepared matching serial numbers. These can sometimes be identified by the faulty alignment of the serial number.

The star (★) was also used after 1935 to complete a numbered series of 100,000,000 for all small-size notes. Since the highest number that can be printed by an eight digit numbering cylinder is 99,999,999, the 100,000,000th note was, in some instances, a hand-inserted star note with a random serial number. Doug Murray and Frank Nowak have confirmed from Bureau records that serial number 100,000,000 was printed for many and could have been printed for all notes prior to 1935. All observed large-size notes with number 100,000,000 appear to have been hand-stamped (see No. H380). It is possible that some, perhaps many, of these scarce, attractive, serial-numbered large- and small-size notes could have been held back as presentation pieces, with a star note inserted to complete a pack of 100 notes, thus accounting for their rarity.

Throughout this catalog replacement notes are listed as a variety of the major entry. These are indicated by a star (☆) after the primary entry. Also listed is the number of known star notes issued, printed or delivered. Listed as well are figures received from collectors who have reported replacements for an issue.

A DESCRIPTION OF NOTE TYPES

Demand Notes

Congressional Acts of July 17 and August 5, 1861 authorized $60 million in demand notes, or "greenbacks" as they were soon called. At $1200 annually, seventy recruits from the United States Treasury Department were assigned the task of signing each of these notes for the two designated Treasury officials. At first, "For the", "For The", or "for the" was written as a prefix to the words "Treasurer" and "Register of the Treasury." The engraved plates were altered in late August 1861 to include the words "For the". A letter dated 27 August from American Bank Note Company (ABNCo) to the Treasury Department acknowledges the request for this change. Three days later, as requested, ABNCo wrote to say they would suspend the printing of demand notes payable at Cincinnati and St. Louis. These notes are now the rarest.

Demand notes are the only United States currency, excluding fractional currency, that do not bear the United States Treasury Seal. Nor do they include the names of the United States Treasurer and Register of the Treasury, but they do include the names of those who signed for them.

These notes, payable on demand, bore no interest as did Treasury notes authorized by the same two acts, and they were not redeemable in coin. However, a circular from the office of the Secretary of the Treasury, prior to specie payment suspension on 21 December 1861, declared them payable in coin, on a par with gold. Prior to, and after the circular issuance, demand notes were acceptable at discount rates.

United States (Legal Tender) Notes

The first of five, large-size issues in denominations of $5 to $1,000 bears the date of March 10, 1862. Two different obligations appear on the back of the first issue.

First Obligation: "This note is legal tender for all debts, public and private, except duties on imports and interest on the public debt, and is exchangeable for U.S. six-percent, twenty-year bonds, redeemable at the pleasure of the United States after five years."

Second obligation: "This note is legal tender for all debts, public and private, except duties on imports and interest on the public debt, and is receivable in payment of all loans made to the United States."

The second issue, dated August 1, 1862, included notes of $1 and $2 only.

The third issue, dated August 1, 1863, once again included denominations from $5 to $1,000. The Congressional Act of March 3, 1863 authorized the fourth issue; it included denominations of $1 to $10,000. Seven series are included in this issue: 1869 (labeled a Treasury Note), 1874, 1878, 1880, 1907, 1917 and 1923. A $10 note was the only denomination included in the fifth issue, series of 1901. In July 1873 the United States Treasury Department decided that the term United States notes would replace "legal tender notes" as the official designation for large-size notes.

Small-size United States notes of $1 (1928), $2 and $5 (1928, 1953 and 1963), and $100 (1966) have been issued. The latter denomination accounted for most of the $346,681,016 that technically remained in circulation as required by the Act of May 31, 1878 and the Old Series Currency Adjustment Act. In late 1986 it was announced that this obligation would be discontinued upon the passage of required legislation. Although still legal tender, as is all circulating U.S. currency since 1861, the few red seal U.S. notes still in circulation are withdrawn as they come into banks.

Section 602(g)(14) of the Riegle Community Development and Regulatory Improvement Act of September 23, 1994 amended Section 5119(b)(2) of title 31 of the United States Code to read: "The Secretary shall not be required to reissue United States currency notes upon redemption." The 1878 requirement to keep "legal tender" notes in circulation was thus repealed.

History of Interest-bearing Treasury Notes

The first United States interest-bearing Treasury notes were issued in 1812. Their recommendation came from Secretary of the Treasury Albert Gallatin on May 14, 1812, one month before war was declared against Great Britain on June 18. These notes, and most of those that were periodically issued during the following 53 years, gained interest. The lower denominations, at times including notes as high as $20, circulated as currency. Higher denominations were often held by banks "as high-powered reserves for the expansion of their own notes and deposits, and as clearing media for adverse balances with other banks" (Timberlake 15). These notes did not enjoy legal tender status, but were nevertheless receivable for government debts, taxes and duties.

Section two of the Act of June 30, 1812 authorized the issue of Treasury notes stating:

That the said treasury notes shall be reimbursed by the United States, at such places, respectively, as may be expressed on the face of the said notes, one year, respectively, after the day on which the same shall have been issued; from which day of issue they shall bear interest at the rate of five and two-fifths per centum a year, payable to the owner and owners of such notes, at the treasury, or by the proper commissioner of loans, at the places and times respectively designated on the face of said notes for the payment of principal.

The first Treasury notes were signed by designees of the President of the United States at a compensation of $1.25 for each 100 notes signed. These notes were then countersigned by United States Commissioner of Loans for the state in which the respective notes were payable. As part of the Act of December 26, 1814, signers had their fee reduced to .75¢ per 100 notes signed. The length of the loan for Treasury notes issued between 1812 and 1860 was one year. Interest rates on Treasury notes issued during this period ranged from 2 to 6 percent. There were three exceptions; those issued under the Acts of October 12, 1837, March 3, 1843 and June 22, 1846 bore interest at a minimum of 1 mill percent.

Interest accrued at the rate of 5, 6 and 7.3 percent over a period of sixty days to three years for Treasury notes issued between 1861 and 1865. Three-year notes included five coupons, each redeemable after intervals of six months. The final payment was made when the note itself was redeemed. The acts that authorized some Treasury notes also allowed for their reissuance, provided the outstanding amount did not exceed the authorized amount.

Beginning with emissions authorized under the Act of February 24, 1815, Treasury notes received the countersignature of the United States Register of the Treasury. Treasury notes issued under the Act of October 12, 1837 and all that followed through 1865, bore the signature of the United States Treasurer and the countersignature of the United States Register of the Treasury.

"In April of 1864 $4,000 in interest-bearing [Treasury] notes of unspecified denominations were issued misdated from 5-12-64 to 5-16-64, thus accounting for a [$20 note] dated 5-14-64" (Gengerke 48).

After 1865, bonds, which had been issued concurrently, seemed to suffice as United States interest-bearing fiscal paper. United States treasury notes regained popularity in the 1970s. However, since a book entry is made at the time of purchase, a statement is received instead of a certificate.

Interest-bearing treasury notes, compound interest treasury notes in denominations of $10 and $20, and refunding certificates often circulated as currency.

INTEREST-BEARING TREASURY NOTES 1812-1860

The original body of this catalog, without the following treasury notes (1812-1860), is arranged by denomination. However, due to the greater variety of interest rates that often apply to early treasury notes, those issued between 1812 and 1860 will be listed and illustrated separately under each act at the beginning of the catalog. The illustrations comparatively reflect the actual size of these larger notes. Interest-bearing treasury notes issued after 1860 are listed by denomination in this catalog. And, although catalog numbers are essential, they can be a nuisance. Rather than introduce yet another set of catalog numbers, those used to identify the following treasury notes as they first appeared in *An Illustrated History of Loans, 1775-1898* will be used here.

To avoid confusion, an "X" was placed before all numbers in the work just mentioned so that easy reference can be made. Thus, HX100 identifies Treasury notes issued under the Act of 21 May 1838; H100 refers to 1969B, $1 Federal Reserve notes, listed under $1 notes in this catalog.

Compound Interest Treasury Notes

Notes of $10, $20, $50, $100, $500 and $1,000, bearing interest at 6 percent annually were authorized by Congressional Acts of March 3, 1863 and June 30, 1864. They were issued to force the retirement of 5 percent treasury notes issued under the latter act. All compound interest treasury notes had bronze overprints; the notes ceased to earn interest after maturity. Two and one-half years after these notes were issued 3 percent certificates were issued for their redemption.
An unknown number of these notes were issued with the incorrect act date of July 2, 1864. Two $10 notes (8275, plate B, and 9582, plate C) have been recorded.

Refunding Certificates

On February 26, 1879 the United States government authorized what was thought to be an appealing fiscal instrument of $10 that would pay 4 percent interest annually with an indefinite accumulation. In 1907 Congress passed a law that discontinued interest after July 1 of that year. At that time the notes with accrued interest were worth $21.30. The first of two types (Nos. 603 & 604 in this catalog) is extremely rare; only two are known.

Currency Certificates of Deposit

By the Act of June 8, 1872 the Secretary of the Treasury was authorized to issue certificates in denominations of $5,000 and to receive certificates of $10,000. The $10,000 notes were receivable on deposit without interest from national banking houses but were not to be included in the legal reserve. The $5,000 notes were payable on demand (in United States notes) at the place of deposit but were accepted in settlement of clearing house balances at the locations where such deposits were made. On March 14, 1900 the act authorizing these large denomination certificates was repealed.

Silver Certificates

All silver certificates were authorized by the Acts of February 28, 1878 and August 4, 1886. The first of five, large-size issues had "Certificate of Deposit" printed on the face of $10 to $10,000 notes. The notes of 1878 all have the countersignature of the United States Assistant Treasurer. Notes of $1 through $1,000 made up the second issue of 1886, 1891 and 1908. Notes of $1, $2 and $5 account for the third issue of 1896 and the fourth issue, Series of 1899. The fifth issue, series of 1923, included only $1 and $5 notes.

Small-size silver certificates in denominations of $1 (1928, 1934, 1935 and 1957), $5 (1934 and 1953), and $10 (1933, 1934 and 1953) are no longer printed. Series of 1934 $1 notes were the first to have the Treasury signatures overprinted on the notes; previous signatures were engraved into the printing plates. After June 24, 1968, silver certificates were no longer redeemable for silver.

Treasury (or Coin) Notes

The Legal Tender Act of July 14, 1890, passed with the help of the silver mining lobby, authorized the "Coin" notes of $1 through $1,000, Series of 1890 and 1891. The $50 note was issued only as Series 1891; only an essay for the $500 design was made.

Treasury, or coin, notes were used to purchase silver bullion, at inflated prices. They were received in payment, then redeemed for gold when possible; the Secretary of the Treasury could decide if the notes were to be payable in gold or silver. This ludicrous scenario continued until President Cleveland had the silver purchasing act repealed in 1893, thereby averting a serious panic in 1893.

Federal Reserve Notes

The Federal Reserve Act of 1913 authorized all Federal Reserve notes. The series of 1914 included only notes of $5 through $100; the higher denominations, $500 through $10,000, bore the series date of 1918. Series 1914 was issued in two types one with red treasury seal and serial number, the other with blue seal and number; the type in red is the scarcest. The red and blue ink that was used for the seals on these notes came from Germany. World War I interrupted the flow from the normal source. The last supplies, less red than blue, came to the U.S. through the Netherlands. In 1918, with the help of the American Chemical Society, the BEP was "able to purchase a very satisfactory American product...(*History BEP* 92)." The obligation on the Federal Reserve notes was borne by the United States government and not by the individual banks.

Small-size Federal Reserve notes have been printed in denominations of $1 through $10,000; the $100 note is the largest denomination printed today. These small-size notes ($5 to $10,000) were first printed in 1929 with a series date of 1928. (Notes of $1 were not printed until 1963.)

Until 1934 the obligation of all Federal Reserve notes made a reference to redemption in gold. Following the passage of the Gold Reserve Act in 1933, United States paper money was no longer redeemable in gold and the obligation was changed to read, "redeemable in lawful money." All notes issued today by the United States government are Federal Reserve notes.

With the introduction of Series 1996, Federal Reserve notes have a new universal Federal Reserve seal. Seals on previous notes included letters, numerals, or both, to indicate a specific Federal Reserve district. Now, the district is identified with an extra letter and numeral below the serial number on the upper left.

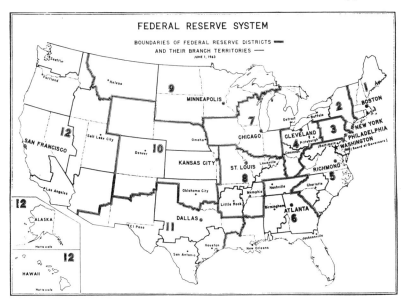

Photo by Coin World.

Federal Reserve Bank Notes

There were two issues of large-size Federal Reserve Bank notes 1915 ($5, $10 and $20) and 1918 ($1-$50) authorized by Federal Reserve Acts of December 23, 1913 and April 23, 1918. Not all banks within the Federal Reserve system issued notes of the first series, but all banks issued notes bearing the series date of 1918. The obligation to pay is made by the individual bank, not by the United States government. Approximately $760 million in notes was issued; only $2 million remain outstanding.

These notes were issued to make up for retired national bank notes and to compensate for silver purchased from the United States Treasury by Great Britain. Silver certificates accumulated by Federal Reserve Banks were transferred to the U.S. Treasury for Pittman (Act of April 1918) certificates of indebtedness, an asset included in Federal Reserve credit. Canceled silver certificates released the silver Great Britain purchased and then sent to India, which was on the silver standard.

The small-size Federal Reserve Bank notes were authorized by the Act of March 9, 1933 and were issued to alleviate the shortage of paper money due to the massive withdrawal of Federal Reserve notes. National bank note plates with the date 1929 were adapted for this issue, which is similar to the earlier national bank notes with the exception of the overprinting, to accommodate the appropriate signatures and a larger brown seal.

National Gold Bank Notes

These gold-tinted notes are extremely beautiful as well as extremely rare. To alleviate the burden of handling gold in the form of dust and nuggets in business transactions, the United States Congress authorized ten banks nine in California and one in Boston to issue paper money in denominations of $5 through $500 redeemable in gold. The Kidder National Bank in Boston had $120,000 in notes prepared. However, none were issued. Three pairs of $50 and $100 specimen notes are known to exist from this bank.

These gold banks were also national banks, and it was therefore necessary for them to deposit United States Bonds as security with the U.S. Treasurer. Notes of up to 80 percent of the deposited bonds could circulate but gold coins equaling 25 percent of the note issue had to remain in the bank's vaults. The obligation on these notes is similar to that on national bank notes except that the gold bank notes were payable in "gold coin."

Fewer than 300 pieces most in a poor state of preservation in all denominations for all banks, are known. However, United States Treasury records show that 6,639 notes remain outstanding.

Gold Certificates

There were nine issues of large-size gold certificates, but only four issues were circulated widely. The first three (issued between 1865 and 1875), the fifth (1888), and the sixth (1900) were used primarily among banks and clearing houses. The 1882 series, the fourth issue, in denominations of $20 through $10,000, was the first to circulate widely. The seventh issue, series of 1905, 1906 and 1907, included two denominations only $10 and $20. Series 1907, the eighth issue, was limited to the $1,000 note. The ninth and final issue consisted of two series 1913 ($50) and 1922 ($10-$1,000).

Small-size gold certificates dated 1928 ($10-$10,000) had a short life; they were recalled following the Gold Reserve Act of 1933. Secretary of the Treasury Dillon's order of April 24, 1964 made it legal for collectors, and others, to hold gold certificates.

National Bank Notes

As the Civil War entered its third year, it became necessary to centralize and standardize paper money in the United States needed to be centralized and standardized. In addition to demand notes, United States (legal tender) notes, and those interest-bearing treasury notes that, out of necessity, circulated, there was a plethora of state bank notes, many of dubious origin, that also continued to circulate. Secretary of the Treasury Salmon P. Chase initiated the National Bank Act of February 25, 1863. Notes of $1 through $1,000 were authorized. A $3 note was included but not issued.

The Act of 1863 allowed participating chartered banks to issue bank notes up to 90 percent of the value of specific United States bonds which had been deposited with the Treasurer of the United States. A circulating limit of $300 million for national banks was established on June 3, 1864. On March 3, 1865 legislation was enacted that apportioned the preceding figure based on population and banking capital. It was this act that imposed the 10 percent tax on all state bank notes in circulation; this sealed the doom of the wildcat banking period.

An additional $54 million in circulating notes was authorized in 1870, and a circulation limit of $500,000 was placed on each chartered bank. Five years later all restrictions were removed, and in 1900 banks were granted the privilege of issuing notes equaling 100 percent of the bonds deposited. When the last of these bonds were recalled, in July 1935, no more were issued.

Prior to 1875 national bank notes were prepared exclusively by three private bank note companies American Bank Note Co., National Bank Note Co. and Continental Bank Note Co. The United States Treasury seal and both sets of serial numbers, treasury and bank, were added in Washington. Commencing in September 1875 face plates were sent to Washington for printing, but most backs continued to be printed by the private bank note companies. Beginning in January 1877 all currency printing was done at the National Currency Bureau in Washington.

Large-size currency was authorized under three 20-year charters. The first included two issues; the second and third, three issues each. Charters were granted from the time of application. Consequently, notes from different periods, issued by a variety of banks, were in circulation at the same time With the exception of most of the original First Charter notes, all subsequent national bank notes had the charter number printed on the face of the notes. First Charter ...of the notes. The "1902-1908" on the backs of the third charter, second issue notes, refer to the Currency Act of April 12, 1902 and the Aldrich-Vreeland Act of May 30, 1908. The latter act, at a time of currency shortage, allowed national banks to deposit other securities, in addition to the required bonds, and issue additional notes equivalent to 75% of these additional securities. Two types of small-size notes were issued; type II had the charter number printed two additional times on each note.

After 1935 the Federal Reserve Banking System, established in 1913, took precedence and the most fascinating chapter in the history of United States currency came to an end. The general rarity of national bank notes by state ranges from

R(arity) 1, the most common, to R(arity) 9, the rarest. The table printed herein is arranged accordingly.

FREQUENTLY USED PORTRAITS ON UNITED STATES PAPER MONEY

Portraits of 13 Americans have frequently appeared on United States paper money since 1961. Brief biographical sketches of these famous Americans along with the catalog numbers of the notes on which their portraits appear follow. Additional information pertaining to these and the portraits of the lesser known personalities that have appeared on United States currency is included with the respective listing.

Salmon P. Chase, b. Cornish, NH 13 Jan. 1808, d. New York City 7 May 1873. After moving to Ohio as a boy he attended Dartmouth; Chase returned to Ohio to practice law in Cincinnati. He served as President Lincoln's Secretary of the Treasury and practically established the National Banking System singlehandedly. In 1864 Chase was appointed to the United States Supreme Court and remained in that position until his death. (Nos. 1-4, 493-496, 945b, 1396-1398 and 1493-1497)

Steven Grover Cleveland, b. Caldwell, NJ 18 Mar. 1837, d. Princeton, NJ 24 June 1908. He practiced law in New York, served there as governor, and was twice elected to the U.S. Presidency. (Nos. 848-850 and all small-size $1,000 notes)

Benjamin Franklin, b. Boston, MA 17 Jan. 1706, d. Philadelphia, PA 17 April 1790. Franklin is recognized by philatelists for his contributions to the postal service. In 1727 he was appointed Postmaster in Philadelphia. In 1753, along with William Hunter, Franklin was placed in charge of the Colonial Postal Service. (Nos. 603-604, 929-941, 1244-1245, X115A, all small-size $100 notes and 30-cent encased postage)

Ulysses S. Grant, b. Point Pleasant, OH 27 April 1822, d. Mount McGregor, NY 23 July 1885. Grant served his country as a military officer and eighteenth U. S. President. (Nos. 349-360, 1040-1042, 1044-1046 and all small-size $50 notes)

Alexander Hamilton, b. Nevis, W. Indies 11 Jan. 1757, d. New York City 12 July 1804. It was through the genius of Hamilton that the financial chaos left by the American Revolution was resolved. As the first Secretary of the Treasury (1789-1795) he established the Bank of the United States and a sensible federal monetary system. In 1799, along with Aaron Burr (Hamilton died from a gunshot wound in a duel with Burr) Hamilton founded the Manhattan Company in New York City. This company, which gave birth to the Bank of the Manhattan Company, survived wars and epidemics and, through a series of mergers, became The Chase Manhattan Bank, one of the largest banks in the nation. Hamilton is one of five Americans of foreign birth to appear on U.S. paper money. The others are R.

Morris (Nos. 578 and 1376), A. Gallatin (No. 1320), E.D. Baker (No. 1441) and G.G. Meade (No. 1425). (Nos. 153, 242-244, 703-723, 926-927, 942, 945a, 1346-1347, 1413-1424, 1429 and all small-size $10 notes)

Andrew Jackson, b. Waxhaw, SC 15 March 1767, d. Nashville, TN 8 June 1845. He studied law in North Carolina and began to practice in Nashville, Tennessee. After serving in the United States House of Representatives and Senate, Jackson served two terms as U.S. President. (Nos. 245-273, 492, 618-620, 1465-1492, all small-size $20 notes and 2-cent encased postage)

Thomas Jefferson, b. Shadwell, Goochland County, VA 13 April 1743, d. Charlottesville, VA 4 July 1826. Jefferson, our third President was knowledgeable in music, architecture, astronomy and agriculture. At age 20 he began building his home, Monticello, on Carter's Mountain; it was completed in his 60th year. Jefferson died on the 15th anniversary of the signing of the Declaration of Independence. (Nos. 154-170 203-207, 1502-1505, 1548-1551 all small-size $2 notes and 5-cent encased postage)

Abraham Lincoln, b. Hodgenville, Harrison County, KY 12 Feb. 1809, d. Washington, DC 15 April 1865. In 1861, during the first administration of the 16th U.S. President, the first demand notes, or greenbacks, were issued. After George Washington and Alexander Hamilton, Abraham Lincoln is the most frequently portrayed person on United States currency. (Nos. 372, 380-382, 463-465, 1122-1136, 1359-1369, 1624-1625, and all small-size $5 notes)

William McKinley, b. Niles, OH 29 Jan. 1843, d. Buffalo, NY 14 Sept. 1901. The 25th U.S. President he was shot at the Pan-American Exposition in Buffalo, New York on 6 September 1901 and died soon thereafter. (Nos. 540-566 and 1372-1375)

James Madison, b. Port Conway, VA 16 Mar. 1751, d. Montpelier, VA 28 June 1836. Madison was a member of the Continental Congress (1780-1783, 1787-1788) and was elected as the fourth U.S. President. He did not favor government-issued paper money and voted against the establishment of the Bank of the United States. (Nos. 1435, 1446-1464)

James Monroe, b. Westmoreland County, VA 28 April 1758, d. New York City 4 July 1831. He studied law under Thomas Jefferson. He became Governor of Virginia, was appointed Secretary of State by President Madison, and became the fifth U.S. President. (Nos. 1212-1221)

Robert Morris, b. Liverpool, England 20 Jan. 1734, d. Philadelphia, PA 8 May 1806. Morris, United States Senator (1789-1795), was one of the signers of the Declaration of Independence. As Superintendent of Finance (1781-1784), he was instrumental in founding the Bank of North America. (Nos. 578-589 and 1376-1378)

George Washington, b. Pope's Creek, VA 22 Feb. 1732, d. Mt. Vernon, VA 14 Dec. 1799. President Washington was much involved in the production of the first U.S. coins. It is possible that the half dismes struck by Robert Birch in 1792 were minted with table silver from the Washington home. Although it does remain controversial, it does seem that Washington financed the purchase of the silver bullion that was used. Washington rejected the idea that his portrait should appear on the new coinage (Nos. 5–28, 45-46, 59-61, 187-196, 300-315, 834-842, 953-986, 1013–1014f, 1137-1140, 1340, 1343, 1393b, 1403-1404, 1461, 1499-1501, 1506-1509, 1514-1529, 1522-1558, 1568-1572, X110C, X113, X115A, X121A, all small-size $1 notes and 90-cent encased postage)

ANNOUNCEMENT OF SMALL-SIZE CURRENCY

A few months before small-size currency entered circulation in 1929, circulars, the same size as the new notes, were distributed by banks and businesses. The backs of these provided a splendid opportunity for advertisement.

TEST PIECES

In January 1972 it was revealed that the Bureau of Engraving and Printing had sent experimental plates to Germany for a test run on new Giori presses, which were later purchased by the Bureau. An examples from this test is illustrated here. One has black printing on the face and a reddish-brown back, another has green face printing and black back printing, a third, discovered in 1980, has black face printing and a light brown back.

At least four examples of these notes, the colors of three are unknown, bear serial numbers with an "A" prefix. The lowest is A000993??A, the highest is A99998109A on a black back.

In 1976 another test piece appeared; it had been printed in Geneva, New York on a Magna press. These pieces have green face designs and black backs   A portrait of George Washington replaced the one of Thomas Jefferson. These test pieces should have been destroyed. However, they are now legal to hold as collectors' pieces.

In the late 1980s a remarkable test piece surfaced. With the exception of the portrait of Thomas de la Rue, the founder of the company that undoubtedly provided for the test, the piece is exactly the same as the 1935-1957, $1 silver certificates. A plate of this type was indeed used to perform trial runs after the Giori presses were acquired by the Bureau of Engraving and Printing. Only four of these uniface, test pieces with the de la Rue portrait are known to exist. The color of this piece is brown, green and blue.

Some test pieces produced by Hamilton-Stevens Group, Inc. entered the market place about 1993. These "TEST PLATE" pieces, produced by the new (continuous) web-fed press have a portrait of Abraham Lincoln on the left and a factory scene on the right. They were printed in three individual colors— brown, green and black; the latter is the scarcest. In addition, there are also examples with an imprint only; without ink they appear to be embossed.

CHAPTER THREE

Catalog of United States Paper Money

USING THE CATALOG

THE catalog is organized by denomination from $1 to $100,000. Within each denomination, the various issues are cataloged by major type. The system of numbering used here is the simplest possible; each piece has been numbered consecutively. Occasionally a letter follows the number, this usually coincides with a series change.

In the case of Federal Reserve notes the letters of the respective districts have been added to the number. In addition, another suffix letter is sometimes included to differentiate between the maximum five-signature combinations. At the end of each listing for Federal Reserve note denominations that are current ($1-$100), additional numbers have been left unassigned for future issues.

Any numbering system is only a type of shorthand reference. Unwieldy cataloging systems that try to include as much information in the catalog number as in the description itself sometimes become redundant and difficult. It should also be remembered that there is no necessity to use a number at all. It is simply a convenience and form of reference for those who wish to use it.

Written permission is required for the use of the numbering system used in this catalog if cited in any book, pamphlet or catalog. Publishers of magazines, newspapers, periodicals, journals and auction catalogs are free to cite this numbering system. Dealers in stamps, coins and currency who send price lists to customers are encouraged to use this system for identification providing reference is made to the book and author.

A Note About Grading

Few syngraphists agree completely when it comes to the grading of paper money. Notwithstanding, a grading scale must be included in any catalog of this type. The following descriptions of grades or conditions are merely guides. If you are novice collector, obtain a "second opinion" before you spend a lot of money for a note. Some people have been known to "doctor" notes so the note appears to be in a higher state of preservation.

Uncirculated (Unc). This note is in the same state as when it was printed with no sign of circulation. The paper is firm and crisp with no discoloration. A perfectly centered note with extremely bright colors and even margins may be called gem uncirculated. A choice uncirculated note has more appeal than the uncirculated note but less than the gem uncirculated one. Any fault, regardless how minor, must be mentioned in a description. Prior to 1952 all federal paper money was printed on wet paper. After the paper dried, some notes had a "ripple effect."

About Uncirculated (AU). A note that appears to be in uncirculated condition, but after close observation minute signs of handling are visible, such as minute corner folds, but no hard creases.

Extra Fine (EFine). A crisp bright note, that might have evidence of handling, such as minor creases and folds. Corners might begin to lose their squared edges.

Very Fine (VFine). A moderately circulated note that retains some crispness, but with folds and creases. Signs of handling must be minimal with no tears on the edges; the corners begin to lose their sharpness.

Fine. Paper that feels soft with multiple folds, creases, smudges, minor tears, and colors that are beginning to fade identifies a note in this condition. These notes have sometimes been washed. Very Good (VGood). Well circulated notes with tears, heavy smudges, faded colors, heavy creases and folds that might have created a separation of the paper in the center of the note. Notwithstanding the folds, the note must be in one piece.

Good. Notes in this condition will have blemishes as the preceding only more severe. Corners of the note might be missing from wear.

A Note About Valuations
Values listed throughout this catalog are suggested or average prices. These figures reflect numerous price lists consulted as well as prices realized from recent auctions. Supply and demand and varying degrees of interest will affect the price of any note. All prices listed for national bank notes are for the most common pieces in the R1 category. LARGE-SIZE NOTES THAT HAVE SURVIVED IN UNCIRCULATED CONDITION AND ARE WELL CENTERED WITH EVEN MARGINS COMMAND A PREMIUM HIGHER THAN THOSE LISTED FOR UNC NOTES.

Many notes listed here are extremely rare, occasionally unique. These pieces do not change hands often, and valuations are therefore difficult, if not impossible, to establish.

The appropriate terms to describe paper money or any type of fiscal document is FACE and BACK. Obverse and reverse are correct when applied to coins and medals. But, as any engraver of fiscal paper will confirm, its FACE and BACK when one describes paper money and related material.

Miscellaneous Information

If more than one-half of a damaged piece of U.S. paper money is presented to a bank, it will be replaced with a new note of the same denomination.

If a note or a group of notes has been damaged or mutilated by fire or was immersed in water so that individual notes cannot be separated, *do not attempt* to isolate from purse or wallet. Package the notes in cotton and send the (insured) note(s) and container to: the Department of the Treasury, Bureau of Engraving and Printing, Office of Currency Standards, P.O. Box 37038, Washington, DC 20013. Every effort will be made to determine the amount of money in such a circumstance and you will receive a check for the deciphered amount. In 1995 over 22,000 processed claims yielded $86 million.

During fiscal year 1995, 6.1 billion Federal Reserve notes were produced at the Bureau of Engraving and Printing in Washington, an additional 3.8 billion notes were printed in Ft. Worth. This 9.9 billion total was a 6 percent increase over 1994.

In 1996 over 10 billion notes will be produced at the BEP at a cost of about 4 cents per note. That is an increase from 3.8 cents in previous years. New features in Series 1996 notes account for the increase. The Washington, DC facilities employ about 1800 people. The Ft. Worth plant, which began operation in 1991, will be at full capacity in 1996; a staff of 700 will produce 5 billion notes annually. (The notes printed in Texas, on ten De La Rue Giori Model I-10 sheet-fed presses, bear "FW" as an identifying mark.)

One sheet-fed press is capable of printing 8,000 32-subject sheets per hour. Operating five days a week, 24 hours a day without interruption, one press can produce a maximum of 737,280,000 in 24 weeks. The Bureau of Engraving and Printing uses over 2500 tons of paper and over 1000 tons of ink every year.

The dollar sign evolved from a variety of symbols and what Chauncey Lee in 1797 called characteristics; these probably included the hastily-written abbreviation of pesos, "ps", in the 17th century. (Gradually the "s" was superimposed over the "p.") The earliest use of the written "$" was in 1776 (Newman 1995, 7). The earliest probable use of the "$" on an American government obligation was on a U.S. Loan Office certificate issued to George Washington on January 17, 1792 (Newman 1995, 32). The same "$" symbol, (*cifrão* in Portuguese) was first used in 1797 to indicate 1000. Since 1911 it is used by the Portuguese to designate a decimal. Thus, 25 75 would indicate 25 escudos and 75 centavos.

The approximate life of U.S. paper money depends on the denomination: $1 and $10 notes 18 months; $5 notes 15 months; $20 notes two years; $50 and $100 notes 8½ years.

Current notes are 6.14 x 2.61 inches and 0.0043 inches thick. Without compressing them, a stack of 233 new notes will equal one inch. It will take 490 notes to weigh one pound. One million new bills will weigh about 2000 pounds.

The percentage of current notes produced are: $1 (45 percent); $5 and $10 (12 percent each); $20 (26 percent); $50 (2 percent); and $100 (3 percent).

Counterfeit U.S. paper money amounts to about one-tenth of one percent of the amount made at the BEP each year. The $20 denomination is the most commonly counterfeited note followed by the $100.

MEMPHIS COIN CLUB'S
INTERNATIONAL PAPER MONEY SHOW
THIRD WEEKEND OF
JUNE

COOK CONVENTION CENTER
255 N. Main St., Memphis, TN 38103-0016

Convention Hotel: Holiday Inn-Crowne Plaza
250 N. Main St., Memphis, TN 38103
901-527-7300

Approximately 150 Dealers
Bureau of Engraving and Printing's Billion Dollar Exhibit
American Bank Note Commemoratives, Inc. Exhibit
Commemorative Souvenir Cards
U. S. P. S. Temporary Postal Station
Fantastic Paper Money Exhibits by Collectors
Society Meetings
Paper Money Auction by leading Auctioneers

free admission

Buy, Sell, Trade, Free Appraisals
Friday & Saturday, 9:00-6:00, Sunday 9:00-
U. S. & World Paper Money, Checks, Stocks & Bonds,
Documents, Autographs, Paper Collectibles, etc.

Information: Mike Crabb
P. O. Box 17871, Memphis, TN 38187-0871
phone 901-754-6118

Society of Paper Money Collectors

It would be to your advantage to join the Society of Paper Money Collectors, organized in 1961 to further the following objectives:

1. Encourage the collecting and study of paper money.
2. Cultivate fraternal collector relations with opportunities for discussion trading, etc.
3. Furnish information and knowledge through experts, particularly through the Society's *PAPER MONEY* magazine.
4. Promote legislation favorable to collectors, providing it is in accord with the general welfare.
6. Advance the prestige of the hobby.
7. Promote exhibits at numismatic and syngraphic meetings.
8. Encourage realistic and consistent market valuations.

PAPER MONEY, the society bimonthly journal, is sent to all members. In addition to informative articles, it lists new members, the collecting specialty of each, and identifies each as a collector or dealer. Members are encouraged to submit articles for publication.

BOOKS that catalog the obsolete currency of individual states are available to members at reduced prices.

DUES are $20 ($30 outside the United States) per year and are payable in U. S. funds. Members who join the Society prior to October 1 receive the magazines already issued in the year in which they join. Members who join after October 1 will have their dues paid through December of the following year. They will also receive, as a bonus, a copy of the magazine issued in November of the year in which they join.

JUNIOR and LIFE MEMBERS, from 12 to 17 years of age, are required to have a parent or guardian sign their application. The "J" that will precede membership numbers will be removed upon notification to the secretary that the member has reached 18 years of age. Life memberships are $300.

MEETINGS, national and regional, take place throughout the year.

Annual dues in US funds: $24 in the U.S.; $29 for Canada and Mexico; $34 for other countries.

To join the SPMC send dues to SPMC, P. O. Box 117060, Carrollton, TX 75011. For a complimentary copy of *PAPER MONEY,* send $2 for postage and handling.

Act of 30 June 1812/One-year Notes/5²/₅%

No.	Denomination	Amount Authorized and Issued	Printer
X69	$100	$5,000,000	MDF&Co

Remarks: The design is the same as X74C.

One-year notes/Act of 25 February 1813/5²/₅%

No.	Denomination	Amount Authorized and Issued	Printer
X72	$100	$5,000,000	MDF&Co

Act of 4 March 1814/One-Year Notes/5²/₅%

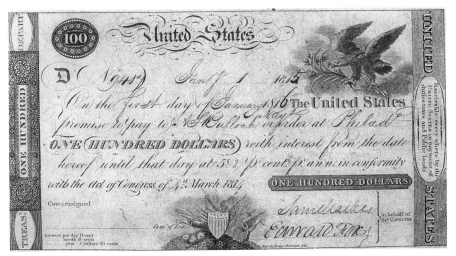

No.	Denomination	Amount Authorized and Issued	Printer
X74A	$20		
X74B	$50 (issue uncertain)	$10,000,000	MDF&Co
X74C	$100		

Remarks: Uncanceled interesting-bearing notes in this section without signatures are remainders, or left-over notes.

Act of 26 December 1814/One-year Notes/5 ²/s%

No.	Denomination	Amount Authorized	Amount Issued	Printer
X80A	₡20			
X80B	₡50	$10,500,000	$8,318,400	MDF&Co
X80C	₡100			

Act of 24 February 1815

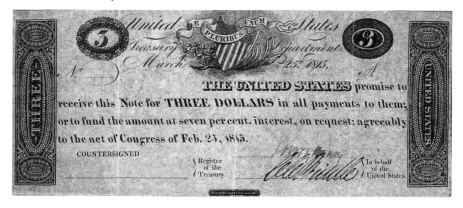

Act of 24 February 1815 *(continued)*

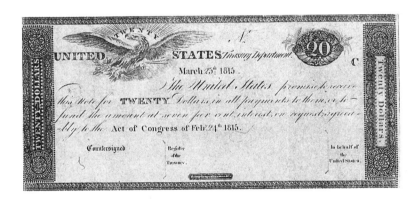

No.		Amount Authorized	Amount Issued	Printer
X83A	$3			
X83B	$5			
X83C	$10	$25,000,000	$3,392,994	MDF&Co
X83D	$20			
X83E	$50			

Remarks: These notes were redeemable at the pleasure of the government.

Act of 24 February 1815 (Section 3)/5²/₅%

No.	Denomination	Amount Issued	Printer
X85	$100	$4,969,400	MDF&Co

Act of 12 October 1837

Mercury was drawn and engraved by George W. Hatch. *Wealth* was designed, drawn and engraved by Freeman Rawdon. *Justice* cannot be specifically attributed.

Remarks: No. X85 was redeemable at the pleasure of the government.

Act of 12 October 1837 *(continued)*

The amount was to be inserted on No. X99I.

The number of notes that were issued at these percentages.

No.		1 mil%	2%	5%	6%
X99A	$50	3,445	4,465	—	
X99B	$50*	2,912	2,490	12,523	1,588
X99C	$100	2,850	9,975	—	12
X99D	$100*	2,306	1,941	10,902	3,533
X99E	$500	—	—	—	—
X99F	$500*	622	151	3,027	794
X99G	$1,000	252	1,039	—	6
X99H	$1,000*	353	113	1,020	335
X99I	Blanks	59	109	—	—
X99J	Blanks*	43	73	—	—

Remarks: These one-year, two and one-half month notes were redeemable one year from date of issue. They are the first U.S. Treasury notes with back designs.

* Dated 1838.

Act of 21 May 1838/7¹/₃ Months/6%

No.		Amount Authorized	NotesIssued	Printer
X100A	$50		12,172	
X100B	$100	$10,000 000	5,907	RW&H
X100C	$500		886	
X100D	$1,000		1,326	

Remarks: These notes were redeemable one year from date of issue.

Act of 2 March 1839

The number of notes that were issued at these percentages.

No.		2%	6%	No.		2%	6%
X101A	$50	80	423	**X101C**	$500	8	309
X101B	$100	50	821	**X101D**	$1,000	—	2216

Remarks: The amount authorized for these four-month notes consisted of the remainder unissued under the Act of 21 May 1838; the issued amount was $3,857,276.21. (RW&H)

Act of 31 March 1840/One-year notes

The number of notes that were issued at these percentages.

No.		2%	5%	5²/₅%	6%
X102A	$50	1,279	2,121	—	—
X102B	$50*	695	1,017	—	2,077
X102C	$100	1,016	1,670	80	—
X102D	$100*	614	805	—	1.989
X102E	$500	174	540	1,212	—
X102F	$500*	126	104	—	555
X102G	$1,000	44	224	1,386	—
X102H	$1,000	6	—	—	—
X102I	$10,000	—	—	—	—
X102J	$10,000	—	—	—	—
X102K	Blanks	—	—	—	—
X102L	Blanks*	—	—	—	—

Remarks: The amount authorized and to be outstanding at any one time was $5,000,000; $7,114,251.31 was issued, including reissues. (RW&H)

* Dated 1841

Act of 15 February 1841/One-year Notes

See No. X99 for designer and engraver information.

No.		2%	5%	5²/₅%	5½%	6%
X103A	$50	2,254	—	973	—	1,700
X103B	$50*	—	—	—	—	3,601
X103C	$100	2,344	—	878	—	2,249
X103D	$100*	—	—	—	—	3,079
X103E	$500	925	—	980	300	1,515
X103F	$500*	—	—	—	—	661
X103G	$1,000	90	—	358	150	2,527
X103H	$1,000*	—	—	—	—	210
X103I	Blanks	20	—	20	—	88
X103J	Blanks*	—	—	—	—	153

Remarks: The amount authorized to be outstanding at any one time for these notes was $5,000,000; $7,529,062.75 was issued, including reissues. (RW&H)

* Dated 1841.

Act of 31 January 1842/One-year Notes 2 & 6%

No.		Notes Issued	No.		Notes Issued
X105A	$50	26,985	X105D	$1,000	915
X105B	$100	24,462	X105E	Blanks	426
X105C	$500	3,360			

Remarks: The amount authorized to be outstanding at any one time for these one-year notes was $5,000,000; $7,959,994.83 was issued. See No. 1139b for the same $100 design. (RW&H)

Act of 31 August 1842/7½ Months/2 & 6% *(continued)*

No.		Amount Authorized	Amount Issued
X107A	$50		
X107B	$100		
X107C	$500	$6,000,000	$3,025,554.89
X107D	$1,000		
X107E	Blanks		

Act of 3 March 1843/Indefinite/1 mill & 4%

X108 $50   See X110A for the same design.

Act of 22 July 1846/One-year notes/1 mill & 5²/₅%

Justice, E Pluribus Unum and *Liberty*.

Washington, *E Pluribus Unum* and *Liberty*.

No.		Amount Authorized	Amount Issued	Printer
X110A	$50			
X110B	$100			
X110C	$500	$10,000,000	$7,787,800	RW&H
X110D	$1,000			
X110E	Blanks			

Remarks: Nos. X107A-E do not bear the date of the act and therefore are indistinguishable from those notes issued under the preceding act (RW&H). The amount authorized for No. X108 was indefinite. According to Bayley (p. 4) $1,806,950 was issued; Knox (p. 452) said $850,000.

Act of 28 January 1847, 5²/₅ & 6%

(X114-115)

The amount issued under this act was $23,000,000, with reissues the amount totaled $26,122,000. These six-month notes were redeemable one and two years after date of issue. (RW&H; RWH&E; TC)

One-Year Notes 5²/₅%

The following notes bear the same vignettes, although arranged differently on each. *Mercury* was drawn and engraved by George W. Hatch; *Wealth* was drawn and engraved by Freeman Rawdon; *Justice* cannot be specifically attributed. Back designs are similar to X114C. (RW&H)

X114A $50   See X99A for the same design.
X114B $100   See 1139b for the same design.

X114C $500   Face Design

Act of 28 January 1847/One-year Notes/5²/₅% *(continued)*

X114D	$1,000	Face Design
X114E	$5,000	
X114F	Blanks	

Two-Year Notes 6%

X115A $50   Benjamin Franklin, *Indian Maiden as America*, Washington, and female representing *Industry, Music and Art*. (TC) The back design has an interest table.

Act of 28 January 1847/Two-year Notes/6% *(continued)*

X115B $100   Female portrait, *E Pluribus Unum* and *Liberty* holding an olive branch. (RWH&E)

Act of 28 January 1847/Two-year Notes/6% *(continued)*

X115C $500   *Minerva, E Pluribus Unum* and *Justice*. (RWH&E)

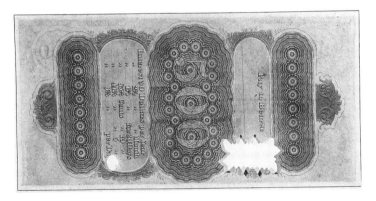

The back design has an interest table.

Act of 28 January 1847/Two-year Notes/6%

X115D $1,000   Portraits of Alexander Dallas and Albert Gallatin, eagle and ships, and an *Indian Maiden as America*. (TC)

The back design has an interest table.

Act of 28 January 1847/Two-year Notes/6% *(continued)*

X115E $5,000   *Agriculture*, eagle and harbor scene, Washington medallion head and *Minerva as America*. (TC) R8. The back design has an interest table.

X115F   Blanks

Act of 23 December 1857/One-year Notes/3 & 6%

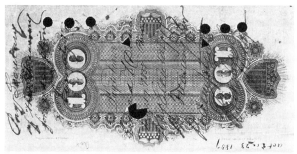

X121A $100   *E Pluribus Unum* as seen on the $10 demand and first United States notes (H463-465); *Union* and the *Prince of Wales* were both engraved by Alfred Jones. The Prince at age six was originally painted by F. Winterhalter. *The Apotheosis of Washington* was engraved by Louis Delnoce. The color is rust (TC).

The back design is blue.

X121B $500   Green and black. At the left is a portrait of Secretary of the Treasury Howell Cobb. The color is green and black (RWH&E). Unique.

Act of 23 December 1857/One-year Notes/3 & 6% *(continued)*

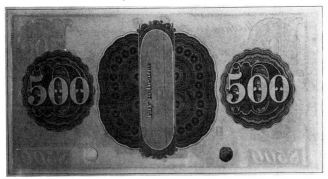

The back design is green and black and is the same as H1340.

X121C $1,000 See X124D for face and back designs. (RWH&E)

Remarks: The amount authorized to be outstanding at any one time for these notes was $20,000,000; $52,778,900 was issued. (RWH&E; TC)

Act of 17 December 1860/One-year Notes/6–12%

Justice, E Pluribus Unum and the portrait of James Buchanan on this uniface proof are believed to be the work of engraver Charles Burt. This note was altered from X121C and bears the additional credit of American Bank Note Co. RWH&E was one of the seven firms that joined together in 1858 to form ABNCo.

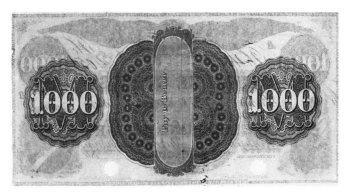

No.		Amount Authorized and Issued
X124A	$50	
X124B	$100	$10,000,000
X124C	$500	
X124D	$1,000	

United States Notes/1862/Red Seal

The portrait of Salmon P. Chase by Henry Ulke was engraved by Joseph P. Ourdan. The illustrated note with serial number "1" and plate position "A" from Series 1 was presented to Secretary of the Treasury Chase.

No.	Description	Fine	EFine	Unc
1	"National Bank Note Company—American Bank Note Company" on face at lower border	$200.	$500.	$1500.
2	as preceding with "American Bank Note Company" at upper right	175.	450.	1100.
3	"National Bank Note Company" printed twice at lower border	160.	350.	675.
4	as preceding with "American Bank Note Company" at upper right	160.	350.	675.

Remarks: The series designation is found at the upper left or right. A total of 28,351,348 notes were issued for Nos. 1 through 4; all have signatures of Chittenden-Spinner. For No. 2, Martin Gengerke has recorded serial number "1" for Series 7, 19 20 & 126. Known for Nos. 1–6; 4–21.

United States Notes/Series 1869/Red Seal

The portrait of George Washington was engraved by Alfred Sealey. *Columbus Discovery of Land,* a painting by Charles Schussele, was engraved by Joseph P. Ourdan.

No.	Signatures	Notes Printed	Fine	EFine	Unc
5	Allison-Spinner	41,868,000	$175.	$450.	$1250.

Remarks: There were 42,456,812 notes issued. Reissues could account for the excess of the official figure above. An example of No. 5, printed on "US" watermarked paper intended for fractional currency, in fine to very fine condition appeared in the November 13, 1979 NASCA auction (see Nos. 154 and 245).

Face design for series 1917; back design is on the following page.

United States Notes/Series 1874-1917

The back has the legal tender and counterfeiting clause. The face design is on the preceding page.

No.	Series	Signatures	Notes Printed	Fine	EFine	Unc
Nos. 6–14 have a small red seal on the left and a red ornament that circles "ONE DOLLAR" on the right.						
6	1874	Allison-Spinner	18,988,000	$175.	$400.	$1250.
7	1875A	Allison-New (12 known)	1,000,000	250.	500.	1250.
8	1875B	Allison-New (10 known)	1,000,000	300.	750.	1950.
9	1875C	Allison-New (18 known)	1,000,000	250.	500.	1250.
10	1875D	Allison-New (10 known)	1,000,000	100.	300.	1500.
11	1875E	Allison-New (15 known)	1,000,000	300.	750.	1950.
12	1875	Allison-New	10,000,000	65.	200.	400.
13	1875	Allison-Wyman	11,212,000	65.	200.	400.
14	1878	Allison-Gilfillan	12,512,000	65.	200.	400.
Nos. 15–17 have red serial numbers and a large brown seal to the right.						
15	1880	Scofield-Gilfillan	15,308,000	65.	115.	300.
16	1880	Bruce-Gilfillan	22,192,000	50.	100.	275.
17	1880	Bruce-Wyman	19,344,000	50.	100.	275.
		Blue serial numbers				
		Seal				
17a	1880	Bruce-Wyman	lg. red	1,636,000	delivered; not issued	
18	1880	Rosecrans-Huston	lg. red	—	265.	575.	2100.
19	1880	Rosecrans-Huston	lg. brn	420,000	265.	575.	2100.
20	1880	Rosecrans-Nebeker	lg. brn	200,000	275.	600.	2250.
21	1880	Rosecrans-Nebeker	sm. red	1,000,000	50.	75.	300.
22	1880	Tillman-Morgan	sm. red	2,000,000	50.	75.	275.
		Red serial numbers				
23	1917	Teehee-Burke	269,684,000	30.	65.	200.
23☆	86 reported		—	—	—	—
24	1917	Elliott-Burke	299,132,000	30.	65.	200.
24☆	116 reported		—	—	—	—
25	1917	Burke-Elliott	incl. in No. 24	50.	165.	675.
26	1917	Elliott-White	304,812,000	30.	65.	125.
26☆	40 reported		—	—	—	—
27	1917	Speelman-White	92,740,000	35.	80.	200.
27☆	151 reported		—	—	—	—

Remarks: An unspecified number of No. 6, commencing with serial number E8347xxx, have been reported in a hoard. For No.14, a note with blue in the top margin, as on fourth issue fractinal currency, and another with a "U.S." watermark intended for fractional currency have been reported. No. 17a was sent to the Treasury Department unsealed; all were apparently destroyed since none are known. The approximate serial numbers reported for No. 20 are A27983xx. The signatures for No. 26 were reversed in error on the plate.

United States Notes/Series 1923/Red Seal

The Gilbert Stuart portrait of George Washington was engraved by G.F.C. Smillie.

This back design was reduced and used as the model for small-size $1 notes first issued in 1928.

No.	Signatures	Notes Printed	Fine	EFine	Unc
28	Speelman-White	81,872,000	$40.	$100.	$225.
28☆	130 reported	—	50.	150.	275.

National Bank Notes/First Charter Period

Concordia, by artist T.A. Liebler, was engraved by Charles Burt.

The *Landing of the Pilgrims*, by Edwin White, was also engraved by Charles Burt.

No.	Series	Signatures	Red Seal	VGood	VFine	Unc
29	orig.	Colby-Spinner	rays	$150.	$ 300.	$ 950.
30	orig.	Jeffries-Spinner	rays	900.	1350.	3500.
31	orig.	Allison-Spinner	rays	150.	300.	900.
32	1875	Allison-New	scallops	100.	300.	900.
33	1875	Allison-Wyman	scallops	100.	300.	900.
34	1875	Allison-Gilfillan	scallops	100.	300.	900.
35	1875	Scofield-Gilfillan	scallops	100.	300.	950.

Remarks: A total of 23,167,677 notes were printed; 339,723 notes are outstanding. The original series had no series date on the face. The values for the above and other national bank notes in this catalog are for common banks. Values increase significantly for notes issued by scarcer banks.

Silver Certificates/Series 1886 & 1891

The Jalabert portrait of Martha Washington was engraved by Charles Burt. She is the only non-idealized woman to appear on U.S. currency.

No.	Signatures	Seal	Notes Printed	Fine	EFine	Une
36	Rosecrans-Jordan	sm. red	14,000,000	$150.	$300.	$750.
37	Rosecrans-Hyatt	sm. red	7,000,000	150.	315.	850.
38	Rosecrans-Hyatt	lg. red	18,648,000	150.	300.	750.
39	Rosecrans-Huston	lg. red	14,648,000	150.	300.	750.
40	Rosecrans-Huston	lg. brn.	10,000,000	150.	300.	750.
41	Rosecrans-Nebeker	lg. brn.	4,200,000	175.	325.	800.
42	Rosecrans-Nebeker	sm. red	4,284,000	175.	325.	800.

The face design now dated 1891 is the same as series 1886; the green back has been redesigned.

Series of 1891

43	Rosecrans-Nebeker	sm. red	13,000,000	$150.	$275.	$850.
44	Tillman-Morgan	sm. red	52,408,000	125.	200.	750.

Remarks: Delivery of this denomination, series 1886 notes began on September 20, 1886. A hoard of No. 37 in uncirculated condition exists with serial numbers B20601553-600.

Silver Certificates/Series 1896/Red Seal

Low's original painting hangs in the Bureau of Engraving and Printing. This is the first note in the educational series (see Nos. 185 & 358).

Thomas F. Morris made some design changes before Charles Schlecht engraved *History Instructing Youth.*

Thomas F. Morris designed this back. Alfred Sealey engraved the portrait of George Washington and Charles Burt engraved the portrait of Martha. Additional engravers for the face and back were L.F. Ellis, J. Kennedy, D.S. Ronaldson, G.U. Rose, Jr. and E.M. Hall.

No.	Signatures	Notes Printed	Fine	EFine	Une
45	Tillman-Morgan	33,400,000	$125.	$350.	$850.
46	Bruce-Roberts	23,944,000	125.	375.	900.

Silver Certificates/Series 1899/Blue Seal

The *Eagle of the Capitol* spreads its wings over portraits of Lincoln and Grant; all three were engraved by G.F.C. Smillie. The Lincoln portrait was based on a photograph by Anthony Berger. The wreaths that surround the portraits were engraved by Marcus W. Baldwin.

No.	Signatures	Notes Printed	Fine	EFine	Unc
		Series above serial number on the right			
47	Lyons-Roberts	500,000	$40.	$50.	$200.
		Series below serial number on the right			
48	Lyons-Roberts	included in above	30.	50.	175.
49	Lyons-Treat	117,112,000	30.	50.	150.
50	Vernon-Treat	316,887,600	25.	40.	150.
51	Vernon-McClung	251,404,000	30.	50.	175.
51☆	14 reported				
		Series vertically to the right of the seal			
51a	Vernon-McClung	included in above, 11 known	30.	100.	300.
51a☆	2 reported		—	—	—
52	Napier-McClung	469,200,000	25.	40.	150.
52☆	26 reported		—	—	—
53	Napier-Thompson	6,740,000	125.	275.	600.
54	Parker-Burke	354,268,000	25.	40.	150.
54☆	30 reported		—	—	—
55	Teehee-Burke	790,444,000	25.	40.	150.
55☆	86 reported		—	—	—
56	Elliott-Burke	30,452,000	35.	50.	175.
56☆	33 reported		—	—	—
57	Elliott-White	326,536,000	25.	40.	150.
57☆	88 reported		—	—	—
58	Speelman-White	530,992,000	25.	40.	150.
58☆	94 reported				

Silver Certificates/Series 1923/Blue Seal

This design is similar to No. 28.

These notes have blue serial numbers.

No.	Signatures	Notes Issued	Fine	EFine	Une
59	Speelman-White	2,431,837,347	$13.	$30.	$50.
59☆	604 reported	—	—	—	—
60	Woods-White	223,472,467	18.	40.	60.
60☆	204 reported	—	—	—	—
61	Woods-Tate	4,686,186	40.	125.	200.
61☆	8 reported	—	—	—	—

Remarks: The number of notes issued was compiled by Frank Nowak and printed in *PAPER MONEY*, Vol. 10, No. 1.

Treasury or Coin Notes/Series 1890

The designer of this note was George W. Casilear. The portrait of Edwin M. Stanton was engraved by Charles Burt. Stanton was Secretary of War under Presidents Lincoln and Johnson. The back design is on following page.

Treasury or Coin Notes/Series 1890 *(continued)*

The engravers of the back were: D.M. Cooper, W.A. Coppenhaver, W.H. Dougal, E.E. Hall, E.E. Myers and G.U. Rose, Jr.

No.	Signatures	Seal	Notes Printed	Fine	EFine	Une
62	Rosecrans-Huston	brown	3,948,000	$200.	$600.	$1750.
63	Rosecrans-Nebeker	brown	802,000	275.	700.	2000.
64	Rosecrans-Nebeker	red	2,410,000	225.	600.	1750.

Treasury or Coin Notes/Series 1891/Red Seal

The face design is the same as the preceding note except for the smaller seal.

The engravers of the back were H.L. Chorlton, E.M. Hall, J. Kennedy and S.B. Many.

Treasury or Coin Notes/Series 1891/Red Seal *(continued)*

No.	Signatures	Notes Printed	Fine	EFine	Unc
65	Rosecrans-Nebeker	14,000,000	$60.	$165.	$400.
66	Tillman Morgan	35,000,000	60.	150.	400.
67	Bruce-Roberts	8,544,000	65.	175.	475.

Remarks: Known for Nos. 62–104; 63–16; 64–34.

Federal Reserve Bank Notes/Series 1918

The portrait of George Washington was engraved by G.F.C. Smillie.

The *Eagle with Flag* was engraved by Robert Ponickau.

No.	Bank	Signatures U.S.	Signatures Bank	Notes Issued	EFine	Unc
68A1	Boston	T-B	Bullen-Morss		$50.	$135.
68A1☆	7 reported				—	—
68A2	Boston	T-B	Willet-Morss	39,600,000	100.	275.
68A3	Boston	E-B	Willet-Morss		50.	135.
68A3☆	13 reported				—	—
68B1	New York	T-B	Sailer-Strong		50.	135.
68B1☆	10 reported				—	—
68B2	New York	T-B	Hendricks-Strong	106,724,000	50.	135.
68B2☆	22 reported				—	—
68B3	New York	E-B	Hendricks-Strong		50.	135.
68B3☆	19 reported				—	—
68C1	Philadelphia	T-B	Hardt-Passmore		50.	135.
68C1☆	7 reported				—	—
68C2	Philadelphia	T-B	Dyer-Passmore		50.	135.
68C2☆	7 reported			51,056,000	—	—
68C3	Philadelphia	E-B	Dyer-Passmore		50.	135.
68C3☆	1 reported				—	—
68C4	Philadelphia	E-B	Dyer-Norris		50.	135.
68C4☆	14 reported				—	—
68D1	Cleveland	T-B	Baxter-Fancher		50.	135.
68D1☆	13 reported				—	—
68D2	Cleveland	T-B	Davis Fancher		50.	135.
68D2☆	4 reported				—	—
68D3	Cleveland	E-B	Davis-Fancher		50.	135.
68D3☆	6 reported				—	—

U.S. government signatures: T(eehee)-B(urke); E(lliott)-B(urke).

Federal Reserve Bank Notes *(continued)*

No.	Bank	Signatures U.S.	Bank	Notes Issued	EFine	Unc
68E1	Richmond	T-B	Keesee-Seay		$50.	$135.
68E1☆	7 reported			23,384,000	—	—
68E2	Richmond	E-B	Keesee-Seay		50.	135.
68E2☆	7 reported				—	—
68F1	Atlanta	T-B	Pike-McCord		50.	135.
68F1☆	2 reported				—	—
68F2	Atlanta	T-B	Bell-McCord		50.	135.
68F2☆	3 reported				—	—
68F3	Atlanta	T-B	Bell-Wellborn		50.	135.
68F3☆	3 reported				—	—
68F4	Atlanta	E-B	Bell-Wellborn		50.	135.
68F4☆	4 reported				—	—
68G1	Chicago	T-B	McCloud-McDougal		50.	135.
68G1☆	14 reported				—	—
68G2	Chicago	T-B	Cramer-McDougal	64,432,000	50.	135.
68G2☆	1 reported				—	—
68G3	Chicago	E-B	Cramer-McDougal		50.	135.
68G3☆	12 reported				—	—
68H1	St. Louis	T-B	Attebery-Wells		50.	135.
68H1☆	8 reported				—	—
68H2	St. Louis	T-B	Attebery-Biggs		50.	135.
68H2☆	4 reported			27,908,000	—	—
68H3	St. Louis	E-B	Attebery-Biggs		50.	135.
68H4	St. Louis	E-B	White-Biggs		50.	135.
68H4☆	4 reported				—	—
68I1	Minneapolis	T-B	Cook-Wold		85.	165.
68I1☆	2 reported				—	—
68I2	Minneapolis	T-B	Cook-Young		700.	2000.
68I2☆	2 reported				—	—
68I3	Minneapolis	E-B	Cook-Young		100.	225.
68I3☆	5 reported				—	—
68J1	Kansas City	T-B	Anderson-Miller		50.	135.
68J1☆	5 reported				—	—
68J2	Kansas City	E-B	Anderson-Miller	24,820,000	50.	135.
68J2☆	3 reported				—	—
68J3	Kansas City	E-B	Helm-Miller		50.	135.
68J3☆	3 reported				—	—
68K1	Dallas	T-B	Talley-VanZandt		50.	135.
68K1☆	7 reported				—	—
68K2	Dallas	E-B	Talley-VanZandt	17,864,000	135.	600.
68K2☆	4 reported				—	—
68K3	Dallas	E-B	Lawder-VanZandt		50.	135.
68K3☆	7 reported				—	—

Federal Reserve Bank Notes *(continued)*

No.	Bank	Signatures U.S.	Bank	Notes Issued	EFine	Unc
68L1	San Francisco	T-B	Clerk-Lynch		50.	135.
68L1☆	11 reported				—	—
68L2	San Francisco	T-B	Clerk-Calkins		50.	135.
68L2☆	3 reported			23,784,000	—	—
68L3	San Francisco	E-B	Clerk-Calkins		50.	135.
68L3☆	1 reported				—	—
68L4	San Francisco	E-B	Ambrose-Calkins		50.	135.
68L4☆	2 reported				—	—

U.S. government signatures: T(eehee)-B(urke); E(lliott)-B(urke).

United States Notes/Series 1928/Red Seal

The Gilbert Stuart portrait of George Washington on all small-size $1 notes was engraved by G.F.C. Smillie in 1918.

No.	Signatures	Notes Printed	VFine	EFine	Unc
69	Woods-Woodin	1,872,012	$ 20.	$ 40.	$ 85.
69☆		—	500.	950.	2000.

Silver Certificates/Blue Seal/1928

The back design is similar to No. 69.

Silver Certificate/Series 1928/1934/Blue Seal

No.		Signatures	Notes Printed	VFine	EFine	Unc
70	1928	Tate-Mellon	638,296,908	$ 8.	$ 10.	$ 20.
70☆			—	—	—	—
71	1928A	Woods-Mellon	2,267,809,500	6.	8.	20.
71☆			—	—	—	—
72	1928B	Woods-Mills	674,597,808	8.	10.	25.
72☆			—	—	—	—
73	1928C	Woods-Woodin	5,364,348	100.	200.	500.
73☆			—	—	—	—
74	1928D	Julian-Woodin	14,451,372	40.	75.	250.
74☆			—	—	—	—
75	1928E	Julian-Morgenthau	3,519,324	200.	375.	1000.
75☆			—	---------- extremely rare ----------		

Silver Certificate/Series 1934/Blue Seal

No.	Signatures	Notes Printed	VFine	EFine	Unc
	The seal, now blue, is on the right, and the large "1" is on the left.				
76	Julian-Morgenthau	682,176,000	$ 8.	$ 10.	$ 25.
76☆		7,680,000	30.	60.	150.

The proposed back design by E.M. Weeks for the 1935, $1 note shows a number of approval initials below the crossed out signature of Franklin D. Roosevelt, who after reconsidering, made changes as indicated. This change inappropriately placed the obverse of the Great Seal on the right. This was the first time both the obverse and reverse of the Great Seal appeared on one note. The engravers were J.C. Benzing, E.M. Hall, D.R. McLeod, R. Ponickau and W.B. Wells.

The revised design has the signatures of the President F.D. Roosevelt and Secretary of the Treasury Henry Morgenthau, Jr.

Silver Certificates/Series 1935/Blue Seal

No.	Series	Notes Printed	VFine	EFine	Unc
77	1935	1,681,552,000	$ 3.	$ 5.	$ 8.
77☆	—	—	—	15.	75.
78	1935A	6,111,832,000	—	—	3.
78☆	—	—	—	—	15.
79	1935A	35,052,000	8.	10.	28.
79☆	—	—	50.	75.	300.
80	1935A	26,916,000	6.	10.	35.
80☆	—	—	50.	75.	300.

Remarks: All bear the signatures of Julian-Morgenthau. No. 79 bears the overprint "HAWAII" on the face and back. No. 80 bears a yellow seal for use in North Africa. Both were used during World War II.

EXPERIMENTAL NOTES
Series 1928A and 1928B

To test the durability of another type of paper, an experimental run of $1 silver certificates, series 1928A and 1928B was issued during the early 1930s. These extremely scarce notes have blocks X-B (10,728,000 printed), Y-B and Z-B (10,248,000 printed for each).

Series of 1935

The *Numismatic Scrapbook* (October 1964, p. 2664 and February 1968, p. 196) published the following letter from the Director of the Bureau of Engraving and Printing to R.H. Lloyd dated 23 December 1938:

Dear Sir:

Receipt is acknowledged of your letter of December 16, 1938, enclosing silver certificate No. C01263845B, and inquiring as to the reason for the suffix letter 'B.' Your certificate is one of the 3,300,000 $1 silver certificates, series 1935, delivered in the latter part of the calendar year 1937, numbered from C00000001B to C03300000B, which was regular work. At the same time there was delivered an equal number of $1 silver certificates, series 1935, numbered from B00000001B to B03300000B. This was platered by a new method. These two deliveries were made for the purpose of determining any objectionable condition due to the new method of platering. The silver certificate is returned herewith.

Very Truly yours,
A.W. Hall, Director

Remarks: The letter fails to mention that 6,180,000 pieces with A-B serial numbers were printed.

Silver Certificates/Series 1935/Blue Seal

No.	Series	Signatures	Notes Printed	Fine	EFine	Unc
81	1935A(R)	Julian-Morgenthau	1,184,000	$14.	$35.	$ 135.
81☆			12,000	—	—	1500.
82	1935A(S)	Julian-Morgenthau	1,184,000	14.	35.	100.
82☆			12,000	—	—	1500.

Nos. 81 and 82 were issued as part of a paper experiment by the Bureau. The "R" signified the regular issue; the "S" identified the special paper.

No.	Series	Signatures	Notes Printed	Fine	EFine	Unc
83	1935B	Julian-Vinson	806,612,000	—	—	4.
83☆			—	13.	25.	50.
84	1935C	Julian-Snyder	3,088,108,000	—	—	4.
84☆			—	—	5.	20.
85	1935D	Clark-Snyder	4,656,968,000	—	—	3.
85☆			—	—	—	6.
86	1935D(ND)	Clark-Snyder	included in above	—	—	3.
86☆			—	—	—	6.
87	1935E	Priest-Humphrey	5,134,056,000	—	—	3.
87☆			—	—	—	6.
88	1935F	Priest-Anderson	1,173,360,000	—	—	3.
88☆			53,200,000	—	—	6.
89	1935G	Smith-Dillon	194,600,000	—	—	3.
89☆			8,640,000	—	—	6.

Remarks: During the printing of series 1935D (No. 86) the back design was narrowed by about 1/16 of an inch. All subsequent $1 issues were printed with this narrow design. No. 89 is without the motto "IN GOD WE TRUST."

Silver Certificates/Series 1935 & 1957/Blue Seal

In addition to those who engraved series 1935, C.A. Brooks, G.L. Huber and R.J. Jones engraved the back for series 1957.

No.	Series	Signatures	Notes Printed	EFine	Unc
90	1935G	Smith-Dillon	31,320,000	$—	$ 5.
90☆	1,080,000			4.	10.
91	1935H	Granahan-Dillon	30,520,000	—	3.
91☆	1,436,000			3.	8.
92	1957	Priest-Anderson	2,609,600,000	—	3.
92☆	307,640,000			—	6.
93	1957A	Smith-Dillon	1,594,080,000	—	3.
93☆	94,720,000			—	4.
94	1957B	Granahan-Dillon	718,400,000	—	3.
94☆	49,280,000			—	6.

Remarks: During the printing of Series 1935G the motto "IN GOD WE TRUST" was added. The 1935G listings above are for notes with the motto.

Federal Reserve Notes/Series 1963, 1963A & 1963B/Green Seal

Series 1963, Granahan-Dillon

No.	Bank	Notes Printed	Unc
95A	Boston	87,680,000	$3.
95A☆		6,400,000	4.
95B	New York	219,200,000	3.
95B☆		15,360,000	4.
95C	Philadelphia	123,680,000	3.
95C☆		10,880,000	4.
95D	Cleveland	108,320,000	3.
95D☆		8,320,000	4.
95E	Richmond	159,520,000	3.
95E☆		12,160,000	4.
95F	Atlanta	221,120,000	3.
95F☆		19,200,000	4.
95G	Chicago	279,360,000	3.
95G☆		19,840,000	4.
95H	St. Louis	99,840,000	3.
95H☆		9,600,000	4.
95I	Minneapolis	44,800,000	3.
95I☆		5,120,000	4.
95J	Kansas City	88,760,000	3.
95J☆		8,960,000	4.
95K	Dallas	85,760,000	3.
95K☆		8,960,000	4.
95L	San Francisco	199,999,999	3.
95L☆		14,720,000	4.

For one year, some Series 1963 $1 notes, and perhaps other denominations, were printed on paper supplied by the Gilbert Paper Company. Some $1 notes are identifiable by serial numbers beginning with C60800000A.

Series 1963A, Granahan-Fowler

No.	Bank	Notes Printed	Unc
96A	Boston	319,840,000	$3.
96A☆		19,840,000	4.
96B	New York	657,600,000	3.
96B☆		48,800,000	4.
96C	Philadelphia	375,520,000	3.
96C☆		26,240,000	4.
96D	Cleveland	337,120,000	3.
96D☆		21,120,000	4.
96E	Richmond	532,000,000	3.
96E☆		41,600,000	4.
96F	Atlanta	636,480,000	3.
96F☆		40,960,000	4.
96G	Chicago	784,480,000	3.
96G☆		52,640,000	4.
96H	St. Louis	264,000,000	3.
96H☆		17,920,000	4.
96I	Minneapolis	112,160,000	3.
96I☆		7,040,000	4.
96J	Kansas City	219,200,000	3.
96J☆		14,720,000	4.
96K	Dallas	288,960,000	3.
96K☆		19,184,000	4.
96L	San Francisco	576,800,000	3.
96L☆		43,040,000	4.

Series 1963B, Granahan-Barr

No.	Bank	Notes Printed	Unc
97B	New York	123,040,000	$3.
97B☆		3,680,000	4.
97E	Richmond	93,600,000	3.
97E☆		3,200,000	4.
97G	Chicago	91,040,000	3.
97G☆		2,400,000	4.
97J	Kansas City	44,800,000	3.
97J☆		not printed	—
97L	San Francisco	106,400,000	3.
97L☆		3,040,000	4.

Federal Reserve Notes/Series 1969, 1969A, 1969B & 1969C/Green Seal

Series 1969, Elston-Kennedy

No.	Bank	Notes Printed	Unc
98A	Boston	99,200,000	$2.
98A☆		1,120,000	3.
98B	New York	269,120,000	2.
98B☆		14,080,000	3.
98C	Philadelphia	68,480,000	2.
98C☆		3,616,000	3.
98D	Cleveland	120,480,000	2.
98D☆		5,760,000	3.
98E	Richmond	250,560,000	2.
98E☆		10,880,000	3.
98F	Atlanta	85,120,000	2.
98F☆		7,680,000	3.
98G	Chicago	359,530,000	2.
98G☆		12,160,000	3.
98H	St. Louis	74,880,000	2.
98H☆		3,840,000	3.
98I	Minneapolis	48,000,000	2.
98I☆		1,920,000	3.
98J	Kansas City	95,360,000	2.
98J☆		5,760,000	4.
98K	Dallas	113,440,000	2.
98K☆		5,120,000	3.
98L	San Francisco	226,240,000	2.
98L☆		9,600,000	3.

Series 1969A, Kabis-Kennedy

No.	Bank	Notes Printed	Unc
99A	Boston	40,480,000	$2.
99A☆		1,120,000	3.
99B	New York	122,400,000	2.
99B☆		6,240,000	3.
99C	Philadelphia	44,960,000	2.
99C☆		1,760,000	3.
99D	Cleveland	30,080,000	2.
99D☆		1,280,000	3.
99E	Richmond	66,080,000	2.
99E☆		3,200,000	3.
99F	Atlanta	70,560,000	2.
99F☆		2,400,000	3.
99G	Chicago	75,680,000	2.
99G☆		4,480,000	3.
99H	St. Louis	41,420,000	2.
99H☆		1,280,000	3.
99I	Minneapolis	21,760,000	2.
99I☆		640,000	5.
99J	Kansas City	40,480,000	2.
99J☆		1,120,000	3.
99K	Dallas	27,520,000	2.
99K☆		not printed	—
99L	San Francisco	51,840,000	2.
99L☆		3,480,000	3.

Series 1969B, Kabis-Connally

No.	Bank	Notes Printed	Unc
100A	Boston	94,720,000	$2.
100A☆		1,920,000	3.
100B	New York	329,144,000	2.
100B☆		7,040,000	3.
100C	Philadelphia	133,280,000	2.
100C☆		3,200,000	3.
100D	Cleveland	91,520,000	2.
100D☆		4,480,000	3.
100E	Richmond	180,000,000	2.
100E☆		3,840,000	3.
100F	Atlanta	200,000,000	2.
100F☆		3,840,000	3.
100G	Chicago	204,480,000	2.
100G☆		4,480,000	3.
100H	St. Louis	59,520,000	2.
100H☆		1,920,000	3.
100I	Minneapolis	33,290,000	2.
100I☆		3,200,000	3.
100J	Kansas City	67,200,000	2.
100J☆		2,560,000	3.
100K	Dallas	116,640,000	2.
100K☆		5,120,000	3.
100L	San Francisco	208,960,000	2.
100L☆		5,760,000	3.

Series 1969C, Banuelos-Connally

No.	Bank	Notes Printed	Unc
101A	Boston	not printed	$—
101A☆		not printed	—
101B	New York	49,920,000	2.
101B☆		not printed	—
101C	Philadelphia	not printed	—
101C☆		not printed	—
101D	Cleveland	8,480,000	2.
101D☆		480,000	6.
101E	Richmond	61,600,000	2.
101E☆		480,000	6.
101F	Atlanta	61,360,000	2.
101F☆		3,680,000	3.
101G	Chicago	137,120,000	2.
101G☆		1,748,000	3.
101H	St. Louis	23,680,000	2.
101H☆		640,000	5.
101I	Minneapolis	25,600,000	2.
101I☆		3,200,000	3.
101J	Kansas City	98,560,000	2.
101J☆		1,120,000	3.
101K	Dallas	29,440,000	2.
101K☆		640,000	5.
101L	San Francisco	101,280,000	2.
101L☆		2,560,000	20.

Federal Reserve Notes/Series 1969D, 1974, 1977 & 1977A/Green Seal

Series 1969D, Banuelos-Shultz

No.	Bank	Notes Printed	Unc
102A	Boston	187,040,000	$2.
102A☆		1,120,000	3.
102B	New York	468,484,000	2.
102B☆		4,480,000	3.
102C	Philadelphia	218,560,000	2.
102C☆		4,320,000	3.
102D	Cleveland	161,440,000	2.
102D☆		2,400,000	3.
102E	Richmond	374,240,000	2.
102E☆		4,320,000	3.
102F	Atlanta	377,240,000	2.
102F☆		5,280,000	3.
102G	Chicago	378,080,000	2.
102G		5,280,000	3.
102H	St. Louis	168,480,000	2.
102H☆		1,760,000	3.
102I	Minneapolis	63,200,000	2.
102I☆		not printed	—
102J	Kansas City	185,760,000	2.
102J☆		3,040,000	3.
102K	Dallas	158,240,000	2.
102K☆		6,240,000	3.
102L	San Francisco	400,640,000	2.
102L☆		6,400,000	3.

Series 1974, Neff-Simon

No.	Bank	Notes Printed	Unc
103A	Boston	269,760,000	$2.
103A☆		2,400,000	3.
103B	New York	730,320,000	2.
103B☆		8,800,000	3.
103C	Philadelphia	308,960,000	2.
103C☆		1,760,000	3.
103D	Cleveland	240,960,000	2.
103D☆		1,120,000	3.
103E	Richmond	644,160,000	2.
103E☆		5,600,000	3.
103F	Atlanta	599,840,000	2.
103F☆		7,520,000	3.
103G	Chicago	473,600,000	2.
103G☆		6,880,000	3.
103H	St. Louis	291,520,000	2.
103H☆		3,040,000	3.
103I	Minneapolis	144,160,000	2.
103I☆		480,000	5.
103J	Kansas City	330,720,000	2.
103J☆		3,200,000	3.
103K	Dallas	330,720,000	2.
103K☆		1,760,000	3.
103L	San Francisco	737,120,000	2.
103L☆		4,320,000	3.

Series 1977, Morton-Blumenthal

No.	Bank	Notes Printed	Unc
104A	Boston	188,160,000	$2.
104A☆		3,072,000	3.
104B	New York	635,520,000	2.
104B☆		10,112,000	3.
104C	Philadelphia	216,960,000	2.
104C☆		4,480,000	3.
104D	Cleveland	213,120,000	2.
104D☆		3,328,000	3.
104E	Richmond	418,560,000	2.
104E☆		6,400,000	3.
104F	Atlanta	565,120,000	2.
104F☆		8,960,000	3.
104G	Chicago	615,680,000	2.
104G☆		9,472,000	3.
104H	St. Louis	199,680,000	2.
104H☆		2,048,000	3.
104I	Minneapolis	115,200,000	2.
104I☆		2,944,000	3.
104J	Kansas City	223,360,000	2.
104J☆		3,840,000	3.
104K	Dallas	289,280,000	2.
104K☆		4,608,000	3.
104L	San Francisco	516,480,000	2.
104L☆		8,320,000	3.

Series 1977A, Morton-Miller

No.	Bank	Notes Printed	Unc
105A	Boston	204,800,000	$2.
105A☆		2,432,000	3.
105B	New York	592,000,000	2.
105B☆		9,472,000	3.
105C	Philadelphia	196,480,000	2.
105C☆		2,688,000	3.
105D	Cleveland	174,120,000	2.
105D☆		2,560,000	3.
105E	Richmond	377,600,000	2.
105E☆		6,400,000	3.
105F	Atlanta	396,160,000	2.
105F☆		5,376,000	3.
105G	Chicago	250,880,000	2.
105G☆		2,560,000	3.
105H	St. Louis	103,680,000	2.
105H☆		1,664,000	3.
105I	Minneapolis	38,400,000	2.
105I☆		384,000	6.
105J	Kansas City	266,880,000	2.
105J☆		4,864,000	3.
105K	Dallas	313,600,000	2.
105K☆		6,016,000	3.
105L	San Francisco	433,280,000	2.
105L☆		5,888,000	3.

Federal Reserve Notes/Series 1981, 1981A, 1985 & 1988/Green Seal

Series 1981, Buchanan-Regan

No.	Bank	Notes Printed	Unc
106A	Boston	308,480,000	$ 2.
106A☆		3,200,000	3.
106B	New York	963,840,000	2.
106B☆		11,776,000	3.
106C	Philadelphia	359,680,000	2.
106C☆		1,536,000	10.
106D	Cleveland	295,680,000	2.
106D☆		1,792,000	3.
106E	Richmond	603,520,000	2.
106E☆		3,840,000	3.
106F	Atlanta	741,760,000	2.
106F☆		3,200,000	8.
106G	Chicago	629,760,000	2.
106G☆		5,184,000	8.
106H	St. Louis	163,840,000	2.
106H☆		1,056,000	5.
106I	Minneapolis	105,600,000	2.
106I☆		1,152,000	10.
106J	Kansas City	302,080,000	2.
106J☆		3,216,000	8.
106K	Dallas	385,920,000	2.
106K☆		1,920,000	10.
106L	San Francisco	677,760,000	2.
106L☆		4,992,000	8.

Series 1981A, Ortega-Regan

No.	Bank	Notes Printed	Unc
107A	Boston	204,800,000	$2.
107A☆		not printed	—
107B	New York	537,600,000	2.
107B☆		9,216,000	3.
107C	Philadelphia	99,200,000	2.
107C☆		not printed	—
107D	Cleveland	188,800,000	2.
107D☆		not printed	—
107E	Richmond	441,600,000	2.
107E☆		6,400,000	3.
107F	Atlanta	483,200,000	2.
107F☆		not printed	—
107G	Chicago	432,000,000	2.
107G☆		3,200,000	3.
107H	St. Louis	182,400,000	2.
107H☆		not printed	—
107I	Minneapolis	102,400,000	2.
107I☆		not printed	—
107J	Kansas City	176,000,000	2.
107J☆		not printed	—
107K	Dallas	188,800,000	2.
107K☆		3,000,000	12.
107L	San Francisco	659,200,000	2.
107L☆		3,200,000	3.

Series 1985, Ortega-Baker

No.	Bank	Notes Printed	Unc
108A	Boston	553,600,000	$2.
108A☆		not printed	—
108B	New York	1,795,200,000	2.
108B☆		not printed	—
108C	Philadelphia	422,400,000	2.
108C☆		not printed	—
108D	Cleveland	636,800,000	2.
108D☆		not printed	—
108E	Richmond	1,190,400,000	2.
108E☆		6,400,000	—
108F	Atlanta	1,414,400,000	3.
108F☆		not printed	—
108G	Chicago	1,190,400,000	—
108G☆		5,120,000	—
108H	St. Louis	400,000,000	—
108H☆		640,000	10.
108I	Minneapolis	246,400,000	2.
108I☆		2,560,000	3.
108J	Kansas City	390,400,000	2.
108J☆		not printed	—
108K	Dallas	697,600,000	2.
108K☆		3,200,000	3.
108L	San Francisco	1,881,600,000	2.
108L☆		9,600,000	3.

Series 1988, Ortega-Brady

No.	Bank	Notes Printed	Unc
109A	Boston	214,400,000	$2.
109A☆		3,200,000	3.
109B	New York	921,600,000	2.
109B☆		2,560,000	3.
109C	Philadelphia	96,000,000	2.
109C☆		not printed	—
109D	Cleveland	195,200,000	2.
109D☆		not printed	—
109E	Richmond	728,800,000	2.
109E☆		2,688,000	3.
109F	Atlanta	390,400,000	2.
109F☆		3,840,000	8.
109G	Chicago	416,400,000	2.
109G☆		not printed	—
109H	St. Louis	396,800,000	2.
109H☆		not printed	—
109I	Minneapolis	124,800,000	3.
109I☆		not printed	—
109J	Kansas City	137,600,000	2.
109J☆		3,200,000	3.
109K	Dallas	80,000,000	3.
109K☆		1,248,000	4.
109L	San Francisco	585,600,000	2.
109L☆		3,200,000	3.

Federal Reserve Notes/Series 1988A & 1993/Green Seal

Series 1988A, Villalpando-Brady

No.	Bank	Notes Printed	Unc
110A	Boston	672,000,000	82.
110A☆		not printed	—
110B	New York	2,127,200,000	—
110B☆	DC	16,000,000	2.
110C	Philadelphia	473,600,000	—
110C☆		not printed	—
110D	Cleveland	460,800,000	2.
110D☆	DC	6,400,000	3.
110E	Richmond	1,542,400,000	—
110E☆	DC	9,600,000	3.
110F	Atlanta†	2,291,200,000	—
110F☆	DC	12,800,000	3.
110G	Chicago†	2,233,600,000	—
110G☆	FW	25,600,000	3.
110H	St. Louis†	793,600,000	—
110H☆	DC	3,200,000	3.
110I	Minneapolis†	921,600,000	—
110I☆	FW	9,600,000	3.
110J	Kansas City†	377,600,000	—
110J☆		not printed	—
110K	Dallas†	861,000,000	—
110K☆		3,200,000	3.
110L	San Francisco†	2,291,200,000	—
110L☆	FW	28,800,000	3.

Series 1993, Withrow-Bentsen

No.	Bank	Notes Printed	Unc
111A	Boston	140,800,000	8—
111A☆		not printed	—
111B	New York	716,800,000	—
111B☆		5,760,000	—
111C	Philadelphia	70,400,000	—
111C☆		640,000	5.
111D	Cleveland	108,800,000	—
111D☆	not printed	—	
111E	Richmond	460,800,000	—
111E☆	not printed	—	
111F	Atlanta	723,200,000	—
111F☆	9,600,000	—	
111G	Chicago†	96,000,000	—
111G☆	not printed	—	
111H	St. Louis†	217,600,000	—
111H☆	not printed	—	
111I	Minneapolis FW	25,600,000	—
111I☆	not printed	—	
111J	Kansas City	not printed	—
111J☆	not printed	—	
111K	Dallas FW	300,000	10.
111K☆	not printed	—	
111L	San Francisco†	921,600,000	—
111L☆	not printed	—	

† Some notes were printed in Fort Worth: see "FW" to the right of Treasury seal.

Web Press Note. (Courtesy of *Coin World*)

Federal Reserve Notes/Series 1988A, 1993 & 1995/Green Seal *(Continued)*

Web notes lack the face check letter. The back has a check number above "E" in ONE. There were 640,000 Series 1988A Web Press notes printed with stars for district F. Web star notes have been reported for Series 1993, district B. The following block figures for $1 notes printed on the discontinued Web Press are included in the listings for Series 1988A, 1993 and 1995.

1988A				**1993**		
Boston	A-E	19,200,000		New York	B-H	12,800,000
	A-F	25,600,000		Philadelphia	C-A	12,800,000
	A-G	19,200,000		**1995**		
New York	B-L	1,920,000		Boston	A-C	12,800,000
Philadelphia	C-A	12,800,000		New York	B-H	12,800,000
Richmond	E-I	19,200,000		Cleveland	D-C	6,400,000
	E-K	19,200,000		Atlanta	F-D	12,800,000
Atlanta	F-L	12,800,000		Atlanta	F-D	12,800,000
	F-M	6,400,000				
	F-N	12,800,000				
	F-U	19,200,000				
	F-V	38,400,000				
Chicago	G-P	12,800,000				
	G-Q	6,400,000				

Series 1995, Withrow-Rubin

No.	Bank	Notes Printed	Unc		No.	Bank	Notes Printed	Unc
112A	Boston†				**112G**	Chicago#		
112A☆					**112G**☆			
112B	New York				**112H**	St. Louis		
112B☆					**112H**☆			
112C	Philadelphia				**112I**	Minneapolis		
112C☆					**112I**☆			
112D	Cleveland				**112J**	Kansas City#		
112D☆					**112J**☆			
112E	Richmond				**112K**	Dallas		
112E☆					**112K**☆			
112F	Atlanta				**112L**	San Francisco#		
112F☆					**112L**☆			

This series was in production when this catalog was printed.

† Some notes were printed in Fort Worth.
# All notes were printed in Fort Worth. Series 1995 was in production when this catalog was printed.

United States Notes/1862/Red Seal

The portrait of Alexander Hamilton was engraved by Joseph P. Ourdan.

No.	Signatures	Notes Printed	Fine	EFine	Unc
153	Chittenden-Spinner; "American Bank Note Company" in left border	} 17,035,514	$250.	$575.	$1500.
153a	Chittenden-Spinner; "National Bank Note Company" in left border		250.	575.	1500.

Remarks: Both have "National Bank Note Company Patented April 23, 1860" in lower face border.

United States Notes/Series 1869/Red Seal

The portrait of Thomas Jefferson was engraved by Charles Burt. The *Capitol* was engraved by Louis Delnoce and William Chorlton.

No.	Signatures	Notes Printed	Fine	EFine	Unc
154	Allison-Spinner	24,796,000	$275.	$750.	$2100.

Remarks: There were 25,255,960 notes issued. Reissues could account for the excess of the the official figure above. A note of this type (U50336) in uncirculated condition, printed on paper watermarked "US" (intended for fractional currency) appeared in the November 13, 1979, NASCA auction (see Nos. 5 and 245).

United States Notes/Series 1874–1917

The face design is similar to No. 154 with a red ornament behind "Washington, D.C." The back design was changed as illustrated.

No.	Series	Signatures		Notes Printed	Fine	EFine	Unc
		Nos. 155–159 have red seals with rays.					
155	1874	Allison-Spinner		8,260,000	$ 125.	$ 275.	$ 625.
155A	1875A	Allison-New		1,000,000	150.	450.	1300.
155B	1875B	Allison-New		1,000,000	150.	450.	1300.
156	1875	Allison-New		4,160,000	125.	275.	600.
157	1875	Allison-Wyman		5,358,000	125.	275.	600.
158	1878	Allison-Gilfillan		4,676,000	125.	275.	600.
159	1878	Scofield-Gilfillan		included in above	750.	1850.	4500.
		Numbers 15–17 have red serial numbers and a large, brown seal on the right.					
160	1880	Scofield-Gilfillan		5,808,000	60.	135.	325.
161	1880	Bruce-Gilfillan		10,132,000	60.	135.	325.
162	1880	Bruce-Wyman		9,636,000	60.	135.	325.
Nos. 162a–166 have blue serial numbers.			**Seal**				
162a	1880	Bruce-Wyman	lg. red	1,052,000	delivered; not issued		
163	1880	Rosecrans-Huston	lg. red	400,000	215.	650.	2100.
164	1880	Rosecrans-Huston	lg. brn	180,000	------- 13 known -------		
165	1880	Rosecrans-Nebeker	lg. brn	920,000	65.	135.	300.
166	1880	Tillman-Morgan	sm. red	1,200,000	50.	100.	250.
		Nos. 167–170 have red serial numbers and red seals with scallops.					
167	1917	Teehee-Burke		69,072,000	25.	65.	175.
167☆	33 reported			—	—	—	—
168	1917	Elliott-Burke		57,136,000	25.	65.	200.
168☆	26 reported			—	—	—	—
169	1917	Elliott-White		17,792,000	35.	75.	225.
169☆	17 reported			—	—	—	—
170	1917	Speelman-White		173,416,000	25.	65.	150.
170☆	129 reported			—	—	—	—

Remarks: No. 162a was sent to the Treasury Department unsealed; all were apparently destroyed since none are known. Known for Nos. 155A–16; 159B–19; 159–11; 163–25; 165–19 (Gengerke).

National Bank Notes/First Charter Period/Red Seals

This design is generally referred to as the "Lazy Two." *Stars and Stripes* was engraved by Louis Delnoce. James B. Chaffee, whose signature is on this note, was the first president of the First National Bank of Denver founded in 1865.

Louis Delnoce engraved *Sir Walter Raleigh Presenting Corn and Tobacco to the English.* Lettering on the face and back was engraved by W.D. Nichols and G.W. Thurber.

No.	Series	Signatures	Red Seal	VGood	VFine	Unc
171	orig.	Colby-Spinner	rays	$ 500.	$1000.	$2500.
172	orig.	Jeffries-Spinner	rays	1650.	2750.	6500.
173	orig.	Allison-Spinner	rays	500.	1000.	2500.
174	1875	Allison-New	scallops	500.	1000.	2500.
175	1875	Allison-Wyman	scallops	500.	1000.	2500.
176	1875	Allison-Gilfillan	scallops	500.	1000.	2500.
177	1875	Scofield-Gilfillan	scallops	500.	1000.	2500.

Remarks: A total of 7,747,519 notes were issued; 80,844 are outstanding. The original series had no series date printed on the face.

Silver Certificates/Series 1886

General Winfield Scott Hancock held the rank of Commanding General of the U.S. Army for 20 years. The portrait was engraved by Charles Schlecht. The back design was engraved by E.M. Hall, S.S. Hurlbut, D.M. Cooper and L. Delnoce.

No.	Signatures	Seal	Notes Printed	Fine	EFine	Unc
178	Rosecrans-Jordan	sm. red	5,000,000	$250.	$600.	$1250.
179	Rosecrans-Hyatt	sm. red	1,400,000	275.	650.	1400.
180	Rosecrans-Hyatt	lg. red	6,796,000	250.	600.	1250.
181	Rosecrans-Huston	lg. red	4,564,000	250.	600.	1250.
182	Rosecrans-Huston	lg. brn.	3,240,000	265.	625.	1300.

Remarks: A hoard of No. 179 in uncirculated condition exists commencing with B6117xxx. No. 180 in the same condition is also known in hoards: B10596xx, B6459xx, B77292xx, and B130550xx-B130552xx. Delivery of this $2 note began on November 27, 1886.

Silver Certificates/Series 1891/Red Seal

William Windom was born in Belmont, OH on May 10, 1827. He moved to Minnesota and served as United States senator. In 1881 Windom resigned to become Secretary of the Treasury; he died in 1891 holding that office. His portrait was engraved by W.G. Phillips.

No.	Signatures	Notes Printed	Fine	EFine	Unc
183	Rosecrans-Nebeker	6,148,000	$225.	$625.	$2850.
184	Tillman-Morgan	14,840,000	200.	525.	2300.

Remarks: *The New York Times* of August 15, 1897 reported that "Secret Service officers say that the reason why the Windom two, raised to a ten, was successfully passed was because the Windom note was not long enough in circulation to become well known to users."

Silver Certificates/Series 1896/Red Seal

The painting of the original design, as a $50 note, hangs in the Bureau of Engraving and Printing.

Science Presenting Steam and Electricity to Industry and Commerce was designed by Edwin H. Blashfield; it was engraved by Charles Schlecht and G.F.C. Smillie. The remainder of the face and the entire back was designed by Thomas F. Morris.

The portrait of R. Fulton, after a painting by Benjamin West, was engraved by Charles Burt. Charles Schlecht engraved the portrait of Samuel F.B. Morse.

This is the second note in the educational series (see Nos. 45 & 358).

No.	Signatures	Notes Printed	Fine	EFine	Une
185	Tillman-Morgan	9,200,000	$325.	$1000.	$3000.
186	Bruce-Roberts	11,452,000	300.	925.	2500.

Remarks: Observed serial numbers exceed the official figures listed above. Roso Marston, a teenage actress, posed for the figure on the left and modeled for some of the other figures. Miss Marston also modeled for Augustus Saint Gaudens (F. Del Witt, *The Numismatist*, July 1940, p. 501).

Silver Certificates/Series 1899/Blue Seal

A portrait of Washington is flanked by *Mechanics and Agriculture*. The engravers were G.F.C. Smillie and M.W. Baldwin. The illustrated note has the autograph of Register of the Treasury Houston B. Teehee.

The back design was engraved by E.M. Hall, W.F. Lutz, J.P. Prender, R. Ponickau, D.S. Ronaldson and G.U. Rose.

No.	Signatures	Notes Printed	Fine	EFine	Unc
		Series above serial number on the right			
187	Lyons-Roberts	119,408,000	$ 85.	$175.	$375.
		Series below serial number on right			
188	Lyons-Treat	13,206,000	100.	215.	475.
189	Vernon-Treat	74,712,000	85.	175.	375.
190	Vernon-McClung	45,852,000	85.	185.	400.
190☆	6 reported	—	—	—	—
		Series vertically to the right of the seal			
191	Napier-McClung	78,936,000	85.	175.	375.
191☆	9 reported	—	—	—	—
192	Napier-Thompson	1,816,000	200.	500.	2000.
193	Parker-Burke	61,600,000	85.	175.	375.
193☆	6 reported	—	—	—	—
194	Teehee-Burke	93,284,000	85.	175.	375.
194☆	19 reported	—	—	—	—
195	Elliott-Burke	11,716,000	100.	215.	475.
195☆	10 reported	—	—	—	—
196	Speelman-White	38,204,000	85.	175.	375.
196☆	25 reported	—	—	—	—

Remarks: Known for Nos. 188–12; 190–34; 192–44; 195–33 (Gengerke).

Treasury or Coin Notes/Series 1890

General James B. McPherson was born on November 14, 1828 in Sandusky, Ohio. He graduated from West Point and eleven years later, in 1864, was killed in an attack against Confederate troops. This portrait was engraved by Charles Burt.

The back design was engraved by W.H. Dougal, E.M. Hall, A.L. Helm and G.U. Rose, Jr.

No.	Signatures	Seal	Notes Printed	Fine	EFine	Unc
197	Rosecrans-Huston	brown	2,650,000	$400.	$1100.	$3500.
198	Rosecrans-Nebeker	brown	450,000	450.	1400.	4000.
199	Rosecrans-Nebeker	red	1,832,000	425.	1200.	3750.

Treasury or Coin Notes/Series 1891/Red Seal

The face design is the same as the preceding type except with a smaller seal.

No.	Signatures	Notes Printed	Fine	EFine	Unc
200	Rosecrans-Nebeker	4,152,000	$135.	$300.	$ 950.
201	Tillman-Morgan	12,348,000	115.	275.	800.
202	Bruce-Roberts	3,472,000	135.	325.	1000.

Federal Reserve Bank Notes/Series 1918/Blue Seal

The portrait of Thomas Jefferson was engraved by Charles Burt. The "A–1" in the four corners indicates the first Federal Reserve District.

The World War I battle-ship *New York* was engraved by C.M. Chalmers.

		Signatures				
No.	**Bank**	**U.S.**	**Bank**	**Notes Issued**	**EFine**	**Unc**
203A1	Boston	T-B	Bullen-Morss		$225.	$475.
203A1☆	3 reported				—	—
203A2	Boston	T-B	Willet-Morss		225.	475.
203A2☆	2 reported			12,468,000	—	—
203A3	Boston	E-B	Willet-Morss		225.	475.
203A3☆	7 reported				—	—
203B1	New York	T-B	Sailer-Strong		225.	475.
203B1☆	5 reported				—	—
203B2	New York	T-B	Hendricks-Strong		225.	475.
203B2☆	3 reported			15,216,000	—	—
203B3	New York	E-B	Hendricks-Strong		225.	475.
203B3☆	1 reported				—	—
203C1	Philadelphia	T-B	Hardt-Passmore		225.	475.
203C1☆	1 reported				—	—
203C2	Philadelphia	T-B	Dyer-Passmore		225.	475.
203C3	Philadelphia	E-B	Dyer-Passmore	8,004,000	265.	675.
203C4	Philadelphia	E-B	Dyer-Norris		225.	475.
203C4☆	4 reported				—	—
203D1	Cleveland	T-B	Baxter-Fancher		225.	475.
203D1☆	3 reported				—	—
203D2	Cleveland	T-B	Davis Fancher		225.	475.
203D2☆	1 reported				—	—
203D3	Cleveland	E-B	Davis-Fancher		225.	475.
203D3☆	1 reported				—	—

U.S. government signatures: T(eehee)-B(urke); E(lliott)-B(urke).

Federal Reserve Notes/Series 1918/Blue Seal (*continued*)

No.	Bank	Signatures U.S.	Bank	Notes Issued	EFine	Une
203E1	Richmond	T-B	Keesee-Seay		265.	675.
203E1☆	5 reported			3,736,000	—	—
203E2	Richmond	E-B	Keesee-Seay		225.	475.
203F1	Atlanta	T-B	Pike-McCord		225.	475.
203F2	Atlanta	T-B	Bell-McCord		290.	750.
203F2☆	1 reported			2,300,000	—	—
203F3	Atlanta	T-B	Bell-Wellborn		265.	675.
203F4	Atlanta	E-B	Bell-Wellborn		265.	675.
203G1	Chicago	T-B	McCloud-McDougal		225.	475.
203G1☆	4 reported				225.	475.
203G2	Chicago	T-B	Cramer-McDougal	9,528,000	225.	475.
203G3	Chicago	E-B	Cramer-McDougal		225.	475.
203G3☆	3 reported				—	—
203H1	St. Louis	T-B	Attebery-Wells		250.	625.
203H2	St. Louis	T-B	Attebery-Biggs	3,300,000	265.	675.
203H3	St. Louis	E-B	Attebery-Biggs		290.	750.
203H4	St. Louis	E-B	White-Biggs		265.	675.
203I1	Minneapolis	T-B	Cook-Wold		265.	675.
203I1☆	2 reported				—	—
203I2	Minneapolis	T-B	Cook-Young		265.	675.
203I3	Minneapolis	E-B	Cook-Young		265.	675.
203J1	Kansas City	T-B	Anderson-Miller		265.	675.
203J1☆	2 reported				—	—
203J2	Kansas City	E-B	Anderson-Miller	2,652,000	265.	675.
203J3	Kansas City	E-B	Helm-Miller		265.	675.
203K1	Dallas	T-B	Talley-VanZandt		265.	675.
203K1☆	1 reported				—	—
203K2	Dallas	E-B	Talley-VanZandt	1,252,000	265.	675.
203K3	Dallas	E-B	Lawder-VanZandt		265.	675.
203L1	San Francisco	T-B	Clerk-Lynch		265.	675.
203L2	San Francisco	T-B	Clerk-Calkins		265.	675.
203L2☆	7 reported				—	—
203L3	San Francisco	E-B	Clerk-Calkins	3,188,000	265.	675.
203L3☆	7 reported				—	—
203L4	San Francisco	E-B	Ambrose-Calkins		265.	675.

U.S. government signatures: T(eehee)-B(urke); E(lliott)-B(urke).

United States Notes/Series 1928/Red Seal

The portrait of Thomas Jefferson, based on a painting by Gilbert Stuart, was engraved by Charles Burt in 1867. A portrait of James Garfield was originally considered for this note.

The engraving of *Monticello*, Jefferson's home, is the work of J.C. Benzing. *Monticello*, now a museum, houses numerous inventions by Jefferson, who was also an architect, a musician and lawyer.

No.	Series	Signatures	Notes Printed	VFine	EFine	Unc
204	1928	Tate-Mellon	55,889,424	$ 5.	$ 7.	$ 25.
204☆			—	25.	50.	150.
204A	1928A	Woods-Mellon	46,859,136	15.	30.	165.
204A☆			—	250.	400.	850.
204B	1928B	Woods-Mills	9,001,632	90.	165.	425.
204B☆			—	1200.	2500.	5000.
204C	1928C	Julian-Morgenthau	86,584,008	8.	18.	65.
204C☆			—	100.	175.	400.
204D	1928D	Julian-Morgenthau	146,381,364	5.	8.	12.
204D☆			—	20.	35.	125.
204E	1928E	Julian-Vinson	5,261,016	6.	12.	40.
204E☆			—	1200.	2000.	4000.
204F	1928F	Julian-Snyder	43,349,292	6.	8.	12.
204F☆			—	20.	35.	100.
204G	1928G	Clark-Snyder	52,208,000	6.	8.	10.
204G☆			—	15.	25.	75.

United States Notes/Series 1953 & 1963/Red Seal

A grey "2" replaces the seal at the left, which is now on the right. "TWO" is also reduced in size.

The back design, engraved by A. Dintaman and G.A. Payne, is the same as the preceding note.

No.	Series	Signatures	Notes Printed	VFine	EFine	Unc
205	1953	Priest-Humphrey	45,360,000	$—	$5.	$7.
205☆			2,160,000	—	—	15.
205A	1953A	Priest-Anderson	18,000,000	—	4.	6.
205A☆			720,000	2.	5.	25.
205B	1953B	Smith-Dillon	10,800,000	—	4.	7.
205B☆			720,000	2.	5.	12.
205C	1953C	Granahan-Dillon	5,760,000	—	4.	7.
205C☆			360,000	4.	7.	20.

The face design is similar to Nos. 204 and 205. "IN GOD WE TRUST" was added to the back of Series 1963.

No.	Series	Signatures	Notes Printed	VFine	EFine	Unc
206	1963	Granahan-Dillon	15,360,000	—	$—	$5.
206☆			640,000	—	5.	10.
206A	1963A	Granahan-Fowler	3,200,000	—	3.	5.
206A☆			640,000	—	5.	10.

Federal Reserve Notes/Series 1976 & 1995/Green Seal

This issue is the first, small-size, $2 Federal Reserve note. The portrait of Thomas Jefferson is based on a painting by Gilbert Stuart, as are numbers 204–206.

The presentation of *The Declaration of Independence* by John Trumbull hangs in the Trumbull Gallery at Yale University (see No. 1151).

Series 1976, Neff-Simon				**Series 1976, Neff-Simon**			
No.	**Bank**	**Notes Printed**	**Unc**	**No.**	**Bank**	**Notes Printed**	**Unc**
207A	Boston	29,440,000	$4.	**207G**	Chicago	75,520,000	$4.
207A☆		1,280,000	5.	**207G☆**		1,280,000	5.
207B	New York	67,200,000	4.	**207H**	St. Louis	39,040,000	4.
207B☆		2,560,000	5.	**207H☆**		1,280,000	5.
207C	Philadelphia	33,280,000	4.	**207I**	Minneapolis	23,680,000	4.
207C☆		1,280,000	5.	**207I☆**		640,000	7.
207D	Cleveland	31,360,000	4.	**207J**	Kansas City	24,960,000	4.
207D☆		1,280,000	5.	**207J☆**		640,000	7.
207E	Richmond	59,960,000	4.	**207K**	Dallas	41,600,000	4.
207E☆		640,000	7.	**207K☆**		1,280,000	5.
207F	Atlanta	60,800,000	4.	**207L**	San Francisco	82,560,000	4.
207F☆		1,280,000	5.	**207L☆**		920,000	5.

Series 1995, Withrow-Rubin
Printed in Fort Worth, these notes were in production when this catalog was printed.

Remarks: The following signed the *Declaration* but are not included in the original painting: Matthew Thornton, NH, John Hart, NJ, John Morton, James Smith, George Taylor and George Ross, PA, Caesar Rodney, DE, Thomas Stone, MD, Thomas Nelson, Jr, Francis Lightfoot Lee and Carter Braxton, VA, John Penn, NC, Button Gwinnett and Lyman Hall, GA.

The portraits of George Wythe, VA, William Whipple and Josiah Bartlet, NH, Thomas Lynch, SC, Thomas McKean, DE, and Philip Livingston, NY were deleted from the above engraving, however they appear on Nos. 1151–1162.

Demand Notes/1861

Freedom, which adorns the top of the Capitol in Washington, was created by Thomas Crawford. The statue as seen here was engraved by Owen G. Hanks. The engraved portrait of Alexander Hamilton is based on a painting by Archibald Robertson.

No.	Payable at	Notes Printed	Known	VGood	Fine	VFine
242A	Boston	1,340,000	76 (1)	$ 600.	$ 1250.	$ 2000.
242B	New York	1,500,000	87 (7)	600.	1250.	2000.
242C	Philadelphia	1,400,000	74	600.	1250.	2000.
242D	Cincinnati	44,000	5	6500.	8000.	15000.
242E	St. Louis	76,000	8	6000.	7500.	12000.

Remarks: A total of 4,360,000 notes were printed. According to records of 1931, 4,249½ notes were outstanding. These notes, all without the U.S. Treasury Seal, were signed by representatives of the U.S. Treasurer and the Register of the Treasury. "For the" was originally written as the signatures were inscribed (see No. 463 for an example). The number of these notes known, not included in the other total, are in parentheses above. These notes are extremely rare and command a higher premium. After a brief time "For the" was engraved into the plate. Serial number "1" notes are known for No. 242A Series 7, and No. 242C with no series.

United States Notes/1862 & 1863/Red Seal

This issue is similar to the preceding with the addition of the U.S. Treasury Seal and the deletion of the words "ON DEMAND." (Photo courtesy of Jack H. Fisher)

Back with first obligation.

Back with second obligation.

Nos. 243 and 243a have the first obligation back, remaining notes have the second obligation.

No.	Date	Description	Notes issued	Fine	EFine	Unc
243	1862	"American Bank Note Company" in upper border, no "Series"	100,000	$2600.	$ —	$ —
243a	1862	"American Bank Note Company" with "Series" on face		150.	400.	1250.
243b	1862	"American Bank Note Company" and "National Bank Note Company" in lower border		150.	400.	1250.
244	1863	"American Bank Note Company" twice in lower border; one serial number		135.	350.	1000.
244a	1863	as 243b; one serial number		135.	350.	1000.
244b	1863	as 244; two serial numbers		135.	350.	1000.

Remarks: All have signatures of Chittenden-Spinner. A total of 20,200,000 notes were printed; 19,332,714 were issued, and 99,726 were outstanding in 1889. Known for Nos. 243–6; 243b–19; 244–54; 244a–57; 244b–19 (Gengerke).

United States Notes/Series 1869/Red Seal

The portrait of Andrew Jackson, based on a painting by Thomas Sully, was engraved by Alfred Sealey. *The Pioneer* was engraved by Henry Gugler.

No.	Date	Signatures	Notes Printed	Fine	EFine	Unc
245	1869	Allison-Spinner	10,068,000	$225.	$600.	$2000.

Remarks: An example of No. 245, printed on paper watermarked "US" (intended for fractional currency) in new condition appeared in the November 13, 1979 NASCA auction (see Nos. 5 and 154).

United States Notes/Series 1875–1880

The face design is similar to the preceding note. This back design was engraved by G.L. Huber.

No.	Series	Signatures	Seal	Notes Printed	Fine	EFine	Unc
		Nos. 246A–249 have a red seal with rays.					
246A	1875A	Allison-New		1,000,000	$ 135.	$ 375.	$1175.
246B	1875B	Allison-New		1,000,000	110.	325.	775.
247	1875	Allison-New		3,860,000	70.	160.	400.
248	1875	Allison-Wyman		3,436,000	70.	160.	400.
249	1878	Allison-Gilfillan		6,032,000	150.	225.	475.
		Series of 1880					
250		Scofield-Gilfillan	lg. brown	3,800,000	350.	925.	3000.
251		Bruce-Gilfillan	lg. brown	7,200,000	75.	150.	475.
252		Bruce-Wyman	lg. brown	6,600,000	75.	150.	475.
		Nos. 253–263 have blue serial numbers and a large seal.					
253		Bruce-Wyman	red, scallops	2,500,000	100.	200.	875.
254		Bruce-Wyman	red, spikes			none observed	
255		Rosecrans-Jordan	red, scallops	6,500,000	85.	200.	825.
256		Rosecrans-Hyatt	red, scallops	1,460,000	100.	225.	1000.
257		Rosecrans-Huston	red, spikes	4,540,000	70.	275.	925.
258		Rosecrans-Huston	brown	4,000,000	70.	275.	925.
259		Rosecrans-Nebeker	brown	600,000	365.	1000.	1750.
		Nos. 260–263 have a small red seal with scallops.					
260		Rosecrans-Nebeker		8,992,000	75.	150.	400.
261		Tillman-Morgan		12,316,000	60.	100.	325.
262		Bruce-Roberts		7,000,000	75.	150.	400.
263		Lyons-Roberts		7,484,000	75.	150.	400.

Remarks: Known for Nos. 250–16; 256–13; 259–24; 263–16. The following hoards (by serial number) are known, all in uncirculated condition: No. 246A, unspecified number commencing with A7808xx; No. 246B, B257945–65 and B981331–83; No. 252, unspecified number commencing with Z12373xx; No. 262, unspecified number commencing with A435117xx

United States Notes/Series 1907

Nos. 264–273 have a red "V" and the word "Dollars" added; serial numbers are red, and the seals are red with scallops.

No.	Signatures	Notes Printed	Fine	EFine	Unc
264	Vernon-Treat	36,010,000	$ 45.	$ 80.	$200.
265	Vernon-McClung	32,120,000	45.	80.	200.
265☆	5 reported	—	—	—	—
266	Napier-McClung	54,004,000	45.	80.	200.
266☆	6 reported	—	—	—	—
267	Napier-Thompson	1,596,000	200.	450.	850.
267☆	not confirmed	—	—	—	—
268	Parker-Burke	47,116,000	45.	80.	200.
268☆	5 reported	—	—	—	—
269	Teehee-Burke	99,500,000	45.	80.	200.
269☆	25 reported	—	—	—	—
270	Elliott-Burke	4,300,000	60.	115.	300.
270☆	5 reported	—	—	—	—
271	Elliott-White	13,700,000	60.	100.	225.
271☆	5 reported	—	—	—	—
272	Speelman-White	155,384,000	45.	65.	200.
272☆	74 reported	—	—	—	—
273	Woods-White	18,304,000	50.	100.	225.
273☆	5 reported	—	—	—	—

Remarks: The number printed for No. 272 could be higher or lower. "M" block, after M24796001, was printed concurrently with notes of Woods-White. It is possible that additional notes were printed for No. 273. Known for Nos. 265–18; 270–20; 271–29; 273–29 (Gengerke).

National Bank Notes/First Charter Period

Columbus in Sight of Land, by artist Charles Fenton, was engraved by Louis Delnoce. *America Presented to the Old World*, by T.A. Liebler, was engraved by W.W. Rice.

The Landing of Columbus is based on the painting by John Vanderlyn. James Bannister, Louis Delnoce and Walter Shirlaw each engraved a version for the Continental Bank Note Co.

No.	Series	Signatures	VGood	VFine	Unc
		Red seal with rays			
274	orig.	Chittenden-Spinner	$150.	$350.	$1250.
275	orig.	Colby-Spinner	150.	350.	1250.
276	orig.	Jeffries-Spinner	775.	1900.	5000.
277	orig.	Allison-Spinner	150.	350.	1250.
		Red seal with scallops			
278	1875	Allison-New	150.	350.	1100.
279	1875	Allison-Wyman	150.	350.	1100.
280	1875	Allison-Gilfillan	150.	350.	1100.
281	1875	Scofield-Gilfillan	150.	350.	1100.
282	1875	Bruce-Gilfillan	175.	400.	1500.
283	1875	Bruce-Wyman	190.	475.	2000.
284	1875	Bruce-Jordan	---------------------- Rare ----------------------		
285	1875	Rosecrans-Jordan	190.	400.	2000.
286	1875	Rosecrans-Huston	190.	400.	2000.
286a	1875	Rosecrans-Nebeker	----------------- Extremely rare --------------		
286b	1875	Tillman-Morgan	--------------------- Unique ---------------------		

Remarks: The original series had no series date on the face. For additional information concerning the varieties of the back design see Hessler (1979, 142–146).

National Bank Notes/Series 1882/Second Charter Period/First Issue/Brown Seal

James A. Garfield was born in Orange, OH on November 18, 1831. After serving in the Ohio Senate he was elected to the presidency; Garfield was assassinated seven months later. This portrait, based on an autotype by Edward Bierstadt, was engraved by Lorenzo Hatch.

The back is brown.

No.	Signatures	VGood	VFine	Unc
287	Bruce-Gilfillan	$ 90.	$225.	$700.
288	Bruce-Wyman	90.	225.	700.
289	Bruce-Jordan	90.	225.	700.
290	Rosecrans-Jordan	90.	225.	700.
291	Rosecrans-Hyatt	90.	225.	700.
292	Rosecrans-Huston	90.	225.	700.
293	Rosecrans-Nebeker	90.	225.	700.
294	Rosecrans-Morgan	165.	425.	1000.
295	Tillman-Morgan	90.	225.	700.
296	Tillman-Roberts	90.	225.	700.
297	Bruce-Roberts	90.	225.	700.
298	Lyons-Roberts	90.	225.	700.
299	Vernon-Treat	125.	300.	975.

National Bank Notes/Series 1882/Second Charter Period/Second Issue/Blue Seal

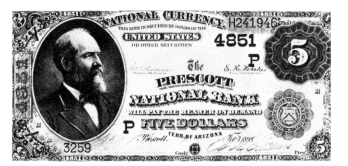

See preceding note for face design information.

The back is green.

No.	Signatures	VGood	VFine	Unc
300	Rosecrans-Huston	$ 90.	$150.	$ 600.
301	Rosecrans-Nebeker	90.	150.	600.
302	Rosecrans-Morgan	225.	550.	1250.
303	Tillman-Morgan	90.	150.	600.
304	Tillman-Roberts	90.	150.	650.
305	Bruce-Roberts	90.	150.	650.
306	Lyons-Roberts	90.	150.	600.
307	Vernon-Treat	90.	150.	700.
307a	Vernon-McClung		unknown	
308	Napier-McClung	425.	825.	1500.

National Bank Notes/Series 1882/Second Charter Period/Third Issue/Blue Seal

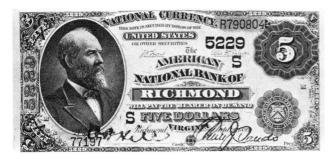

See No. 287 for face design information.

The back is green.

No.	Signatures	VGood	VFine	Unc
309	Tillman-Morgan	$100.	$250.	$1000.
310	Tillman-Roberts	150.	450.	1750.
311	Bruce-Roberts	150.	450.	1750.
311a	Lyons-Treat	---------------------------- Unknown ----------------------------		
312	Lyons-Roberts	135.	250.	1000.
313	Vernon-Treat	135.	450.	1250.
314	Napier-McClung	200.	450.	1500.
315	Teehee-Burke	------------------------------- Rare -------------------------------		

National Bank Notes/Series 1902/Third Charter Period

Benjamin Harrison, 23rd President of the U.S., was born on August 20, 1833. His great-grandfather was a signer of the Declaration of Independence; his grandfather was the ninth president, and his father served in the House of Representatives. The note was designed by Ostrander Smith and engraved by G.F. C. Smillie.

The green back design, with the *Landing of the Pilgrims* engraved by G.F.C. Smillie, is the same for all three issues, however, the second issue only has "1902–1908" added.

No.	Signatures	VGood	VFine	Unc
	First Issue—red seal			
316	Lyons-Roberts	$ 90.	$150.	$ 600.
317	Lyons-Treat	90.	175.	700.
318	Vernon-Treat	100.	200.	750.
	Second issue—blue seal			
319	Lyons-Roberts	35.	60.	375.
320	Lyons-Treat	35.	60.	375.
321	Vernon-Treat	35.	60.	375.
322	Vernon-McClung	35.	60.	375.
323	Napier-McClung	40.	70.	400.
324	Napier-Thompson	50.	115.	450.
325	Napier-Burke	40.	70.	375.
326	Parker-Burke	40.	70.	375.
327	Teehee-Burke	60.	165.	500.
	Third issue—blue seal			
328	Lyons-Roberts	30.	50.	275.
329	Lyons-Treat	30.	50.	275.
330	Vernon-Treat	30.	50.	275.
331	Vernon-McClung	30.	50.	275.
332	Napier-McClung	30.	50.	275.
333	Napier-Thompson	40.	115.	375.
334	Napier-Burke	30.	50.	275.
335	Parker-Burke	30.	50.	275.
336	Teehee-Burke	30.	50.	275.
337	Elliott-Burke	30.	50.	275.
338	Elliott-White	30.	50.	275.
339	Speelman-White	30.	50.	275.
340	Woods-White	30.	50.	275.
341	Woods-Tate	40.	80.	300.
342	Jones-Woods	150.	375.	1250.

National Gold Bank Notes/Red Seal

See Nos. 274–286 for face design information.

The gold coin vignette was engraved by James Smillie. Notes

No.	Date	Issuing Bank	City	Notes Issued	Known	VGood	Fine
343	1870	First National Gold Bank	San Francisco	33,000	192	$ 900.	$1750.
344	1872	National Gold Bank and Trust Company	San Francisco	17,840	6	1400.	2250.
345	1872	National Gold Bank of D.O. Mills and Company	Sacramento	7,960	26	1250.	2000.
346	1873	First National Gold Bank	Santa Barbara	2,000	10	1400.	2250.
347	1873	First National Gold Bank	Stockton	4,000	12	1250.	2000.
348	1874	Farmers National Gold Bank	San Jose	8,028	28	1000.	1850.

Remarks: The signatures of Allison-Spinner appear on these notes. A total of 3,451 notes are outstanding.

Silver Certificates/Series 1886

Lorenzo Hatch engraved the portrait of Ulysses S. Grant.

"In God We Trust," as seen on the reverses of the silver dollars, was not adopted for use on U.S. paper money until 1957.

No.	Signatures	Seal	Notes Printed	Fine	EFine	Unc
349	Rosecrans-Jordan	sm. red	1,500,000	$450.	$1200.	$3000.
350	Rosecrans-Hyatt	sm. red	7,345,800	375.	1000.	2800.
351	Rosecrans-Hyatt	lg. red	12,171,000	350.	1000.	2700.
352	Rosecrans-Huston	lg. red	3,548,000	375.	1100.	2900.
353	Rosecrans-Huston	lg. brown	7,400,000	350.	1000.	2800.
354	Rosecrans-Nebeker	sm. red	1,000,000	450.	1200.	3000.
355	Rosecrans-Nebeker	lg. brown	880,000	500.	1350.	3250.

Series of 1891

The back design has changed; the face design is similar to the preceding note.

356	Rosecrans-Nebeker	red, scallops	6,464,000	$300.	$700.	$3000.
357	Tillman-Morgan	red	25,092,000	250.	600.	2350.

Remarks: Delivery for Nos. 349–355 began on Feb. 9, 1887. The following hoards have been reported: No. 351 (B8845901–15); No. 353 (unknown number commencing with B310794x); No. 357 (E2761001–34).

Silver Certificates/Series 1896/Red Seal

This painting by Walter Shirlaw, about four feet across, the original model for Nos. 358–360 hangs in the Bureau of Engraving and Printing. For this design the artist was paid $600.

Mr. Shirlaw's central design, *Electricity Presenting Light to the World*, was retained; Thomas F. Morris redesigned the remaining portions. G.F.C. Smillie engraved the figures.

T.F. Morris designed the back; the female head, which greatly resembles the designer's wife, was engraved by G.F.C. Smillie. The portraits of U.S. Grant and Gen. Philip Sheridan were engraved by Lorenzo Hatch. This is the third note in the educational series (see Nos. 45 & 185).

No.	Signatures	Notes Printed	Fine	EFine	Unc
358	Tillman-Morgan	15,650,000	$400.	$1250.	$3500.
359	Bruce-Roberts	12,850,000	425.	1300.	3650.
360	Lyons-Roberts	6,432,000	500.	1400.	3850.

Remarks: A total of 35,012,000 notes were printed. This note is considered by many to be one of the most beautiful notes prepared by the Bureau of Engraving and Printing. It is possible that Anthony Comstock, Secretary of the Society for Suppression of Vice, pressured the U.S. Treasury to withdraw these "dirty dollars." An essay, dated 1897, with additional clothing on the central figure was prepared but not issued.

Silver Certificates/Series 1899/Blue Seal

The model for this portrait was *Chief Running Antelope*, a Sioux. The headdress is a Pawnee war bonnet, which the model supposedly refused to wear. G.F.C. Smillie engraved this portrait.

Additional engravers were: W. Montgomery, E.M. Hall, E.E. Myers, R. Ponickau and G.U. Rose, Jr. who also engraved the back.

No.	Signatures	Notes Issued	Fine	EFine	Unc
361	Lyons-Roberts	154,276,000	$185.	$400.	$1000.
362	Lyons-Treat	36,212,000	200.	450.	1100.
363	Vernon-Treat	94,282,000	185.	400.	1000.
364	Vernon-McClung	46,020,000	200.	425.	1100.
364☆	4 reported	—	—	—	—
365	Napier-McClung	62,780,000	185.	400.	1000.
365☆	4 reported	—	—	—	—
366	Napier-Thompson	2,234,000	235.	700.	2100.
367	Parker-Burke	40,572,000	200.	425.	1100.
367☆	7 reported	—	—	—	—
368	Teehee-Burke	47,804,000	200.	425.	1100.
368☆	10 reported	—	—	—	—
369	Elliott-Burke	18,520,000	210.	500.	1200.
369☆	10 reported	—	—	—	—
370	Elliott-White	32,212,000	200.	425.	1100.
370☆	15 reported	—	—	—	—
371	Speelman-White	30,952,000	200.	425.	1100.
371☆	5 reported	—	—	—	—

Remarks: A total of 556,054,000 notes were printed. Known for Nos. 363–42; 364–26; 366–28; 369–53.

Silver Certificates/Series 1923/Blue Seal

The "porthole" portrait of Lincoln was based on a photograph by Anthony Berger, a partner of Matthew Brady; it was engraved by Charles Burt.

The obverse of the *Great Seal of the United States*, as seen on the back, was engraved by Robert Ponickau.

No.	Signatures	Notes Printed	Fine	EFine	Unc
372	Speelman-White	6,316,000	$225.	$450.	$1200.
372☆	36 reported	—	200.	550.	1850.

Remarks: Other notes with nicknames include the "buffalo bill" (No. 483) and the "tombstone note" (No. 590).

Treasury or Coin Notes/Series 1890 & 1891

George W. Thomas was born in Southhampton, VA on July 11, 1816. He graduated from West Point where he served as an instructor from 1851 to 1854. He won numerous battles during the Civil War. The portrait of Thomas was engraved by Lorenzo Hatch.

No.	Signatures	Seal	Notes Printed	Fine	EFine	Unc
373	Rosecrans-Huston	brown	3,500,000	$275.	$675.	$1950.
374	Rosecrans-Nebeker	brown	300,000	375.	850.	3500.
375	Rosecrans-Nebeker	red	3,400,000	275.	675.	1950.

The face design is similar to the preceding note with the new back design.

Series 1891/Red Seal

376	Rosecrans-Nebeker	2,700,000	225.	450.	1200.
377	Tillman-Morgan	11,344,000	200.	375.	950.
378	Bruce-Roberts	2,456,000	225.	450.	1200.
379	Lyons-Roberts	760,000	300.	800.	2200.

Remarks: The following serial numbers have been observed in uncirculated condition for No. 373: A2829002, –010, and –079. Many of the numbers between exist in the same condition. The following serial numbers have been observed in uncirculated condition for No. 375: A7192317, –330, –379, –399 and 400, indicating that many of the numbers between probably exist in the same condition. For the 1891 issue 16,948,000 notes were issued. Known for Nos. 374–8; 379–8.

Federal Reserve Notes/Series of 1914/Red Seal

Charles Burt's engraving of the Lincoln portrait was based on a photograph by Anthony Berger, a partner of Matthew Brady.

Columbus Discovery of Land and *Landing of the Pilgrims* were probably engraved by Joseph I. Pease.

No.	Bank	VFine	Unc	No.	Bank	VFine	Unc
380A	Boston	$65.	$400.	**380G**	Chicago	$65.	$300.
380B	New York	65.	300.	**380H**	St. Louis	65.	400.
380C	Philadelphia	65.	350.	**380I**	Minneapolis	65.	375.
380D	Cleveland	65.	350.	**380J**	Kansas City	65.	375.
380E	Richmond	65.	400.	**380K**	Dallas	65.	375.
380F	Atlanta	65.	400.	**380L**	San Francisco	75.	500.

Remarks: The first day of issue was November 16, 1914. The signatures of Burke-McAdoo appear on these notes. Type I was printed for all 12 districts. Type II, with small district number and letter in upper left and lower right corners, was printed for all districts.

Federal Reserve Notes/Series 1914/Blue Seal

No.	Bank	Signatures	Printed	Delivered	VFine	Unc
			Notes			
381A1	Boston	Burke-McAdoo			$30.	$90.
381A1☆	4 reported				—	—
381A2	Boston	Burke-Glass			30.	90.
381A2☆	1 reported		92,168,000	90,400,000	—	—
381A3	Boston	Burke-Houston			30.	90.
381A3☆	6 reported				—	—
381A4	Boston	White-Mellon (b,c)			30.	90.
381A4☆	13 reported		(872,000)		—	—
381B1	New York	Burke-McAdoo			30.	90.
381B1☆	5 reported				—	—
381B2	New York	Burke-Glass			30.	90.
381B2☆	3 reported				—	—
381B3	New York	Burke-Houston	297,852,000		30.	90.
381B3☆	16 reported				—	—
381B4	New York	White Mellon (b,c)			30.	90.
381B4☆	51 reported	(4 "b",10 "c")	(2,400,000)		—	—
381C1	Philadelphia	Burke-McAdoo			30.	90.
381C1☆	2 reported				—	—
381C2	Philadelphia	Burke-Glass			30.	90.
381C2☆	1 reported				—	—
381C3	Philadelphia	Burke-Houston	103,824,000		30.	90.
381C3☆	8 reported				—	—
381C4	Philadelphia	White-Mellon (b,c)			30.	90.
381C4☆	19 reported	(1 "b", 4 "c")	(1,204,000)		—	—
381D1	Cleveland	Burke-McAdoo			30.	90.
381D1☆	1 reported				—	—
381D2	Cleveland	Burke-Glass			30.	90.
381D3	Cleveland	Burke-Houston	73,216,000		30.	90.
381D3☆	3 reported				—	—
381D4	Cleveland	White-Mellon (b,c)			30.	90.
381D4☆	17 reported	(1 "b", 4 "c")	(752,000)		—	—
381E1	Richmond	Burke-McAdoo			30.	90.
381E2	Richmond	Burke-Glass			30.	90.
381E3	Richmond	Burke-Houston	49,444,000	45,932,000	30.	90.
381E3☆	7 reported				—	—
381E4	Richmond	White-Mellon (b,c)			35.	110.
381E4☆	5 reported		(496,000)		—	—
381F1	Atlanta	Burke-McAdoo			30.	90.
381F2	Atlanta	Burke-Glass			45.	135.
381F3	Atlanta	Burke-Houston	55,000,000	54,476,000	30.	90.
381F3☆	5 reported				—	—
381F4	Atlanta	White-Mellon (b,c)			30.	90.
381F4☆	4 reported		(504,000)		—	—
381G1	Chicago	Burke-McAdoo			30.	90.
381G1☆	2 reported				—	—
381G2	Chicago	Burke-Glass			30.	90.
381G2☆	5 reported				—	—
381G3	Chicago	Burke-Houston	164,876,000		30.	90.
381G3☆	16 reported				—	—
381G4	Chicago	White-Mellon (b,c)			30.	90.
381G4☆	34 reported	(1 "b", 3 "c")	(1,524,000)		—	—

Federal Reserve Notes/Series 1914/Blue Seal *(continued)*

No.	Bank	Signatures	Printed	Delivered	VFine	Unc
			Notes			
381H1	St. Louis	Burke-McAdoo			30.	90.
381H1☆	2 reported				—	—
381H2	St. Louis	Burke-Glass			30.	90.
381H2☆	7 reported		41,704,000		—	—
381H3	St. Louis	Burke-Houston			30.	90.
381H3☆	6 reported				—	—
381H4	St. Louis	White-Mellon (b)			30.	90.
381H4☆	4 reported		(476,000)		—	—
381I1	Minneapolis	Burke-McAdoo			30.	90.
381I1☆	1 reported				—	—
381I2	Minneapolis	Burke-Glass			30.	90.
381I2☆	1 reported				—	—
381I3	Minneapolis	Burke-Houston	30,116,000	29,280,000	35.	110.
381I3☆	5 reported				—	—
381I4	Minneapolis	White-Mellon			30.	90.
381I4☆	5 reported		(244,000)		—	—
381J1	Kansas City	Burke-McAdoo			30.	90.
381J1☆	1 reported				30.	90.
381J2	Kansas City	Burke-Glass			30.	90.
381J2☆	2 reported				—	—
381J3	Kansas City	Burke-Houston	44,396,000	43,928,000	30.	90.
381J3☆	7 reported				—	—
381J4	Kansas City	White-Mellon (b)			30.	90.
381J4☆	10 reported		(372,000)		—	—
381K1	Dallas	Burke-McAdoo			45.	135.
381K2	Dallas	Burke-Glass			45.	135.
381K2☆	2 reported				—	—
381K3	Dallas	Burke-Houston	29,416,000	28,526,000	30.	90.
381K3☆	2 reported				—	—
381K4	Dallas	White-Mellon (b,c)			30.	90.
381K4☆	7 reported		(272,000)		—	—
381L1	San Francisco	Burke-McAdoo			30.	90.
381L1☆	1 reported				—	—
381L2	San Francisco	Burke-Glass			30.	90.
381L3	San Francisco	Burke-Houston	92,168,000	91,848,000	30.	90.
381L3☆	1 reported				—	—
381L4	San Francisco	White-Mellon (b,c)			30.	90.
381L4☆	11 reported	(1 "b")	(892,000)		—	—

| Type "a" | Type "b" | Type "c" |

Remarks: The total for each district is for regular issues only. The figure in parenthesis, the last replacement serial number, is the total number of replacement notes of this denomination printed for that bank; the number printed by signatures is not available. White-Mellon plate variations, in parenthesis, exist for some districts, identified as type "b" (small district number and letter in lower left) and type "c" (space of 23 mm horizontal from left seal to the engraved border). Star, replacement notes reported in the main listing above are type "a" if not identified by type.

Federal Reserve Bank Notes/Blue Seal

See No. 380 for portrait information. The "G–7" in the four corners indicates the seventh Federal Reserve District.

The back design is similar to No. 380.

No.	Bank	Date	Bank Signatures	Notes Issued	VFine	Unc
382A1	Boston	1918	Bullen-Morss	440,000	$800.	$2750.
382A1☆	1 reported				—	—
382B1	New York	1918	Hendricks-Strong	6,400,000	100.	475.
382C1	Philadelphia	1918	Hardt-Passmore	1,600,000	100.	475.
382C2	Philadelphia	1918	Dyer-Passmore	included in above	100.	475.
382D1	Cleveland	1918	Baxter-Fancher	—	100.	400.
382D1☆	3 reported			—	—	—
382D2	Cleveland	1918	Davis Fancher	—	120.	525.
382D3	Cleveland	1918	Davis-Fancher@	—	120.	525.
382F1	Atlanta	1915	Bell-Wellborn	—	200.	625.
382F2	Atlanta	1915	Pike-McCord	—	150.	575.
382F3	Atlanta	1918	Pike-McCord	—	125.	575.
382F4	Atlanta	1918	Bell-Wellborn	—	125.	575.
382F5	Atlanta	1918	Bell-Wellborn@	—	125.	575.
382G1	Chicago	1915	McLalllen-McDougal	—	125.	550.
382G2	Chicago	1918	McCloud-McDougal	—	100.	425.
382G2☆	3 reported			—	—	—
382G3	Chicago	1918	Cramer-McDougal	—	175.	675.
382H1	St. Louis	1918	Attebery-Wells		125.	500.
382H2	St. Louis	1918	Attebery-Biggs	51,524,000	100.	425.
382H3	St. Louis	1918	White-Biggs@		100.	425.
382I1	Minneapolis	1918	Cook-Wold	—	125.	525.

Federal Reserve Bank Notes/Blue Seal *(continued)*

No.	Bank	Date	Bank Signatures	Notes Issued	VFine	Unc
382J1	Kansas City	1915	Anderson-Miller	⎫	170.	600.
382J2	Kansas City	1915	Cross-Miller	⎪	150.	550.
382J3	Kansas City	1915	Helm-Miller	⎬ 4,802,000	170.	550.
382J4	Kansas City	1918	Anderson-Miller	⎪ —	150.	550.
382J4☆	2 reported			⎭ —	—	—
382J5	Kansas City	1918	Helm-Miller@	—	170.	550.
382K1	Dallas	1915	Hoopes-VanZandt	128,000	150.	500.
382K2	Dallas	1915	Talley-VanZandt	included in above	185.	600.
382K3	Dallas	1918	Talley-VanZandt	500,000	240.	650.
382L1	San Francisco	1915	Clerk-Lynch	336,000	150.	550.
382L2	San Francisco	1918	Clerk-Lynch	500,000	150.	550.
382L3	San Francisco	1914	Clerk-Lynch	—	800.	3000.
382L3☆	7 reported			—	—	—
382L4	San Francisco	1918	Ambrose-Calkins@	incl. in No. 382L2	—	—

Remarks: For No. 382A, 375 pieces are outstanding. No. 382L3 has the incorrect date, May 18; it should be May 20. All have Teehee-Burke signatures except those with (@), which have Elliott-Burke signatures. Observed: 382J1 hand-signed; 382J2 Cross, hand-signed, as Acting Cashier; 382J5 Helm as Acting Cashier.

United States Notes/Series 1928/Red Seal

Charles Burt's 1869 engraving of Abraham Lincoln was based on a photograph by Anthony Berger, a partner of Matthew Brady.

The *Lincoln Memorial* on the back was engraved by J.C. Benzing. On May 30, 1922, 57 years after the idea was conceived, the memorial was dedicated; Henry Bacon was the architect. The 36 columns represent the 36 states of the Union in 1865. The 19-foot statue of Lincoln was carved by Daniel C. French.

No.	Series	Signatures	Notes Printed	VFine	EFine	Unc
383	1928	Woods-Mellon	267,209,616	$ —	$ 8.	$ 30.
383☆			—	20.	50.	200.
383A	1928A	Woods-Mills	58,194,600	15.	25.	75.
383A☆			—	250.	400.	1000.
383B	1928B	Julian-Morgenthau	147,827,340	—	10.	15.
383B☆			—	20.	35.	175.
383C	1928C	Julian-Morgenthau	214,735,765	—	10.	15.
383C☆			—	20.	35.	175.
383D	1928D	Julian-Vinson	9,297,120	25.	35.	150.
383D☆			—	200.	350.	900.
383E	1928E	Julian-Snyder	109,952,760	—	10.	15.
383E☆			—	35.	60.	150.
383F	1928F	Clark-Snyder	104,194,704	—	10.	15.
383F☆			—	15.	25.	75.

United States Notes/Series 1953 & 1963/Red Seal

A grey "5" replaces the seal, which is now on the left. "FIVE" is also reduced in size. The back design is the same as the preceding note.

No.	Series	Signatures	Notes Printed	VFine	EFine	Unc
384	1953	Priest-Humphrey	120,880,000	—	8—	$15.
384☆			5,760.000	—	15.	35.
384A	1953A	Priest-Anderson	90,760,000	—	—	10.
384A☆			5,400,000	—	25	65.
384B	1953B	Smith-Dillon	44,640,000	—	—	10.
384B☆			2,160,000	—	10.	20.
384C	1953C	Granahan-Dillon	8,640,000	—	—	10.
384C☆			320,000	—	10.	35.

"IN GOD WE TRUST" was added to the 1963 series.

385	1963	Granahan-Dillon	63,360,000	—	—	10.
385☆			3,840,000	—	—	15.

Silver Certificates/Blue Seal

No.	Series	Signatures	Notes Printed	VFine	EFine	Unc
386	1934	Julian-Morgenthau	393,088,368	$ —	$ 8.	$ 15.
386☆			3,960,000	10.	20.	50.
386A	1934A	Julian-Morgenthau	656,265,948	—	—	12.
386A☆				10.	20.	35.

Nos. 387 and 387A have yellow seals; they were issued for the North African invasion during World War II.

No.	Series	Signatures	Notes Printed	VFine	EFine	Unc
387	1934	Julian-Morgenthau	—		none reported	
387A	1934A	Julian Morgenthau	16,710,000	15.	25.	80.
387A☆		included in above	50.	75.	150.	
387B	1934B	Julian-Vinson	59,128,500	8.	10.	30.
387B☆			—	20.	50.	135.
387C	1934C	Julian-Snyder	403,328,964	—	—	15.
387C☆			—	—	15.	25.
387D	1934D	Clark-Snyder	486,146,148	—	—	15.
387D☆			—	—	15.	25.

The "5" on the left is grey; the blue seal is smaller.

No.	Series	Signatures	Notes Printed	VFine	EFine	Unc
388	1953	Priest-Humphrey	339,600,000	—	—	10.
388☆			15,120,000	—	10.	25.
388A	1953A	Priest-Anderson	232,400,000	—	—	10.
388A☆			12,960,000	—	10.	25.
388B	1953B	Smith-Dillon	73,000,000	—	—	10.
388B☆			3,240,000	—	175.	600.
388C	1953C	Granahan-Dillon	90,640,000		never released	

Remarks: For No. 388B only 14,196,000 notes were released. The figure for No. 388C includes an uncut sheet of star notes at the BEP.

Federal Reserve Bank Notes/Series 1929/Brown Seal

Back design is similar to No. 383.

Signatures of Jones-Woods

No.	Bank	Notes Printed	VFine	EFine	Unc
389A	Boston	3,180,000	$ 10.	$ 15.	$ 60.
389A☆		—	—	—	—
389B	New York	2,100,200	10.	15.	50.
389B☆		—	—	—	—
389C	Philadelphia	3,096,000	10.	15.	60.
389C☆		—	—	—	—
389D	Cleveland	4,236,000	8.	12.	45.
389D☆		—	—	—	—
389E	Richmond	not issued	—	—	—
389F	Atlanta	1,848,000	12.	20.	85.
389F☆		—	—	—	—
389G	Chicago	5,988,000	8.	12.	35.
389G☆		—	—	—	—
389H	St. Louis	276,000	75.	125.	550.
389H☆		—	—	—	—
389I	Minneapolis	684,000	20.	35.	125.
389J	Kansas City	2,460,000	10.	15.	60.
389J☆		—	—	—	—
389K	Dallas	996,000	15.	25.	60.
389L	San Francisco	360,000	350.	500.	2500.
389L☆		—	—	—	—

National Bank Notes/Series 1929/Brown Seal

Type I

Type II has the charter number printed a second time near the serial number.

No.	Rarity	Type I			Type II		
		VFine	EFine	Une	VFine	EFine	Une
	1	$ 15.	$20.	$ 40.	$ 20.	$ 30.	$ 50.
	2	18.	25.	50.	25.	35.	60.
	3	22.	35.	60.	30.	45.	85.
	4	30.	45.	75.	40.	60.	100.
390	5	40.	55.	100.	50.	75.	125.
	6	50.	80.	150.	60.	100.	165.
	7	75.	115.	200.	100.	165.	250.
	8	150.	250.	400.	250.	400.	500.
	9	1500.	2750.	5000.	3500.	5000.	7500.

Remarks: A total of 170,229,387 notes were issued for both types; both bear the signatures of Jones-Woods. The Chase National Bank, now The Chase Manhattan Bank, issued 6,346,530 type I notes, the largest amount issued by any national bank.

Federal Reserve Notes/Series 1928 & 1928A/Green Seal

The number in the seal indicates the Federal Reserve district.   The back design is similar to No. 383.

Series 1928, Tate-Mellon

No.	Bank	Notes Printed	Une
391A	Boston	8,025,300	$ 50.
391A☆			200.
391B	New York	14,701,884	50.
391B☆			200.
391C	Philadelphia	123,680,000	50.
391C☆			200.
391D	Cleveland	9,048,500	50.
391D☆			200.
391E	Richmond	6,027,000	50.
391E☆			200.
391F	Atlanta	10,964,000	50.
391F☆			200.
391G	Chicago	12,326,052	50.
391G☆			200.
391H	St. Louis	4,765,000	50.
391H☆			200.
391I	Minneapolis	4,284,000	50.
391I☆			300.
391J	Kansas City	4,480,000	50.
391J☆			200.
391K	Dallas	8,137,000	35.
391K☆			200.
391L	San Francisco	9,792,000	100.
391L☆			400.

Series 1928A, Woods-Mellon

No.	Bank	Notes Printed	Une
392A	Boston	9,404,724	$ 40.
392A☆			275.
392B	New York	42,878,196	40.
392B☆			275.
392C	Philadelphia	10,806,012	40.
392C☆			275.
392D	Cleveland	6,822,424	40.
392D☆			275.
392E	Richmond	2,409,900	60.
392E☆			275.
392F	Atlanta	13,386,420	40.
392F☆			275.
392G	Chicago	37,882,176	40.
392G☆			250.
392H	St. Louis	2,731,824	50.
392H☆			275.
392I	Minneapolis	652,000	200.
392I☆			500.
392J	Kansas City	3,572,400	50.
392J☆			275.
392K	Dallas	2,564,400	60.
392K☆			500.
392L	San Francisco	6,565,500	50.
392L☆			275.

Federal Reserve Notes/Series 1928B, 1928C & 1928D/Green Seal

Series 1928B, Woods-Mellon

No.	Bank	Notes Printed	Unc
393A	Boston	28,430,724	$ 40.
393A☆			200.
393B	New York	51,157,536	40.
393B☆			200.
393C	Philadelphia	25,698,396	40.
393C☆			200.
393D	Cleveland	28,874,272	40.
393D☆			200.
393E	Richmond	15,151,932	40.
393E☆			200.
393F	Atlanta	13,386,420	40.
393F☆			200.
393G	Chicago	17,157,036	40.
393G☆			200.
393H	St. Louis	20,251,716	40.
393H☆			200.
393I	Minneapolis	6,954,060	40.
393I☆			200.
393J	Kansas City	10,677,636	40.
393J☆			200.
393K	Dallas	4,334,400	40.
393K☆			200.
393L	San Francisco	28,840,080	40.
393L☆		not issued	200.

A letter replaces the numeral in the Federal Reserve seal on No. 393. Notes with with a light green seal command an aditional premium.

Series 1928C, Woods-Mills

No.	Bank	Notes Printed	Unc
394D	Cleveland	3,293,640	$600.
394F	Atlanta	2,056,200	500.
394L	San Francisco	266,304	700.

Series 1928D, Woods-Woodin

No.	Bank	Notes Printed	Unc
395F	Atlanta	1,281,600	$750.

For Series 1928C and 1928D, $20 notes were printed only for the districts listed.

Federal Reserve Notes/Series 1934/Green Seal

Series 1934, Julian-Morgenthau				Series 1934, Julian Morgenthau			
No.	Bank	Notes Printed	Unc	No.	Bank	Notes Printed	Unc
396A	Boston	30,510,000	$ 35.	396G	Chicago	131,299,156	$ 25.
396A☆			125.	396G☆			125.
396B	New York	47,888,760	30.	396H	St. Louis	48,737,280	30.
396B☆			125.	396H☆			125.
396C	Philadelphia	47,327,760	30.	396I	Minneapolis	16,795,392	30.
396C☆			125.	396I☆			125.
396D	Cleveland	62,273,508	30.	396J	Kansas City	31,854,432	30.
396D☆			125.	396J☆			125.
396E	Richmond	62,128,452	30.	396K	Dallas	33,332,208	30.
396E☆			125.	396K☆			125.
396F	Atlanta	50,548,608	30.	396L	San Francisco	39,324,168	30.
396F☆			125.	396L☆			125.
396LL	Hawaii	3,000,000	150.	396LL☆			900.

Remarks: Notes with a dark green seal command an additional premium. No. 396LL was overprinted with "HAWAII" for use in the Pacific theater during World War II. Notes of $1 (No. 79), $5 (No. 397LL) $10 (No. 633LL) and $20 (No. 858LL) also bear this overprint.

Federal Reserve Notes/Series 1934A, 1934B, 1934C & 1934D/Green Seal

Series 1934A, Julian-Morgenthau

No.	Bank	Notes Printed	Unc
397A	Boston	23,231,566	$ 25.
397A☆			100.
397B	New York	143,199,336	20.
397B☆			100.
397C	Philadelphia	30,691,632	25.
397C☆			100.
397D	Cleveland	1,610,676	50.
397D☆			100.
397E	Richmond	6,555,168	25.
397E☆			115.
397F	Atlanta	22,811,168	25.
397F☆			100.
397G	Chicago	88,376,376	25.
397G☆			100.
397H	St. Louis	7,843,452	25.
397H☆			115.
397I	Minneapolis	not issued	—
397I☆		not issued	—
397J	Kansas City	not issued	—
397J☆		not issued	—
397K	Dallas	not issued	—
397K☆		not issued	—
397L	San Francisco	72,118,452	25.
397L☆			100.
397LL	(Hawaii ovpt)	6,416,000	100.
397LL☆			250.

Series 1934B, Julian-Vinson

No.	Bank	Notes Printed	Unc
398A	Boston	3,457,000	$ 25.
398A☆			200.
398B	New York	14,099,580	25.
398B☆			200.
398C	Philadelphia	8,306,820	25.
398C☆			200.
398D	Cleveland	11,348,184	25.
398D☆			200.
398E	Richmond	5,902,848	25.
398E☆			200.
398F	Atlanta	4,314,048	25.
398F☆			200.
398G	Chicago	9,070,932	25.
398G☆			200.
398H	St. Louis	4,307,712	25.
398H☆			200.
398I	Minneapolis	2,482,000	25.
398I☆			200.
398J	Kansas City	738,000	300.
398J☆			200.
398K	Dallas	not issued	
398K☆		not issued	—
398L	San Francisco	9,910,296	25.
398L☆			200.

Series 1934C, Julian-Snyder

No.	Bank	Notes Printed	Unc
399A	Boston	14,463,600	$ 25.
399A☆			100.
399B	New York	74,383,248	25.
399B☆			75.
399C	Philadelphia	22,879,212	25.
399C☆			75.
399D	Cleveland	19,898,256	25.
399D☆			75.
399E	Richmond	23,800,524	25.
399E☆			75.
399F	Atlanta	23,572,968	25.
399F☆			115.
399G	Chicago	60,598,812	25.
399G☆			75.
399H	St. Louis	20,393,340	25.
399H☆			75.
399I	Minneapolis	5,089,200	25.
399I☆		not issued	—
399J	Kansas City	8,313,504	25.
399J☆			100.
399K	Dallas	5,107,800	25.
399K☆			115.
399L	San Francisco	9,451,944	25.
399L☆			100.

Series 1934D, Clark-Snyder

No.	Bank	Notes Printed	Unc
400A	Boston	12,660,552	$ 30.
400A☆			100.
400B	New York	50,976,676	25.
400B☆			100.
400C	Philadelphia	12,106,740	30.
400C☆			100.
400D	Cleveland	8,969,052	30.
400D☆			175.
400E	Richmond	13,333,032	30.
400E☆			125.
400F	Atlanta	9,599,352	30.
400F☆			125.
400G	Chicago	36,601,680	30.
400G☆			100.
400H	St. Louis	8,093,412	30.
400H☆			100.
400I	Minneapolis	3,594,900	30.
400I☆			125.
400J	Kansas City	6,538,740	30.
400J☆			125.
400K	Dallas	4,139,016	30.
400K☆			125.
400L	San Francisco	11,704,200	30.
400L☆			125.

Federal Reserve Notes/Series 1950, 1950A, 1950B & 1950C/Green Seal

The size of the Federal Reserve seal is reduced.

Series 1950, Clark-Snyder

No.	Bank	Notes Printed	Unc
401A	Boston	30,672,000	$ 30.
401A☆		408,000	100.
401B	New York	106,768,000	30.
401B☆		1,464,000	100.
401C	Philadelphia	44,784,000	30.
401C☆		600,000	100.
401D	Cleveland	54,000,000	30.
401D☆		744,000	175.
401E	Richmond	47,088,000	30.
401E☆		684,000	125.
401F	Atlanta	52,416,000	30.
401F☆		696,000	125.
401G	Chicago	85,104,000	30.
401G☆		1,176,000	100.
401H	St. Louis	36,864,000	30.
401H☆		552,000	100.
401I	Minneapolis	11,796,000	30.
401I☆		144,000	125.
401J	Kansas City	25,428,000	30.
401J☆		360,000	125.
401K	Dallas	22,848,000	30.
401K☆		372,000	125.
401L	San Francisco	55,008,000	30.
401L☆		744,000	125.

Series 1950A, Priest-Humphrey

No.	Bank	Notes Printed	Unc
402A	Boston	53,568,000	$15.
402A☆		2,808,000	20.
402B	New York	186,472,000	15.
402B☆		9,216,000	20.
402C	Philadelphia	69,616,000	15.
402C☆		4,320,000	20.
402D	Cleveland	45,360,000	15.
402D☆		2,376,000	20.
402E	Richmond	76,672,000	15.
402E☆		5,400,000	20.
402F	Atlanta	86,464,000	15.
402F☆		5,040,000	20.
402G	Chicago	129,296,000	15.
402G☆		6,264,000	20.
402H	St. Louis	54,936,000	15.
402H☆		3,384,000	20.
402I	Minneapolis	11,232,000	15.
402I☆		864,000	25.
402J	Kansas City	29,952,000	15.
402J☆		1,088,000	20.
402K	Dallas	24,984,000	15.
402K☆		1,368,000	20.
402L	San Francisco	90,712,000	15.
402L☆		6,336,000	20.

Series 1950B, Priest-Anderson

No.	Bank	Notes Printed	Unc
403A	Boston	30,880,000	$15.
403A☆		2,520,000	20.
403B	New York	85,960,000	15.
403B☆		4,680,000	20.
403C	Philadelphia	43,560,000	15.
403C☆		2,880,000	20.
403D	Cleveland	38,800,000	15.
403D☆		2,880,000	20.
403E	Richmond	52,920,000	15.
403E☆		2,008,000	20.
403F	Atlanta	80,560,000	15.
403F☆		3,960,000	20.
403G	Chicago	104,320,000	15.
403G☆		6,120,000	20.
403H	St. Louis	25,840,000	15.
403H☆		1,440,000	20.
403I	Minneapolis	20,880,000	15.
403I☆		792,000	25.
403J	Kansas City	32,400,000	15.
403J☆		2,520,000	20.
403K	Dallas	52,120,000	15.
403K☆		3,240,000	20.
403L	San Francisco	56,080,000	15.
403L☆		3,600,000	20.

Series 1950C, Smith-Dillon

No.	Bank	Notes Printed	Unc
404A	Boston	20,880,000	$15.
404A☆		720,000	50.
404B	New York	47,440,000	15.
404B☆		2,880,000	20.
404C	Philadelphia	29,520,000	15.
404C☆		1,800,000	20.
404D	Cleveland	33,840,000	15.
404D☆		1,800,000	20.
404E	Richmond	33,460,000	15.
404E☆		1,160,000	20.
404F	Atlanta	54,360,000	15.
404F☆		3,240,000	20.
404G	Chicago	56,880,000	15.
404G☆		3,240,000	20.
404H	St. Louis	22,680,000	15.
404H☆		720,000	50.
404I	Minneapolis	12,960,000	15.
404I☆		720,000	50.
404J	Kansas City	24,760,000	15.
404J☆		1,800,000	20.
404K	Dallas	3,960,000	15.
404K☆		360,000	75.
404L	San Francisco	25,920,000	15.
404L☆		1,440,000	20.

Federal Reserve Notes/Series 1950D, 1950E, 1963 & 1963A/Green Seal

Series 1950D, Granahan-Dillon

No.	Bank	Notes Printed	Unc
405A	Boston	25,200,000	$15.
405A☆		1,080,000	20.
405B	New York	102,160,000	15.
405B☆		5,040,000	20.
405C	Philadelphia	21,520,000	15.
405C☆		1,080,000	20.
405D	Cleveland	23,400,000	15.
405D☆		1,080,000	20.
405E	Richmond	42,400,000	15.
405E☆		1,080,000	20.
405F	Atlanta	35,200,000	15.
405F☆		1,800,000	20.
405G	Chicago	67,240,000	15.
405G☆		3,600,000	20.
405H	St. Louis	20,160,000	15.
405H☆		14,400,000	20.
405I	Minneapolis	7,920,000	15.
405I☆		360,000	50.
405J	Kansas City	11,160,000	15.
405J☆		720,000	35.
405K	Dallas	7,200,000	15.
405K☆		360,000	40.
405L	San Francisco	53,280,000	15.
405L☆		3,600,000	20.

Series 1950E, Granahan-Fowler

No.	Bank	Notes Printed	Unc
406B	New York	82,000,000	$15.
406B☆		6,678,000	20.
406G	Chicago	14,760,000	15.
406G☆		1,080,000	35.
406L	San Francisco	24,400,000	15.
406L☆		1,800,000	35.

"In God We Trust" was added to the back of Series 1963 and all subsequent $1 notes.

Series 1963, Granahan-Dillon

No.	Bank	Notes Printed	Unc
407A	Boston	4,480,000	$15.
407A☆		640,000	20.
407B	New York	12,160,000	15.
407B☆		1,280,000	18.
407C	Philadelphia	8,320,000	15.
407C☆		1,920,000	18.
407D	Cleveland	10,240,000	15.
407D☆		1,920,000	18.
407E	Richmond	not printed	—
407E☆		not printed	—
407F	Atlanta	17,920,000	15.
407F☆		2,560,000	18.
407G	Chicago	22,400,000	15.
407G☆		3,200,000	18.
407H	St. Louis	14,080,000	15.
407H☆		1,920,000	18.
407I	Minneapolis	not printed	—
407I☆		not printed	—
407J	Kansas City	1,920,000	18.
407J☆		640,000	20.
407K	Dallas	5,760,000	15.
407K☆		1,920,000	25.
407L	San Francisco	18,560,000	15.
407L☆		1,920,000	18.

Series 1963A, Granahan-Fowler

No.	Bank	Notes Printed	Unc
408A	Boston	77,440,000	$10.
408A☆		5,760,000	15.
408B	New York	98,080,000	10.
408B☆		7,680,000	15.
408C	Philadelphia	106,400,000	10.
408C☆		10,240,000	15.
408D	Cleveland	83,840,000	10.
408D☆		7,040,000	15.
408E	Richmond	118,560,000	10.
408E☆		10,880,000	15.
408F	Atlanta	117,920,000	10.
408F☆		9,600,000	15.
408G	Chicago	213,440,000	10.
408G☆		16,640,000	15.
408H	St. Louis	56,960,000	10.
408H☆		5,120,000	15.
408I	Minneapolis	32,640,000	10.
408I☆		3,200,000	15.
408J	Kansas City	55,040,000	10.
408J☆		5,760,000	15.
408K	Dallas	64,000,000	10.
408K☆		3,840,000	20.
408L	San Francisco	128,900,000	10.
408L☆		12,153,000	15.

Federal Reserve Notes/Series 1969, 1969A, 1969B & 1969C/Green Seal

Series 1969, Elston-Kennedy

No.	Bank	Notes Printed	Unc
409A	Boston	51,200,000	$10.
409A☆		1,920,000	15.
409B	New York	198,560,000	10.
409B☆		8,960,000	12.
409C	Philadelphia	69,120,000	10.
409C☆		2,560,000	15.
409D	Cleveland	56,320,000	10.
409D☆		2,560,000	15.
409E	Richmond	84 480,000	10.
409E☆		3,200,000	12.
409F	Atlanta	84,480,000	10.
409F☆		3,840,000	15.
409G	Chicago	125,600,000	10.
409G☆		5,120,000	12.
409H	St. Louis	27,520,000	10.
409H☆		1,280,000	15.
409I	Minneapolis	16,640,000	10.
409I☆		640,000	20.
409J	Kansas City	48,640,000	10.
409J☆		3,292,000	12.
409K	Dallas	39,680,000	10.
409K☆		1,920,000	15.
409L	San Francisco	103,840,000	10.
409L☆		4,480,000	12.

Series 1969A, Kabis-Connally

No.	Bank	Notes Printed	Unc
410A	Boston	23,040,000	$10.
410A☆		1,280,000	20.
410B	New York	62,240,000	10.
410B☆		2,394,000	20.
410C	Philadelphia	41,160,000	10.
410C☆		1,920,000	20.
410D	Cleveland	21,120,000	10.
410D☆		640,000	30.
410E	Richmond	37,920,000	10.
410E☆		1,120,000	20.
410F	Atlanta	25,120,000	10.
410F☆		480,000	30.
410G	Chicago	60,800,000	10.
410G☆		1,920,000	20.
410H	St. Louis	15,360,000	10.
410H☆		640,000	30.
410I	Minneapolis	8,960,000	10.
410I☆		640,000	30.
410J	Kansas City	17,920,000	10.
410J☆		640,000	30.
410K	Dallas	21,120,000	10.
410K☆		640,000	30.
410L	San Francisco	44,800,000	10.
410L☆		1,920,000	20.

Series 1969B, Banuelos-Connally

No.	Bank	Notes Printed	Unc
411A	Boston	5,040,000	$15.
411A☆		not printed	—
411B	New York	34,560,000	15.
411B☆		634,000	40.
411C	Philadelphia	5,120,000	15.
411C☆		not printed	—
411D	Cleveland	12,160,000	15.
411D☆		not printed	—
411E	Richmond	15 360,000	15.
411E☆		640,000	40.
411F	Atlanta	18,560,000	15.
411F☆		640,000	40.
411G	Chicago	27,040,000	15.
411G☆		480,000	50.
411H	St. Louis	5,120,000	15.
411H☆		not printed	—
411I	Minneapolis	8,320,000	15.
411I☆		not printed	—
411J	Kansas City	8,320,000	15.
411J☆		640,000	40.
411K	Dallas	12,160,000	15.
411K☆		not printed	—
411L	San Francisco	23,160,000	15.
411L☆		640,000	40.

Series 1969C, Banuelos-Shultz

No.	Bank	Notes Printed	Unc
412A	Boston	50,720,000	$10.
412A☆		1,920,000	20.
412B	New York	120,000,000	10.
412B☆		2,400,000	20.
412C	Philadelphia	53,760,000	10.
412C☆		1,280,000	20.
412D	Cleveland	43,680,000	10.
412D☆		1,120,000	20.
412E	Richmond	73,760,000	10.
412E☆		640,000	30.
412F	Atlanta	81,440,000	10.
412F☆		3,200,000	20.
412G	Chicago	54,400,000	10.
412G☆		not printed	—
412H	St. Louis	37,760,000	10.
412H☆		1,820,000	20.
412I	Minneapolis	14,080,000	10.
412I☆		not printed	—
412J	Kansas City	41,120,000	10.
412J☆		1,920,000	20.
412K	Dallas	41,120,000	10.
412K☆		1,920,000	20.
412L	San Francisco	80,800,000	10.
412L☆		3,680,000	20.

Federal Reserve Notes/Series 1974, 1977, 1977A & 1981/Green Seal

Series 1974, Neff-Simon

No.	Bank	Notes Printed	Unc
413A	Boston	58,240,000	$10.
413A☆		1,468,000	20.
4013	New York	153,120,000	10.
413B☆		3,200,000	20.
413C	Philadelphia	53,920,000	10.
413C☆		3,200,000	20.
413D	Cleveland	78,240,000	10.
413D☆		1,920,000	20.
413E	Richmond	135,200,000	10.
413E☆		1,920,000	20.
413F	Atlanta	127,520,000	10.
413F☆		3,200,000	20.
413G	Chicago	95,520,000	10.
413G☆		3,200,000	20.
413H	St. Louis	64,800,000	10.
413H☆		1,920,000	20.
413I	Minneapolis	41,600,000	10.
413I☆		2,560,000	20.
413J	Kansas City	42,240,000	10.
113J☆		3,200,000	20.
413K	Dallas	23,680,000	10.
413K☆		1,920,000	20.
413L	San Francisco	139,680,000	10.
413L☆		6,400,000	20.

Series 1977, Morton-Blumenthal

No.	Bank	Notes Printed	Unc
414A	Boston	60,800,000	$10.
414A☆		1,664,000	20.
414B	New York	163,040,000	10.
414B☆		3,072,000	20.
414C	Philadelphia	78,720,000	10.
414C☆		1,280,000	20.
414D	Cleveland	72,960,000	10.
414D☆		1,152,000	20.
414E	Richmond	110,720,000	10.
414E☆		1,816,000	20.
414F	Atlanta	127,360,000	10.
414F☆		1,920,000	20.
414G	Chicago	177,920,000	10.
414G☆		2,816,000	20.
414H	St. Louis	46,080,000	10.
414H☆		128,000	25.
414I	Minneapolis	21,760,000	10.
414I☆		not printed	—
414J	Kansas City	78,080,000	10.
414J☆		1,408,000	20.
414K	Dallas	60,800,000	10.
414K☆		1,040,000	20.
414L	San Francisco	135,040,000	10.
414L☆		2,432,000	20.

Series 1977A, Morton-Miller

No.	Bank	Notes Printed	Unc
415A	Boston	48,000,000	$10.
415A☆		512,000	15.
415B	New York	113,920,000	15.
415B☆		2,304,000	10.
415C	Philadelphia	55,680,000	15.
415C☆		384,000	15.
415D	Cleveland	58,880,000	15.
415D☆		1,280,000	10.
415E	Richmond	77,440,000	15.
415E☆		768,000	15.
415F	Atlanta	76,160,000	15.
415F☆		1,152,000	10.
415G	Chicago	80,640,000	15.
415G☆		1,408,000	10.
415H	St. Louis	42,240,000	15.
415H☆		640,000	15.
415I	Minneapolis	10,240,000	15.
415I☆		256,000	25.
415J	Kansas City	52,480,000	10.
415J☆		1,024,000	15.
415K	Dallas	76,160,000	10.
415K☆		1,408,000	15.
415L	San Francisco	106,880,000	10.
415L☆		1,152,000	15.

Series 1981, Buchanan-Regan

No.	Bank	Notes Printed	Unc
416A	Boston	73,600,000	$10.
416A☆		16,000	—
416B	New York	250,800,000	10.
416B☆		3,968,000	15.
416C	Philadelphia	74,240,000	10.
416C☆		640,000	20.
416D	Cleveland	130,560,000	10.
416D☆		384,000	20.
416E	Richmond	176,000,000	10.
416E☆		1,664,000	15.
416F	Atlanta	155,520,000	10.
416F☆		768,000	20.
416G	Chicago	186,240,000	10.
416G☆		1,280,000	20.
416H	St. Louis	58,240,000	10.
416H☆		256,000	20.
416I	Minneapolis	31,360,000	10.
416I☆		128,000	25.
416J	Kansas City	111,360,000	10.
416J☆		272,000	20.
416K	Dallas	96,000,000	10.
416K☆		640,000	25.
416L	San Francisco	240,640,000	10.
416L☆		1,792,000	20.

Federal Reserve Notes/Series 1981A, 1985, 1988 & 1988A/Green Seal

Series 1981A, Ortega-Regan

No.	Bank	Notes Printed	Unc
417A	Boston	54,400,000	$10.
417A☆		not printed	—
417B	New York	112,000,000	10.
417B☆		1,920,000	15.
417C	Philadelphia	25,600,000	10.
417C☆		not printed	—
417D	Cleveland	51,200,000	10.
417D☆		not printed	—
417E	Richmond	96,000,000	10.
417E☆		not printed	—
417F	Atlanta	102,400,000	15.
417F☆		not printed	—
417G	Chicago	115,200,000	10.
417G☆		not printed	—
417H	St. Louis	32,000,000	10.
417H☆		not printed	—
417I	Minneapolis	19,200,000	10.
417I☆		not printed	—
417J	Kansas City	48,000,000	10.
417J☆		not printed	—
417K	Dallas	35,200,000	10.
417K☆		not printed	—
417L	San Francisco	150,400,000	10.
417L☆		3,200,000	15.

Series 1985, Ortega-Brady

No.	Bank	Notes Printed	Unc
418A	Boston	192,000,000	$10.
418A☆		not printed	—
418B	New York	448,000,000	10.
418B☆		128,000	15.
418C	Philadelphia	169,600,000	10.
418C☆		4,608,000	15.
418D	Cleveland	214,400,000	10.
418D☆		not printed	—
418E	Richmond	332,800,000	10.
418E☆		256,000	15.
418F	Atlanta	352,000,000	10.
418F☆		3,840,000	15.
418G	Chicago	345,600,000	10.
418G☆		3,584,000	15.
418H	St. Louis	128,000,000	10.
418H☆		not printed	—
418I	Minneapolis	73,600,000	10.
418I☆		not printed	—
418J	Kansas City	134,400,000	10.
418J☆		not printed	—
418K	Dallas	176,000,000	10.
418K☆		3,200,000	15.
418L	San Francisco	457,600,000	10.
418L☆		2,560,000	15.

Series 1988, Ortega-Brady

No.	Bank	Notes Printed	Unc
419A	Boston	86,400,000	$10.
419A☆		768,000	15.
419B	New York	195,200,000	10.
419B☆		3,200,000	15.
419C	Philadelphia	54,400,000	10.
419C☆		not printed	—
419D	Cleveland	111,200,000	10.
419D☆		not printed	—
419E	Richmond	131,200,000	10.
419E☆		not printed	—
419F	Atlanta	137,200,000	10.
419F☆		2,048,000	10.
419G	Chicago	134,400,000	10.
419G☆		not printed	—
419H	St. Louis	51,200,000	10.
419H☆		not printed	—
419I	Minneapolis	9,600,000	10.
419I☆		not printed	—
419J	Kansas City	44,800,000	10.
419J☆		not printed	—
419K	Dallas	54,400,000	10.
419K☆		not printed	—
419L	San Francisco	70,400,000	10.
419L☆		not printed	—

Series 1988A, Villalpando-Brady

No.	Bank	Notes Printed	Unc
420A	Boston	140,800,000	$10.
420A☆		3,200,000	15.
420B	New York	640,000,000	10.
420B☆		6,400,000	15.
420C	Philadelphia	121,600,000	10.
420C☆		not printed	—
420D	Cleveland	230,400,000	10.
420D☆		6,400,000	15.
420E	Richmond	486,400,000	10.
420E☆		6,400,000	15.
420F	Atlanta†	300,800,000	10.
420F☆	DC & FW	9,600,000	15.
420G	Chicago†	755,200,000	10.
420G☆	FW	3,200,000	15.
420H	St. Louis	185,600,000	10.
420H☆	FW	3,200,000	15.
420I	Minneapolis	169,600,000	10.
420I☆		3,200,000	15.
420J	Kansas City	140,800,000	10.
420J☆		not printed	—
420K	Dallas†	172,800,000	10.
420K☆		not printed	—
420L	San Francisco†	620,800,000	10.
420L☆	FW	3,200,000	15.

† Some notes were printed in Fort Worth.

Series 1993, Withrow-Bentsen				Series 1995, Withrow-Rubin			
No.	**Bank**	**Notes Printed**	**Unc**	**No.**	**Bank**	**Notes Printed**	**Unc**
421A	Boston	19,200,000	$—	**422A**	Boston		
421A☆		3,200,000	—	**422A**☆			
421B	New York†	102,400,000	—	**422B**	New York		
421B☆		3,200,000	—	**422B**☆			
421C	Philadelphia	38,400,000	—	**422C**	Philadelphia		
421C☆		not printed	—	**422C**☆			
421D	Cleveland	not printed	—	**422D**	Cleveland		
421D☆		not printed	—	**422D**☆			
421E	Richmond	76,800,000	—	**422E**	Richmond		
421E☆		1,920,000	—	**422E**☆			
421F	Atlanta	70,400,000	—	**422F**	Atlanta		
421F☆		not printed	—	**422F**☆			
421G	Chicago#	64,000,000	—	**422G**	Chicago		
421G☆		not printed	—	**422G**☆			
421H	St. Louis#	64,000,000	—	**422H**	St. Louis#		
421H☆		not printed	—	**422H**☆			
421I	Minneapolis#	64,000,000	—	**422I**	Minneapolis		
421I☆		not printed	—	**422I**☆			
421J	Kansas City#	32,000,000	—	**422J**	Kansas City		
421J☆		not printed	—	**422J**☆			
421K	Dallas#	57,600,000	—	**422K**	Dallas		
421K☆		not printed	—	**422K**☆			
421L	San Francisco#	185,600,000	—	**422L**	San Francisco		
421L☆		not printed	—	**422L**☆			

† Some notes were printed in Fort Worth.
# All notes were printed in Fort Worth.
Series 1995 was in production when this catalog was printed.

American Numismatic Association
Application for Membership

☐ **Yes,** I want to be a part of America's Coin Club. I understand that I will receive the association's award winning monthly journal, *The Numismatist;* access to over 40,000 books, videos and slide sets in the world's largest Numismatic library, discounts on numismatic books, the opportunity to be a part of the ANA School of Numismatics and dozens of other member benefits.

Name _____

Address _____

C/S/Z _____

Signature _____

Date of Birth _____ (required for jr. and sr. members)

I herewith make application for membership in the American Numismatic Association, subject to the bylaws of the Association. I also agree to abide by the Code of Ethics adopted by the Association.

☐ **Enclosed is $29 for a 1 yr. membership**
☐ **Enclosed is $26 for a 1 yr. Senior membership (age 65 and over)**
☐ **Enclosed is $11 for a 1 yr Junior Membership (under age 18)**
☐ **Enclosed is $79 for 3 years (Seniors $69)**
☐ **Enclosed is $130 for 5 years (Seniors $110)**

American Numismatic Association
818 N. Cascade Avenue
Colorado Springs, CO 80903-3279
1-800-367-9723

Chartered by Congress in 1912 to promote the hobby and science of numismatics.

Demand Notes/1861

The Frederick Girsch engraving of Lincoln was based on a photograph by C.S. German. A symbolic figure of *Art* (or *Painting*), is on the right. The eagle, *E Pluribus Unum*, was originally engraved for Toppan Carpenter. (ABNCo)

Demand notes are the original "greenbacks."

No.	Payable at	Notes Printed	Known	VGood	Fine	VFine
463A	Boston	660,000	32 (1)	$1000.	$1750.	$3000.
463B	New York	640,000	35 (5)	1000.	1750.	3000.
463C	Philadelphia	580,000	33	1100.	2000.	3500.
463D	Cincinnati	75,000	5 (1)	-------------- extremely rare --------		
463E	St. Louis	48,000	4	-------------- extremely rare --------		

Remarks: A total of 2,003,000 (including 3,000 reissues) were printed. Records of 1931 indicate that 1,964 notes were outstanding. No. 463C with serial number "1," once held by S.P. Chase, is in a private collection. Recorded notes for No. 463E are: 31133, 35202, 41122 and 47760.

These notes, all without the U.S. Treasury Seal, were signed by representatives of the U.S. Treasurer and the Register of the Treasury. "For the" was originally written as the signatures were inscribed; the number of these notes known, not included in the other total, is in parentheses above. After a brief period, "For the" was engraved into the plate. Demand notes with the handwritten "For the" command a higher premium than the latter type.

"For the" as written.   "For the" as engraved.

United States Notes/1862 & 1863/Red Seal

Face design is similar to the preceding note; the Treasury Seal has been added and "On Demand" has been deleted.

Back design with second obligation.

Back design with first obligation.

No.	Series	Description	Fine	EFine	Une
464	1862	"American Bank Note Company" in upper border	$325.	$750.	$1950.
465	1862	"American Bank Note Company" in lower border	325.	650.	1850.
465a	1863	"National Bank Note Company" in lower border	325.	650.	1750.
465b	1863	same as 465 but, one serial numbers	300.	650.	1600.
465c	1863	same as 465 but, two serial numbers	325.	650.	1750.

Remarks: A total of 11,800,505 notes were printed; all except No. 464 bear the second obligation back. Signatures of Chittenden-Spinner appear on all notes. Catalog numbers have been changed since the previous edition. No. 464, unique with handwritten signatures, sold for $21,500 in Stack's Sept. 1994 auction. This note was issued without printed signatures. Paymaster Maj. D. Bannister returned the note to the U.S. Treasury, where officials handsigned the note. Known for Nos. 464–75; 465–11; 465a–14; 465b–14; 465c–66 (Gengerke).

United States Notes/Series 1869–1878

The portrait of Daniel Webster was engraved by Alfred Sealey. If the note is inverted, the small eagle engraved by Henry Gugler, takes on the appearance of a jackass, the name given to this note. The scene on the right is *Introduction of the Old World to the New World*, or *Pocahontas Presented at Court*; it is believed the artist and engraver are T.A. Liebler and W.W. Rice, respectively.

No.	Series	Signatures	Seal	Notes Printed	Fine	EFine	Unc
466	1869	Allison-Spinner	lg. red	8,376,000	$300.	$625.	$1900.
		The following have "TEN" in red on the right.					
467	1875	Allison-New	sm. red	1,500,000	350.	675.	1850.
467A	1875A	Allison-Gilfillan	sm. red	866,000	400.	775.	2400.
468	1878	Allison-Gilfillan	sm. red	2,600,000	300.	625.	1750.

Remarks: The back design for Nos. 467 and 468 is on the following page. There were 8,522,124 notes for No. 466 issued. Reissues could account for the excess of the official figure above. Known for Nos. 467–21; 467A–10; 468–43.

The following hoards of No. 466 in uncirculated condition have been observed by Gengerke: H42651xx-H42653xx, H42658xx-H42659xx, H68400xx-H68402xx, H71784xx-H71787xx, H73584xx-H73587xx.

United States Notes/Series 1880

The face design is similar to No. 466. This back design is for Nos. 467–482.

The red "TEN" is replaced with a large seal; serial numbers are red.

No.	Signatures	Seal	Notes Printed	Fine	EFine	Unc
469	Scofield-Gilfillan	lg. brown	1,560,000	$200.	$350.	$900.
470	Bruce-Gilfillan	lg. brown	1,872,000	200.	350.	900.
471	Bruce-Wyman	lg. brown	2,732,000	185.	335.	850.
		Serial numbers are blue				
472	Bruce-Wyman	lg. red	1,000,000	225.	475.	1100.
473	Rosecrans-Jordan	lg. red	1,084,000	225.	475.	1100.
474	Rosecrans-Hyatt	lg. red	1,616,000	225.	475.	1100.
475	Rosecrans-Hyatt	lg. red, spikes	2,552,000	200.	450.	1000.
476	Rosecrans-Huston	lg. red, spikes	2,748,000	200.	450.	1000.
477	Rosecrans-Huston	lg. brown	1,508,000	225.	475.	1100.
478	Rosecrans-Nebeker	lg. brown	200,000	---------- Unique -----------		
479	Rosecrans-Nebeker	sm. red, scallops	3,792,000	265.	375.	950.
480	Tillman-Morgan	sm. red, scallops	9,900,000	265.	375.	950.
481	Bruce-Roberts	sm. red, scallops	960,000	250.	475.	1450.
482	Lyons-Roberts	sm. red, scallops	11,840,000	165.	375.	1000.

Remarks: The following hoards (by serial number) are known, all in uncirculated condition: No. 471, Z26029506–85; No. 472, A289308–43; No. 475, A4093333–54. Known for Nos. 469–19; 470–13; 471–41; 472–45; 473–16; 474–14; 475–52; 476–47; 477–41; 478–2; 479–41; 480–73; 481–18; 482–92 (Gengerke).

United States Notes/Series 1901/Red Seal

Ostrander Smith based his bison design of *Pablo* on a sketch by Charles Knight; M.W. Baldwin was the engraver. The portraits of Lewis and Clark were engraved by G.F.C. Smillie. This "buffalo bill" could have been designed to stimulate interest in the Lewis and Clark Centennial Exposition in 1905. The same bison appears on the 30–cent stamp of 1923 and the $1 military payment certificate Series 692.

No.	Signatures	Notes Issued	Fine	EFine	Unc
483	Lyons-Roberts	46,500,000	$275.	$550.	$1400.
484	Lyons-Treat	101,000,000	250.	525.	1400.
485	Vernon-Treat	17,030,000	275.	550.	1400.
486	Vernon-McClung	5,760,000	275.	550.	1500.
486☆	2 reported	—	—	—	—
487	Napier-McClung	8,476,000	275.	550.	1500.
487☆	1 reported	—	—	—	—
488	Parker-Burke	11,592,000	275.	550.	1400.
488☆	2 reported	—	—	—	—
489	Teehee-Burke	10,621,000	275.	550.	1400.
489☆	6 reported	—	—	—	—
490	Elliott-White	10,621,000	275.	550.	1400.
490☆	20 reported	—	—	—	—
491	Speelman-White	32,359,000	275.	550.	1400.
491☆	34 reported	—	—	—	—

Remarks: Plates with signatures of Napier-Thompson were prepared. Observed, uncirculated examples of No. 488 are known as E19477xx, and E98964xx-E98965xx. Known for Nos. 486–18; 487–19; 488–66; 489–44.

United States Notes/Series 1923/Red Seal

The portrait of Andrew Jackson was engraved by Alfred Sealey.

No.	Signatures	Notes Printed	Fine	EFine	Une
492	Speelman-White	696,000	$425.	$1000.	$2850.
492☆	2 reported	—	—	—	—

Remarks: A minimum of 250 notes in new condition are known including the first note, A1B, and the last note, A696,000B, both in the same collection. Many of the observed notes have serial numbers within A387xxxB, A5023xxB, and A6958xxB to A6959xxB.

Compound Interest Treasury Notes/Red Seals

Charles Burt engraved the portrait of Salmon P. Chase; the *Eagle of the Capitol* was engraved by James Bannister. "COMPOUND INTEREST TREASURY NOTE" AND "10" in the center are in bronze.

Redemption values are listed in the center of the back.

No.	Signatures	Dated	Printed	Issued	Outstanding	Fine
		Act of March 3, 1863				
493	Chittenden-Spinner	June 10, 1864	92,420	84,940	164	rare
		Act of June 30, 1864				
494	Chittenden-Spinner	July 5, 1864	—	206,000	2007	$2200.
494a	Chittenden-Spinner	July 15, 1864	(error, Act of July 2, 1864)			4 known
495	Colby-Spinner	Aug. 15, 1864	—	210,500	—	1950.
495a	Colby-Spinner	Oct. 15, 1864	included in preceding			2500.
495b	Colby-Spinner	Dec. 15, 1864	. —	176,500	—	2200.

Remarks: Known for Nos. 493–10; 494–16; 495–72; 495a–6; 495b–15 (Gengerke). An extra fine example of No. 495 was advertised at $6250 in 1991. An unspecified number of No. 494a were issued with the incorrect Act of July 2, 1864 printed on the note. The three recorded serial numbers are 8275, 9592 and 14072.

Interest-Bearing Notes/5%

The face design is similar to the preceding note.

The back design includes the obligation and a warning to counterfeiters.

Signatures of Chittenden-Spinner

No.	Dated		Known	No.	Dated		Known
	Feb. 29,	1864 (ABNCo)	1		April 1,	1864 (ABNCo)	2
	March 1,	1864 (ABNCo)	1		April 4,	1864	1
	March 3,	1864	1		April 6,	1864	1
	March 5,	1864 (ABNCo)	1		April 8,	1864	2
	March 9,	1864	1		April 9,	1864	2
	March 15,	1864	2		April 13,	1864	1
496	March 15,	1864 (ABNCo)	1	**496**	April 16,	1864	1
	March 16,	1864	2		April 18,	1864 (ABNCo)	1
	March 23,	1864	2		April 20,	1864	1
	March 28,	1864	3		May 18,	1864 (ABNCo)	1
	March 30,	1864	3		May 28,	1864	1
	March 31,	1864 (ABNCo)	1		May 30,	1864	3

Remarks: A total of 620,000 notes were issued; 503½ remain outstanding. The dated portion of the note with serial number 156281 C5 is missing (Gengerke 47). An example dated March 31, 1864 in fine condition was advertised at $4750 in 1989. In addition, the following have been recorded: Nos. 52239 (ABNCo); 14126, 30537, 95324 all (BEP).

National Bank Notes/First Charter Period

Franklin and Electricity, 1752 was engraved by Alfred Jones and James Smillie for ABNCo. T.A. Liebler's *America Seizing Lightning* was engraved by Charles Burt.

DeSoto Discovering the Mississippi was engraved by Frederick Girsch (see No. 1370).

No.	Series	Signatures	VGood	VFine	Unc
		The red seal has rays.			
497	orig.	Chittenden-Spinner	$250.	$ 475.	$3250.
498	orig.	Colby-Spinner	225.	500.	2750.
499	orig.	Jeffries-Spinner	575.	1400.	6000.
500	orig.	Allison-Spinner	200.	525.	2500.
		The red seal has scallops.			
501	1875	Allison-New	225.	500.	2000.
502	1875	Allison-Wyman	225.	500.	2000.
503	1875	Allison-Gilfillan	200.	45.	3250.
504	1875	Scofield-Gilfillan	200.	475.	3250.
505	1875	Bruce-Gilfillan	200.	475.	3250.
506	1875	Bruce-Wyman	200.	475.	3250.
507	1875	Rosecrans-Huston	350.	600.	3500.
508	1875	Rosecrans-Nebeker	375.	650.	3750.
508a	1875	Tillman-Morgan	------------------ Rare ----------------------		

Remarks: The original series had no series date on the face.

National Bank Notes/Second Charter Period/First Issue/Series 1882/Brown Seal

See preceding note for design information.

The color of the back is brown.

No.	Signatures	VGood	VFine	Une
509	Bruce-Gilfillan	$100.	$200.	$ 850.
510	Bruce-Wyman	100.	200.	850.
511	Bruce-Jordan	125.	250.	1100.
512	Rosecrans-Jordan	100.	200.	850.
513	Rosecrans-Hyatt	100.	200.	850.
514	Rosecrans-Huston	100.	200.	850.
515	Rosecrans-Nebeker	100.	200.	850.
516	Rosecrans-Morgan	325.	625.	2350.
517	Tillman-Morgan	100.	200.	850.
518	Tillman-Roberts	125.	250.	1100.
519	Bruce-Roberts	100.	200.	850.
520	Lyons-Roberts	100.	200.	850.
521	Lyons-Treat	150.	325.	1600.
522	Vernon-Treat	150.	325.	1600.

National Bank Notes/Second Charter Period/Second Issue/Series 1882/Blue Seal

The design is the same as the preceding.

The portrait of William P. Fessenden, Secretary of the Treasury, was engraved by Charles Skinner. The figure on the right is *Mechanics*.

No.	Signatures	VGood	VFine	Unc
523	Rosecrans-Huston	$ 90.	$225.	$ 900.
524	Rosecrans-Nebeker	90.	225.	900.
525	Rosecrans-Morgan	300.	700.	1300.
526	Tillman-Morgan	90.	225.	900.
527	Tillman-Roberts	90.	250.	900.
528	Bruce-Roberts	90.	250.	1000.
529	Lyons-Roberts	90.	225.	900.
530	Vernon-Treat	90.	250.	900.
531	Vernon-McClung	135.	300.	1100.
532	Napier-McClung	135.	300.	1100.
532a	Parker-Burke	------------------------ unique ------------------------		

National Bank Notes/Second Charter Period/Third Issue/Blue Seal/Series 1882

The design is the same as the preceding.

"TEN DOLLARS" replaces "1882–1908" on the back.

No.	Signatures	VGood	VFine	Unc
533	Tillman-Morgan	$115.	$350.	$1350.
534	Tillman-Roberts	115.	350.	1350.
535	Bruce-Roberts	115.	350.	1350.
536	Lyons-Roberts	115.	350.	1350.
536a	Lyons-Treat	---------------------------- Unknown ----------------------------		
537	Vernon-Treat	225.	600.	1500.
538	Napier-McClung	200.	500.	1400.
538a	Parker-Burke	---------------------------- Unknown ----------------------------		
539	Teehee-Burke	---------------------------- Rare ----------------------------		

National Bank Notes/Third Charter Period/Series 1902

The Courtney photograph of William McKinley was engraved by G.F.C. Smillie.

G.F.C. Smillie is also the engraver of Walter Shirlaw's *Liberty and Progress*. Only the back of the second issue has "1902–1908."

No.	Signatures	VGood	VFine	Unc
		First issue red seal		
540	Lyons-Roberts	$110.	$165.	$700.
541	Lyons-Treat	110.	185.	800.
542	Vernon-Treat	125.	225.	900.
		Second issue blue seal		
		"1902–1908" on back		
543	Lyons-Roberts	30.	60.	325.
544	Lyons-Treat	30.	60.	325.
545	Vernon-Treat	30.	60.	325.
546	Vernon-McClung	30.	60.	325.
547	Napier-McClung	30.	60.	325.
548	Napier-Thompson	30.	100.	425.
549	Napier-Burke	30.	60.	325.
550	Parker-Burke	30.	60.	325.
551	Teehee-Burke	40.	125.	475.

National Bank Notes/Third Charter Period/Series 1902

The face design is the same as the preceding note. The dates have been deleted from the back.

No.	Signatures	VGood	VFine	Unc
		Third issue blue seal		
552	Lyons-Roberts	$ 30.	$ 50.	$ 275.
553	Lyons-Treat	30.	50.	275.
554	Vernon-Treat	30.	50.	275.
555	Vernon-McClung	30.	50.	275.
556	Napier-McClung	30.	50.	275.
557	Napier-Thompson	60.	115.	500.
558	Napier-Burke	35.	50.	275.
559	Parker-Burke	35.	50.	275.
560	Teehee-Burke	35.	50.	275.
561	Elliott-Burke	35.	50.	275.
562	Elliott-White	35.	50.	275.
563	Speelman-White	35.	50.	275.
564	Woods-White	40.	65.	300.
565	Woods-Tate	50.	150.	500.
566	Jones-Woods	115.	400.	1250.

National Gold Bank Notes

Franklin and Electricity, 1752 was engraved by Alfred Jones and Louis Delnoce for ABNCo. T.A. Liebler's *America Seizing Lightning* was engraved by Charles Burt.

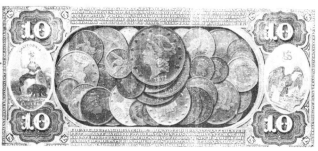

The gold coin vignette was engraved by James Smillie.

No.	Date	Issuing Bank	City	Notes Issued	Known	Good	VGood
567	1870	First Nat'l Gold Bank	San Francisco	18,004	24	$ 850.	$1500.
568	1872	Nat'l Gold Bank & T Co.	San Francisco	12,669	9	900.	1650.
569	1872	National Gold Bank of D.O. Mills & Company	Sacramento	3,723	5	1000.	1750.
570	1873	First Nat'l Gold Bank	Stockton	15,000	14	850.	1500.
570a	1875	First Nat'l Gold Bank	Stockton	779	5	1000.	1750.
571	1873	First Nat'l Gold Bank	Santa Barbara	2,400	3	1200.	1850.
572	1874	Farmers Nat'l Gold Bank	San Jose	8,547	9	1000.	1600.
573	1874	First Nat'l Gold Bank	Petaluma	6,000	7	1000.	1600.
574	1875	First Nat'l Gold Bank	Petaluma	600	6	1000.	1750.
574a	1875	as preceding on white paper		489	2	1350.	1900.
575	1875	First Nat'l Gold Bank	Oakland	4,800	7	1000.	1650.
575a	1875	First Nat'l Gold Bank	Oakland	36	0		—
576	1875	Union Nat'l Gold Bank	Oakland	1,500	3	1350.	1900.

Remarks: The signatures of Allison-Spinner appear on these notes except for Nos. 575 and 574a, which have Scofield-Gilfillan signatures. A total of 2,481 notes are outstanding.

Silver Certificates/Series 1878 & 1880

The portrait of Robert Morris, by Robert Edge Pine, was engraved by Charles Schlecht.

The back is black and brown.

The following bear the signatures of Scofield-Gilfillan.
Nos. 578–583a have red seals; 584 & 585 have brown seals.

No.	Series	Countersignatures	Payable at	Notes Issued	Known	VGood	VFine
578	1878	W.G. White*	New York	20,000	1	$ —	$ —
579	1878	J.C. Hopper*	New York	incl. in above	5	12000.	—
580	1878	T. Hillhouse*	New York	16,000	0		
581	1878	T. Hillhouse	New York	incl. in above	2	18700.	—
582	1878	R.M. Anthony*	San Francisco	3,400	0		
583	1878	A.U. Wyman*	Washington, DC	4,000	2	18500.	—
583a	1878	A.U. Wyman	Washington, DC	182,000	7	10000.	—
584	1880	T. Hillhouse	New York	196,000	14	8000.	—
585	1880	A.U. Wyman	Washington, DC	—	0		

Remarks: The (*) indicates autographed countersignatures. A total of 1,734 notes for Nos. 578–583a were outstanding in 1893. A private sale of No. 578 in fine condition has been recorded at $35,000. No. 579 ($27,500) in VF-EF and No. 583 ($35,200) in uncirculated conditions were sold by Christie's in 1995. Robert Morris is one of five Americans of foreign birth to appear on U.S. paper money; the others are A. Hamilton, E.D. Baker (No. 1441), A. Gallatin (No. 1320) and G.G. Meade No. 1425).

Silver Certificates/Series 1880

An "X" has been added to all but No. 589. The back design is the same as the preceding note.

No.	Signatures	Seal	Notes Issued	Fine	EFine	Unc
586	Scofield-Gilfillan	brown	2,772,000	$675.	$1250.	$3250.
587	Bruce-Gilfillan	brown	1,832,000	700.	1350.	3500.
588	Bruce-Wyman	brown	3,102,000	675.	1200.	3000.
589	Bruce-Wyman	red	304,000	800.	1600.	5500.

Remarks: Known for Nos. 586–45; 587–54; 588–108; 589–34 (Gengerke). A group of as many as 29 consecutively-numbered notes in uncirculated condition of No. 587, commencing with B34387xx has been reported. As many as 44 in the same condition of No. 588 commencing with B71133xx have been reported.

Silver Certificates/Series 1886

Thomas A. Hendricks was Vice-President of the U.S. for nine months; he died on November 25, 1865 in Indianapolis, where he spent most of his academic and political life. This portrait was engraved by Charles Schlecht. Due to the shape of the portrait frame, this bill is often called the "tombstone note."

No.	Signatures	Seal	Notes Printed	Fine	EFine	Unc
590	Rosecrans-Jordan	sm. red	400,000	$600.	$1200.	$8000.
591	Rosecrans-Hyatt	sm. red	2,560,000	450.	1000.	5000.
592	Rosecrans-Hyatt	lg. red	5,640,000	425.	900.	4000.
593	Rosecrans-Huston	lg. red	2,036,000	450.	1000.	5000.
594	Rosecrans-Huston	lg. brn	1,764,000	500.	1100.	5000.
595	Rosecrans-Nebeker	lg. brown	1,600.000	500.	1100.	5000.
596	Rosecrans-Nebeker	sm. red-scallops	204,000	650.	1300.	9000.

Remarks: Known for Nos. 590–13; 591–42; 592–78; 593–43; 594–29; 595–34; 596–9 (Gengerke).

Silver Certificates/Series 1891 & 1908

The face design is similar to the preceding note.

No.	Series	Signatures	Seal	Notes Printed	Fine	EFine	Unc
597	1891	Rosecrans-Nebeker	red	3,500,000	$250.	$575.	$1800.
598	1891	Tillman-Morgan	red	16,500,000	225.	550.	1600.
599	1891	Bruce-Roberts	red	7,776,000	225.	550.	1600.
600	1891	Lyons-Roberts	red	6,644,000	225.	550.	1600.
		Blue "X" added to face					
601	1908	Vernon-Treat	blue	4,500,000	250.	575.	1850.
601☆	1 reported			—	—	—	—
601a	1908	Vernon-McClung	blue	1,756,000	275.	600.	2000.
602	1908	Parker-Burke	blue	3,952,000	250.	575.	1750.
602☆	1 reported			—	—	—	—

Remarks: Known for Nos. 597–42; 598–108; 599–42; 600–64; 601–64; 601a–55; 602–94 (Gengerke).

Refunding Certificates

The portrait of Benjamin Franklin is based on the painting by James Barton Longacre.

No.	Notes Issued	Outstanding	Known	VGood	VFine	EFine
603	5,850	2	2	$ —	$ —	$ —
604	3,995,425	800	119	450.	1000.	1500.

No. 604 is payable to bearer.

Gold Certificates/Series 1907 & 1922

Michael Hillegas was born in Philadelphia on April 22, 1729; he died there on September 29, 1804. With George Clymer he held the office of co-Treasurer of the U.S. They were the first to hold this office. The portrait of Hillegas, originally painted by A.M. Archambault, was engraved by G.F.C. Smillie. The illustrated note has small serial numbers.

The bright yellow back was engraved by H.L. Chorlton, E.M. Hall and G.U. Rose, Jr.

No.	Series	Signatures	Notes Issued	VFine	EFine	Une
605	1907	Vernon-Treat	21,366,800	$ 80.	$115.	$ 400.
606	1907	Vernon McClung	17,746,000	80.	140.	500.
606☆	1907	2 reported	—	—	—	—
607	1907	Napier-McClung	⎫	90.	165.	500.
607☆	1907	3 reported	⎬ 33,436,000	90.	165.	500.
607a	1907	Napier-McClung	⎭ —	—	—	—
608	1907	Napier-Thompson	2,276,000	350.	750.	3000.
608a	1907	Napier-Thompson	incl. in above	350.	750.	3000.
609	1907	Parker-Burke	16,176,000	80.	140.	400.
609☆	1907	3 reported	—	—	—	—
610	1907	Teehee-Burke	44,364,000	80.	115.	350.
610☆	1907	9 reported	—	—	—	—
611	1922	Speelman-White (sm. sn)	13,504,000	90.	165.	500.
611☆	1922	7 reported	—	—	—	—
611a	1922	Speelman-White (lg. sn)	147,100,000	75.	. 100.	350.
611a☆	1922	118 reported	—	—	—	—

Remarks: "Act of July 12, 1882" appears on Nos. 607 and 608; "Act of March 4, 1907" is on Nos. 607a and 608a (sn=serial number). See Nos. 1042 and 1042a for examples of large and small sn. Known for Nos. 605–15; 606–14; 607–41; 608–8; 608a–20; 609–38; 610–53; 611–57 (Gengerke).

Treasury or Coin Notes/Series 1890

General Philip Sheridan was born in Albany, NY on March 6, 1831, He graduated from West Point in 1853 and fought in the Civil War. This portrait was engraved by Lorenzo Hatch.

The back was engraved by D.M. Cooper, W.A. Copenhaver, W.H. Hall, A.L. Helm, W.G. Phillips and D.M. Russell.

No.	Signatures	Seal	Notes Printed	Fine	EFine	Unc
612	Rosecrans-Huston	brn.	2,876,000	$500.	$1000.	$3000.
613	Rosecrans-Nebeker	brown	324,000	700.	1200.	4500.
614	Rosecrans-Nebeker	red	1,400,000	600.	1100.	3400.

Series of 1891

The face design is similar to the preceding note. This back was engraved by J.A. Allen, D.M. Cooper, W.H. Dougal, E.M. Hall, A.L. Helm, J.R. Hill, E.E. Myers, E.G. Rose and G.U. Rose, Jr.

No.	Signatures	Seal	Notes Issued	Fine	EFine	Unc
615	Rosecrans-Nebeker	red	976,000	$375.	$650.	$1500.
616	Tillman-Morgan	red	4,552,000	325.	575.	1450.
617	Bruce-Roberts	red	500,000	425.	750.	1650.

Remarks: Six notes (four in uncirculated condition) are known for No. 613. No. 614 could exist as a hoard; Nos. A4483529, -568, 569 and -585 have been observed in uncirculated condition. No. 615 could also exist as a hoard; B543627, -636, -660, -678 and 683 have been observed in uncirculated condition. Known for Nos. 612–46; 613–10; 614–58; 615–51; 616–26; 617–20 (Gengerke).

Federal Reserve Notes/Series 1914/Red Seal

The portrait of Andrew Jackson was engraved by G.F.C. Smillie.

The back design is the same as No. 620.

Signatures of Burke-McAdoo

No.	Bank	VGood	VFine	Unc
618A	Boston	$50.	$100.	$525.
618B	New York	40.	75.	425.
618C	Philadelphia	40.	75.	425.
618D	Cleveland	40.	75.	425.
618E	Richmond	40.	75.	425.
618F	Atlanta	40.	75.	425.
618G	Chicago	40.	75.	425.
618H	St. Louis	40.	75.	425.
618I	Minneapolis	40.	75.	425.
618J	Kansas City	40.	75.	425.
618K	Dallas	50.	100.	525.
618L	San Francisco	50.	100.	525.

Remarks: The first day of issue was November 16, 1914. Type I and type II were printed for all districts. Type II has the small district number and letter in the upper left and lower right corners. See No. 380 for illustrations. Known for types I & II: A–8 & 1; B–21 & 33; C–2 & 12; D–3 & 7; E–3 & 6; F–8 & 2; G–23 & 18; H–13 & 5; I–12 & 2; J–7 & 2; K–11 & 5; L–6 & 5 (Gengerke).

Federal Reserve Notes/Series 1914/Blue Seal

No.	Bank	Signatures	Notes Printed	Delivered	VFine	Unc
619A1	Boston	Burke-McAdoo			$ 30.	$110.
619A1☆	1 reported				—	—
619A2	Boston	Burke-Glass			35.	125.
619A3	Boston	Burke-Houston	69,756,000	69,756,000	30.	110.
619A3☆	7 reported				—	—
619A4	Boston	White-Mellon (b)			30.	110.
619A4☆	8 reported	(1 "b")	(568,000)		—	—
619B1	New York	Burke-McAdoo			30.	110.
619B1☆	1 reported				—	—
619B2	New York	Burke-Glass			35.	125.
619B2☆	4 reported				—	—
619B3	New York	Burke-Houston	176,728,000	176,728,000	30.	110.
619B3☆	11 reported				—	—
619B4	New York	White Mellon (b,c)			30.	110.
619B4☆	11 reported	(4 "b", 8 "c")	(1,396,000)		—	—
619C1	Philadelphia	Burke-McAdoo			30.	110.
619C2	Philadelphia	Burke-Glass			35.	125.
619C2☆	2 reported				—	—
619C3	Philadelphia	Burke-Houston	56,616,000	56,616,000	30.	110.
619C3☆	5 reported				—	—
619C4	Philadelphia	White Mellon (o)			30.	110.
619C4☆	7 reported	(1 "c")	(476,000)		—	—
619D1	Cleveland	Burke-McAdoo			30.	110.
619D1☆	1 reported				—	—
619D2	Cleveland	Burke-Glass			35.	125.
619D2☆	2 reported				—	—
619D3	Cleveland	Burke-Houston	43,856,000	43,856,000	30.	110.
619D3☆	5 reported				—	—
619D4	Cleveland	White-Mellon b,c)			30.	110.
619D4☆	10 reported		(360,000)		—	—
619E1	Richmond	Burke-McAdoo			30.	110.
619E2	Richmond	Burke-Glass			35.	125.
619E2☆	2 reported				—	—
619E3	Richmond	Burke-Houston	27,528,000	27,528,000	30.	110.
619E3☆	4 reported				—	—
619E4	Richmond	White-Mellon			30.	110.
619E4☆	1 reported		(236,000)		—	—
619F1	Atlanta	Burke-McAdoo			30	110.
619F1☆	2 reported				—	—
619F2	Atlanta	Burke-Glass			35	125.
619F2j	1 reported		31,400,000	31,400,000	—	—
619F3	Atlanta	Burke-Houston			30	110.
619F4	Atlanta	White-Mellon (b)			30	110.
619F4☆	1 reported		(228,000)		—	—
619G1	Chicago	Burke-McAdoo			30	110.
619G1☆	1 reported				—	—
619G2	Chicago	Burke-Glass			35	125.
619G2☆	4 reported				—	—
619G3	Chicago	Burke-Houston	84,804,000	84,804,000	30	110.
619G3☆	23 reported				—	—
619G4	Chicago	White-Mellon (b,c)			30	110.
619G4☆	18 reported	(3 "b", 1 "c")	(680,000)		—	—

Federal Reserve Notes/Series 1914/Blue Seal *(continued)*

No	Bank	Signatures	Notes Printed	Delivered	VFine	Unc
619H1	St. Louis	Burke-McAdoo			$30	$110.
619H1☆	5 reported				—	—
619H2	St. Louis	Burke-Glass			35	125.
619H2☆	1 reported		21,508,000	21,508,000	—	—
619H3	St. Louis	Burke-Houston			30	110.
619H3☆	7 reported				—	—
619H4	St. Louis	White-Mellon	(236,000)		30	110.
619I1	Minneapolis	Burke-McAdoo			30	110.
619I1☆	1 reported				—	—
619I2	Minneapolis	Burke-Glass			35	125.
619I2☆	5 reported				—	—
619I3	Minneapolis	Burke-Houston	14,376,000	14,376,000	30	110.
619I3☆	6 reported				—	—
619I4	Minneapolis	White-Mellon			30	110.
619I4☆	4 reported		(124,000)		—	—
619J1	Kansas City	Burke-McAdoo			30	110.
619J1☆	2 reported				—	—
619J2	Kansas City	Burke-Glass			35	125.
619J3	Kansas City	Burke-Houston	16,448,000	16,448,000	30	110.
619J3☆	10 reported				—	—
619J4	Kansas City	White-Mellon	(144,000)		30	110.
619K1	Dallas	Burke-McAdoo			30	110.
619K1☆	3 reported				—	—
619K2	Dallas	Burke-Glass			35	125.
619K3	Dallas	Burke-Houston	13,400,000	12,988,000	30	110.
619K3☆	4 reported				—	—
619K4	Dallas	White-Mellon	(112,000)		30	110.
619L1	San Francisco	Burke-McAdoo			30	110.
619L2	San Francisco	Burke-Glass			35	125.
619L2☆	1 reported		41,432,000	41,432,000	—	—
619L3	San Francisco	Burke-Houston			30	110.
619L4	San Francisco	White-Mellon (b,c)			30	110.
619L4☆	4 reported	(1 "c")	(352,000)		—	—

Remarks: The totals are for regular issues The figures in parenthesis, the last replacement serial number, is the total number of replacement notes of this denomination printed for that bank; the number printed by signatures is not available White-Mellon plate variations, in parenthesis, exist for some districts, identified as type "b" (small district number and letter in lower left) and type "c" (space of 20 mm horizontal from left seal to the engraved border) Star, replacement notes reported in the main listing above are type "a" or notes not identified by type See $5 Federal Reserve notes for examples.

Federal Reserve Bank Notes/Series 1915 & 1918/Blue Seal

The portrait of Andrew Jackson was engraved by G.F.C. Smillie.

The back was designed by C.A. Huston *Farming,* a scene in Manchester Township, York County, PA, was engraved by Marcus W. Baldwin; *Industry,* a mill in Joliet, Illinois, was engraved by H.L. Chorlton.

No	Bank	Series	Bank Signatures	Issued	VFine	EFine	Unc
620B	New York	1918	Hendricks-Strong	200,000	$450.	$ 800.	$3000.
620F1	Atlanta	1915	Bell-Wellborn	300,000	350.	550.	2550.
620F2	Atlanta	1918	Bell-Wellborn	incl. in above	350.	550.	2500.
620G1	Chicago	1915	McLallen-McDougal	300,000	350.	550.	2500.
620G2	Chicago	1918	McCloud-McDougal	incl. in above	350.	550.	2500.
620H	St. Louis	1918	Attebery-Wells	100,000	450.	1000.	4000.
620H☆	1 reported			—	—	—	—
620J1	Kansas City	1915	Anderson-Miller		400.	800.	3000.
620J2a	Kansas City	1915	Cross-Miller		350.	475.	2750.
620J2b	as above with large signatures				350.	475.	2750.
620J4	Kansas City	1915	Helm-Miller	504,000	350.	550.	4000.
620K1	Dallas	1915	Hoopes-VanZandt		400.	800.	3000.
620K2	Dallas	1915	Gilbert-VanZandt		350.	525.	2850.
620K3	Dallas	1915	Talley-VanZandt		350.	475.	2750.

Remarks: Government signatures of Teehee-Burke appear on all except No. 620F2, which has Elliott-Burke On 620J2b, Cross is "Acting Secretary." Respectively, 343 and 237 notes are outstanding for Nos. 620B and 620H. For the latter, 17 notes are known Known for B–17; F1–3 ;F2–20; G1–32; G2–14; H–17; J1–20; J2a–49; J4–4; K1–35; K2–3; K3–7 (Gengerke)

Silver Certificate/Series 1933–1934A/Blue Seal

John Trumbull's portrait of Alexander Hamilton was engraved in 1906 by G.F.C. Smillie.

The U.S. Treasury Building was engraved by L.S. Schofield.

No	Series	Signatures	Notes Printed	VFine	EFine	Unc
621	1933	Julian-Woodin	216,000			
			(156,000 released)	$1250	$1750	$4500
621A	1933A	Julian-Morgenthau	336,000			
			(28,000 released)	------------- Unique -------------		

Series of 1934
The seal is moved to the right; a blue "10" is on the left The back design is the same as No. 621.

No	Series	Signatures	Notes Printed	VFine	EFine	Unc
622	1934	Julian-Morgenthau	88,692,000	15	25	50.
622☆			—	—	—	75.

Yellow seals for the invasion of North Africa

No	Series	Signatures	Notes Printed	VFine	EFine	Unc
623	1934	Julian-Morgenthau	21,860,000	1250	2750	6500.
623☆			—	-------------- Rare --------------		
623A	1934A	Julian-Morgenthau	included in above	20	35	100.
623☆			—	40	100	200.

Silver Certificates/Series 1934A-1953D/Blue Seal

No	Series	Signatures	Notes Printed	VFine	EFine	Une
624A	1934A	Julian-Morgenthau	42,346,428	$ 15	$ 25	$ 60.
624A☆			—	—	—	—
624B	1934B	Julian-Vinson	337,740	125	250	1400.
624B☆			—	375	600	2000.
624C	1934C	Julian-Snyder	20,032,632	—	18	40.
624C☆			—	—	—	—
624D	1934D	Clark-Snyder	11,801,112	—	18	45.
624D☆			—	—	30.	75.

Series 1953

The "10" on the left is now grey The back design is the same as No. 621.

No	Series	Signatures	Notes Printed	VFine	EFine	Une
625	1953	Priest-Humphrey	10,440,000	15	25	70.
625☆			576,000	20	35	100.
625A	1953A	Priest-Anderson	1,080,000	15	30	150.
625A☆			144,000	30	50	200.
625B	1953B	Smith-Dillon	720,000	15	25	60.

Federal Reserve Bank Notes/Series 1929/Brown Seal

John Trumbull's portrait of Alexander Hamilton was engraved in 1906 by G.F.C. Smillie The back design is the same as No. 621.

Signatures of Jones-Woods

No	Bank	Notes Printed	VFine	EFine	Unc
626A	Boston	1,680,000	$ 18.	$ 40.	$ 60.
626A☆	1 reported	—	—	—	500.
626B	New York	5,556,000	15.	20.	30.
626B☆	8 reported	—	—	—	200.
626C	Philadelphia	1,416,000	18.	40.	50.
626C☆	2 reported	—	—	—	350.
626D	Cleveland	2,412,000	18.	30.	35.
626D☆	3 reported	—	—	—	300.
626E	Richmond	1,356,000	18.	40.	60.
626E☆	2 reported	—	—	—	350.
626F	Atlanta	1,056,000	18.	40.	60.
626F☆	2 reported	—	—	—	350.
626G	Chicago	3,156,000	15.	20.	30.
626G☆	1 reported	—	—	—	600
626H	St. Louis	1,584,000	18.	40.	60.
626H☆	4 reported	—	—	—	300.
626I	Minneapolis	588,000	30.	60.	225.
626I☆	2 reported	—	—	—	500.
626J	Kansas City	1,284,000	18.	40.	60.
626J☆	5 reported	—	—	—	300.
626K	Dallas	504,000	30.	60.	250.
626K☆	2 reported	—	—	—	2000.
626L	San Francisco	1,080,000	30.	50.	300.
626L☆	3 reported	—	—	—	500.

National Bank Notes/Series 1929/Brown Seal

Type I with the G.F.C. Smillie portrait of Alexander Hamilton.

Type II has the bank charter number printed a second time near the serial number The back design is the same as No. 621.

| | | Signatures of Jones-Woods | | | | | |
| | | Type I | | | | Type II | |
No	Rarity	VFine	EFine	Une	VFine	EFine	Une
	1	$ 15	$ 25	$ 50	$ 20	$ 35.	$ 60.
	2	20.	30.	60.	25.	40	70.
	3	25.	40.	75.	30.	50	90.
	4	30.	60.	90.	35.	70	110.
627	5	40.	75.	115.	50.	85	140.
	6	50.	90.	135.	65.	100	175.
	7	80.	140.	225.	100.	150	275.
	8	150.	350.	500.	250.	425	600.
	9	1650.	3000	5000	3500	5000	7500.

Remarks: The total issue for both types was 124,236,394 notes.

Federal Reserve Notes/Series 1928 & 1928A/Green Seal

The numeral in the seal represents the second Federal Reserve district The back design is the same as No. 621.

Series 1928, Tate-Mellon

No	Bank	Notes Printed	Unc
628A	Boston	9,804,552	$ 50.
628A☆			200.
628B	New York	11,295,000	60.
628B☆			200.
628C	Philadelphia	8,114,412	60.
628C☆			200.
628D	Cleveland	7,570,000	60.
628D☆			200.
628E	Richmond	4,534,800	60.
628E☆			225.
628F	Atlanta	6,807,720	60.
628F☆			200.
628G	Chicago	8,130,000	50.
628G☆			200.
628H	St. Louis	4,124,100	60.
628H☆			200.
628I	Minneapolis	3,874,440	60.
628I☆			225.
628J	Kansas City	3,620,400	60.
628J☆			225.
628K	Dallas	4,855,500	60.
628K☆			225.
628L	San Francisco	7,086,900	70.
628L☆			325.

Series 1928A, Woods-Mellon

No	Bank	Notes Printed	Unc
629A	Boston	2,893,440	$ 80.
629A☆			300.
629B	New York	18,631,056	75.
629B☆			300.
629C	Philadelphia	2,710,680	80.
629C☆			300.
629D	Cleveland	5,610,000	75.
629D☆			300.
629E	Richmond	552,300	150.
629E☆			325.
629F	Atlanta	3,033,480	80.
629F☆			300.
629G	Chicago	8,715,000	80.
629G☆			300.
629H	St. Louis	531,000	100.
629H☆			325.
629I	Minneapolis	102,600	175.
629I☆			400.
629J	Kansas City	410,400	125.
629J☆			275.
629K	Dallas	410,400	100.
629K☆			275.
629L	San Francisco	2,547,900	80.
629L☆			225.

Federal Reserve Notes/Series 1928B & 1928C/Green Seal

Series 1928B, Woods-Mellon

No	Bank	Notes Printed	Unc
630A	Boston	33,218,088	$ 50.
630A☆			300.
630B☆			300.
630B	New York	44,458,308	40.
630C☆			300.
630C	Philadelphia	22,689,216	40.
630D	Cleveland	17,418,024	40.
630D☆			250.
630E	Richmond	12,714,504	55.
630E☆			250.
630F	Atlanta	5,246,700	60.
630G	Chicago	38,035,000	40.
630G☆			250.
630H	St. Louis	10,814,664	50.
630H☆			300.
630I	Minneapolis	5,294,460	50.
630I☆			300.
630J	Kansas City	7,748,040	50.
630K	Dallas	3,396,096	75.
630L	San Francisco	22,695,300	60.
630L☆	1 reported		—

Series 1928C, Woods-Mills

No	Bank	Notes Printed	Unc
631B	New York	2,902,678	$125.
631D	Cleveland	4,230,428	175.
631D☆	1 reported		5000.
631E	Richmond	304 800	—
631F	Atlanta	688,380	—
631G	Chicago	2,423,400	100.

Series 1928C $10 notes were printed for these districts only.

Letter replaces numeral on No. 630.

Federal Reserve Notes/Series 1934, 1934A, 1934B & 1934C/Green Seal

Series 1934, Julian-Morgenthau

No	Bank	Notes Printed	Unc
632A	Boston	46,276,152	$ 25.
632A☆			125.
632B	New York	177,298,000	25.
632B☆			125.
632C	Philadelphia	34,770,768	25.
632C☆			125.
632D	Cleveland	28,764,108	25.
632D☆			125.
632E	Richmond	16,437,252	25.
632E☆			175.
632F	Atlanta	20,656,872	25.
632F☆			125.
632G	Chicago	69,962,064	20.
632G☆			125.
632H	St. Louis	22,593,204	25.
632H☆			125.
632I	Minneapolis	16,840,000	25.
632I☆			175.
632J	Kansas City	22,627,824	25.
632J☆			125.
632K	Dallas	21,403,488	25.
632K☆			175.
632L	San Francisco	37,402,308	25.
632L☆			125.

Series 1934A, Julian-Morgenthau

No	Bank	Notes Printed	Unc
633A	Boston	104,540,088	$ 25.
633A☆			85.
633B	New York	281,940,996	25.
633B☆			85.
633C	Philadelphia	95,338,032	25.
633C☆			85.
633D	Cleveland	93,332,048	25.
633D☆			85.
633E	Richmond	101,037,912	25.
633E☆			85.
633F	Atlanta	85,478,160	25.
633F☆			85.
633G	Chicago	177,285,960	25.
633G☆			85.
633H	St. Louis	50,694,312	25.
633H☆			85.
633I	Minneapolis	16,340,000	25.
633I☆			85.
633J	Kansas City	31,069,978	25.
633J☆			85.
633K	Dallas	28,263,156	25.
633K☆			85.
633L	San Francisco	125,537,592	25.
633L☆			85.
633LL	(HAWAII ovpt.)	10,424,000	250.
633LL☆			1000.

Series 1934B, Julian-Vinson

No	Bank	Notes Printed	Unc
634A	Boston	3,999,600	$ 30.
634A☆			100.
634B	New York	34,815,948	25.
634B☆			100.
634C	Philadelphia	10,339,020	25.
634C☆			100.
634D	Cleveland	1,394,700	35.
634D☆			125.
634E	Richmond	4,018,272	25.
634E☆			125.
634F	Atlanta	6,764,076	25.
634F☆			125.
634G	Chicago	18,130,836	25.
634G☆			100.
634H	St. Louis	6,849,348	30.
634H☆			100.
634I	Minneapolis	2,254,800	30.
634I☆		not printed	125.
634J	Kansas City	3,835,200	25.
634J☆		not printed	125.
634K	Dallas	3,085,200	30.
634K☆		not printed	125.
634L	San Francisco	9,076,800	25.
634L☆			125.

Series 1934C, Julian-Snyder

No	Bank	Notes Printed	Unc
635A	Boston	42,431,404	$ 20.
635A☆			100.
635B	New York	115,675,644	20.
635B☆			100.
635C	Philadelphia	46,874,760	20.
635C☆			100.
635D	Cleveland	332,400	50.
635D☆			100.
635E	Richmond	37,422,600	20.
635E☆			100.
635F	Atlanta	44,838,264	20.
635F☆			100.
635G	Chicago	105,875,412	20.
635G☆			100.
635H	St. Louis	36,541,404	20.
635H☆			100.
635I	Minneapolis	11,944,848	20.
635I☆			125.
635J	Kansas City	10,874,072	20.
635J☆			100
635K	Dallas	25,642,620	20.
635K☆			125.
635L	San Francisco	49,164,480	20.
635L☆			100.

Federal Reserve Notes/Series 1934D, 1950, 1950A & 1950B/Green Seal

Series 1934D, Clark-Snyder

No.	Bank	Notes Printed	Une
636A	Boston	19,917,900	$ 25.
636A☆			100.
636B	New York	64,067,904	25.
636B☆			100.
636C	Philadelphia	18,432,000	25.
636C☆			100.
636D	Cleveland	20,291,316	25.
636D☆			100.
636E	Richmond	18,090,312	25.
636E☆			125.
636F	Atlanta	17,064,816	25
636F☆			100.
636G	Chicago	55,943,844	25.
636G☆			100.
636H	St. Louis	15,828,048	25.
636H☆			100.
636I	Minneapolis	5,237,220	25.
636I☆			100.
636J	Kansas City	7,992,500	25.
636J☆			100.
636K	Dallas	7,178,196	25.
636K☆			125.
636L	San Francisco	23,956,584	25.
636L☆			125.

Series 1950, Clark-Snyder

No.	Bank	Notes Printed	Une
637A	Boston	70,992,000	$ 25.
637A☆		1,008,000	125.
637B	New York	218,567,000	25.
637B☆		2,568,000	125.
637C	Philadelphia	76,320,000	25.
637C☆		1,008,000	125.
637D	Cleveland	76,032,000	25.
637D☆		1,008,000	125.
637E	Richmond	61,776,600	25.
637E☆		876,000	125.
637F	Atlanta	63,792,000	25.
637F☆		864,000	125.
637G	Chicago	161,056,000	25.
637G☆		2,088,000	125.
637H	St. Louis	47,808,000	25.
637H☆		648,000	125.
637I	Minneapolis	18,864,000	25.
637I☆		252,000	125.
637J	Kansas City	36,332,000	25.
637J☆		456,000	125.
637K	Dallas	33,264,000	25.
637K☆		480,000	125.
637L	San Francisco	76,896,000	25.
637L☆		1,152,000	125.

Smaller letter and Federal Reserve seal on No. 637.

Series 1950A, Priest-Humphrey

No.	Bank	Notes Printed	Une
638A	Boston	104,248,000	$25.
638A☆		5,112,000	75.
638B	New York	356,664,000	25.
638B☆		16,992,000	75.
638C	Philadelphia	71,920,000	25.
638C☆		3,672,000	75.
638D	Cleveland	75,088,000	25.
638D☆		3,672,000	75.
638E	Richmond	82,144,000	25.
638E☆			75.
638F	Atlanta	73,288,000	25.
638F☆		3,816,000	75.
638G	Chicago	235,064,000	25.
638G☆		11,160,000	75.
638H	St. Louis	46,512,000	25.
638H☆		2,880,000	75.
638I	Minneapolis	8,136,000	25.
638I☆		432,000	75.
638J	Kansas City	25,448,000	25.
638J☆		2,304,000	75.
638K	Dallas	21,816,000	25.
638K☆		1,584,000	75.
638L	San Francisco	101,584,000	25.
638L☆		6,408,000	75.

Series 1950B, Priest-Anderson

No.	Bank	Notes Printed	Une
639A	Boston	49,240,000	$20.
639A☆		2,880,000	50.
639B	New York	170,840,000	20.
639B☆		8,280,000	50.
639C	Philadelphia	66,880,000	20.
639C☆		3,240,000	50.
639D	Cleveland	55,360,000	20.
639D☆		2,880,000	50.
639E	Richmond	51,120,000	20.
639E☆		2,880,000	50.
639F	Atlanta	66,520,000	20.
639F☆		2,880,000	50.
639G	Chicago	165,080,000	15.
639G☆		6,480,000	50.
639H	St. Louis	33,040,000	20.
639H☆		1,800,000	50.
639I	Minneapolis	13,320,000	20.
639I☆		720,000	50.
639J	Kansas City	33,480,000	20.
639J☆		2,520,000	50.
639K	Dallas	26,280,000	20.
639K☆		1,440,000	50.
639L	San Francisco	55,000,000	20.
639L☆		2,880,000	50.

Federal Reserve Notes/Series 1950C, 1950D, 1950E & 1963/Green Seal

Series 1950C, Smith-Dillon

No.	Bank	Notes Printed	Unc
640A	Boston	52,120,000	$25.
640A☆		2,160,000	40.
640B	New York	126,520,000	25.
640B☆		6,840,000	40.
640C	Philadelphia	22,200,000	25.
640C☆		720,000	50.
640D	Cleveland	33,120,000	25.
640D☆		1,640,000	40.
640E	Richmond	46,640,000	25.
640E☆		1,800,000	40.
640F	Atlanta	38,880,000	25.
640F☆		1,800,000	40.
640G	Chicago	69,400,000	25.
640G☆		3,600,000	40.
640H	St. Louis	23,040,000	25.
640H☆		1,080,000	40.
640I	Minneapolis	9,000,000	25.
640I☆		720,000	40.
640J	Kansas City	23,320,000	25.
640J☆		800,000	50.
640K	Dallas	17,640,000	25.
640K☆		720,000	50.
640L	San Francisco	35,640,000	25.
640L☆		1,800,000	40.

Series 1950D, Granahan-Dillon

No.	Bank	Notes Printed	Unc
641A	Boston	38,800,000	$25.
641A☆		1,800,000	40.
641B	New York	150,320,000	25.
641B☆		6,840,000	40.
641C	Philadelphia	19,080,000	25.
641C☆		1,808,000	40.
641D	Cleveland	24,120,000	25.
641D☆		720,000	50.
641E	Richmond	33,840,000	25.
641E☆		720,000	50.
641F	Atlanta	36,000,000	25.
641F☆		1,440,000	40.
641G	Chicago	115,480,000	25.
641G☆		5,040,000	40.
641H	St. Louis	10,440,000	25.
641H☆		720,000	50.
641I	Minneapolis	no record	—
641I☆		not printed	—
641J	Kansas City	15,480,000	25.
641J☆		1,080,000	50.
641K	Dallas	18,280,000	25.
641K☆		800,000	50.
641L	San Francisco	62,560,000	25.
641L☆		3,600,000	40.

Series 1950E, Granahan-Fowler

No.	Bank	Notes Printed	Unc
642A	Boston	not printed	$—
642A☆		not printed	—
642B	New York	12,600,000	35.
642B☆		2,621,000	50.
642G	Chicago	65,080,000	30.
642G☆		4,320,000	50.
642L	San Francisco	17,280,000	35.
642L☆			75.

Series 1950E $10 notes were printed
for these districts only.

Series 1963, Granahan-Dillon

No.	Bank	Notes Printed	Unc
643A	Boston	5,760,000	$20.
643A☆			30.
643B	New York	24,960,000	20.
643B☆			30.
643C	Philadelphia	6,400,000	20.
643C☆			30.
643D	Cleveland	7,040,000	20.
643D☆			30.
643E	Richmond	4,480,000	20.
643E☆			30.
643F	Atlanta	10,880,000	25.
643F☆			30.
643G	Chicago	35,200,000	20.
643G☆			30.
643H	St. Louis	13,440,000	20.
643H☆			30.
643I	Minneapolis	not printed	—
643I☆		not printed	—
643J	Kansas City	3,120,000	20.
643J☆			30.
643K	Dallas	5,120,000	20.
643K☆			30.
643L	San Francisco	14,080,000	20.
643L☆			30.

"IN GOD WE TRUST" added to back of
Series 1963 and all subsequent notes.

Federal Reserve Notes/Series 1963A, 1969, 1969A & 1969B/Green Seal

Series 1963A, Granahan-Fowler

No.	Bank	Notes Printed	Unc
644A	Boston	131,360,000	$20.
644A☆		6,400,000	30.
644B	New York	199,360,000	20.
644B☆		9,600,000	30.
644C	Philadelphia	100,000,000	20.
644C☆		4,480,000	30.
644D	Cleveland	72,960,000	20.
644D☆		3,840,000	30.
644E	Richmond	114,720,000	20.
644E☆		5,120,000	30.
644F	Atlanta	80,000,000	20.
644F☆		3,840,000	30.
644G	Chicago	195,520,000	20.
644G☆		9,600,000	30.
644H	St. Louis	43,520,000	20.
644H☆		1,920,000	30.
644I	Minneapolis	16,640,000	20.
644I☆		640,000	30.
644J	Kansas City	31,360,000	20.
644J☆		1,920,000	30.
644K	Dallas	51,200,000	20.
644K☆		1,920,000	30.
644L	San Francisco	87,200,000	20.
644L☆		5,120,000	30.

Series 1969, Elston-Kennedy

No.	Bank	Notes Printed	Unc
645A	Boston	74,880,000	$20.
645A☆		2,560,000	30.
645B	New York	247,560,000	20.
645B☆		10,240,000	30.
645C	Philadelphia	56,960,000	20.
645C☆		2,560,000	30.
645D	Cleveland	57,620,000	20.
645D☆		2,560,000	30.
645E	Richmond	56,960,000	20.
645E☆		2 560,000	30.
645F	Atlanta	53,760,000	20.
645F☆		2,560,000	30.
645G	Chicago	142,240,000	20.
645G☆		6,400,000	30.
645H	St. Louis	22,400,000	20.
645H☆		640,000	30.
645I	Minneapolis	12,800,000	20.
645I☆		280,000	40.
645J	Kansas City	31,360,000	20.
645J☆		1,280,000	30.
645K	Dallas	30,800,000	20.
645K☆		1,280,000	30.
645L	San Francisco	56,320,000	20.
645L☆		3,185,000	30.

Series 1969A, Kabis-Connally

No.	Bank	Notes Printed	Unc
646A	Boston	41,120,000	$20.
646A☆		1,920,000	25.
646B	New York	111,840,000	20.
646B☆		3,840,000	25.
646C	Philadelphia	24,320,000	20.
646C☆		1,920,000	25.
646D	Cleveland	23,680,000	20.
646D☆		1,276,000	25.
646E	Richmond	26,600,000	20.
646E☆		640,000	30.
646F	Atlanta	20,480,000	20.
646F☆		640,000	30.
646G	Chicago	80,160,000	20.
646G☆		3,560,000	25.
646H	St. Louis	15,360,000	20.
646H☆		640,000	30.
646I	Minneapolis	8,320,000	20.
646I☆			30.
646J	Kansas City	10,880,000	$20.
646J☆			30.
646K	Dallas	20,480,000	20.
646K☆		640,000	30.
646L	San Francisco	27,520,000	20.
646L☆		1,280,000	25.

Series 1969B, Banuelos-Connally

No.	Bank	Notes Printed	Unc
647A	Boston	16,640,000	$20.
647A☆		not printed	—
647B	New York	60,320,000	20.
647B☆		1,920,000	35.
647C	Philadelphia	16,880,000	20.
647C☆		not printed	—
647D	Cleveland	12,800,000	20.
647D☆		not printed	—
647E	Richmond	12,160,000	25.
647E☆		640,000	50.
647F	Atlanta	13,440,000	20.
647F☆		640,000	50.
647G	Chicago	32,640,000	20.
647G☆		1,268,000	40.
647H	St. Louis	8,960,000	20.
647H☆		1,280,000	40.
647I	Minneapolis	3,200,000	25.
647I☆		not printed	—
647J	Kansas City	5,120,000	25.
647J☆		640,000	50.
647K	Dallas	5,760,000	25.
647K☆		not printed	—
647L	San Francisco	23,840,000	25.
647L☆		640,000	50.

Federal Reserve Notes/Series 1969C, 1974, 1977 & 1977A/Green Seal

Series 1969C, Banuelos-Shultz

No.	Bank	Notes Printed	Unc
648A	Boston	44,800,000	$15.
648A☆		640,000	25.
648B	New York	203,200,000	12.
648B☆		7,040,000	20.
648C	Philadelphia	69,920,000	15.
648C☆		1,280,000	25.
648D	Cleveland	46,880,000	15.
648D☆		2,400,000	25.
648E	Richmond	45,600,000	15.
648E☆		1,120,000	25.
648F	Atlanta	46,240,000	15.
648F☆		1,920,000	25.
648G	Chicago	55,200,000	15.
648G☆		880,000	25.
648H	St. Louis	29,800,000	15.
648H☆		128,000	35.
648I	Minneapolis	11,520,000	15.
648I☆		640,000	25.
648J	Kansas City	23,040,000	15.
648J☆		640,000	25.
648K	Dallas	24,960,000	15.
648K☆		640,000	20.
648L	San Francisco	56,960,000	15.
648L☆		640,000	25.

Series 1974, Neff-Simon

No.	Bank	Notes Printed	Unc
649A	Boston	104,480,000	$15.
649A☆		2,560,000	20.
649B	New York	239,040,000	15.
649B☆		4,480,000	20.
649C	Philadelphia	69,280,000	15.
649C☆		2,560,000	20.
649D	Cleveland	82,080,000	15.
649D☆		640,000	30.
649E	Richmond	105,760,000	15.
649E☆		3,220,000	20.
649F	Atlanta	75,680,000	15.
649F☆		3,200,000	20.
649G	Chicago	104,480,000	15.
649G☆		5,120,000	20.
649H	St. Louis	46,240,000	15.
649H☆		1,280,000	20.
649I	Minneapolis	27,520,000	15.
649I☆		2,560,000	20.
649J	Kansas City	34,032,000	15.
649J☆		640,000	25.
649K	Dallas	39,840,000	15.
649K☆		1,920,000	20.
649L	San Francisco	70,560,000	15.
649L☆		1,920,000	20.

Series 1977, Morton-Blumenthal

No.	Bank	Notes Printed	Unc
650A	Boston	96,640,000	$15.
650A☆		2,688,000	20.
650B	New York	277,440,000	15.
650B☆		7,296,000	20.
650C	Philadelphia	83,200,000	15.
650C☆		896,000	20.
650D	Cleveland	83,200,000	15.
650D☆		768,000	20.
650E	Richmond	71,040,000	15.
650E☆		1,920,000	20.
650F	Atlanta	88,960,000	15.
650F☆		1,536,000	20.
650G	Chicago	174,720,000	15.
650G☆		3,968,000	20.
650H	St. Louis	46,720,000	15.
650H☆		896,000	20.
650I	Minneapolis	10,240,000	15.
650I☆		256,000	25.
650J	Kansas City	50,560,000	15.
650J☆		1,024,000	20.
650K	Dallas	53,760,000	15.
650K☆		640,000	25.
650L	San Francisco	73,600,000	15.
650L☆		1,792,000	20.

Series 1977A, Morton-Miller

No.	Bank	Notes Printed	Unc
651A	Boston	83,840,000	$15.
651A☆		1,792,000	20.
651B	New York	252,800,000	15.
651B☆		6,016,000	20.
651C	Philadelphia	96,000,000	15.
651C☆		2,048,000	20.
651D	Cleveland	60,160,000	15.
651D☆		2,176,000	20.
651E	Richmond	113,280,000	15.
651E☆		3,072,000	20.
651F	Atlanta	49,280,000	15.
651F☆		1,024,000	20.
651G	Chicago	122,240,000	15.
651G☆		3,200,000	20.
651H	St. Louis	27,520,000	15.
651H☆		768,000	25.
651I	Minneapolis	7,680,000	15.
651I☆		128,000	50.
651J	Kansas City	41,600,000	15.
651J☆		2,048,000	20.
651K	Dallas	60,160,000	15.
651K☆		3,712,000	20.
651L	San Francisco	68,480,000	15.
651L☆		2,048,000	20.

Federal Reserve Notes/Series 1981, 1981A, 1985 & 1988A/Green Seal

Series 1981, Buchanan-Regan

No.	Bank	Notes Printed	Unc
652A	Boston	172,160,000	$15.
652A☆		1,280,000	25.
652B	New York	381,440,000	15.
652B☆		1,920,000	25.
652C	Philadelphia	94,720,000	15.
652C☆		384,000	25.
652D	Cleveland	68,480,000	15.
652D☆		896,000	25.
652E	Richmond	122,080,000	15.
652E☆		2,576,000	25.
652F	Atlanta	72,960,000	15.
652F☆		1,536,000	25.
652G	Chicago	179,840,000	15.
652G☆		1,280,000	25.
652H	St. Louis	55,680,000	15.
652H☆		not printed	—
652I	Minneapolis	23,680,000	15.
652I☆		256,000	30.
652J	Kansas City	53,120,000	15.
652J☆		not printed	—
652K	Dallas	50,560,000	15.
652K☆		not printed	—
652L	San Francisco	144,000,000	15.
652L☆		1,280,000	25.

Series 1981A, Ortega-Regan

No.	Bank	Notes Printed	Unc
653A	Boston	112,000,000	$ 15.
653A☆		not printed	—
653B	New York	259,200,000	—
653B☆		24,000	100.
653C	Philadelphia	48,000,000	15.
653C☆		not printed	—
653Dj	Cleveland	80,000,000	15.
653D☆		not printed	—
653E	Richmond	92,800,000	15.
653E☆		3,200,000	20.
653F	Atlanta	83,200,000	15.
653F☆		4,736,000	20.
653G	Chicago	99,200,000	15.
653G☆		not printed	—
653H	St. Louis	25,600,000	15.
653H☆		not printed	—
653I	Minneapolis	19,200,000	15.
653I☆		not printed	—
653J	Kansas City	48,000,000	12.
653J☆		not printed	—
653K	Dallas	48,000,000	15.
653K☆		not printed	—
653L	San Francisco	115,200,000	15.
653L☆		not printed	—

Series 1985, Ortega-Baker

No.	Bank	Notes Printed	Unc
654A	Boston	380,800,000	$15.
654A☆		7,296,000	20.
654B	New York	1,027,200,000	15.
654B☆			20.
654C	Philadelphia	163,200,000	15.
654C☆		not printed	—
654D	Cleveland	304,000,000	15.
654D☆		not printed	—
654E	Richmond	211,200,000	15.
654E☆		not printed	—
654F	Atlanta	297,600,000	15.
654F☆		384,000	25.
654G	Chicago	358,400,000	15.
654G☆		not printed	—
654H	St. Louis	131,200,000	15.
654H☆		3,200,000	25.
654I	Minneapolis	64,000,000	15.
654I☆		not printed	—
654J	Kansas City	86,400,000	15.
654J☆		not printed	—
654K	Dallas	115,200,000	15.
654K☆		3,136,000	20.
654L	San Francisco	300,800,000	15.
654L☆		2,688,000	25.

Series 1988A, Villalpando-Brady

No.	Bank	Notes Printed	Unc
655A	Boston	198,400,000	$15.
655A☆		64,000,000	20.
655B	New York	352,000,000	15.
655B☆		32,000,000	20.
655C	Philadelphia	57,600,000	15.
655C☆		not printed	—
655D	Cleveland	128,000,000	15.
655D☆		32,000,000	20.
655E	Richmond	102,400,000	15.
655E☆		not printed	—
655F	Atlanta	236,800,000	15.
655F☆		not printed	—
655G	Chicago	262,400,000	15.
655G☆		not printed	—
655H	St. Louis	70,400,000	15.
655H☆		not printed	—
655I	Minneapolis	19,200,000	15.
655I☆		not printed	—
655J	Kansas City	51,200,000	15.
655J☆		not printed	—
655K	Dallas	115,200,000	15.
655K☆		not printed	—
655L	San Francisco	217,600,000	15.
655L☆		32,000,000	20.

Federal Reserve Notes/Series 1990, 1993/Green Seal

Series 1990, Villalpando-Brady

No.	Bank	Notes Printed	Unc
656A	Boston	128,000,000	$15.
656A☆		not printed	—
656B	New York	742,400,000	15.
656B☆		19,200,000	20.
656C	Philadelphia	115,200,000	15.
656C☆		3,200,000	20.
656D	Cleveland	185,600,000	15.
656D☆		not printed	—
656E	Richmond	192,000,000	15.
656E☆		not printed	—
656F	Atlanta	160,000,000	15.
656F☆		not printed	—
656G	Chicago	307,200,000	15.
656G☆		2,560,000	20.
656H	St. Louis	166,400,000	15.
656H☆		3,200,000	20.
656I	Minneapolis	108,800,000	15.
656I☆		3,200,000	20.
656J	Kansas City	166,400,000	15.
656J☆		not printed	—
656K	Dallas	153,600,000	15.
656K☆		not printed	—
656L	San Francisco	179,200,000	15.
656L☆		not printed	—

Series 1993, Withrow-Bentsen

No.	Bank	Notes Printed	Unc
657A	Boston	121,600,000	$15.
657A☆		not printed	—
657B	New York	153,600,000	—
657B☆		not printed	—
657C	Philadelphia	76,800,000	—
657C☆		1,920,000	20.
657D	Cleveland	140,800,000	—
657D☆		not printed	—
657E	Richmond	not printed	—
657E☆		not printed	—
657F	Atlanta	121,600,000	—
657F☆		not printed	—
657G	Chicago	128,000,000	—
657G☆		2,560,000	15.
657H	St. Louis	38,400,000	—
657H☆		not printed	—
657I	Minneapolis	not printed	—
657I☆		not printed	—
657J	Kansas City	19,200,000	15.
657J☆		not printed	—
657K	Dallas	not printed	—
657K☆		not printed	—
657L	San Francisco	76,800,000	—
657L☆		not printed	—

Gold Certificate/Series 1928 & 1928A

The Hamilton portrait was engraved by G.F.C. Smillie. Additional engravers were H.K. Earle, H.S. Nutter, F. Pauling and W.B. Wells. The back design is the same for all small-size $10 notes.

No.	Series	Signatures	Notes Printed	VFine	EFine	Unc
699	1928	Woods-Mellon	130,812,000	$30.	$ 50.	$200.
699☆			—	65.	135.	600.
699A	1928A	Woods-Mills	2,544,000		never released	

Demand Notes/1861

America was engraved by Alfred Jones.

No.	Payable at	Notes Printed	Known	VGood	VFine
700A	Boston	300,000	4	$8500.	$17,500.
700B	New York	320,000	7	8000.	15,500.
700C	Philadelphia	240,000	6	8500.	16,500.
700D	Cincinnati	25,000	1	—	—
700E	St. Louis	25,000	1	—	—

Remarks: Records of 1931 indicate that 606 notes are outstanding; 10 are known in collections. Treasurer F.E. Spinner was presented with the first sheet of second emission $20 demand notes; unsigned and canceled, the sheet was cut. Spinner gave two notes to government officials and retained the illustrated note and the remaining one.

These notes, all without the U.S. Treasury Seal, were signed by representatives of the U.S. Treasurer and the Register of the Treasury. "For the" was originally written as the signatures were inscribed. These notes are extremely rare, and command a higher premium, because after a brief time "For the" was engraved on the plate (see No. 463 for an example).

United States Notes/1862 & 1863/Red Seal

The face design is similar to the preceding note with the addition of the U.S. Treasury Seal; "On Demand" has been deleted.

First obligation back on No. 701, remaining have second obligation.

Second obligation back.

No.	Date	Description	Fine	EFine	Unc
701	1862	"American Bank Note Company" in lower border	$700.	$1500.	$3550.
701a	1862	as preceding but second obligation	650.	1400.	3000.
701b	1863	"American Bank Note Company" and			
		"National Bank Note Company" in lower border	800.	1600.	3750.
701c	1863	"American Bank Note Company" in lower border,	750.	1700.	4000.
		one serial number	750.	1700.	4000.
702	1863	same as 701c but two serial numbers	700.	1500.	3550.

Remarks: Catalog numbers have been changed since the previous edition. A total of 5,146,000 notes were printed; all bear signatures of Chittenden-Spinner. Examples of Nos. 701b and 702 in uncirculated condition have been recorded between serial numbers 28655–28775 and 41634–41758; remaining unobserved notes within this range could also be similar condition. Known for Nos. 701–60; 701a–21; 701b–17; 701c–6; 702–94 (Gengerke).

United States Notes/Series 1869/Red Seal

The portrait of Alexander Hamilton was engraved by Charles Burt. *Liberty*, sketched by John W. Casilear, was engraved by Alfred Jones.

An enlarged portion of the back.

No.	Signatures	Notes Printed	Fine	EFine	Unc
703	Allison-Spinner	3,648,000	$800.	$2650.	$5000.

United States Notes/Series 1875 & 1878/Red Seal

The face design is similar to No. 703 with the addition of "XX" on either side of "20."

The back bears the imprint of the Columbian Bank Note Company.

No.	Series	Signatures	Notes Printed	Fine	EFine	Unc
704	1875	Allison-New	1,240,000	$650.	$ 1200.	$2500.
705	1878	Allison-Gilfillan	1,740,000	550.	900.	2200.

Remarks: Numerous examples of No. 705 between A1013651 and A1013988, and an unspecified number commencing with A682xxx, all in new condition have been observed; these could represent hoards. No. 705 with serial number 1013688 on "US" watermarked paper, intended for fourth issue fractional currency, was in Stack's, March 14, 1989 sale. Known for Nos. 704–47; 705–104.

United States Notes/Series 1880

The "XX" has been deleted. The back design is the same as Nos. 704 & 705.

Serial numbers for Nos. 706–721 are blue; red for Nos. 722 & 723.

No.	Signatures	Seal	Notes Printed	Fine	EFine	Unc
706	Scofield-Gilfillan	lg. brown	316,000	$200.	$600.	$2200.
707	Bruce-Gilfillan	lg. brown	484,000	200.	600.	2100.
708	Bruce-Wyman	lg. brown	640,000	185.	650.	2000.
	Serial numbers are blue except for Nos. 722 & 723 which have red numbers.					
709	Bruce-Wyman	lg. red	500,000	200.	600.	2000.
710	Rosecrans-Jordan	lg. red	550,000	200.	600.	2000.
711	Rosecrans-Hyatt	lg. red	810,000	150.	500.	1800.
712	Rosecrans-Hyatt	lg. red, spikes	1,890,000	150.	500.	1700.
713	Rosecrans-Huston	lg. red, spikes	1,700,000	150.	500.	1700.
714	Rosecrans-Huston	lg. brown	1,050,000	150.	500.	1750.
715	Rosecrans-Nebeker	lg. brown	120,000	300.	750.	—-
	Numbers 716–723 have small red seals with scallops.					
716	Rosecrans-Nebeker		1,380,000	200.	450.	1200.
717	Tillman-Morgan		2,500,000	175.	400.	1100.
718	Bruce-Roberts		2,500,000	175.	400.	1100.
719	Lyons-Roberts		1,560,000	200.	450.	1200.
720	Vernon-Treat		404,000	250.	600.	2000.
721	Vernon-McClung		408,000	250.	600.	2000.
722	Teehee-Burke		400,000	250.	600.	2000.
722☆	3 reported		—	—	—	—
723	Elliott-White		4,580,000	175.	450.	1000.
723☆	19 reported		—	—	—	—

Remarks: The official total of notes issued is 20,792,000. However, higher serial numbers have been recorded by Walter Breen, who believes the total could be 21,252,000. Known for Nos. 706–10; 707–13; 708–34; 709–12; 710–31; 711–29; 714–38; 715–13; 720–29; 721–38; 722–32 (Gengerke). Numerous examples of No. 716 between A768005 and A768072, in uncirculated condition, have been observed and recorded; more within this range could exist. As many as 78 consecutively numbered examples of No. 717, commencing with A9652xx, might exist. As many as 35 examples of No. 718, in uncirculated condition, starting with A119041xx, might exist. The 400,000 for No. 722 could prove to be incomplete.

Compound Interest Treasury Notes/6%/Red Seal

Act of March 3, 1863

The design of this note is similar to the following note.

No.	Signatures	Notes Printed	Notes Issued
724	Chittenden-Spinner	152,000	0

The portrait of Abraham Lincoln was engraved by Henry Gugler. The two vignettes are entitled *Victory* and *Mortar Firing*; the latter was engraved by James Smillie.

The back design includes an interest-rate table.

Act of June 30, 1864

No.	Signatures	Dated		Printed	Issued	Outstanding	VFine
725	Chittenden-Spinner	July	15, 1864	696,000	677,600	1,715	3 known
725a	Chittenden-Spinner	July	15, 1864	(error, Act of July 2, 1864)			unknown
726	Colby-Spinner	Aug.	15, 1864	194,000	included in above		$5,000.
726a	Colby-Spinner	Oct.	15, 1864		included in above		10,000.
726b	Colby-Spinner	Dec.	15, 1864	—	90,400	—	7,000.
726c	Colby-Spinner	Aug.	1, 1865	—	41,000	—	3 known
726d	Colby-Spinner	Sept.	1, 1865	—	—	—	unique
726e	Colby-Spinner	Sept.	15, 1865	—	55,600	—	2 known
726f	Colby-Spinner	Oct.	15, 1865	—	—	—	unknown

Remarks: Known for Nos. 726–47; 726a–4; 726b–12. For No. 725a four $10 notes are known with this incorrect date, and the July 7, 1885 edition of *The New York Times* confirms that $50 notes were issued. It is therefore possible that $20 notes could also bear this incorrect date.

Interest-bearing Notes/One-year/5%/Red Seal

The face design, without the overprint, is similar to the preceding note. A counterfeiting clause appears on the back.

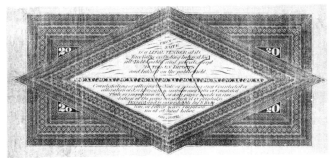

Act of March 3, 1863
Signatures of Chittenden-Spinner

No.	Dated		Known	No.	Dated		Known
	Feb. 15,	1864 (ABNCo)	1		March 23, 1864		1
	Feb. 13,	1864 (ABNCo)	1		March 30, 1864		2
	Feb. 26,	1864	1		April 1,	1864 (ABNCo)	1
	March 3,	1864 (ABNCo)	1		April 5,	1864	2
	March 5,	1864	1		April 7,	1864	1
727	March 7,	1864	2	**727**	April 9,	1864	1
	March 12,	1864	1		April 14,	1864	1
	March 15,	1864	1		May 14,	1864	1
	March 16,	1864	1		April 15,	1864	3
	March 18,	1864 (ABNCo)	2		April 18,	1864	2 *
	March 19,	1864	1		May 25,	1864	1

Remarks: A total of 822,000 notes were issued; 602 remain outstanding. The note dated May 14, 1864, serial number 180741, was dated in error; it should have been April 14. Only a few entered circulation. Serial number 75168 has been recorded, but not the date and variety. One of the notes with the (*) bears the imprint of ABNCo (Gengerke).

National Bank Notes/First Charter Period/Red Seal

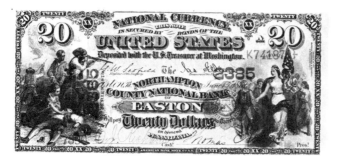

Felix O.C. Darley's painting of the *Battle of Lexington, 1775* was engraved by Joseph I. Pease; *Loyalty* was engraved by Alfred Jones. (ABNCo)

The *Baptism of Pocahontas*, by John G. Chapman, was engraved by Charles Burt.

No.	Series	Signatures	VGood	VFine	Unc
		Red seals with rays			
728	orig.	Chittenden-Spinner	$ 550.	$1000.	$3850.
729	orig.	Colby-Spinner	550.	1000.	3850.
730	orig.	Jeffries-Spinner	1500.	2850.	—
731	orig.	Allison-Spinner	550.	1000.	3850.
		Red seals with scallops			
732	1875	Allison-New	550.	900.	3600.
733	1875	Allison-Wyman	550.	900.	3600.
734	1875	Allison-Gilfillan	550.	900.	3600.
735	1875	Scofield-Gilfillan	550.	900.	3600.
736	1875	Bruce-Gilfillan	550.	950.	3600.
737	1875	Bruce-Wyman	550.	1000.	3800.
738	1875	Rosecrans-Huston	600.	1000.	4000.
739	1875	Rosecrans-Nebeker	700.	1200.	4200.
740	1875	Tillman-Morgan	----------------- extremely rare -----------------		

Remarks: The original series had no series date on the face. A total of 340,082 notes are outstanding.

National Bank Notes/Second Charter Period/First Issue/Series 1882/Brown Seal

The face design is similar to the preceding note.

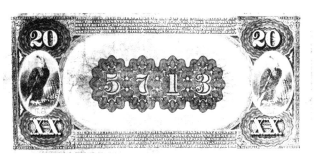

The back design is brown.

No.	Signatures	VGood	VFine	Unc
		First issue—brown seal		
741	Bruce-Gilfillan	$135.	$300.	$1000.
742	Bruce-Wyman	135.	300.	1000.
743	Bruce-Jordan	150.	350.	1100.
744	Rosecrans-Jordan	135.	300.	1000.
745	Rosecrans-Hyatt	135.	300.	1000.
746	Rosecrans-Huston	135.	300.	1000.
747	Rosecrans-Nebeker	135.	300.	1000.
748	Rosecrans-Morgan	350.	900.	2400.
749	Tillman-Morgan	135.	300.	1000.
750	Tillman-Roberts	150.	350.	1100.
751	Bruce-Roberts	135.	300.	1000.
752	Lyons-Roberts	135.	300.	1000.
753	Lyons-Treat	185.	550.	1400.
754	Vernon-Treat	150.	350.	1100.

National Bank Notes/Second Charter Period/Second Issue/Series 1882/Blue Seal

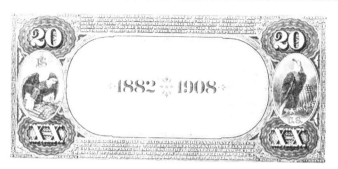

The back design now includes "1882–1908." The face design is similar to the preceding note.

No.	Signatures	VGood	VFine	Unc
		Second issue—blue seal		
755	Rosecrans-Huston	$100.	$250.	$1000.
756	Rosecrans-Nebeker	100.	250.	1000.
757	Rosecrans-Morgan	275.	600.	1800.
758	Tillman-Morgan	100.	250.	1000.
759	Tillman-Roberts	100.	250.	1000.
760	Bruce-Roberts	125.	275.	1200.
761	Lyons-Roberts	100	250.	1000.
762	Vernon-Treat	125.	275.	1000.
762a	Vernon-McClung		Unknown	
763	Napier-McClung	175.	500.	1750.

Third issue—blue seal

The back design now includes "TWENTY DOLLARS." The face design is similar to the preceding note.

No.	Signatures	VGood	VFine	Unc
764	Tillman-Morgan	$150.	$400.	$2000.
765	Tillman-Roberts		Rare, no recent sale.	
766	Bruce-Roberts		Rare, no recent sale.	
767	Lyons-Roberts	135.	350.	1900.
768	Lyons-Treat	175.	450.	2200.
769	Vernon-Treat	175.	450.	2200.
770	Napier-McClung	135.	350.	2100.
771	Parker-Burke		Rare, no recent sale.	
772	Teehee-Burke	135.	350.	2100.

National Bank Notes/Third Charter Period/Series 1902

Hugh McCulloch held the office of Secretary of the Treasury twice, 1865–1869 and 1884–1885. Ostrander Smith designed this note; Alfred Sealey engraved the portrait.

The back design is the same for all three issues; only the second issue has "1902–1908." *Union and Civilization* was engraved by G.F.C. Smillie. *The Capitol* was engraved by Marcus W. Baldwin.

No.	Signatures	VGood	VFine	Unc
		First Issue—red seal		
773	Lyons-Roberts	$160.	$275.	$1000.
774	Lyons-Treat	175.	315.	1150.
775	Vernon-Treat	175.	350.	1150.
		Second issue—blue seal		
		"1902–1908" on back		
776	Lyons-Roberts	55.	85.	425.
777	Lyons-Treat	55.	85.	425.
778	Vernon-Treat	55.	85.	425.
779	Vernon-McClung	55.	85.	425.
780	Napier-McClung	55.	85.	475.
781	Napier-Thompson	75.	125.	550.
782	Napier-Burke	55.	85.	475.
783	Parker-Burke	55.	85.	425.
784	Teehee-Burke	75.	125.	550.

National Bank Notes/Third Charter Period/Series 1902 *(continued)*

The face and back designs
are the same as the
preceding note.

Third issue—blue seal

No.	Signatures	VGood	VFine	Unc
785	Lyons-Roberts	$ 50.	$ 75.	$300.
786	Lyons-Treat	50.	75.	300.
787	Vernon-Treat	50.	75.	300.
788	Vernon-McClung	50.	75.	300.
789	Napier-McClung	50.	75.	300.
790	Napier-Thompson	75.	135.	400.
791	Napier-Burke	50.	90.	350.
792	Parker-Burke	50.	90.	350.
793	Teehee-Burke	50.	75.	300.
794	Elliott-Burke	50.	75.	300.
795	Elliott-White	50.	75.	300.
796	Speelman-White	50.	75.	300.
797	Woods-White	100.	200.	500.
798	Woods-Tate	135.	300.	650.
798a	Jones-Woods		Rare, no recent sale.	

National Gold Bank Notes/Red Seal

The face design is similar to Nos. 728–754.

The gold coin vignette was engraved by James Smillie. The signatures of Bruce-Gilfillan appear on No. 800; Scofield-Gilfillan on Nos. 802a, 804a and 804b. Remaining notes have signatures of Allison-Spinner.

No.	Date	Issuing Bank	City	Issued	Known	VGood	Fine
799	1870*	First Nat'l Gold Bank	San Francisco	11,248	27	$3000.	$4700.
800	1875	First Nat'l Gold Bank	San Francisco	3,600	7	3000.	6000.
800a	1875	as preceding on white paper			4	3500.	6500.
801	1872	National Gold Bank of D.O. Mills & Company	Sacramento	3,641	3	3500.	6500.
802	1873*	First Nat'l Gold Bank	Stockton	5,000	6	3500.	6250.
802a	1875	First Nat'l Gold Bank	Stockton	293	1	—	—
803	1874	Farmers Nat'l Gold Ban	San Jose	2,849	7	3500.	6250.
804	1874*	First Nat'l Gold Bank	Petaluma	2,000	1	—	—
804a	1875	First Nat'l Gold Bank	Petaluma	200	2		
804b	1875	as preceding on white paper		163	1	—	—
805	1875*	First Nat'l Gold Bank	Oakland	1,600	8	3500.	6250.
805a	1875	First Nat'l Gold Bank	Oakland	12	0		
806	1875	Union Nat'l Gold Bank	Oakland	500	2	—	—
807	1873*	First Nat'l Gold Bank	Santa Barbara	800	1	—	—

Remarks: The (*) indicates the note is from the original series. A total of 506 notes is outstanding. No. 807, in good condition, sold for $10,500 in Christie's May 1995 sale.

Silver Certificates/Series 1878 & 1880

The portrait of U.S. Naval Commander Stephen Decatur was engraved by Charles Schlecht. Decatur was killed in 1820 in a duel with James Baron.

Nos. 808–813 have the signatures of Scofield-Gilfillan; they have red seals with the exception of No. 813, which has a brown seal. On Nos. 808–812 the key is reversed in the treasury seal.

No.	Series	Countersignatures	Payable at	Issued	Known	VGood	Fine
808	1878	W.G. White	New York	20,000	0	$ —	$ —
809	1878	J.C. Hopper	New York	incl. in above	3	—	—
809a	1878	T. Hillhouse	New York	—	3	—	20000.
810	1878	R.M. Anthony	San Francisco	3,300	0	—	—
811	1878	A.U. Wyman*	Washington, DC	4,000	2	—	—
812	1878	A.U. Wyman	Washington, DC	88,000	15	1500.	8000.
813	1880	T. Hillhouse	New York	182,000	6	4000.	10000.

			Series 1880				
No.	Signatures	Seal	Notes Issued	Known	VGood	VFine	Unc
814	Scofield-Gilfillan	brown	1,216,000	37	500.	1250.	5500.
815	Bruce-Gilfillan	brown	556,000	30	650.	1400.	7500.
816	Bruce-Wyman	brown	1,960,000	99	500.	1250.	5500.
817	Bruce-Wyman	red	124,000	27	1250.	2750.	10000.

Remarks: The (*) indicates autographed countersignature. Nos. 809 and 811, both in VF condition, sold for $23,100 and $35,200 respectively in May 1995 at Christie's. For No. 810, 40,000 notes were printed; all but 3,300 were burned on October 19, 1881. A "XX" appears in the center of Nos. 813–816. Plates were made for the No. 814–817 type with signatures of Rosecrans-Jordan.

Silver Certificates/Series 1886

Daniel Manning was Secretary of the Treasury, 1865–1887. His portrait was engraved by Lorenzo Hatch. The two allegorical figures represent *Agriculture* and *Industry*.

The back design was engraved by D.M. Cooper and G.U. Rose.

No.	Signatures	Seal	Notes Printed	Known	Fine	EFine	Unc
818	Rosecrans-Hyatt	lg. red	12,000	13	$2000.	$6250.	$ —
819	Rosecrans-Huston	lg. brown	616,000	52	1700.	4250.	10000.
820	Rosecrans-Nebeker	lg. brown	872,000	17	1600.	4000.	9000.
821	Rosecrans-Nebeker	sm. red	212,000	19	1800.	5000.	11000.

Series 1891

The face design is similar to the preceding note.

No.	Signatures	Seal	Notes Printed	Known	Fine	EFine	Unc
822	Rosecrans-Nebeker	red	1,180,000	38	350.	900.	3250.
823	Tillman-Morgan	red	5,920,000	74	250.	750.	2800.
824	Bruce-Roberts	red	1,500,000	31	350.	900.	2950.
825	Lyons-Roberts	red	504,000	34	400.	1000.	—
826	Parker-Burke	blue	1,500,000	144	300.	900.	3250.
826☆		blue		5	$3,300 in VF, 1995 sale		
827	Teehee-Burke	blue	424,000	57	400.	900.	—

Remarks: Nos. 826 and 827 have "XX" in blue on the face. As many as 24 of No. 825 exist in uncirculated condition commencing with E86814xx. As many as 34 consecutively numbered notes of No. 826 exist in uncirculated condition commencing with H14412xx. E1, the first No. 822 note is known.

Gold Certificates/Act of March 3, 1863/First Issue

E Pluribus Unum was engraved by Charles Skinner.

The back design is gold.

No.	Signatures	Payable at	Printed	Issued	Outstanding	Known
827a	Colby-Spinner	New York	100,000	48,000	9	1
827b	Colby-Spinner	New York	included in above		—	3

Remarks: No. 827a has an autographed countersignature. No. 827b has a printed countersignature. Serial number 36621 is at the Bureau of the Public Debt; 41146 was sold in 1979 for $100,000; 48545 is at the Smithsonian Institution.

Gold Certificates/Series 1882

The portrait of President James Garfield was engraved by Charles Burt.

Ocean Telegraph, which commemorated the completion of the Atlantic Cable in 1858, was engraved by George D. Baldwin. The back design is gold.

No.	Signatures	Seal	Notes Printed	Known	VGood	VFine	Unc
828	Bruce-Gilfillan	brown	14,000	2		no recent sale	
829	Bruce-Gilfillan	brown	586,000	20	$3000.	$6500.	$ —
830	Bruce-Gilfillan	brown	448,000	8		no recent sale	
831	Bruce-Wyman	brown	232,000	14	2250.	4750.	—
832	Rosecrans-Huston	lg. brown	200,000	22	1850.	4250.	—
833	Lyons-Roberts	sm. red	16,344,000	92	125.	400.	1850.

Remarks: Both No. 828 & 829, payable at New York, are countersigned by Thomas C. Acton; No. 828 bears the autographed countersignature. Martin Gengerke has recorded the following serial numbers for No. 828 (A1 and A2205), and No. 830 (A337644, A338121, A370769 and A399371).

Gold Certificates/Series 1905–1922

The portrait of George Washington was engraved by Alfred Sealey.

The Great Seal of the U.S. on this gold back was engraved by Robert Ponickau.

No.	Series	Signatures	Notes Issued	VFine	EFine	Unc
834	1905	Lyons-Roberts	1,664,000	$1000.	$3000.	$8000.
835	1905	Lyons-Treat	3,012,000	900.	2600.	7500.
836	1906	Vernon-Treat	12,176,000	100.	200.	500.
837	1906	Vernon McClung	6,924,000	100.	200.	550.
838	1906	Napier-McClung	8,248,000	100.	200.	550.
838☆	1906	8 reported	—	400.	800.	1850.
839	1906	Napier-Thompson	2,276,000	125.	200.	750.
840	1906	Parker-Burke	8,316,000	100.	200.	525.
840☆	1906	6 reported	—	500.	900.	2000.
841	1906	Teehee-Burke	10,064,000	100.	200.	500.
841☆	1906	1 reported				
842	1922	Speelman-White	87,120,000	100.	185.	450.
842☆	1922	83 reported	—	350.	550.	1200.

Remarks: Serial number 1 has been recorded for No. 834; serial numbers A1, A7 and A8 for No. 835. No. 840 exists as a hoard, H567728–800. Known for Nos. 834–37; 835–69; 836–19; 837–11; 838–26; 839–21; 840–39; 841–36; 842–265 (Gengerke).

Treasury or Coin Notes/Series 1890

John Marshall served as Secretary of State and Chief Justice of the Supreme Court. He was born in Virginia in 1755 and died in Philadelphia in 1835. The Henry Inman portrait of Marshall was engraved by Charles Schlecht.

No.	Signatures	Seal	Notes Printed	Known	Fine	EFine	Unc
843	Rosecrans-Huston	brown	488,000	25	$1250.	$3750.	$10000.
844	Rosecrans-Nebeker	brown	100,000	7	no recent sale		
845	Rosecrans-Nebeker	red	704,000	60	1000.	3500.	9500.

Remarks: Known for Nos. 843–41; 844–8; 845–78.

Treasury or Coin Notes/Series 1891

The face design is similar to the preceding note.

No.	Signatures	Seal	Printed	Issued	Known	Fine	EFine	Unc
				Notes				
846	Tillman-Morgan	red	820,000	496,000	52	$2250.	$5250.	$14500.
847	Bruce-Roberts	red	328,000	incl. in above	2		no recent sale	

Remarks: Known for Nos. 846–69; 847–2 (Gengerke).

Federal Reserve Notes/Series 1914/Red Seal

The portrait of Grover Cleveland was engraved by G.F.C. Smillie. *Land, Sea and Air*, which represents the four methods of transportation, was engraved by Marcus W. Baldwin.

Signatures of Burke-McAdoo

No.	Bank	VFine	Unc	No.	Bank	VFine	Unc
848A	Boston	$250.	$1400.	**848G**	Chicago	$150.	$1250.
848B	New York	200.	1250.	**848H**	St. Louis	150.	1250.
848C	Philadelphia	200.	1250.	**848I**	Minneapolis	150.	1250.
848D	Cleveland	200.	1250.	**848J**	Kansas City	150.	1250.
848E	Richmond	200.	1250.	**848K**	Dallas	150.	1250.
848F	Atlanta	200.	1250.	**848L**	San Francisco	175.	1400.

Remarks: The first day of issue for this issue was November 16, 1914. Type II, as illustrated with small district number and letter in the upper left and lower right corners, was printed for all districts except Atlanta and Dallas. See No. 380 for additional illustrations. Known for type I & II: A–9 & 2; B–18 & 25; C–4 & 3; D–3 & 9; E–5 & 1; F–4 & 0; G–17 & 8; H–6 & 4; I–4 & 2; J–8 & 11; K–11 & 0; L–4 & 2 (Gengerke).

Federal Reserve Notes/Series 1914/Blue Seal

No.	Bank	Signatures	Notes Printed	Delivered	VFine	Unc
849A1	Boston	Burke-McAdoo			$ 40.	$150.
849A1☆	2 reported				—	—
849A2	Boston	Burke-Glass			45.	175.
849A2☆	2 reported		26,024,000	25,760,000	—	—
849A3	Boston	Burke-Houston			40.	150.
849A3☆	7 reported				225.	—
849A4	Boston	White-Mellon	(200,000)		40.	150.
849B1	New York	Burke-McAdoo			40.	150.
849B1☆	2 reported				—	—
849B2	New York	Burke-Glass			45.	175.
849B2☆	2 reported				—	—
849B3	New York	Burke-Houston	59,848,000	58,704,000	40.	150.
849B3☆	9 reported				—	—
849B4	New York	White Mellon (b,c)			40.	150.
849B4☆	13 reported		(472,000)		—	—
849C1	Philadelphia	Burke-McAdoo			40.	150.
849C1☆	3 reported				—	—
849C2	Philadelphia	Burke-Glass			45.	175.
849C3	Philadelphia	Burke-Houston	30,088,000	30,088,000	40.	150.
849C3☆	9 reported				—	—
849C4	Philadelphia	White-Mellon			40.	150.
849C4☆	6 reported		(216,000)		—	—
849D1	Cleveland	Burke-McAdoo			40.	150.
849D1☆	1 reported				—	—
849D2	Cleveland	Burke-Glass			45.	175.
849D2☆	1 reported				—	—
849D3	Cleveland	Burke-Houston	38,544,000	38,544,000	40.	150.
849D3☆	7 reported				—	—
849D4	Cleveland	White-Mellon (b)			40.	150.
849D4☆	7 reported		(280,000)		—	—
849E1	Richmond	Burke-McAdoo			40.	150.
849E1☆	2 reported				—	—
849E2	Richmond	Burke-Glass	17,336,000	16,944,000	45.	175.
849E3	Richmond	Burke-Houston			40.	150.
849E3☆	1 reported				—	—
849E4	Richmond	White-Mellon (b)			40.	150.
849E4☆	2 reported		(136,000)		—	—
849F1	Atlanta	Burke-McAdoo			40.	150.
849F1☆	6 reported				200.	—
849F2	Atlanta	B-G, not printed			45.	175.
849F3	Atlanta	Burke-Houston	16,384,000	15,956,000	40.	150.
849F3☆	3 reported				—	—
849F4	Atlanta	White-Mellon (b)			40.	150.
849G1	Chicago	Burke-McAdoo			40.	150.
849G1☆	1 reported				—	—
849G2	Chicago	Burke-Glass			45.	175.
849G2☆ 5 reported			46,776,000	46,776,000	—	—
849G3	Chicago	Burke-Houston			40.	150.
849G3☆	21 reported				200.	—
849G4	Chicago	White-Mellon (b,c)			40.	150.
849G4☆	5 reported		(364,000)		—	—

Federal Reserve Notes/Series 1914/Blue Seal *(continued)*

No.	Bank	Signatures	Notes Printed	Delivered	VFine	Unc
849H1	St. Louis	Burke-McAdoo			$ 40.	$150.
849H1☆	7 reported				—	—
849H2	St. Louis	Burke-Glass			45.	175.
849H2☆	1 reported	10,748,000	10,748,000		—	—
849H3	St. Louis	Burke-Houston			40.	150.
849H3☆	10 reported				—	—
849H4	St. Louis	White-Mellon	(144,000)		40.	150.
849I1	Minneapolis	Burke-McAdoo			40.	150.
849I1☆	3 reported				—	—
849I2	Minneapolis	Burke-Glass			45.	175.
849I3	Minneapolis	Burke-Houston	6,872,000	6,600,000	40.	150.
849I3☆	3 reported				1100.	—
849I4	Minneapolis	White-Mellon	(76,000)		40.	150.
849J1	Kansas City	Burke-McAdoo			40.	150.
849J2	Kansas City	B-G, not printed			45.	175.
849J3	Kansas City	Burke-Houston	9,172,000	9,172,000	40.	150.
849J3☆	6 reported				—	—
849J4	Kansas City	White-Mellon	(56,000)		40.	150.
849K1	Dallas	Burke-McAdoo			40.	150.
849K1☆	10 reported				—	—
849K2	Dallas	Burke-Glass	7,064,000	6,872,000	45.	175.
849K3	Dallas	Burke-Houston			40.	150.
849K4	Dallas	White-Mellon	(76,000)		40.	150.
849L1	San Francisco	Burke-McAdoo			40.	150.
849L1☆	2 reported				400.	—
849L2	San Francisco	Burke-Glass			45.	175.
849L2☆	2 reported				—	—
849L3	San Francisco	Burke-Houston	35,756,000	35,756,000	40.	150.
849L3☆	5 reported				—	—
849L4	San Francisco	White-Mellon (b,c)			40.	150.
849L4☆	9 reported	(1 "b")	(296,000)		300.	—

Remarks: The figure in parenthesis, the last replacement serial number, is the total number of replacement notes of this denomination printed for that bank; the number printed by signatures is not available. White-Mellon plate variations in parenthesis exist for some districts identified as type "b" (small district number and letter in lower left) and type "c" (space of 18 mm horizontal from left seal to the engraved border). Star, replacement notes reported in the main listing above are type "a."

Tom Conklin star notes in CAA Oct. 1995 sale: B1 in G-VG $187; B3 in F $99; C3 in VG-F $99; D4 in F $132; E1 in VG $935; E4 in F $1045; G2 in VG $198; H1 in VG $176; H3 in F $143; J3 in F $154.

Federal Reserve Bank Notes/Series 1915 & 1918/Blue Seal

The portrait of Grover Cleveland was engraved by G.F.C. Smillie.

The back design is the same as No. 848.

No.	Bank	Series	Bank Signatures	Issued	Fine	EFine	Unc
850F1	Atlanta	1915	Bell-Wellborn (Bell as cashier)		---------- Unique --------		
850F1a	Atlanta	1915	Bell-Wellborn (Bell as secretary)	24,000			
850F3	Atlanta	1915	Pike-McCord	—	---------- Unique --------		
850F4	Atlanta	1918	Bell-Wellborn	96,000	$400.	$1000.	$2500.
850G1	Chicago	1915	McLallen-McDougal	84,000	400.	1000.	2500.
850H1	St. Louis	1918	Attebery-Wells	24,000	500.	1250.	2950.
850J1	Kansas City	1915	Anderson-Miller		400.	1100.	2700.
850J2	Kansas City	1915	Cross Miller	180,000	400.	1100.	2700.
850J2a	Kansas City	1915	Cross-Miller		400.	1100.	2700.
850K1	Dallas	1915	Hoopes-Van Zandt		------------ 5 known ------		
850K2	Dallas	1915	Gilbert-Van Zandt	100,000	------------ 4 known ------		
850K3	Dallas	1915	Talley-Van Zandt		------------ 2 known ------		

Remarks: Government signatures are Teehee-Burke except for No. 850F4, which has Elliott-Burke. On No. 850J2a signatures are large; Cross is "Acting Secretary." For Nos. 850G, H and K, respectively, 170, 93 and 230 notes are outstanding. Known for F1–3; F2–3; F3–1; F4–30; G1–22; H1–15; J1–17; J2–20; K1–18; K2–5; K3–3 (Gengerke).

Federal Reserve Bank Notes/Series 1929/Brown Seal

The portrait of Andrew Jackson was engraved by Alfred Sealey in 1867.

The White House.

Signatures of Jones-Woods

No.	Bank	Notes Printed	VFine	EFine	Une
851A	Boston	927,000	$ 35.	$ 65.	$100.
851A☆		24,000	125.	350.	1000.
851B	New York	2,568,000	35.	45.	60.
851B☆		24,000	60.	350.	1000.
851C	Philadelphia	1,008,000	40.	60.	90.
851C☆		24,000	60.	350.	1000.
851D	Cleveland	1,020,000	35.	45.	60.
851D☆		24,000	175.	750.	1000.
851E	Richmond	1,632,000	25.	50.	65.
851E☆		24,000	135.	350.	1000.
851F	Atlanta	960,000	35.	65.	90.
851F☆		8,000	175.	1000.	1850.
851G	Chicago	2,028,000	30.	40.	75.
851H	St. Louis	444,000	35.	40.	75.
851H☆		24,000	75.	300.	750.
851I	Minneapolis	864,000	35.	40.	75.
851I☆		12,000	175.	1000.	1500.
851J	Kansas City	612,000	35.	50.	75.
851J☆		24,000	125.	350.	650.
851K	Dallas	468,000	35.	100.	250.
851K☆		24,000	700.	1500.	2250.
851L	San Francisco	888,000	35.	75.	100.

National Bank Notes/1929/Brown Seal

Type I with Alfred Sealey portrait of Andrew Jackson.

Type II has the bank charter number printed a second time near the serial number.

		Type I			Type II		
No.	Rarity	VFine	EFine	Unc	VFine	EFine	Unc
	1	$ 25.	$ 35.	$ 60.	$ 30.	$ 50.	$ 75.
	2	30.	40.	70.	35.	55.	80.
	3	35.	50.	80.	40.	65.	100.
	4	45.	60.	90.	55.	80.	120.
852	5	60.	75.	115.	70.	100.	150.
	6	75.	100.	140.	100.	135.	180.
	7	90.	125.	200.	135.	180.	275.
	8	150.	250.	400.	300.	500.	900.
	9	2000.	3000.	5000.	2500.	3250.	7500.

Remarks: The total issue for both types was 22,531,578 notes; both have the signatures of Jones-Woods.

Federal Reserve Notes/Series 1928, 1928A, 1928B & 1928C/Green Seal

The back design is similar to No. 851.

Series 1928, Tate-Mellon

No.	Bank	Notes Printed	Une
853A	Boston	3,790,880	$ 50.
853A☆			200.
853B	New York	12,797,000	50.
853B☆			200.
853C	Philadelphia	3,787,200	50.
853C☆			200.
853D	Cleveland	10,626,900	50.
853D☆			200.
853E	Richmond	4,119,600	50.
853E☆			200.
853F	Atlanta	3,842,000	50.
853F☆			200.
853G	Chicago	10,891,740	50.
853G☆			200.
853H	St. Louis	2,523,300	50.
853H☆			200.
853I	Minneapolis	2,633,100	50.
853I☆			200.
853J	Kansas City	2,584,500	50.
853J☆			200.
853K	Dallas	1,568,500	50.
853K☆			200.
853L	San Francisco	8,404,800	50.
853L☆			200.

Series 1928A, Woods-Mellon

No.	Bank	Notes Printed	Une
854A	Boston	1,293,900	$ 75.
854A☆			900.
854B	New York	1,055,800	75.
854B☆	1 reported		900.
854C	Philadelphia	1,717,200	75.
854C☆			900.
854D	Cleveland	625,200	100.
854D☆			900.
854E	Richmond	1,534,500	75.
854E☆	1 reported		900.
854F	Atlanta	1,442,400	75.
854F☆			900.
854G	Chicago	822,000	75.
854G☆			900.
854H	St. Louis	573,300	100.
854H☆			900.
854I	Minneapolis	not printed	—
854I☆		not printed	—
854J	Kansas City	113,400	125.
854J☆			900.
854K	Dallas	1,032,000	75.
854K☆			900.
854L	San Francisco	9,689,124	75.
854L☆			900.

A letter replaces numeral in Federal Reserve seal on No. 855.

Series 1928B, Woods-Mellon

No.	Bank	Notes Printed	Une
855A	Boston	7,749,636	$ 50.
855A☆			175.
855B	New York	19,448,436	40.
855B☆			175.
855C	Philadelphia	8,095,548	50.
855C☆			175.
855D	Cleveland	11,648,196	50.
855D☆			175.
855E	Richmond	4,413,900	60.
855E☆			175.
855F	Atlanta	2,390,240	75.
855F☆			175.
855G	Chicago	17,220,276	50.
855G☆			175.

Series 1928B, Woods-Mellon (cont'd)

No.	Bank	Notes Printed	Une
855H	St. Louis	3,834,600	$ 60.
855H☆			175.
855I	Minneapolis	3,298,920	60.
855I☆			175.
855J	Kansas City	4,941,252	60.
855J☆			175.
855K	San Francisco	8,404,800	60.
855K☆			175.

Series 1928C, Woods-Mills

No.	Bank	Notes Printed	Une
856G	Chicago	3,363,300	500.
856L	San Francisco	1,420,000	600.

Federal Reserve Notes/Series 1934, 1934A & 1934B/Green Seal

The back design is similar to No. 851.

Series 1934, Julian-Morgenthau

No.	Bank	Notes Printed	Unc
857A	Boston	27,673,000	$ 35.
857A☆			275.
857B	New York	27,573,264	35.
857B☆			275.
857C	Philadelphia	53,209,968	35.
857C☆			275.
857D	Cleveland	48,301,416	35.
857D☆			275.
857E	Richmond	36,259,224	35.
857E☆			275.
857F	Atlanta	41,547,660	35.
857F☆			275.
857G	Chicago	20,777,832	35.
857G☆			275.
857H	St. Louis	27,174,552	35.
857H☆			275
857I	Minneapolis	16,795,000	40.
857I☆			275.
857J	Kansas City	20,852,160	35.
857J☆			275.
857K	Dallas	20,852,160	35.
857K☆			275.
857L	San Francisco	32,203,956	35.
857L☆			275.
857LL	(HAWAII)	incl. in 858LL	750.
857LL☆			1800.

Series 1934A, Julian-Morgenthau

No.	Bank	Notes Printed	Unc
858A	Boston	3,202,416	$ 40.
858A☆			150.
858B	New York	102,555,538	35.
858B☆			110.
858C	Philadelphia	3,371,316	40.
858C☆			125.
858D	Cleveland	23,475,108	35.
858D☆			125.
858E	Richmond	46,816,224	35.
858E☆			125.
858F	Atlanta	6,756,816	40.
858F☆			125.
858G	Chicago	91,141,452	35.
858G☆			100.
858H	St. Louis	3,701,568	40.
858H☆			125.
858I	Minneapolis	1,162,500	40.
858I☆			150.
858J	Kansas City	3,221,184	40.
858J☆			125.
858K	Dallas	2,531,700	40.
858K☆			150.
858L	San Francisco	94,454,112	35.
858L☆			125.
858LL	(HAWAII)	11,246,000	425.
858LL☆			2000.

Series 1934B, Julian-Vinson

No.	Bank	Notes Printed	Unc	No.	Bank	Notes Printed	Unc
859A	Boston	3,904,800	$ 40.	**859G**	Chicago	9,084,600	$ 40.
859A☆			350.	**859G☆**			375.
859B	New York	14,876,436	30.	**859H**	St. Louis	5,817,300	40.
859B☆			375.	**859H☆**			375.
859C	Philadelphia	3,271,452	40.	**859I**	Minneapolis	2,817,300	50.
859C☆			375.	**859I☆**			375.
859D	Cleveland	2,814,600	40.	**859J**	Kansas City	3,524,244	40.
859D☆			375.	**859J☆**			300.
859E	Richmond	9,451,632	40.	**859K**	Dallas	2,807,388	50.
859E☆			375.	**859K☆**			375.
859F	Atlanta	6,887,640	40.	**859L**	San Francisco	5,289,540	40.
859F☆			375	**859L☆**			375.

Federal Reserve Notes/Series 1934C & 1934D/Green Seal

On 20 July 1948 an altered version of the *White House* was first used on backs of $20 notes, Series 1934C; consequently, this series can be found with the old and new version. The plate, engraved by Charles Brooks, shows two additional chimneys, a second floor balcony and larger trees and shrubbery. All subsequent $20 notes bear this altered back design. Notes with the old back will cost a few dollars more.

Series 1934C, Julian-Snyder

No.	Bank	Notes Printed	Unc
860A	Boston	7,397,352	$35.
860A☆			75.
860B	New York	18,668,148	35.
860B☆			75.
860C	Philadelphia	11,590,752	35.
860C☆			75.
860D	Cleveland	17,912,424	35.
860D☆			90.
860E	Richmond	22,526,568	35.
860E☆			75.
860F	Atlanta	18,858,568	35.
860F☆			90.
860G	Chicago	26,031,660	35.
860G☆			75.
860H	St. Louis	13,276,984	35.
860H☆			75.
860I	Minneapolis	3,490,200	35.
860I☆			90.
860J	Kansas City	9,675,468	35.
860J☆			75.
860K	Dallas	10,205,364	35.
860K☆			75.
860L	San Francisco	20,580,828	35.
860L☆			75.

Series 1934D, Clark-Snyder

No.	Bank	Notes Printed	Unc
861A	Boston	4,520,000	$ 35.
861A☆			100.
861B	New York	27,894,260	30.
861B☆			75.
861C	Philadelphia	6,022,428	35.
861C☆			75.
861D	Cleveland	8,981,688	35.
861D☆			75.
861E	Richmond	14,055,984	35.
861E☆			75.
861F	Atlanta	7,495,440	35.
861F☆			75.
861G	Chicago	15,187,596	35.
861G☆			75.
861H	St. Louis	5,923,248	35.
861H☆			75.
861I	Minneapolis	2,422,000	35.
861I☆			75.
861J	Kansas City	4,211,904	35.
861J☆			100.
861K	Dallas	3,707,364	35.
861K☆			100.
861L	San Francisco	12,015,228	35.
861L☆			100.

Federal Reserve Notes/Series 1950, 1950A, 1950B & 1950C/Green Seal

Series 1950, Clark-Snyder

No.	Bank	Notes Printed	Unc
862A	Boston	23,184,000	$ 50.
862A☆			175.
862B	New York	80,064,000	50.
862B☆			175.
862C	Philadelphia	29,520,000	50.
862C☆			175.
862D	Cleveland	51,120,424	50.
862D☆			175.
862E	Richmond	67,536,000	50.
862E☆			150.
862F	Atlanta	39,312,000	50.
862F☆			150.
862G	Chicago	70,464,000	50.
862G☆			150.
862H	St. Louis	27,352,000	50.
862H☆			150.
862I	Minneapolis	9,216,000	50.
862I☆			175.
862J	Kansas City	22,752,000	50.
862J☆			250.
862K	Dallas	22,658,000	50.
862K☆			250
862L	San Francisco	70,272,000	50.
862L☆			150.

Series 1950A, Priest-Humphrey

No.	Bank	Notes Printed	Unc
863A	Boston	19,656,000	$40.
863A☆			75.
863B	New York	82,568,000	40.
863B☆			75.
863C	Philadelphia	16,560,000	40.
863C☆			75.
863D	Cleveland	50,320,000	40.
863D☆			75.
863E	Richmond	69,544,000	40.
863E☆			75.
863F	Atlanta	27,648,000	40.
863F☆			75.
863G	Chicago	73,720,000	40.
863G☆			75.
863H	St. Louis	22,680,000	40.
863H☆			75.
863I	Minneapolis	5,544,000	45.
863I☆			75.
863J	Kansas City	22,968,000	40.
863J☆			75.
863K	Dallas	10,728,000	40.
863K☆			75.
863L	San Francisco	85,528,000	40.
863L☆			75.

Series 1950B, Priest-Humphrey

No.	Bank	Notes Printed	Unc
864A	Boston	5,040,000	$ 40.
864A☆			100.
864B	New York	49,960,000	40.
864B☆			75.
864C	Philadelphia	7,920,000	40.
864C☆			75.
864D	Cleveland	38,160,424	40.
864D☆			75.
864E	Richmond	42,120,000	40.
864E☆			75.
864F	Atlanta	40,240,000	40.
864F☆			75.
864G	Chicago	80,560,000	40.
864G☆			75.
864H	St. Louis	19,440,000	40.
864H☆			75.
864I	Minneapolis	12,240,000	40.
864I☆			75.
864J	Kansas City	28,440,000	40.
864J☆			75.
864K	Dallas	11,880,000	40.
864K☆			75.
864L	San Francisco	51,040,000	40.
864L☆			75.

Series 1950C, Smith-Dillon

No.	Bank	Notes Printed	Unc
865A	Boston	7,200,000	$ 40.
865A☆		not printed	—
865B	New York	43,200,000	40.
865B☆			100.
865C	Philadelphia	7,560,000	40.
865C☆			100.
865D	Cleveland	28,440,000	40.
865D☆			100.
865E	Richmond	37,004,000	40.
865E☆			100.
865F	Atlanta	19,080,000	40.
865F☆			100.
865G	Chicago	29,160,000	40.
865G☆			100.
865H	St. Louis	12,960,000	40.
865H☆			100.
865I	Minneapolis	6,480,000	40.
865I☆			100.
865J	Kansas City	18,360,000	40.
865J☆			100.
865K	Dallas	9,000,000	40.
865K☆			100.
865L	San Francisco	45,360,000	40.
865L☆			100.

Federal Reserve Notes/Series 1950D, 1950E & 1963/Green Seal

Series 1950D, Granahan-Dillon

No.	Bank	Notes Printed	Une
866A	Boston	9,320,000	$40.
866A☆			75.
866B	New York	64,280,000	40.
866B☆			75.
866C	Philadelphia	5,400,000	40.
866C☆			75.
866D	Cleveland	23,760,000	40.
866D☆			75.
866E	Richmond	30,240,000	40.
866E☆			75.
866F	Atlanta	22,680,000	40.
866F☆			75.
866G	Chicago	67,960,000	40.
866G☆			75.
866H	St. Louis	6,120,000	40.
866H☆			75.
866I	Minneapolis	3,240,000	40.
866I☆			75.
866J	Kansas City	8,200,000	40.
866J☆			75.
866K	Dallas	6,480,000	40.
866K☆			75.
866L	San Francisco	69,400,000	40.
866L☆			75.

Series 1963, Granahan-Fowler

No.	Bank	Notes Printed	Une
868A	Boston	2,560,000	$40.
868A☆			50.
868B	New York	16,640,000	35.
868B☆			40.
868C	Philadelphia	not printed	—
868C☆		not printed	—
868D	Cleveland	7,680,000	35.
868D☆			40.
868E	Richmond	4,480,000	40.
868E☆			50.
868F	Atlanta	10,240,000	40.
868F☆			50.
868G	Chicago	2,560,000	40.
868G☆			50.
868H	St. Louis	3,200,000	40.
868H☆			50.
868I	Minneapolis	not printed	—
868I☆		not printed	—
868J	Kansas City	3,840,072	40.
868J☆			50.
868K	Dallas	2,560,000	40.
868K☆			50.
868L	San Francisco	7,040,000	40.
868L☆			50.

Series 1950E, Granahan-Fowler

No.	Bank	Notes Printed	Une
867B	New York	8,640,000	$ 75.
867B☆			150.
867G	Chicago	9,360,000	50.
867G☆			175.
867L	San Francisco	8,640,000	50.
867L☆			175.

"IN GOD WE TRUST" was added to No. 868 and all subsequent $20 notes.

Federal Reserve Notes/Series 1963A, 1969, 1969A & 1969B/Green Seal

Series 1963A, Granahan-Fowler

No.	Bank	Notes Printed	Unc
869A	Boston	23,680,000	$30.
869A☆		1,280,000	35.
869B	New York	96,600,000	30.
869B☆		3,840,000	30.
869C	Philadelphia	17,920,000	30.
869C☆		640,000	40.
869D	Cleveland	68,480,424	30.
869D☆		2,560,000	30.
869E	Richmond	128,800,000	30.
869E☆		5,760,000	30.
869F	Atlanta	42,880,000	30.
869F☆		1,920,000	35.
869G	Chicago	156,320,000	25.
869G☆		7,040,000	30.
869H	St. Louis	34,400,000	30.
869H☆		1,920,000	35.
869I	Minneapolis	10,240,000	30.
869I☆		640,000	40.
869J	Kansas City	37,120,000	30.
869J☆		1,920,000	35.
869K	Dallas	38,400,000	30.
869K☆		1,280,000	35.
869L	San Francisco	169,120,000	25.
869L☆		8,320,000	30.

Series 1969, Elston-Kennedy

No.	Bank	Notes Printed	Unc
870A	Boston	19,200,000	$30.
870A☆		1,280,000	50.
870B	New York	106,400,000	25.
870B☆		5,106,000	40.
870C	Philadelphia	10,880,000	30.
870C☆		1,280,000	55.
870D	Cleveland	60,160,000	30.
870D☆		2,560,000	50.
870E	Richmond	66,560,000	30.
870E☆		2,560,000	40.
870F	Atlanta	36,480,000	30.
870F☆		1,280,000	50.
870G	Chicago	107,680,000	25.
870G☆		3,202,000	40.
870H	St. Louis	19,200,000	30.
870H☆		640,000	60.
870I	Minneapolis	12,160,000	30.
870I☆		640,000	60.
870J	Kansas City	39,040,000	30.
870J☆		1,280,000	50.
870K	Dallas	25,600,000	30.
870K☆		640,000	60.
870L	San Francisco	103,840,000	30.
870L☆		5,120,000	40.

Series 1969A, Kabis-Connally

No.	Bank	Notes Printed	Unc
871A	Boston	13,440,000	$35.
871A☆		not printed	—
871B	New York	69,760,000	30.
871B☆		2,460,000	40.
871C	Philadelphia	13,440,000	30.
871C☆		not printed	—
871D	Cleveland	29,440,424	30.
871D☆		640,000	60.
871E	Richmond	42,400,000	30.
871E☆		1,920,000	50.
871F	Atlanta	13,440,000	30.
871F☆		not printed	—
871G	Chicago	81,640,000	30.
871G☆		1,920,000	50.
871H	St. Louis	14,080,000	30.
871H☆		640,000	50.
871I	Minneapolis	7,040,000	30.
871I☆		640,000	50.
871J	Kansas City	16,040,000	30.
871J☆		not printed	—
871K	Dallas	14,720,000	30.
871K☆		640,000	50.
871L	San Francisco	50,560,000	30.
871L☆		1,280,000	50.

Series 1969B, Banuelos-Connally

No.	Bank	Notes Printed	Unc
872A	Boston	not printed	$—
872A☆		not printed	—
872B	New York	39,200,000	40.
872B☆			75.
872C	Philadelphia	not printed	—
872C☆		not printed	—
872D	Cleveland	6,400,000	45.
872D☆		not printed	—
872E	Richmond	27,520,000	40.
872E☆		not printed	—
872F	Atlanta	14,080,000	40.
872F☆		640,000	60.
872G	Chicago	14,240,000	40.
872G☆		1,112,000	60.
872H	St. Louis	5,120,000	40.
872H☆		not printed	—
872I	Minneapolis	2,560,000	50.
872I☆		not printed	—
872J	Kansas City	3,840,000	45.
872J☆			75
872K	Dallas	12,160,000	40.
872K☆		not printed	—
872L	San Francisco	26,000,000	40.
872L☆		640,000	60.

Federal Reserve Notes/1969C, 1974, 1977 & 1981/Green Seal

Series 1969C, Banuelos-Shultz

No.	Bank	Notes Printed	Unc
873A	Boston	17,280,000	$30.
873A☆		640,000	50.
873B	New York	135,200,000	25.
873B☆		1,640,000	40.
873C	Philadelphia	40,960,000	30.
873C☆		640,000	50.
873D	Cleveland	57,760,424	30.
873D☆		480,000	50.
873E	Richmond	80,160,000	30.
873E☆		1,920,000	40.
873F	Atlanta	35,840,000	30.
873F☆		640,000	50.
873G	Chicago	78,720,000	30.
873G☆		640,000	50.
873H	St. Louis	33,920,000	30.
873H☆		640,000	50.
873I	Minneapolis	14,080,000	30.
873I☆		640,000	50.
873J	Kansas City	32,000,000	30.
873J☆		640,000	50.
873K	Dallas	31,360,000	30.
873K☆		1,920,000	40.
873L	San Francisco	62,080,000	30.
873L☆		1,120,000	40.

Series 1974, Neff-Simon

No.	Bank	Notes Printed	Unc
874A	Boston	57,120,000	$30.
874A☆		1,280,000	40.
874B	New York	296,800,000	30.
874B☆		8,320,000	35.
874C	Philadelphia	59,680,000	30.
874C☆		1,920,000	40.
874D	Cleveland	148,460,000	30.
874D☆		4,480,000	40.
874E	Richmond	149,920,000	30.
874E☆		5,120,000	40.
874F	Atlanta	53,280,000	30.
874F☆		480,000	45.
874G	Chicago	250,080,000	30.
874G☆		6,880,000	40.
874H	St. Louis	73,120,000	30.
874H☆		1,280,000	40.
874I	Minneapolis	39,040,000	30.
874I☆		1,280,000	40.
874J	Kansas City	74,400,000	30.
874J☆		1,760,000	50.
874K	Dallas	68,640,000	30.
874K☆		1,120,000	40.
874L	San Francisco	128,800,000	30.
874L☆		5,760,000	40.

Series 1977, Morton-Blumenthal

No.	Bank	Notes Printed	Unc
875A	Boston	94,720,000	$30.
875A☆		2,688,000	40.
875B	New York	569,600,000	30.
875B☆		12,416,000	40.
875C	Philadelphia	117,760,000	30.
875C☆		2,816,000	40.
875D	Cleveland	189,632,000	30.
875D☆		5,632,000	40.
875E	Richmond	257,280,000	30.
875E☆		6,272,000	40.
875F	Atlanta	70,400,000	30.
875F☆		2,688,000	40.
875G	Chicago	358,400,000	30.
875G☆		7,552,000	40.
875H	St. Louis	98,560,000	30.
875H☆		1,792,000	40.
875I	Minneapolis	15,360,000	30.
875I☆		512,000	50.
875J	Kansas City	148,480,000	30.
875J☆		4,864,000	40.
875K	Dallas	163,840,000	30.
875K☆		6,656,000	40.
875L	San Francisco	263,680,000	30.
875L☆		6,528,000	40.

Series 1981, Buchanan-Regan

No.	Bank	Notes Printed	Unc
876A	Boston	191,360,000	$30.
876A☆		1,024,000	40.
876B	New York	559,360,000	30.
876B☆		5,312,000	40.
876C	Philadelphia	101,760,000	30.
876C☆		256,000	50.
876D	Cleveland	146,500,000	30.
876D☆		1,280,000	40.
876E	Richmond	296,320,000	30.
876E☆		1,280,000	40.
876F	Atlanta	93,440,000	30.
876F☆		3,200,000	40.
876G	Chicago	361,600,000	30.
876G☆		2,688,000	40.
876H	St. Louis	76,160,000	30.
876H☆		1,536,000	40.
876I	Minneapolis	23,040,000	30.
876I☆		256,000	50.
876J	Kansas City	147,840,000	30.
876J☆		1,280,000	40.
876K	Dallas	95,360,000	30.
876K☆		896,000	40.
876L	San Francisco	404,480,000	30.
876L☆		1,424,000	40.

Federal Reserve Notes/1981A, 1985, 1988A & 1990/Green Seal

Series 1981A, Ortega-Regan

No.	Bank	Notes Printed	Unc
877A	Boston	156,800,000	$30.
877A☆		57,600,000	30.
877B	New York	352,000,000	30.
877B☆		not printed	—
877C	Philadelphia	57,600,000	30.
877C☆		not printed	—
877D	Cleveland	160,000,424	30.
877D☆		3,840,000	40.
877E	Richmond	214,400,000	30.
877E☆		16,000,000	30.
877F	Atlanta	140,800,000	30.
877F☆		3,200,000	30.
877G	Chicago	211,200,000	30.
877G☆		not printed	—
877H	St. Louis	73,600,000	30.
877H☆		not printed	—
877I	Minneapolis	19,200,000	30.
877I☆		not printed	—
877J	Kansas City	86,400,000	30.
877J☆		not printed	—
877K	Dallas	99,200,000	30.
877K☆		not printed	—
877L	San Francisco	457,600,000	30.
877L☆		6,400,000	40.

Series 1985, Ortega-Brady

No.	Bank	Notes Printed	Unc
878A	Boston	416,000,000	$30.
878A☆		3,200,000	40.
878B	New York	1,728,000,000	30.
878B☆		5,760,000	40.
878C	Philadelphia	224,000,000	30.
878C☆		6,400,000	40.
878D	Cleveland	585,600,000	30.
878D☆		3,200,000	40.
878E	Richmond	860,800,000	30.
878E☆		6,400,000	40.
878F	Atlanta	313,600,000	30.
878F☆		not printed	—
878G	Chicago	729,600,000	30.
878G☆		5,760,000	40
878H	St. Louis	230,400,000	30.
878H☆		not printed	—
878I	Minneapolis	112,000,000	30.
878I☆		not printed	—
878J	Kansas City	204,800,000	30.
878J☆		3,200,000	40.
878K	Dallas	192,000,000	30.
878K☆		3,200,000	40.
878L	San Francisco	1,129,600,000	30.
878L☆		3,200,000	40.

Series 1988A, Villalpando-Brady

No.	Bank	Notes Printed	Unc
879A	Boston	313,600,000	$30.
879A☆		not printed	—
879B	New York	979,200,000	30.
879B☆		92,800,000	35.
879C	Philadelphia	96,000,000	30.
879C☆		3,200,000	35.
879D	Cleveland	307,200,424	30.
879D☆		not printed	—
879E	Richmond	281,600,000	30.
879E☆		not printed	—
879F	Atlanta	288,000,000	30.
879F☆		3,200,000	40.
879G	Chicago	563,200,000	30.
879G☆		3,200,000	40.
879H	St. Louis	108,800,000	30.
879H☆		not printed	—
879I	Minneapolis	25,600,000	30.
879I☆		not printed	—
879J	Kansas City	134,400,000	30.
879J☆		not printed	—
879K	Dallas	70,400,000	30.
879K☆		3,200,000	40.
879L	San Francisco	727,600,000	30.
877L☆		not printed	—

Series 1990, Villalpando-Brady

No.	Bank	Notes Printed	Unc
890A	Boston	345,600,000	$30.
890A☆		3,200,000	40.
890B	New York	1,446,400,000	30.
8908B☆		15,360,000	35.
890C	Philadelphia	192,000,000	30.
8908C☆		not printed	—
890D	Cleveland	281,600,000	30.
890D☆		3,200,000	40.
890E	Richmond	307,200,000	30.
890E☆		3,200,000	30.
890F	Atlanta	460,800,000	30.
890F☆		3,200,000	40.
890G	Chicago	652,800,000	30.
890G☆	DC & FW	16,000,000	35.
890H	St. Louis	172,800,000	30.
890H☆		3,200,000	40.
890I	Minneapolis	134,800,000	30.
890I☆	FW	3,200,000	40.
890J	Kansas City	179,200,000	30.
890J☆		not printed	—
890K	Dallas	121,600,000	30.
890K☆		not printed	—
890L	San Francisco	416,000,000	30.
890L☆		not printed	—

Series 1993, Withrow-Bentsen

No.	Bank	Notes Printed	Unc
891A	Boston		$—
891A☆			—
891B	New York		—
891B☆			—
891C	Philadelphia		—
891C☆			—
891D	Cleveland		—
891D☆			—
891E	Richmond		—
891E☆			—
891F	Atlanta†		—
891F☆			—
891G	Chicago#		—
891G☆			—
891H	St. Louis†		—
891H☆			—
891I	Minneapolis		—
891I☆			—
891J	Kansas City#		—
891J☆			—
891K	Dallas†		—
891K☆			—
891L	San Francisco#		—
871L☆	FW		—

Series 1993 was in production when this catalog was printed.
† Some notes were printed in Fort Worth.
# All notes were printed in Fort Worth.

Gold Certificate/Series 1928 & 1928A

The back design is the same as No. 851.

No.	Series	Signatures	Notes Printed	VFine	EFine	Unc
925	1928	Woods-Mellon	66,204,000	$ 40.	$ 70.	$275.
925☆	1928☆	Woods-Mellon	—	125.	275.	475.
925A	1928A	Woods-Mills	1,500,000	never released		

United States Notes/1862 & 1863/Red Seal

The portrait of Alexander Hamilton was engraved by Joseph P. Ourdan.

No. 926 has the first obligation back; the remaining have the second obligation.

Second obligation back.

No.	Date	Description	Printed	VGood	Fine	Unc
926	1862	"American Bank Note Company" upper border	260,000	$2500.	$6500.	—
926a	1862	as above with "National Bank Note Company" added		---------- Unique ---------		
926b	1862	"National Bank Note Company" upper border	341,104	2500.	6500.	—
927	1863	as 926a		2500.	6500.	—
927a	1863	as 926b		2500.	6500.	—

Remarks: A total of 601,104 notes were printed, all with Chittenden-Spinner signatures. For 927 and 927a a group of nine consecutively numbered notes in uncirculated condition has been reported; these commence with 133xx with the implication that there could be more. About 10,000 counterfeit notes of this design circulated. Known for Nos. 926b–26; 927–7; 927a–7.

United States Notes/Series 1869/Red Seal

Henry Clay, self-educated, was admitted to the bar in VA, where he was born in 1777. He was twice elected to the Senate; he also served as Secretary of State from 1825–1829. This portrait of Clay was engraved by Alfred Sealey. *Return of Peace*, on the left, was engraved by Charles Smith.

No.	Series	Signatures	Notes Printed	VGood	VFine	Unc
928	1869	Allison-Spinner	604,000	$4500.	$14,000.	$24,000.

Remarks: At least 52 notes have been recorded. This issue was recalled because of an abundance of counterfeits with plate letter "B." All of these counterfeits lack a flourish between "SERIES OF" and "1869"; and there is no engraving behind the portrait of Clay. The following counterfeits have been recorded by Martin Gengerke: Y29597, Y32790, Y37566 and Y37569.

United States Notes/Series 1874–1880

America, with a crown bearing *E Pluribus Unum*, was engraved by Charles Burt, who probably engraved the Duplessis portrait of Benjamin Franklin.

No.	Series	Signatures	Seal	Notes Printed	Fine	EFine	Unc
		"L" in red on left and right; seal is red.					
929	1874	Allison-Spinner	rays	489,200	$2500.	$5000.	$10000.
930	1875	Allison-Wyman	rays	40,000	------------ 3 known -------------		
931	1878	Allison-Gilfillan	rays	210,000	1650.	4200.	11000.
		"L" is deleted; serial numbers are blue; red seals except for Nos. 932 & 933.					
932	1880	Bruce-Gilfillan	brown	80,000	4000.	6000.	—
933	1880	Bruce-Wyman	brown	160,000	3500.	5000.	12000.
934	1880	Rosecrans-Jordan	large	80,000	4000.	6000.	—
935	1880	Rosecrans-Hyatt	plain	80,000	4000.	6000.	—
936	1880	Rosecrans-Hyatt	spikes	160,000	3500.	5000.	12000.
937	1880	Rosecrans-Huston	spikes	80,000	4000.	6000.	—
938	1880	Rosecrans-Huston	large	100,000	1250.	3000.	7500.
939	1880	Tillman-Morgan	scallops	212,000	1000.	2500.	6000.
940	1880	Bruce-Roberts	scallops	28,000	------------ 5 known -------------		
941	1880	Lyons-Roberts	scallops	300,000	1000.	2000.	5000.

Remarks: Only uncirculated notes between E78416–E78588 have been observed and recorded for No. 929; this suggests that more exist in similar condition. As many as 46 consecutively numbered notes of No. 938 have been reported; all commence with A4485xx. Known for Nos. 929–27; 930–3; 931–16; 932–6; 933–12; 934–7; 935–6; 936–11; 937–10; 938–51; 939–18; 940–4; 941–125 (Gengerke). No. 935 in choice unc brought $20,900 in Christie's May 1995 sale.

Compound Interest Treasury Notes/6%

To the left of the Alexander Hamilton portrait, engraved by Owen G. Hanks, is a symbolic figure of *Loyalty* engraved by Charles Burt. (RWH&E-ABNCo)

No.	Signatures	Dated	Notes Printed	Notes Issued	Outstanding	Known	VFine
		Act of March 3, 1863					
942	Chittenden-Spinner	10 June 1864	55,580	40,180	95	1	—
943	Colby-Spinner	—	208,000	0	0	0	—
		Act of June 30, 1864					
943a	Chittenden-Spinner	July 15, 1864	(error, Act of July 2, 1864)			1	—
944	Chittenden-Spinner	July 15, 1864	880,500	851,200	1213	3	—
944a	Colby-Spinner	Aug. 15, 1864	612,000	306,000	incl above	2	$20,000.
944b	Colby-Spinner	Oct. 15, 1864	—	—	—	3	20,000.
944c	Colby-Spinner	Dec. 15, 1864	—	—	—	4	20,000.
944d	Colby-Spinner	May 15, 1865	—	—	—	1	—
944e	Colby-Spinner	Sep. 1, 1865	—	—	—	1	—

Remarks: Nos. 942 and 944 have signatures of Chittenden-Spinner; all others have Colby-Spinner. The serial number for 943a is 86613. The issued figure for 944a is an estimate. Martin Gengerke has recorded the following counterfeits for No. 944: 12639, 16239, 16450 (at ANS in NYC), 16823, 31407, 39345 and 91239. The July 7, 1885 edition of *The New York Times* confirmed that as much as $15,000,000 in notes bearing the erroneous Act of July 2, 1864 was issued. Three $10 notes have been recorded. See No. 494a.

Interest-bearing Notes/6%/Act of March 2, 1861

Rawdon, Wright, Hatch & Edson prepared this "old style" uniface note. *Mercury* was drawn and engraved by George W. Hatch; *Wealth* was designed and engraved by Freeman Rawdon; *Justice*, on the right, was probably engraved by Hatch or Rawdon.

No.	Term	Notes Issued	
		Old Plates	New Plates
945	60–days	Unknown	30,113

Act of March 3, 1863
One-Year Notes—5%

The back of this note, similar to Nos. 942–944e, has an interest table.

No.	Signatures	Dated	Notes Issued	Out	Known
945a	Chittenden-Spinner	March 15, 1864	164,800	131	1
	Chittenden-Spinner	April 14, 1864	included in above		2

Remarks: No.945, as illustrated, sold for $4,500 in Christie's April 2, 1982 auction. Serial numbers for known notes are 8525, 35145 and 38161.

Interest-bearing Notes/6%/Two Years/Act of March 2, 1861

The John Wood Dodge portrait of Andrew Jackson (also used on the $1,000 Confederate note in 1861) was probably engraved by Charles Burt. Frederick Girsch is believed to have engraved *Justice* and the portrait of Salmon P. Chase. The note is black and red. (NBNCo)

No.	Signatures	Dated	Notes Issued Old Plates	New Plates	Known
945b	Chittenden-Spinner	9 Aug. 1861	7,624	73,316	2

Remarks: Additional notes could have been printed and issued.

G. Luff, H.G. Root and other authorized clerks signed "For the" Register and the Treasurer. "For the" was probably engraved on the new plates. The only circulated note in the hands of a collector is from an old plate and bears plate position "A"; the faded serial number could be 17662C. The second circulated note, with serial number 17119A, is canceled and held by the Bureau of the Public Debt. There are three additional examples: one specimen and two plate proofs. The illustrated specimen was in the Christie's auction of September 17, 1982. One proof bears plate position "B," the other "C." There is no example of this note at the Bureau of Engraving and Printing.

Interest-bearing Notes/5%/Two Years/Act of March 3, 1863

Caduceus, on the left, was sketched by John W. Casilear and engraved by Alfred Jones. *Justice with Shield*, by engraver Charles Burt, occupies the center; *Loyalty*, by Alfred Jones, was engraved by W.W. Rice. (ABNCo)

| | | Signatures of Chittenden-Spinner | | | | |
No.	Dated	Coupons	Printed	Issued	Out	Known
945c	April 1, 1864 April 13, 1864 April 20, 1864 April 22, 1864 May 27, 1864	none	148,000	136,000	115	6
945d		3	199,112	118,112	38	—

Remarks: Serial numbers for No. 945c are 10174, 12114, 20569, 26198, 29419 and 32596 (Gengerke).

Interest-bearing Notes/7.3%/Three-Year Notes

Act of July 17, 1861

The *Great Eagle* by W. Croome was engraved by Alfred Jones (ABNCo)

No.	Dated	Serial Numbers	Issued	Outstanding
946	Aug. 19, 1861	red	71,641	108
947	Oct. 1, 1861	red	82,365	17
948	Oct. 1, 1861	blue	527	10

Act of June 30, 1864

The face and back of this note are similar to the following note.

No.	Dated	Printed	Serial Numbers	Issued	Outstanding
949	Aug. 15, 1864	623,408	red	363,952	270
950	Mar. 3, 1865	42,268		included in above	

Remarks: For Nos. 949 & 950 serial numbers 24346, 65433, 118501, 154721, 203090, 227602 & 261361.

Interest-bearing Notes/7.3%/Three-Year Notes

This large eagle is similar to the small eagle by Henry Gugler on No. 466. (ABNCo & BEP)

No.	Dated	Serial Numbers	Printed	Issued	Out	Known
951	June 15, 1865	blue	226,324	182,324	56	1
952	July 15, 1865	red	368,000	343,320	211	5

Remarks: The following serial numbers have been recorded by Martin Gengerke, Gene Hessler and John Isted. No. 951: 89959; No. 952: 57224, 126378, 142145, 161643 and 196081.

National Bank Notes/First Charter Period/Red Seal

J.P. Major designed the face of this note. *Washington Crossing the Delaware* was engraved by Alfred Jones. *Prayer for Victory* was engraved by Louis Delnoce; his daughters were the models for the three figures above the soldier. The *Embarkation of the Pilgrims* by Robert W. Weir was engraved by W.W. Rice. (ABNCo)

No.	Series	Signatures	VGood	VFine
		The red seal has rays.		
953	orig.	Chittenden-Spinner	$2300.	$5000.
954	orig.	Colby-Spinner	2300.	4750.
955	orig.	Allison-Spinner	2300.	4750.
		The red seal has scallops		
956	1875	Allison-New	2300.	4500.
957	1875	Allison-Wyman	--------------- Unique -----------------	
958	1875	Allison-Gilfillan	2300.	5800.
959	1875	Scofield-Gilfillan	2300.	5800.
960	1875	Bruce-Gilfillan	2500.	5800.
961	1875	Bruce-Wyman	2500.	5800.
962	1875	Rosecrans-Huston	2600.	6000.
963	1875	Rosecrans-Nebeker	2600.	6000.
964	1875	Tillman-Morgan	2600.	6000.

Remarks: The original series had no series date on the faces. A total of 23,871 notes are outstanding for both types; about 60 actually exist.

National Bank Notes/Second Charter Period/First Issue/Series 1882/Brown Seal

See preceding note for engraver information.

The back is brown.

No.	Signatures	VGood	VFine	Unc
965	Bruce-Gilfillan	$525.	$1250.	$4000.
966	Bruce-Wyman	525.	1250.	4000.
967	Bruce-Jordan	525.	1250.	4250.
968	Rosecrans-Jordan	525.	1250.	4000.
969	Rosecrans-Hyatt	525.	1250.	4000.
970	Rosecrans-Huston	525.	1250.	4000.
971	Rosecrans-Nebeker	525.	1250.	4000.
972	Rosecrans-Morgan	700.	1500.	5250.
973	Tillman-Morgan	525.	1250.	4000.
974	Tillman-Roberts	550.	1250.	4250.
975	Bruce-Roberts	525.	1250.	4000.
976	Lyons-Roberts	525.	1250.	4000.
977	Vernon-Treat	750.	1700.	5750.

National Bank Notes/Second Charter Period/Series 1882/Blue Seal

The back design now has "1882–1908." The face design is similar to the preceding note.

No.	Signatures	VGood	VFine	Unc
978	Rosecrans-Huston	$500.	$1000.	$3500.
979	Rosecrans-Nebeker	500.	1000.	3500.
980	Tillman-Morgan	500.	1000.	3500.
981	Tillman-Roberts	500.	1000.	3500.
982	Bruce-Roberts	500.	1000.	3500.
983	Lyons-Roberts	500.	1000.	3500.
984	Vernon-Treat	550.	1100.	3750.
985	Napier-McClung	600.	1200.	4000.

Third issue—blue seal

The face design is similar to the preceding note.

Th back design now includes "FIFTY DOL-LARS."

No.	Signatures	Printed	Issued	Known	VFine
986	Lyons-Roberts	9,300	8,571	4	$25,000.

National Bank Notes/Third Charter Period/Series 1902

The portrait of John Sherman was engraved by G.F.C. Smillie. Sherman was Secretary of the Treasury 1877–1881 and Secretary of State 1897–1898.

The back design is the same for all three issues; only the second issue has "1902–1908." *Mechanics and Navigation* was engraved by G.F.C. Smillie.

No.	Signatures	VGood	VFine	Unc
		First Issue—red seal		
987	Lyons-Roberts	$800.	$2300.	$5500.
988	Lyons-Treat	800.	2400.	6500.
989	Vernon-Treat	900.	2500.	7000.
		Second issue—blue seal		
		"1902–1908" on back		
990	Lyons-Roberts	250.	500.	2000.
991	Lyons-Treat	250.	500.	2000.
992	Vernon-Treat	250.	500.	2000.
993	Vernon-McClung	250.	500.	2000.
994	Napier-McClung	250.	500.	2200.
995	Napier-Thompson	250.	500.	2250.
996	Napier-Burke	250.	500.	2000.
997	Parker-Burke	250.	500.	2000.
998	Teehee-Burke	325.	625.	2400.
		Third issue—blue seal		
999	Lyons-Roberts	200.	450.	1850.
1000	Lyons-Treat	200.	450.	1850.
1001	Vernon-Treat	200.	450.	1850.
1002	Vernon-McClung	200.	450.	1850.
1003	Napier-McClung	200.	450.	1850.
1004	Napier-Thompson	200.	525.	1850.
1005	Napier-Burke	200.	450.	1850.
1006	Parker-Burke	200.	450.	1850.
1007	Teehee-Burke	200.	450.	1850.
1008	Elliott-Burke	200.	450.	1850.
1009	Elliott-White	200.	450.	1850.
1010	Speelman-White	200.	450.	1850.
1011	Woods-White	250.	600.	2250.
1012	Woods-Tate		No examples are known.	

National Gold Bank Notes/Red Seal

The face design is similar to Nos. 953–986. (ABNCo)

The back design is similar to Nos. 799–807.

No.	Date	Issuing Bank	City	Issued	Good	VGood
1013	1870	First National Gold Bank of	San Francisco	2000	$ 9000.	$18,000.
1013a	1875	First National Gold Bank of as No. 1013 on white paper	San Francisco	620	10000.	20,500.
1014	1874	Farmers Nat'l Gold Bank	San Jose	400	—	—
1014a	1872	Nat'l Gold Bank & Trust Co.	San Francisco	2856	—	—
1014b	1872	Nat'l GB of D.O. Mills Co.	Sacramento	604	—	—
1014c	1873	First National Gold Bank of	Stockton	867	—	—
1014d	1873	First National Gold Bank of	Santa Barbara	200	—	—
1014e	1874	First National Gold Bank of	Petaluma	400	—	—
1014f	1873	Union National Gold Bank	Oakland	100	—	—

Remarks: A total of 113 notes are outstanding. Known for Nos. 1013–5; 1013a–1; 1014–1. Listed are recorded serial numbers with bank serial numbers in parentheses:

No. 1013				No. 1013a	No. 1014
321280	(1392)	321558	(1670)	A338681 (20)	43486 (386)
321504	(1616)	321772	(1884)		
321833	(1945)				

Silver Certificates/Series 1878 & 1880

Edward Everett was Professor of Greek at Harvard at age 21. He served in the House of Representatives and as Secretary of State. In 1835 Everett became Governor of Massachusetts. His portrait was engraved by Charles Schlecht.

The back is black and brown.

Series of 1878 notes have large red seals, signatures of Scofield-Gilfillan and "L" below the series. Countersignatures on Nos. 1014g, 1014h, 1016 & 1017 are handwritten.

No.	Series	Countersigned by	Payable at	Issued	Known
1014g	1878	W.G. White	New York	8,000	0
1014h	1878	J.C. Hopper	New York	included in above	0
1015	1878	T. Hillhouse	New York	8,000	2
1016	1878	R.M. Anthony	San Francisco	1,000	1
1017	1878	A.U. Wyman	Washington, DC	4,000	0
1017a	1878	A.U. Wyman	Washington, DC	38,000	3

Series 1880
Seals are brown except for No. 1022.

No.	Signatures	Seal	Notes Printed	Known	VGood	VFine	Unc
1018	Scofield-Gilfillan	rays	16,000	1	$—	$	$ —
1019	Bruce-Gilfillan	rays	80,000	4	—	—	—
1020	Bruce-Wyman	rays	100,000	10	4000.	9000.	—
1021	Rosecrans-Huston	spikes	100,000	27	3000.	8000.	20,000.
1022	Rosecrans-Nebeker	red	120,000	20	3500.	10000.	—

Remarks: No. 1017a in VF condition brought $46,200 in Christie's May 1995 sale.

Silver Certificates/Series 1891

The face design is similar to the preceding note.

The back design was engraved by W.H. Dougal, E.M. Hall, A.L. Helm and G.U. Rose, Jr.

No.	Signatures	Seal	Notes Printed	Known	Fine	EFine	Unc
1023	Rosecrans-Nebeker	red	120,000	5	$3000.	$6000.	$ —
1024	Tillman-Morgan	red	380,000	17	900.	2200	5000.
1025	Bruce-Roberts	red	384,000	15	900.	2200.	5000.
1026	Lyons-Roberts	red	220,000	26	900.	2200.	4800.
1027	Vernon-Treat	blue	200,000	35	750.	2000.	4800.
1028	Parker-Burke	blue	812,000	111	750.	2000.	4200.

Remarks: As many as 13 consecutively numbered notes are known for No. 1027. They commence with H1662xx in addition, at least three uncirculated notes are known. At least four notes in uncirculated condition are known for No. 1028.

Gold Certificates/Series 1882

Silas Wright was born in Amherst, Massachusetts on May 24, 1795. He was a state and U.S. Senator, and was governor of New York. He died on August 27, 1847 in Canton New York. Charles Burt's engraving of Wright's portrait was based on a painting by Alonzo Chappell.

The back is yellow.

No.	Signatures	Seal	Notes Printed	Known	VGood	VFine	Une
1029	Bruce-Gilfillan	brown	9,000	1	$ —	$ —	$ —
1030	Bruce-Gilfillan	brown	191,000	10	3000.	4500.	—
1031	Bruce-Gilfillan	brown	96,000	7	5000.	11000.	—
1032	Bruce-Wyman	brown	40,000	5	6000.	12000.	—
1033	Rosecrans-Hyatt	lg. red	40,000	4		no recent sale	
1034	Rosecrans-Huston	lg. brn	100,000	12	2000.	3250.	—
1034a	Rosecrans-Huston	red	incl. in above	1		no recent sale	
1035	Lyons-Roberts	red	1,724,000	52	350.	600.	3,000.
1036	Lyons-Treat	red	400,000	17	400.	750.	4,250.
1037	Vernon-Treat	red	400,000	25	400.	750.	4,000.
1038	Vernon-McClung	red	400,000	16	400.	750.	4,000.
1039	Napier-McClung	red	1,204,000	77	350.	600.	3,000.

Remarks: Nos. 1029 & 1030 are payable at New York; both are countersigned by Thomas C. Acton. No. 1029 bears an autographed countersignature and No. 1029 sold for $5,700 in 1974.

Gold Certificates/Series 1913–1922

The portrait of Ulysses S. Grant was engraved by G.F.C. Smillie.

The back is yellow.

No.	Series	Signatures	Notes Issued	VFine	EFine	Unc
1040	1913	Parker-Burke	400,000	$500.	$750.	$2750.
1041	1913	Teehee-Burke	1,224,000	350.	600.	1900.
1042	1922	Speelman-White (sm. numbers)	800,000	450.	700.	2250.
1042a	1922	Speelman-White (lg. numbers)	5,184,000	325.	525.	1750.
1042a☆	1922	13 reported				

Remarks: Known for Nos. 1040–25; 1041–44; 1042–27; 1042a--103 (Gengerke).

No. 1042

No. 1042a

Treasury or Coin Notes/Series 1891/Red Seal

The portrait of William H. Seward (1801–1872) was engraved by Charles Schlecht. As Secretary of State (1860–1869), Seward negotiated for foreign land purchases; only the Alaska purchase was successful.

The back design was engraved by D.M. Cooper, W.H. Hall, E.E. Myers and G.U. Rose, Jr.

No.	Signatures	Printed	Issued	Outstanding	Known	VGood	VFine
1043	Rosecrans-Nebeker	80,000	23,500	23	20	$7500.	$27,500.

Remarks: Of the notes outstanding, six are in new condition including the first note, B1, at the American Numismatic Association Museum. Notes with the following serial numbers have been recorded: B2, B3, B7, B8, B1572, B2137, B5082, B12916, B13884, B13890, B14535, B15233, B16876, B17501, B17508, B17510, B17532, B20726 and B79901. A private sale of the uncirculated, illustrated note was reported at more than $100,000.

Federal Reserve Notes/Series 1914/Red Seal

The portrait of U.S. Grant was engraved by John Eissler.

The symbolic figure of *Panama* was engraved by Marcus W. Baldwin. This note was issued in the year the Panama Canal opened.

Signatures of Burke-McAdoo

No.	Bank	Notes Issued	VFine	Unc
1044A-I	Boston	20,000	$350.	$2000.
1044A-II		24,000	350.	2000.
1044B-I	New York	80,000	350.	2000.
1044B-II		40,000	350.	2000.
1044C-I	Philadelphia	12,000	500.	2300.
1044C-II		40,000	350.	2000.
1044D-I	Cleveland	8,000	500.	2400.
1044D-II		40,000	350.	2000.
1044E-I	Richmond	28,000	350.	2000.
1044E-II		40,000	350.	2000.
1044F-I	Atlanta	28,000	350.	2000.
1044F-II		none	—	—
1044G-I	Chicago	20,000	350.	2000.
1044G-II		40,000	350.	2000.
1044H-I	St. Louis	12,000	500.	2300.
1044H-II		16,000	400.	2300.
1044I-I	Minneapolis	8,000	500.	2400.
1044I-II		8,000	500.	2400.
1044J-I	Kansas City	8,000	500.	2400.
1044J-II		8,000	500.	2400.
1044K-I	Dallas	28,000	350.	2000.
1044K-II		none	—	—
1044L-I	San Francisco	8,000	500.	2400.
1044L-II		24,000	350.	2000.

Remarks: The first day of issue for this issue was November 16, 1914. Type II has a small district number and letter in the upper left and lower right corners. The number of notes issued was compiled by Doug Murray. See No. 380 for illustrations. Known for types I & II: A–2 & 2; B–6 & 9; C–8 & 3; D–3 7; E–5 & 9; F–7 & 0; G–4 & 4; H–7 & 9; I–3 & 9; J–4 & 4; K–7 & 0; L–3 & 11 (Gengerke).

Federal Reserve Notes/Series 1918/Blue Seal

No.	Bank	Signatures	Notes Printed	Delivered	EFine	Unc
1045A1	Boston	Burke-McAdoo	⎫		$185.	$950.
1045A2	Boston	Burke-Glass	⎪		200.	1000.
1045A3	Boston	Burke-Houston	1,072,000	1,072,000	185.	950.
1045A4	Boston	White-Mellon	⎭		185.	950.
1045B1	New York	Burke-McAdoo	⎫		185.	950.
1045B2	New York	Burke-Glass	⎪		200.	1000.
1045B3	New York	Burke-Houston	5,264,000	5,264,000	185.	950.
1045B3☆	3 reported		⎪			
1045B4	New York	White Mellon (b)	⎭		185.	950.
1045C1	Philadelphia	Burke-McAdoo	⎫		185.	950.
1045C2	Philadelphia	Burke-Glass	⎪		200.	1000.
1045C3	Philadelphia	Burke-Houston	3,720,000	3,720,000	185.	950.
1045C3☆	1 reported		⎪			
1045C4	Philadelphia	White-Mellon	⎭		185.	950.
1045C4☆	1 reported					
1045D1	Cleveland	Burke-McAdoo	⎫		185.	950.
1045D2	Cleveland	Burke-Glass	⎪		200.	1000.
1045D3	Cleveland	Burke-Houston	6,136,000	6,012,000	185.	950.
1045D4	Cleveland	White-Mellon (b)	⎭		185.	950.
1045D4☆	10 reported					
1045E1	Richmond	Burke-McAdoo	⎫		185.	950.
1045E2	Richmond	Burke-Glass	⎪		200.	1000.
1045E3	Richmond	Burke-Houston	1,688,000	1,664,000	185.	950.
1045E3☆	2 reported		⎪			
1045E4	Richmond	White-Mellon	⎭		185.	950.
1045F1	Atlanta	Burke-McAdoo	⎫		185.	950.
1045F2	Atlanta	Burke-Glass	⎪		200.	1000.
1045F3	Atlanta	Burke-Houston	1,060,000	868,000	185.	950.
1045F4	Atlanta	White-Mellon	⎭		185.	950.
1045G1	Chicago	Burke-McAdoo	⎫		185.	950.
1045G2	Chicago	Burke-Glass	⎪		200.	1000.
1045G2☆	1 reported		⎪			
1045G3	Chicago	Burke-Houston	3,988,000	3,988,000	185.	950.
1045G3☆	2 reported		⎪			
1045G4	Chicago	White-Mellon	⎭		185.	950.
1045H1	St. Louis	Burke-McAdoo	⎫		185.	950.
1045H2	St. Louis	Burke-Glass	⎪		200.	1000.
1045H2☆	1 reported	584,000	572,000			
1045H3	St. Louis	Burke-Houston	⎪		185.	950.
1045H4	St. Louis	White-Mellon	⎭		185.	950.
1045I1	Minneapolis	Burke-McAdoo	⎫		185.	950.
1045I3	Minneapolis	Burke-Houston	164,000	160,000	185.	950.
1045I4	Minneapolis	White-Mellon	⎭		185.	950.
1045J1	Kansas City	Burke-McAdoo	424,000	372,000	185.	950.
1045J4	Kansas City	White-Mellon	included in above		185.	950.

Federal Reserve Notes/Series 1918/Blue Seal (*Continued*)

No.	Bank	Signatures	Notes Printed	Delivered	EFine	Unc
1045K1	Dallas	Burke-McAdoo			185.	950.
1045K3	Dallas	Burke-Houston	216,000	204,000	185.	950.
1045K4	Dallas	White-Mellon			185.	950.
1045L1	San Francisco	Burke-McAdoo			185.	950.
1045L3	San Francisco	Burke-Houston	1,356,000	1,356,000	185.	950.
1045L4	San Francisco	White-Mellon			185.	950.

Remarks: Doug Murray reports that no plates were made for Nos. 1045I2, 1045J2 & 3, 1045K2 and 1045L2. For each of the following districts, A, F, H, I, J, K and L, 4,000 replacement notes were printed; for B, 12,000 notes; C, 28,000; D, 36,000; E & G, 8,000 each. White-Mellon plate variation, in parenthesis, exist for two districts, identified as type "b" (small district number and letter in lower left). Star, replacement notes reported in the main listing above are type "a" notes. See $5 Federal Reserve notes for examples.

Federal Reserve Bank Notes/Series 1918/Blue Seal

The portrait of Ulysses S. Grant was engraved by John Eissler. The back design is similar to No. 1044.

No.	Bank	Government	Signatures Bank	Issued	VFine	Une
1046	St. Louis	Teehee-Burke	Attebery-Wells	4000	$4000.	$9000.

Remarks: Although plates were prepared for all 12 Federal Reserve Banks, St. Louis was the only bank to issue this denomination. In 1956, 64 notes were outstanding. The serial numbers of the known 50 notes are provided by Michael A. Crabb, Jr. and Martin Gengerke. Each note has the "H" prefix and "A" suffix: 46, 103, 110, 115, 117, 118, 122, 138, 140, 151, 153, 161, 168, 176, 508, 608, 649, 656, 671, 674, 678, 682, 683, 689, 741, 751, 753, 768, 770, 774, 797, 821, 898, 899, 991, 1813, 2128, 2320, 2923, 2933, 3213, 3299, 3396, 3402, 3458, 3800, 3862, 3887 and 3917.

Federal Reserve Bank Notes/Series 1929/Brown Seal

This portrait of U.S. Grant was engraved by John Eissler.

An engraving of the *U.S. Capitol* occupies the back.

Signatures of Jones-Woods

No.	Bank	Notes Printed	VFine	EFine	Une
1047A	Boston	not printed	$ —	$ —	$ —
1047B	New York	636,000	75.	90.	125.
1047B☆		24,000	—	300.	500.
1047C	Philadelphia	not printed	—	—	—
1047D	Cleveland	684,000	75.	90.	125.
1047D☆		12,000	—	—	—
1047E	Richmond	not printed	—	—	—
1047F	Atlanta	not printed	—	—	—
1047G	Chicago	300,000	75.	90.	150.
1047G☆		4,000	—	—	—
1047H	St. Louis	not printed	—	—	—
1047I	Minneapolis	132,000	75.	100.	175.
1047I☆		12,000	250.	750.	1000.
1047J	Kansas City	276,000	75.	90.	135.
1047J☆		12,000	100.	350.	500.
1047K	Dallas	168,000	65.	90.	150.
1047K☆		12,000	250.	1000.	1400.
1047L	San Francisco	576,000	75.	125.	175.
1047L☆		12,000	250.	1000.	1400.

National Bank Notes/Series 1929/Brown Seal

Signatures of Jones-Woods

Type I

Type II has the bank charter number printed a second time near the serial number.

		Type I				Type II	
No.	Rarity	VFine	EFine	Unc	VFine	EFine	Unc
	1	$ 80.	$110.	$165.	$ 90.	$120.	$ 475.
	2	85.	120.	175.	95.	130.	500.
	3	90.	130.	200.	100.	150.	525.
	4	100.	155.	225.	120	165.	550.
1048	5	140.	175.	250.	160.	190.	600.
	6	165.	210.	285.	200.	250.	675.
	7	190.	250.	350.	225.	300.	1000.
	8	375.	500.	850.	500.	700.	—
	9	—	—	—	—	—	—

Remarks: The total issue for both types was 1,160,812. Banks in Alabama, Alaska, Arizona, Arkansas, Georgia, Maine, New Mexico and South Carolina did not issue this denomination.

Federal Reserve Notes/Series 1928 & 1928A/Green Seal

The district letter replaces the numeral in the seal on the Series 1928A. The back design is the same as No. 1047.

Series 1928, Woods-Mellon				Series 1928A, Woods-Mellon			
No.	**Bank**	**Notes Printed**	**Unc**	**No.**	**Bank**	**Notes Printed**	**Unc**
1049A	Boston	265,000	$150.	**1050A**	Boston	1,834,989	$150.
1049A☆			750.	**1050A**☆		not printed	—
1049B	New York	1,351,800	150.	**1050B**	New York	3,392,329	150.
1049B☆			500.	**1050B**☆		not printed	—
1049C	Philadelphia	997,560	150.	**1050C**	Philadelphia	3,078,944	150.
1049C☆			500.	**1050C**☆			100.
1049D	Cleveland	1,161,900	150.	**1050D**	Cleveland	2,453,364	150.
1049D☆			500.	**1050D**☆			850.
1049E	Richmond	539,400	150.	**1050E**	Richmond	1,516,500	150.
1049E☆			500.	**1050E**☆			850.
1049F	Atlanta	538,800	150.	**1050F**	Atlanta	338,400	175.
1049F☆			500.	**1050F**☆			850.
1049G	Chicago	1,348,620	150.	**1050G**	Chicago	5,263,956	150.
1049G☆			500.	**1050G**☆			850.
1049H	St. Louis	627,300	150.	**1050H**	St. Louis	880,500	165.
1049H☆			500.	**1050H**☆			850.
1049I	Minneapolis	106,200	150.	**1050I**	Minneapolis	780,240	165.
1049I☆			750.	**1050I**☆			850.
1049J	Kansas City	252,600	150.	**1050J**	Kansas City	791,064	165.
1049J☆			600.	**1050J**☆			850.
1049K	Dallas	109,920	150.	**1050K**	Dallas	701,496	165.
1049K☆			750.	**1050K**☆			850.
1049L	San Francisco	447,600	150.	**1050L**	San Francisco	1,522,000	150.
1049L☆			750.	**1050L**			850.

Federal Reserve Notes/Series 1934, 1934A, 1934B, 1934C & 1934D/Green Seal

Series 1934, Julian-Morgenthau

No.	Bank	Notes Printed	Unc
1051A	Boston	2,265,000	$100.
1051A☆			350.
1051B	New York	17,894,676	100.
1051B☆			350.
1051C	Philadelphia	5,833,200	100.
1051C☆			350.
1051D	Cleveland	8,817,720	100.
1051D☆			350.
1051E	Richmond	4,826,628	100.
1051E☆			350.
1051F	Atlanta	3,069,348	100.
1051F☆			500.
1051G	Chicago	8,675,940	100.
1051G☆			500.
1051H	St. Louis	1,497,144	100.
1051H☆			500.
1051I	Minneapolis	539,700	100.
1051I☆			500.
1051J	Kansas City	1,133,520	100.
1051J☆			500.
1051K	Dallas	1,194,876	100.
1051K☆			500.
1051L	San Francisco	8,101,200	100.
1051L☆			500.

Series 1934A, Julian-Morgenthau

No.	Bank	Notes Printed	Unc
1052A	Boston	406,200	$115.
1052A☆			400.
1052B	New York	4,710,648	100.
1052B☆			400.
1052C	Philadelphia	not printed	—
1052C☆			
1052D	Cleveland	864,164	100.
1052D☆			400.
1052E	Richmond	2,235,372	100.
1052E☆			400.
1052F	Atlanta	416,100	115.
1052F☆			400.
1052G	Chicago	1,014,600	100.
1052G☆			400.
1052H	St. Louis	361,944	115.
1052H☆			400.
1052I	Minneapolis	93,300	125.
1052I☆			500.
1052J	Kansas City	189,300	115.
1052J☆			400.
1052K	Dallas	266,700	115.
1052K☆			400.
1052L	San Francisco	162,000	115.
1052L☆			400.

Series 1934B, Julian-Vinson

No.	Bank	Notes Printed	Unc
1053A	Boston	not printed	$ —
1053B	New York	not printed	—
1045B☆			900.
1053C	Philadelphia	509,100	125.
1053D	Cleveland	359,100	125.
1053D☆			2000.
1053E	Richmond	596,700	125.
1053F	Atlanta	416,710	125.
1053G	Chicago	306,000	100.
1053H	St. Louis	306,000	125.
1053I	Minneapolis	120,000	175.
1053J	Kansas City	221,340	150.
1053J☆			2000.
1053K	Dallas	120,108	175.
1053L	San Francisco	441,000	125.

Series 1934C, Julian-Snyder

No.	Bank	Notes Printed	Unc
1054A	Boston	117,600	$115.
1054B	New York	1,556,400	90.
1054C	Philadelphia	107,283	115.
1054D	Cleveland	374,400	110.
1045D☆			900.
1054E	Richmond	1,821,960	90.
1054F	Atlanta	107,640	115.
1054G	Chicago	294,432	110.
1054H	St. Louis	535,200	110.
1054I	Minneapolis	118,800	115.
1054J	Kansas City	303,600	110.
1054J☆		none reported	—
1054K	Dallas	429,900	110.
1054K☆			900.

Series 1934D, Clark Snyder

No.	Bank	Notes Printed	Unc	No.	Bank	Notes Printed	Unc
1055A	Boston	279,000	$125.	**1055G**	Chicago	494,016	$100.
1055A☆			175.	**1055G**☆			2000.
1055B	New York	898,776	100.	**1055H**	St. Louis	not printed	—
1055C	Philadelphia	699,000	100.	**1055I**	Minneapolis	reported	—
1055D	Cleveland	not printed	—	**1055J**	Kansas City	not printed	—
1055E	Richmond	156,000	200.	**1055K**	Dallas	103,200	100.
1055F	Atlanta	216,000	200.	**1055L**	San Francisco	not printed	—
1055F☆			2000.				

Federal Reserve Notes/Series 1950, 1950A, 1950B & 1950C/Green Seal

Smaller letter and Federal Reserve seal on No. 1056.

Series 1950, Clark-Snyder

No.	Bank	Notes Printed	Unc
1056A	Boston	1,248,000	$ 90.
1056A☆			300.
1056B	New York	10,236,000	90.
1056B☆			300.
1056C	Philadelphia	2,353,000	90.
1056C☆			300.
1056D	Cleveland	6,180,000	90.
1056D☆			300.
1056E	Richmond	5,064,000	90.
1056E☆			325.
1056F	Atlanta	1,812,000	90.
1056F☆			325.
1056G	Chicago	4,212,000	90.
1056G☆			300.
1056H	St. Louis	892,000	90.
1056H☆			325.
1056I	Minneapolis	384,000	100.
1056I☆			325.
1056J	Kansas City	696,000	90.
1056J☆			325.
1056K	Dallas	1,100,000	90.
1056K☆			300.
1056L	San Francisco	3,996,000	90.
1056L☆			325.

Series 1950A, Priest-Humphrey

No.	Bank	Notes Printed	Unc
1057A	Boston	720,000	$ 90.
1057A☆			275.
1057B	New York	6,480,000	90.
1057B☆			275.
1057C	Philadelphia	1,728,000	90.
1057C☆			275.
1057D	Cleveland	1,872,000	90.
1057D☆			275.
1057E	Richmond	2,016,000	90.
1057E☆			275.
1057F	Atlanta	288,000	125.
1057F☆			325.
1057G	Chicago	2,016,000	90.
1057G☆			275.
1057H	St. Louis	576,000	90.
1057H☆			275.
1057I	Minneapolis	not printed	—
1057J	Kansas City	144,000	150.
1057J☆			325.
1057K	Dallas	664,000	90.
1057K☆			275.
1057L	San Francisco	576,000	90.
1057L☆			275.

Series 1950B, Priest-Anderson

No.	Bank	Notes Printed	Unc
1058A	Boston	664,000	$ 80.
1058A☆			275.
1058B	New York	8,352,000	75.
1058B☆			275.
1058C	Philadelphia	2,592,000	75.
1058C☆			275.
1058D	Cleveland	1,728,000	75.
1058D☆			275.
1058E	Richmond	1,584,000	75.
1058E☆			275.
1058F	Atlanta	not printed	—
1058F☆		not printed	—
1058G	Chicago	4,320,000	75.
1058G☆			275.
1058H	St. Louis	576,000	80.
1058H☆			275.
1058I	Minneapolis	not printed	—
1058I☆		not printed	—
1058J	Kansas City	1,008,000	75.
1058J☆			275.
1058K	Dallas	1,008,000	75.
1058K☆			275.
1058L	San Francisco	1,872,000	75.
1058L☆			275.

Series 1950C, Smith-Dillon

No.	Bank	Notes Printed	Unc
1059A	Boston	720,000	$ 80.
1059A☆			225.
1059B	New York	5,328,000	75.
1059B☆			175.
1059C	Philadelphia	1,296,000	75.
1059C☆			225.
1059D	Cleveland	1,296,000	75.
1059D☆			225.
1059E	Richmond	1,296,000	75.
1059E☆			225.
1059F	Atlanta	not printed	—
1059F☆		not printed	—
1059G	Chicago	1,728,000	75.
1059G☆			200.
1059H	St. Louis	576,000	85.
1059H☆			175.
1059I	Minneapolis	144,000	100.
1059I☆			175.
1059J	Kansas City	432,000	85.
1059J☆			225.
1059K	Dallas	720,000	85.
1059K☆			225.
1059L	San Francisco	1,152,000	75.
1059L☆			225.

Federal Reserve Notes/Series 1950D, 1950E, 1963A & 1969/Green Seal

Series 1950D, Granahan-Dillon

No.	Bank	Notes Printed	Unc
1060A	Boston	1,728,000	$ 75.
1060A☆			275.
1060B	New York	7,200,000	75.
1060B☆			275.
1060C	Philadelphia	2,736,000	75.
1060C☆			275.
1060D	Cleveland	2,880,000	75.
1060D☆			275.
1060E	Richmond	2,016,000	75.
1060E☆			275.
1060F	Atlanta	576,000	85.
1060F☆			275.
1060G	Chicago	4,176,000	75.
1060G☆			275.
1060H	St. Louis	1,440,000	75.
1060H☆			275.
1060I	Minneapolis	288,000	90.
1060I☆			275.
1060J	Kansas City	720,000	85.
1060J☆			275.
1060K	Dallas	1,296,000	75.
1060K☆			275.
1060L	San Francisco	2,160,000	75.
1060L☆			275.

Series 1950E, Granahan-Fowler

No.	Bank	Notes Printed	Unc
1061B	New York	3,024,000	$100.
1061B☆			275.
1061G	Chicago	1,008,000	125.
1061L	San Francisco	1,296,000	125.
1061L☆			375.

$50 notes were printed for these districts only.

"IN GOD WE TRUST" added to Series 1963A and all subsequent $50 notes.

Series 1963A, Granahan-Fowler

No.	Bank	Notes Printed	Unc
1062A	Boston	1,536,000	$ 75.
1062A☆		320,000	100.
1062B	New York	11,008,000	65.
1062B☆		1,408,000	90.
1062C	Philadelphia	3,328,000	75.
1062C☆		704,000	90.
1062D	Cleveland	3,584,000	75.
1062D☆		256,000	100.
1062E	Richmond	3,072,000	75.
1062E☆		704,000	90.
1062F	Atlanta	768,000	75.
1062F☆		384,000	90.
1062G	Chicago	6,912,000	75.
1062G☆		768,000	90.
1062H	St. Louis	512,000	90.
1062H☆		128,000	100.
1062I	Minneapolis	512,000	90.
1062I☆		128,000	100.
1062J	Kansas City	512,000	90.
1062J☆		64,000	165.
1062K	Dallas	1,536,000	75.
1062K☆		128,000	100.
1062L	San Francisco	4,352,000	75.
1062L☆		704,000	90.

Series 1969, Elston-Kennedy

No.	Bank	Notes Printed	Unc
1063A	Boston	2,048,000	$ 75.
1063A☆		not printed	—
1063B	New York	12,032,000	75.
1063B☆		384,000	90.
1063C	Philadelphia	3,548,000	75.
1063C☆		128,000	100.
1063D	Cleveland	3,584,000	75.
1063D☆		192,000	100.
1063E	Richmond	2,560,000	75.
1063E☆		64,000	175.
1063F	Atlanta	256,000	90.
1063F☆		not printed	—
1063G	Chicago	9,728,000	75.
1063G☆		256,000	100.
1063H	St. Louis	256,000	100.
1063H☆		not printed	—
1063I	Minneapolis	512,000	75.
1063I☆		not printed	—
1063J	Kansas City	1,280,000	75.
1063J☆		64,000	175.
1063K	Dallas	1,536,000	75.
1063K☆		64,000	125.
1063L	San Francisco	6,912,000	75.
1063L☆		256,000	100.

Federal Reserve Notes/Series 1969A, 1969B, 1969C & 1974/Green Seal

Series 1969A, Kabis-Connally

No.	Bank	Notes Printed	Unc
1064A	Boston	1,536,000	$ 75.
1064A☆		128,000	100.
1064B	New York	9,728,000	75.
1064B☆		704,000	90.
1064C	Philadelphia	2,560,000	75.
1064C☆		704,000	90.
1064D	Cleveland	2,816,000	75.
1064D☆		not printed	—
1064E	Richmond	2,304,000	75.
1064E☆		64,000	185.
1064F	Atlanta	256,000	100.
1064F☆		64,000	185.
1064G	Chicago	3,584,000	75.
1064G☆		192,000	100.
1064H	St. Louis	256,000	100.
1064H☆		not printed	—
1064I	Minneapolis	512,000	90.
1064I☆		not printed	—
1064J	Kansas City	256,000	100.
1064J☆		not printed	—
1064K	Dallas	1,024,000	75.
1064K☆		128,000	185.
1064L	San Francisco	5,120,000	75.
1064L☆		256,000	100.

Series 1969B, Banuelos-Connally

No.	Bank	Notes Printed	Unc
1065A	Boston	1,024,000	$100.
1065A☆		not printed	—
1065B	New York	2,560,000	100.
1065B☆		not printed	—
1065C	Philadelphia	2,048,000	100.
1065C☆		not printed	—
1065E	Richmond	1,536,000	100.
1065F	Atlanta	512,000	100.
1065G	Chicago	1,134,000	100.
1065K	Dallas	1,024,000	100.
1065K☆		128,000	375.

$50 notes were printed for these districts only.

Series 1969C, Banuelos-Shultz

No.	Bank	Notes Printed	Unc
1066A	Boston	1,792,000	$ 70.
1066A☆		64,000	175.
1066B	New York	7,040,000	70.
1066B☆		192,000	100.
1066C	Philadelphia	3,584,000	70.
1066C☆		256,000	100.
1066D	Cleveland	5,120,000	70.
1066D☆		192,000	100.
1066E	Richmond	2,304,000	70.
1066E☆		64,000	175.
1066F	Atlanta	256,000	100.
1066F☆		64,000	175.
1066G	Chicago	6,784,000	70.
1066G☆		576,000	90.
1066H	St. Louis	2,688,000	70.
1066H☆		64,000	175.
1066I	Minneapolis	256,000	100.
1066I☆		64,000	175.
1066J	Kansas City	1,280,000	70.
1066J☆		128,000	125.
1066K	Dallas	3,456,000	70.
1066K☆		64,000	175.
1066L	San Francisco	4,608,000	70.
1066L☆		256,000	100.

Series 1974, Neff-Simon

No.	Bank	Notes Printed	Unc
1067A	Boston	3,840,000	$ 70.
1067A☆		256,000	65.
1067B	New York	38,400,000	65.
1067B☆		768,000	65.
1067C	Philadelphia	7,040,000	65.
1067C☆		384,000	65.
1067D	Cleveland	21,120,000	65.
1067D☆		640,000	65.
1067E	Richmond	14,400,000	65.
1067E☆		576,000	65.
1067F	Atlanta	1,280,000	65.
1067F☆		64,000	65.
1067G	Chicago	30,720,000	65.
1067G☆		1,536,000	55.
1067H	St. Louis	1,920,000	65.
1067H☆		128,000	65.
1067I	Minneapolis	3,200,000	65.
1067I☆		192,000	100.
1067J	Kansas City	4,480,000	65.
1067J☆		192,000	100.
1067K	Dallas	8,320,000	65.
1067K☆		128,000	100.
1067L	San Francisco	8,320,000	65.
1067L☆		64,000	115.

Federal Reserve Notes/Series 1977, 1981, 1981A & 1985/Green Seal

Series 1977, Morton-Blumnenthal

No.	Bank	Notes Printed	Unc
1068A	Boston	15,360,000	$ 65.
1068A☆		1,088,000	75.
1068B	New York	49,920,000	65.
1068B☆		2,112,000	75.
1068C	Philadelphia	5,112,000	65.
1068C☆		128,000	100.
1068D	Cleveland	23,040,000	65.
1068D☆		1,024,000	75.
1068E	Richmond	24,320,000	65.
1068E☆		896,000	80.
1068F	Atlanta	2,560,000	65.
1068F☆		128,000	100.
1068G	Chicago	47,360,000	60.
1068G☆		2,304,000	65.
1068H	St. Louis	3,840,000	65.
1068H☆		512,000	90.
1068I	Minneapolis	3,840,000	65.
1068I☆		128,000	100.
1068J	Kansas City	7,680,000	65.
1068J☆		256,000	90.
1068K	Dallas	14,080,000	65.
1068K☆		576,000	90.
1068L	San Francisco	19,200,000	65.
1068L☆		768,000	75.

Series 1981, Buchanan-Regan

No.	Bank	Notes Printed	Unc
1069A	Boston	18,500,000	$65.
1069A☆		not printed	—
1069B	New York	78,080,000	65.
1069B☆		1,264,000	75.
1069C	Philadelphia	1,280,000	65.
1069C☆		not printed	—
1069D	Cleveland	28,160,000	65.
1069D☆		628,000	75.
1069E	Richmond	5,600,000	65.
1069E☆		not printed	—
1069F	Atlanta	14,080,000	65.
1069F☆		1,904,000	75.
1069G	Chicago	67,200,000	65.
1069G☆		1,252,000	75.
1069H	St. Louis	4,480,000	65.
1069H☆		not printed	—
1069I	Minneapolis	5,760,000	65.
1069I☆		624,000	75.
1069J	Kansas City	18,560,000	65.
1069J☆		624,000	75.
1069K	Dallas	19,840,000	65.
1069K☆		not printed	—
1069L	San Francisco	35,200,000	65.
1069L☆		628,000	75.

Series 1981A, Ortega-Regan

No.	Bank	Notes Printed	Unc
1070A	Boston	9,600,000	$65.
1070A☆		not printed	—
1070B	New York	28,800,000	65.
1070B☆		3,200,000	75.
1070C	Philadelphia	not printed	—
1070C☆		not printed	—
1070D	Cleveland	12,800,000	65.
1070D☆		not printed	—
1070E	Richmond	12,800,000	65.
1070E☆		688,000	75.
1070F	Atlanta	3,200,000	65.
1070F☆		not printed	—
1070G	Chicago	28,800,000	65.
1070G☆		not printed	—
1070H	St. Louis	3,200,000	65.
1070H☆		not printed	—
1070I	Minneapolis	3,200,000	65.
1070I☆		not printed	—
1070J	Kansas City	6,400,000	65.
1070J☆		not printed	—
1070K	Dallas	6,400,000	65.
1070K☆		not printed	—
1070L	San Francisco	22,400,000	65.
1070L☆		640,000	75.

Series 1985, Ortega-Baker

No.	Bank	Notes Printed	Unc
1071A	Boston	51,200,000	$65.
1071A☆		not printed	—
1071B	New York	185,600,000	65.
1071B☆		3,200,000	75.
1071C	Philadelphia	3,200,000	65.
1071C☆		not printed	—
1071D	Cleveland	57,600,000	65.
1071D☆		3,200,000	75.
1071E	Richmond	54,400,000	65.
1071E☆		not printed	—
1071F	Atlanta	16,000,000	65.
1071F☆		not printed	—
1071G	Chicago	128,400,000	65.
1071G☆		6,400,000	75.
1071H	St. Louis	6,400,000	65.
1071H☆		not printed	—
1071I	Minneapolis	12,800,000	65.
1071I☆		not printed	—
1071J	Kansas City	9,600,000	65.
1071J☆		not printed	—
1071K	Dallas	25,600,000	65.
1071K☆		not printed	—
1071L	San Francisco	57,600,000	65.
1071L☆		not printed	—

Federal Reserve Notes/Series 1988, 1990 & 1993/Green Seal

Series 1988, Ortega-Brady

No.	Bank	Notes Printed	Unc
1072A	Boston	9,600,000	$65.
1072A☆		not printed	—
1072B	New York	214,400,000	65.
1072B☆		1,408,000	75.
1072C	Philadelphia	not printed	—
1072C☆		not printed	—
1072D	Cleveland	32,000,000	65.
1072D☆		not printed	—
1072E	Richmond	12,800,000	65.
1072E☆		not printed	—
1072F	Atlanta	not printed	—
1072F☆		not printed	—
1072G	Chicago	80,000,000	65.
1072G☆		not printed	—
1072H	St. Louis	3,200,000	55.
1072H☆		not printed	—
1072I	Minneapolis	not printed	—
1072I☆		not printed	—
1072J	Kansas City	6,400,000	65.
1072J☆		not printed	—
1072K	Dallas	not printed	—
1072K☆		not printed	—
1072L	San Francisco	12,800,000	65.
1072L☆		not printed	—

Series 1990, Villalpando-Brady

No.	Bank	Notes Printed	Unc
1073A	Boston	147,200,000	$60.
1073A☆		not printed	—
1073B	New York	128,000,000	60.
1073B☆		3,200,000	65.
1073C	Philadelphia	140,800,000	60.
1073C☆		3,200,000	65.
1073D	Cleveland	192,000,000	60.
1073D☆		3,200,000	65.
1073E	Richmond	176,000,000	60.
1073E☆		not printed	—
1073F	Atlanta	not printed	—
1073F☆		not printed	—
1073G	Chicago	108,800,000	60.
1073G☆		3,200,000	65.
1073H	St. Louis	115,200,000	60.
1073H☆		not printed	—
1073I	Minneapolis	121,600,000	60.
1073I☆		not printed	—
1073J	Kansas City	134,400,000	60.
1073J☆		3,200,000	65.
1073K	Dallas	115,200,000	60.
1073K☆		not printed	—
1073L	San Francisco	118,400,000	60.
1073L☆		not printed	—

Series 1993 was in production when this catalog was printed.

Series 1993, Withrow-Bentsen

No.	Bank	Notes Printed	Unc
1074A	Boston		$—
1074A☆			—
1074B	New York		—
1074B☆			—
1074C	Philadelphia		—
1074C☆			—
1074D	Cleveland		—
1074D☆			—
1074E	Richmond		—
1074E☆			—
1074F	Atlanta		—
1074F☆			—
1074G	Chicago		—
107G☆			—
1074H	St. Louis		—
1074H☆			—
1074I	Minneapolis		—
1074I☆			—
1074J	Kansas City		—
1074J☆			—
1074K	Dallas		—
1074K☆			—
1074L	San Francisco		—
1074L☆			—

Gold Certificate/Series 1928

The portrait of U.S. Grant was engraved by John Eissler. The back design is similar to No. 1047.

No.	Signatures	Notes Printed	VFine	EFine	Unc
1119	Woods-Mellon	5,520,000	$100.	$200.	$ 650.
1119☆	Woods-Mellon	—	325.	750.	2750.

United States Notes/1862 & 1863/Red Seal

Spread Eagle was engraved by Joseph P. Ourdan.

First obligation back Nos. 1120 & 1120a.

Second obligation back.

No.	Date	Description	VGood	VFine	Unc
1120	1862	"American Bank Note Company" upper left	$2750.	$6000.	$22,000.
1120a	1862	without monogram.	2750.	6000.	22,000.
1120b	1862	"National Bank Note Company" and			
		"American Bank Note Company" in upper border		unique	
1121	1863	as preceding with one serial number		2 known	
1121a	1863	"National Bank Note Company" upper border	2750.	6000.	20,000.
1121b	1863	as preceding, one serial number		unique	

Remarks: A total of 400,000 notes were printed, all with signatures of Chittenden-Spinner. For Nos. 1120–1120a, an estimated 130,000 notes bearing the first obligation were printed. The remaining 270,000 notes bear the second obligation. Recorded serial numbers suggest that as many as 64 notes in uncirculated condition could exist. Known for Nos. 1120–12; 1120a–10; 1121a–25 (Gengerke). Some catalog numbers have been changed from the previous edition.

United States Notes/Series 1869/Red Seal

The portrait of Abraham Lincoln, based on a photograph by Anthony Berger, was engraved by Charles Burt, who also engraved the head of *Liberty* (see No. 1341). *Reconstruction* was engraved by Louis Delnoce

No.	Signatures	Notes Printed	Known	Fine	EFine	Unc
1122	Allison-Spinner	364,000	22	$7500.	$11,000.	$25,000.

Remarks: According to Walter Breen, as many as 371,040 notes were issued; this exceeds the official total. About five of the known notes are in uncirculated condition. The following serial numbers, all with "A" prefix, have been recorded by Martin Gengerke, Gene Hessler and John Isted: 45508, 68701, 68705, 71287, 72701, 88855, 110033, 167928, 175693, 204590, 204599, 211085, 212120, 212366, 213113, 266223, 266227, 277696, 282739, 291200, 329434 & 346542. Four additional notes have been reported but unconfirmed.

United States Notes/Series 1875–1880

Face design is similar to preceding note.

No.	Series	Signatures	Seal	Notes Printed	Fine	EFine	Unc
		Nos. 1123A-1125 have red floral patterns and red seals.					
1123	1875	Allison-New	rays	122,000	$3350.	$8750.	$ —
1124	1875A	Allison-Wyman	rays	40,000	----------	4 known	--------
1125	1878	Allison-Gilfillan	rays	202,000	3150.	9000.	—
		Black floral patterns. All have red seals except for Nos. 1126, 1127 & 1132.					
1126	1880	Bruce-Gilfillan	brown	60,000	2250.	5750.	10500.
1127	1880	Bruce-Wyman	brown	80,000	2250.	5750.	10500.
1128	1880	Rosecrans-Jordan	large	80,000	2250.	5750.	10750.
1129	1880	Rosecrans-Hyatt	large	20,000	----------	2 known	--------
1130	1880	Rosecrans-Hyatt	lg. spikes	80,000	2250.	5750.	10750.
1131	1880	Rosecrans-Huston	spikes	60,000	2250.	5750.	10500.
1132	1880	Rosecrans-Huston	brown	80,000	2250.	5750.	10500.
1133	1880	Tillman-Morgan	scallops	172,000	1750.	4250.	9500.
1134	1880	Bruce-Roberts	scallops	24,000	----------	6 known	--------
1135	1880	Lyons-Roberts	scallops	180,000	1750.	4250.	9500.
1136	1880	Napier-McClung	scallops		existence doubtful		

Remarks: Known for Nos. 1123–11; 1125–16; 1126–10; 1127–8; 1128–13; 130–6; 1131–19; 1132–13; 1133–22; 1135–40 (Gengerke).

Compound Interest Treasury Notes/6%/Red Seal

The *Lansdowne Portrait of Washington* was engraved by Owen G. Hanks. *Justice and Shield* on the right was engraved by Charles Burt; the *Guardian* is on the left.

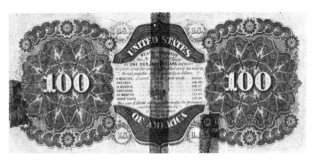

The interest-rate table is on the back.

No.	Signatures	Dated	Notes Printed	Notes Issued	Outstanding	Known
		Act of March 3, 1863				
1137	Chittenden-Spinner	June 10, 1864	40,032	39,176	59	1
		Act of June 30, 1864				
1138	Chittenden-Spinner	July 15, 1864	272,480	260,140	278	2
1139	Colby-Spinner	Aug. 15, 1864	266,800	243,600	incl. above	2
1139a	Colby-Spinner	Dec. 15, 1864	—	—	—	1
1139b	Colby-Spinner	May 15, 1865	—	—	—	6
1139c	Colby-Spinner	Aug. 1, 1865	—	—	—	2
1139d	Colby-Spinner	Sept. 1, 1865	—	—	—	1

Remarks: These notes, especially No. 1139b, were counterfeited extensively. See "A Superb Counterfeit...." by W.P. Koster in *PAPER MONEY*, Vol. XIV, No. 1. 1975, p. 7. As much as $15,000,000 in notes, of all denominations, bearing the erroneous Act of 2 July 1864 was issued with the date of 15 July 1864. To date only two $10 notes have been recorded.

Interest-bearing Notes 6%/Act of March 2, 1861

Wealth was designed and engraved by Freeman Rawdon; *Mercury* was drawn and engraved by G.W. Hatch; *Justice*, on the right, is probably the work of Rawdon or Hatch. Rawdon, Wright, Hatch & Edson prepared this "old-style," uniface note. This illustrated note sold for $4,500 in Christie's April 2, 1982 auction.

		Notes Issued		
No.	Term	Old Plates	New Plates	Known
1139g	60 days	Unknown	30,152	1

One-year Notes, Act of March 3, 1863

The face design is similar to Nos. 1137–1139d.

The back design includes a counterfeit clause.

		Signatures of Chittenden-Spinner		
No.	Dated	Notes Issued	Outstanding	Known
1140	Feb. 17, 1864 March 25, 1864 June 10, 1864	136,400	62	1 1 1

Interest-bearing Notes/6%/Two-year Notes

This is the only example on which this version of *Liberty* and this *Eagle* appear on U.S. federal currency (NBNCo).

Act of March 2, 1861

| No. | Signatures | Notes Issued | | Known |
		Old Plates	New Plates	
1141	Chittenden-Spinner	8,719	95,848	1

Remarks: In addition to the illustration of No. 1141, complete with face and back, there is a uniface, face proof with plate "C" known. This version of *Liberty* is based on a reversed image that is part of the *Hemicycle* by Paul Delaroche, completed in 1841 for the École des Beaux Arts. See "Liberty" by R. Horstman in *The Essay Proof Journal*, Vol. 45, No. 3, p. 110.

The head of *Liberty* was used on an essay for a Confederate 5¢ stamp, 200E-C. "For the" was probably written on notes from old plates by clerks who were authorized to sign for U.S. Treasury officials. Notes from new plates probably had "For the" engraved in the plate. At least 97,390 notes from new plates were printed; additional notes could have been printed and issued.

Interest-bearing Notes/6%/Act of March 3, 1863/Two-year Notes

The vignettes on either side of the U.S. Treasury building are entitled *Farmer and Mechanics* and *In the Turret*. (ABNCo & NBNCo)

The back design includes a counterfeit clause.

			Notes		
No.	Signatures	Coupons	Printed	Issued	Outstanding
1142	Chittenden-Spinner	0	96,800	96,800	19
1143	Chittenden-Spinner	3	144,800	144,800	80

Remarks: In 1961 this heretofore unknown note was discovered at the Citizens National Bank of Lexington, KY; the illustrations are courtesy of the bank. In addition to the illustrated note another is known with serial number 18114.

Interest-bearing Notes, Three-year Notes/7.3%

The portrait of General Winfield Scott was engraved by Alfred Jones. This illustrated note, on India paper, is unique in that uniface face and back are mounted as a complete note. (ABNCo)

The back design is green.

Act of July 17, 1861
Signatures of Chittenden-Spinner

No.	Dated	Serial Numbers	Notes Issued	Outstanding
1144	Aug. 19, 1861	red	90,000	73
1145	Oct. 1, 1861	red	103,074	37
1146	Oct. 1, 1861	blue	1,066	0

Act of June 30, 1864
Signatures of Colby-Spinner

No.	Dated	Printed	Notes Issued	Outstanding
1147	Aug. 15, 1864	550,400	556,039	219
1148	Mar. 3, 1865	86,552	included in above	

Remarks: The coupons attached to these notes were redeemed at six-month intervals; the notes, by the U.S. Treasury and ABNCo, were redeemed after the last interval. In addition to known proofs, two notes are known for No. 1147, serial numbers 213731 and 250812. Nos. 1147 and 1148 are similar to Nos. 1149 and 1150.

Interest-bearing Notes, Three-year Notes/7.3%

This portrait of General Winfield Scott was engraved by George D. Baldwin. Scott, Supreme Commander of the U.S. Army from July 1841 to Nov. 1861, was, due to his vanity, called "Old Fuss'n Feathers." (ABNCo & BEP)

Act of March 3, 1865
Signatures of Colby-Spinner

No.	Dated	Notes Printed	Issued	Outstanding	Known
1149	June 15, 1865	401,048	338,227	122½	1
1150	July 15, 1865	500,000	472,080	215½	2

Remarks: The recorded serial number for No. 1149 is 272963; the serial numbers for No. 1150 are 193083 and 194009.

National Bank Notes/First Charter Period

The *Battle of Lake Erie*, by W.H. Powell, was engraved by Louis Delnoce. *Union*, at the right, was engraved by James Bannister. (ABNCo)

The presentation of the *Declaration of Independence*, by John Trumbull, was engraved by Frederick Girsch.

No.	Series	Signatures	VGood	VFine
		Red seals have rays.		
1151	orig.	Chittenden-Spinner	$3250.	$6000.
1152	orig.	Colby-Spinner	3000.	5500.
1153	orig.	Allison-Spinner	3000.	5500.
		Red seals have scallops.		
1154	1875	Allison-New	2850.	5500.
1155	1875	Allison-Wyman	--------------- Unique -------------	
1156	1875	Allison-Gilfillan	2750.	5500.
1157	1875	Scofield-Gilfillan	2750.	5500.
1158	1875	Bruce-Gilfillan	3250.	6000.
1159	1875	Bruce-Wyman	3250.	6000.
1160	1875	Rosecrans-Huston	3250.	6000.
1161	1875	Rosecrans-Nebeker	—	—
1162	1875	Tillman-Morgan	—	—

Remarks: The original series had no series date on the face. A total of 16,309 notes for both types are outstanding; about 60 actually exist.

National Bank Notes/Second Charter Period/First Issue/Series 1882/Brown Seal

The face design is similar to Nos. 1151–1162. The back design is similar to Nos. 287–299.

No.	Signatures	VGood	VFine	Une
1163	Bruce-Gilfillan	$850.	$1600.	$5500.
1164	Bruce-Wyman	850.	1600.	5500.
1165	Bruce-Jordan	850.	1600.	5500.
1166	Rosecrans-Jordan	850.	1600.	5500.
1167	Rosecrans-Hyatt	850.	1600.	5500.
1168	Rosecrans-Huston	850.	1600.	5500.
1169	Rosecrans-Nebeker	850.	1600.	5500.
1170	Rosecrans-Morgan	950.	1850.	6500.
1171	Tillman-Morgan	850.	1600.	5500.
1172	Tillman-Roberts	850.	1600.	5500.
1173	Bruce-Roberts	850.	1600.	5500.
1174	Lyons-Roberts	950.	1600.	5500.
1174a	Vernon-Treat	-------------------------- extremely rare ----------------------		

Second Charter Period/Second Issue/Series 1882/Blue Seal

Face design is similar to Nos. 1151–1162. The *Eagle* on the left was engraved by Harry L. Chorlton.

No.	Signatures	VGood	VFine	Une
1175	Rosecrans-Huston	$600.	$1300.	$5000.
1176	Rosecrans-Nebeker	625.	1350.	5250.
1177	Tillman-Morgan	625.	1350.	5250.
1178	Tillman-Roberts	625.	1350.	5250.
1179	Bruce-Roberts	625.	1350.	5250.
1180	Lyons-Roberts	600.	1300.	5000.
1181	Vernon-Treat	700.	1450.	5750.
1182	Napier-McClung	-------------------------- extremely rare ----------------------		

National Bank Notes/Second Charter Period/Series 1882

The face design is similar to No. 1151.

Third Issue—Blue Seal Notes

No.	Signatures	Printed	Issued	Known
1183	Lyons-Roberts	3,100	2,857	4

Remarks: The Winters National Bank of Dayton, Ohio and the Canal-Commercial National Bank of New Orleans were the only two banks to issue this denomination. One of these notes note was purchased for $25,000 in 1974; another sold for $52,500 in 1991.

National Bank Notes/Third Charter Period/Series 1902

John Knox (1826–1892) served as Comptroller of the Currency (1872–1884). Ostrander Smith designed this note; G.F.C. Smillie engraved the portrait.

The back design is the same for all three issues; only the second issue has "1902–1908."

No.	Signatures	VGood	VFine	Une
		First Issue—red seal		
1184	Lyons-Roberts	$1200.	$2250.	$6000.
1185	Lyons-Treat	1200.	2250.	6000.
1186	Vernon-Treat	1400.	2400.	7500.
		Second issue—blue seal		
		"1902–1908"		
1187	Lyons-Roberts	300.	550.	2000.
1188	Lyons-Treat	300.	550.	2000.
1189	Vernon-Treat	300.	550.	2000.
1190	Vernon-McClung	300.	550.	2000.
1191	Napier-McClung	300.	550.	2000.
1192	Napier-Thompson	325.	550.	2150.
1193	Napier-Burke	300.	550.	2000.
1194	Parker-Burke	300.	550.	2000.
1195	Teehee-Burke	325.	550.	2150.

National Bank Notes/Third Charter Period/Series 1902 *(continued)*

The face design is similar to the preceding note.

Third issue—blue seal

No.	Signatures	VGood	VFine	Unc
1196	Lyons-Roberts	$300.	$550.	$2000.
1197	Lyons-Treat	300.	550.	2000.
1198	Vernon-Treat	300.	550.	2000.
1199	Vernon-McClung	300.	550.	2000.
1200	Napier-McClung	300.	550.	2000.
1201	Napier-Thompson	350.	600.	2300.
1201a	Napier-Burke	---------------------------- unknown -------------------------		
1202	Parker-Burke	300.	575.	2100.
1203	Teehee-Burke	300.	575.	2000.
1204	Elliott-Burke	300.	575.	2000.
1205	Elliott-White	300.	575.	2000.
1206	Speelman-White	300.	575.	2000.
1206a	Woods-White	---------------------------- 2 known -------------------------		

National Gold Bank Notes/Red Seal

The face design similar to No. 1151.

The gold coin vignette was engraved by James Smillie.

No.	Date	Issuing Bank	City	Issued	Known
1207	1870	First National Gold Bank of	San Francisco	2000	2
1208	1875	as above on white paper	San Francisco	620	2
1209	1873	First National Gold Bank of	Santa Barbara	200	1
1210	1874	First National Gold Bank of	Petaluma	400	2
1211	1875	Union National Gold Bank	Oakland	100	1
1211a	1872	Nationlal Gold Bank & Trust Co.	San Francisco	2856	0
1211b	1872	National Gold Bank of D.O. Mills Co.	Sacramento	604	0
1211c	1873	First National Gold Bank of	Stockton	867	0
1211d	1874	Farmers' National Gold Bank	San Jose	400	0

Remarks: A total of 84 notes are outstanding. No. 1207 (321148) in fine condition was advertised at $14,000. No. 1209 (375737) in very good condition sold for $59,000 in 1989. No. 1210, in fine condition, sold for $10,500 in 1973. No. 1211 sold for $18,000 in 1979. One of the two known for No. 1208 is in new condition.

Silver Certificates/Series 1878

The portrait of James Monroe (1758–1831), fifth President of the U.S., was engraved by Louis, Delnoce; it is based on a portrait by John Vanderlyn.

The back is brown and black.

No. 1213

Series of 1878 notes have large red seals, signatures of Scofield-Gilfillan and "100" below series. Countersignatures on Nos. 1213 & 1214 are handwritten.

No.	Countersigned by	Payable at	Issued	Known
1212	W.G. White	New York		1
1212a	J.C. Hopper	New York	5,000	0
1212b	T. Hillhouse	New York		0
1213	R.M. Anthony	San Francisco	2,400	1
1214	A.U. Wyman	Washington, DC	4,000	1
1214a	A.U. Wyman	Washington, DC	24,000	4

Remarks: For No. 1212, 8,000 notes were printed; 6,800 probably had autographed countersignatures. The remaining 1,200 could have had the engraved countersignature of T. Hillhouse. See "Series 1878 silver certificates..." by W. Breen, *Numismatic News*, May 24, 1975. No. 1214a, in very fine condition, was advertised by Stack's in 1989 for $59,000.

Silver Certificates/Series 1880 & 1891

The face design is similar to the preceding note. The back design is the same as the following note.

Series of 1880

Seals are brown except for No. 1219; large "C" in center except for No. 1218.

No.	Signatures	Seal	Notes Printed	Known	VGood	VFine	Une
1215	Scofield-Gilfillan	rays	16,000	0	$ —	$ —	$ —
1216	Bruce-Gilfillan	rays	40,000	5	7500.	12500.	—
1217	Bruce-Wyman	rays	80,000	11	4000.	7500.	—
1218	Rosecrans-Huston	spikes	100,000	21	5000.	9000.	—
			Small seal at lower right				
1219	Rosecrans-Nebeker	red	40,000	13	7500.	12500.	—

Series of 1891

The face design is similar to the preceding note. In addition to the portrait, engraving is by D.M. Cooper, W.H. Dougal, J.R. Hall, E.E. Myers, W.G. Phillips and G.U. Rose, Jr. The seal is at right-center.

The back design was engraved by D.M. Cooper, W.H. Dougal, E.M. Hall, W.F. Lutz and G.U. Rose, Jr.

No.	Signatures	Seal	Notes Printed	Known	Fine	EFine	Une
1220	Rosecrans-Nebeker	red	192,000	17	$3250.	$7000.	$12,500.
1221	Tillman-Morgan	red	312,000	27	3000.	6500.	11,000.

Remarks: In 1897 there was an attempt to recall all of No. 1221 due to superb counterfeits by W.M. Jacobs. In early January 1898 four eastern cities reported counterfeits that began with serial number 326. In addition, Cincinnati reported counterfeits that began with serial number 323.

Gold Certificates/Series 1863–1875

E Pluribus Unum was engraved by Charles Skinner. For the complete figure of the *Altar of Liberty*, in lower border, see No. 1435a.

Only the first issue had this back design, undoubtedly the work of American Bank Note Co.

Thomas H. Benton (1782–1858), whose portrait appears on the second and third issues, served in the U.S. Senate and the House of Representatives. Benton favored Western development and spoke out against slavery.

No.	Issue	Date	Signatures	Printed	Issued	Out	Known
1222a	Second	Date	Allison Gilfillan	Printed	116,449	Out	Known
1222	First	1863	Colby-Spinner	118,000	116,449	—	3
1222a	First	1863	Colby-Spinner	included in above		44	3
1223	Second	1870	(There is a proof with no signatures at the BEP.)			—	
1224	Second	1871	Colby-Spinner	50,000	48,000	27	—
1225	Third	1875	Allison-New	56,894	35,984	8	5
1225a	Third	1875	Allison-Gilfillan	included in above		—	3

Remarks: No. 1222 has an autographed countersignature; serial number 11811 is at the Smithsonian Institution, 46425 is in private hands. No. 1222a, with serial number 112853, at the Smithsonian Institution, is payable at Washington, others are payable at New York. Nos. 1225 with serial numbers B5298 and B13104 are at the Smithsonian; No. 1225a with serial number B56887 is at the Bureau of the Public Debt. All three are uniface.

Gold Certificates/Series 1882

The portrait of Thomas H. Benton on this and the preceding note was engraved by Charles Burt.

The *Eagle* on the gold back was engraved by Joseph Ourdan.

No.	Signatures	Notes Printed	Known	VGood	VFine	Unc
		Nos. 1226–1229 have brown seals.				
1226	Bruce-Gilfillan	9,000	2			
1227	Bruce-Gilfillan	71,000	3		no recent sales	
1228	Bruce-Gilfillan	80,000	7			
1229	Bruce-Wyman	40,000	3			
		Seal is larger; No. 1230 is red; No. 1231 is brown				
1230	Rosecrans-Hyatt	40,000	4	$ —	$ —	$ —
1231	Rosecrans-Huston	60,000	7	—	—	—
		All have a small red seal				
1232	Lyons-Roberts	1,160,000	29	300.	500.	3250.
1233	Lyons-Treat	296,000	11	500.	850.	4250.
1234	Vernon-Treat	320,000	19	500.	850.	4350.
1235	Vernon-McClung	402,000	31	300.	850.	3750.
1236	Napier-McClung	202,000	15	500.	850.	4000.
1237	Napier-Thompson	198,000	37	350.	800.	3750.
1238	Napier-Burke	200,000	27	375.	850.	3750.
1239	Parker-Burke	200,000	25	375.	850.	3750.
1240	Teehee-Burke	1,020,000	159	300.	500.	2850.
1241	Speelman-White	2,444,000	123	225.	375.	2000.
1241☆	18 reported			375.	750.	—

Remarks: Nos. 1226 & 1227 are payable at New York; both are countersigned by Thomas C. Acton. No. 1226 bears an autographed countersignature. No. 1241 is dated 1922.

Treasury or Coin Notes/Series 1890 & 1891

David G. Farragut (1811–1870) was the first man to hold the rank of admiral in the U.S. Navy. Although he was born in Tennessee, he served in the Union Navy during the Civil War. His portrait was engraved by Charles Schlecht.

The back design was engraved by W.A. Copenhaver, W.H. Dougal, G.U. Rose, Jr. and J.A. Rueff. The shape and color of the zeros prompt collectors to call this the watermelon note. (See No. 1425)

No.	Series	Signatures	Seal	Printed	Known	VGood	VFine	Unc
1242	1890	Rosecrans-Huston	brown	120,000	31	$6,750.	$16,500.	—

The face design is similar to the preceding note; the seal is smaller. The back design was engraved by D.M. Cooper, W.H. Dougal, E.M. Hall and E.E. Myers.

No.	Series	Signatures	Seal	Printed	Known	VGood	VFine	Unc
1243	1891	Rosecrans-Nebeker	red	80,000	11	$12,500.	$30,000.	—

Remarks: For No. 1242, 298 notes are outstanding. For No. 1243, 60,000 were issued. Ten of the known notes are: B3958, B48693, B6388, B7296, B10662, B14471, B17039, B47137, B55602 and B79901. No. B48693 in F-VF condition sold for $16,500 in 1996.

Federal Reserve Notes/Series 1914/Red Seal

The portrait of Benjamin Franklin was engraved by Marcus W. Baldwin.

Labor, Plenty, America, Peace and Commerce by Kenyon Cox was engraved by G.F.C. Smillie. This design was originally intended for all denominations of U.S. small-size currency.

Signatures of Burke-McAdoo

No.	Bank	Notes Issued	VGood	VFine	Unc
1244A-I	Boston	16,000	$275.	$600.	$2200.
1244A-II		28,000	275.	600.	2200.
1244B-I	New York	60,000	275.	600.	2200.
1244B-II		20,000	275.	600.	2200.
1244C-I	Philadelphia	12,000	300.	650.	2300.
1244C-II		40,000	275.	600.	2200.
1244D-I	Cleveland	8,000	350.	650.	2350.
1244D-II		40,000	275.	600.	2200.
1244E-I	Richmond	16,000	275.	600.	2200.
1244E-II		8,000	350.	650.	2350.
1244F-I	Atlanta	16,000	275.	600.	2200.
1244F-II		4,000	350.	650.	2500.
1244G-I	Chicago	16,000	275.	600.	2200.
1244G-II		44,000	275.	600.	2200.
1244H-I	St. Louis	12,000	275.	650.	2300.
1244H-II		20,000	275.	600.	2200.
1244I-I	Minneapolis	8,000	350.	650.	2500.
1244I-II		12,000	300.	600.	2300.
1244J-I	Kansas City	8,000	350.	650.	2400.
1244J-II		12,000	300.	600.	2300.
1244K-I	Dallas	8,000	350.	650.	2400.
1244K-II		8,000	350.	650.	2500.
1244L-I	San Francisco	8,000	350.	650.	2500.
1244L-II					

Remarks: The first day of issue was November 16, 1914. The number of notes issued was compiled by Doug Murray. About 500 notes are probably outstanding. Type II has the small district number and letter in the upper left and lower right corners. See No. 380 for illustrations. Known for types I & II A–21 & 9; B–11 & 4; C–8 & 14; D–4 & 18; E–10 & 4; F–6 & 1; G–6 & 20; H–7 & 6; I–2 & 6; J–8 & 11; K–5 & 5; L–8 & 20 (Gengerke).

Federal Reserve Notes/Series 1914/Blue Seal

No.	Bank	Signatures	Printed	Issued	VFine	Unc
1245A1	Boston	Burke-McAdoo			$225.	$700.
1245A2	Boston	Burke-Glass	728,000	728,000	250.	800.
1245A4	Boston	White-Mellon			225.	700.
1245B1	New York	Burke-McAdoo			225.	700.
1245B1☆	1 reported				225.	700.
1245B2	New York	Burke-Glass			250.	800.
1245B3	New York	Burke-Houston	3,084,000	3,084,000	225.	700.
1245B3☆	1 reported				—	—
1245B4	New York	White Mellon			225.	700.
1245C1	Philadelphia	Burke-McAdoo	666,000	636,000	225.	700.
1245C4	Philadelphia	White-Mellon	included in above		225.	700.
1245D1	Cleveland	Burke-McAdoo			225.	700.
1245D2	Cleveland	Burke-Glass			250.	800.
1245D3	Cleveland	Burke-Houston	668,000	668,000	225.	700.
1245D3☆	1 reported				—	—
1245D4	Cleveland	White-Mellon			225.	700.
1245E1	Richmond	Burke-McAdoo			225.	700.
1245E1☆	1 reported		504,000	416,000	—	—
1245E2	Richmond	Burke-Glass			250.	800.
1245E4	Richmond	White-Mellon			225.	700.
1245F1	Atlanta	Burke-McAdoo			225.	700.
1245F1☆	1 reported				—	—
1245F3	Atlanta	Burke-Houston	540,000	476,000	225.	700.
1245F4	Atlanta	White-Mellon			225.	700.
1245G1	Chicago	Burke-McAdoo			225.	700.
1245G1☆	1 reported		888,000	888,000	—	—
1245G3	Chicago	Burke-Houston			225.	700.
1245G4	Chicago	White-Mellon			225.	700.
1245H1	St. Louis	Burke-McAdoo	188,000	188,000	225.	800.
1245H4	St. Louis	White-Mellon	included in above		225.	700.
1245I1	Minneapolis	Burke-McAdoo	124,000	120,000	225.	700.
1245I4	Minneapolis	White-Mellon	included in above		225.	700.
1245J1	Kansas City	Burke-McAdoo			225.	700.
1245J1☆	1 reported		256,000	256,000	—	—
1245J4	Kansas City	White-Mellon			225.	700.
1245K1	Dallas	Burke-McAdoo			225.	700.
1245K1☆	1 reported		256,000	256,000	—	—
1245K4	Dallas	White-Mellon			225.	700.
1245L1	San Francisco	Burke-McAdoo			225.	700.
1245L1☆	1 reported				—	—
1245L3	San Francisco	Burke-Houston	1,064,000	1,064,000	225.	700.
1245L4	San Francisco	White-Mellon			225.	700.

Remarks: Doug Murray reports that no plates were made for Nos. 1245A3, 1245C2, & 3, 1245E3, 1245F2, 1245G2, 1245H2 & 3, 1245I2 & 3, 1245J2 & 3, 1245 K2 & 3, and 1245L2. A total of 4,000 replacement notes were printed for each district except New York, which had 8,000 printed. Tom Conklin star notes in CAA Oct. 1995 sale, 1245J1☆ at $1650 in fine and 1245K1☆ at $1870 in VF-EF.

United States Notes/Series 1966 & 1966A/Red Seal

The portrait of Benjamin Franklin by J.S. Duplessis, after a portrait by J.B. Longacre, was engraved by John Eissler; it appears on all small-size $100 notes.

The back design with *Independence Hall* in Philadelphia was engraved by F. Lamasure, W.H. Hall, J.C. Benzing and H.S. Nutter.

No.	Series	Signatures	Notes Printed	VFine	Unc
1246	1966	Granahan-Fowler	768,000	$ —	$250.
1246☆			128,000	—	500.
1247	1966A	Elston-Kennedy	512,000	150.	650.

Remarks: As many as 700,000, for both issues, might have entered circulation. These $100 notes were intended to replace the $2 and $5 red seal notes. In October 1976 they were first released in Washington, DC, New York City and perhaps Puerto Rico; remaining $100 notes were held by Federal Reserve Banks. These notes are now being withdrawn as they come into banks.

Federal Reserve Bank Notes/Series 1929/Brown Seal

See No. 1247 for descriptive information.

Signatures of Jones-Woods

No.	Bank	Notes Printed	EFine	Une
1248A	Boston	not printed	$ —	$ —
1248B	New York	480,000	150.	200.
1248B☆		12,000	500.	1850.
1248C	Philadelphia	not printed	—	—
1248D	Cleveland	276,000	150.	225.
1248D☆		—	300.	1000.
1248E	Richmond	192,000	175.	225.
1248E☆		—	500	1000.
1248F	Atlanta	not printed	—	—
1248G	Chicago	384,000	175.	200.
1248G☆		12,000	350.	1000.
1248H	St. Louis	not printed	—	—
1248I	Minneapolis	144,000	175.	200.
1248☆		12,000	350.	1000.
1248J	Kansas City	96,000	175.	275.
1248J☆		12,000	350.	750.
1248K	Dallas	36,000	200.	400.
1248K☆		12,000	500.	2000.
1248L	San Francisco	not printed	—	—

National Bank Notes/Series 1929/Brown Seal

Type I

Type II has the bank charter number printed a second time near the serial number.

		Type I			Type II		
No.	Rarity	VFine	EFine	Une	VFine	EFine	Une
	1	$135	$175.	$200.	$200.	$275.	875.
	2	145.	195.	250.	210.	285.	900.
	3	175.	210.	275.	225.	300.	925.
	4	225.	235.	315.	240.	315.	950.
1249	5	235.	275.	325.	255.	330.	1000.
	6	235.	315.	375.	270.	345.	1050.
	7	275.	365.	500.	285.	375.	1100.
	8	400.	500.	800.	500.	650.	1400.
	9			none were issued			

Remarks: A total of 456,915 notes were issued for both types. Banks in the following states did not issue this denomination: Alabama, Alaska, Arizona, Arkansas, Georgia, Maine, New Mexico, South Carolina and Utah.

Federal Reserve Notes/Series 1928 & 1928A/Green Seal

The district number appears in the seal. The district letter replaces the number.

Series 1928, Woods-Mellon

No.	Bank	Notes Printed	Unc
1250A	Boston	376,000	$175.
1250A☆			475.
1250B	New York	755,400	175.
1250B☆			375.
1250C	Philadelphia	389,000	175.
1250C☆			475.
1250D	Cleveland	542,400	175.
1250D☆			475.
1250E	Richmond	364,416	175.
1250E☆			475.
1250F	Atlanta	357,000	175.
1250F☆			475.
1250G	Chicago	783,000	175.
1250G☆			350.
1250H	St. Louis	187,200	200.
1250H☆			425.
1250I	Minneapolis	102,000	200.
1250I☆			475.
1250J	Kansas City	234,000	175.
1250J☆			475.
1250K	Dallas	80,140	200.
1250K☆			500.
1250L	San Francisco	486,000	175.
1250L☆			425.

Series 1928A, Woods-Mellon

No.	Bank	Notes Printed	Unc
1251A	Boston	980,400	$175.
1251A☆			not printed
1251B	New York	2,938,000	165.
1251B☆			not printed
1251C	Philadelphia	1,496,000	165.
1251C☆			not printed
1251D	Cleveland	993,436	175.
1251D☆			not printed
1251E	Richmond	621,364	175.
1251E☆			not printed
1251F	Atlanta	371,400	175.
1251F☆			not printed
1251G	Chicago	4,010,424	165.
1251G☆			not printed
1251H	St. Louis	749,424	175.
1251H☆		reported	—
1251I	Minneapolis	503,040	175.
1251I☆			not printed
1251J	Kansas City	681,804	175.
1251J☆			not printed
1251K	Dallas	594,456	175.
1251K☆			not printed
1251L	San Francisco	1,228,032	165.
1251L☆			not printed

Federal Reserve Notes/Series 1934/Green Seal *(Continued)*

Series 1934, Julian-Morgenthau

No.	Bank	Notes Printed	Unc	No.	Bank	Notes Printed	Unc
1252A	Boston	3,710,000	$175.	**1252G**	Chicago	7,075,000	$175.
1252A☆			200.	**1252G**☆		—	200.
1252B	New York	3,086,000	175.	**1252H**	St. Louis	2,106,192	175.
1252B☆			200.	**1252H**☆			200,
1252C	Philadelphia	2,776,000	175.	**1252I**	Minneapolis	852,600	175.
1252C☆			250.	**1252I**☆			250.
1252D	Cleveland	3,447,108	175.	**1252J**	Kansas City	1,932,900	175.
1252D☆			250.	**1252J**☆			200.
1252E	Richmond	4,317,600	175.	**1252K**	Dallas	1,506,516	175.
1252E☆			250.	**1252K**☆			200.
1252F	Atlanta	3,264,000	175.	**1252L**	San Francisco	6,521,940	175.
1252F☆			275.	**1252L**☆			200.

Remarks: Some star notes, depending on the light or dark seal, command higher premiums.

Federal Reserve Notes/Series 1934A, 1934B, 1934C, 1934D, 1950 &1950A/Green Seal

Series 1934A, Julian-Morgenthau

No.	Bank	Notes Printed	Une
1253A	Boston	102,000	$225.
1253A☆			250.
1253B	New York	15,278,892	150.
1253B☆			225.
1253C	Philadelphia	588,000	175.
1253D	Cleveland	645,300	175.
1253E	Richmond	770,100	175.
1253F	Atlanta	589,896	175.
1253G	Chicago	3,328,800	175.
1253G☆			250.
1253H	St. Louis	434,208	175.
1253I	Minneapolis	153,000	200.
1253J	Kansas City	455,100	175.
1253K	Dallas	226,164	200.
1253L	San Francisco	1,130,000	175.
1253L☆			250.

Series 1934B, Julian-Vinson

No.	Bank	Notes Printed	Une
1254A	Boston	41,400	$225.
1254A☆		not printed	—
1254B	New York		225.
1254B☆		not printed	—
1254C	Philadelphia	39,600	225.
1254D	Cleveland	61,200	275.
1254E	Richmond	877,400	225.
1254F	Atlanta	645,000	225.
1254F☆		—	—
1254G	Chicago	396,000	225.
1254H	St. Louis	672,200	225.
1254I	Minneapolis	377,000	225.
1254J	Kansas City	364,500	225.
1254K	Dallas	392,700	225.
1254K☆		reported	—
1254L	San Francisco	not printed	—

Series 1934C, Julian-Snyder

No.	Bank	Notes Printed	Une
1255A	Boston	13,800	$200.
1255B	New York	1,556,000	160.
1255C	Philadelphia	13,200	200.
1255D	Cleveland	1,473,200	160.
1255E	Richmond	no record	—
1255F	Atlanta	493,900	175.
1255G	Chicago	612,000	175.
1255H	St. Louis	957,000	175.
1255H☆		—	—
1255I	Minneapolis	392,904	175.
1255J	Kansas City	401,100	175.
1255K	Dallas	280,700	175
1255L	San Francisco	432,600	175.
1255L☆		not printed	—

Series 1934D, Clark-Snyder

No.	Bank	Notes Printed	Une
1256A	Boston	no record	$ —
1256B	New York	156	2500.
1256C	Philadelphia	308,400	175.
1256D	Cleveland	no record	—
1256E	Richmond	no record	—
1256F	Atlanta	260,400	175.
1256G	Chicago	78,000	175.
1256H	St. Louis	166,800	175.
1265H☆			
1256I	Minneapolis	no record	—
1256J	Kansas City	no record	—
1256K	Dallas	66,000	175.
1256K☆		not printed	—
1256L	San Francisco	no record	—

Smaller letter and Federal Reserve seal on No. 1257.

Series 1950, Clark-Snyder

No.	Bank	Notes Printed	Unc
1257A	Boston	768,000	$150.
1257B	New York	3,908,000	135.
1257C	Philadelphia	1,332,000	135.
1257C☆			175.
1257D	Cleveland	1,632,000	135.
1257E	Richmond	4,076,000	135.
1257F	Atlanta	1,824,900	135.
1257G	Chicago	4,428,000	135.
1257H	St. Louis	1,284,000	135.
1257H☆			175.
1257I	Minneapolis	564,000	150.
1257J	Kansas City	864,000	150.
1257K	Dallas	1,216,000	135.
1257L	San Francisco	2,524,000	135.
1257L☆		not printed	—

Series 1950A, Priest-Humphrey

No.	Bank	Notes Printed	Unc
1258A	Boston	1,008,000	$135.
1258B	New York	2,880,000	135.
1258B☆			225.
1258C	Philadelphia	720,000	150.
1258D	Cleveland	432,000	150.
1258E	Richmond	1,008,000	135.
1258F	Atlanta	576,000	150.
1258G	Chicago	2,592,000	135.
1258G☆			150.
1268H	St. Louis	1,152,000	135.
1258I	Minneapolis	288,000	160.
1258J	Kansas City	720,000	150.
1258K	Dallas	1,728,000	135.
1258K☆			150.
1258L	San Francisco	2,880,000	135.

Federal Reserve Notes/1950B, 1950C, 1950D, 1950E & 1963A/Green Seal

Series 1950B, Priest-Anderson

No.	Bank	Notes Printed	Unc
1259A	Boston	720,000	$150.
1259B	New York	6,636,000	130.
1259C	Philadelphia	720,000	150.
1259D	Cleveland	432,000	150.
1259E	Richmond	1,008,000	130.
1259F	Atlanta	576,000	150.
1259G	Chicago	2,592,000	130.
1259G☆			200.
1259H	St. Louis	1,152,000	130.
1259I	Minneapolis	288,000	165.
1259J	Kansas City	720,000	150.
1259K	Dallas	1,728,000	130.
1259K☆			200.
1259L	San Francisco	2,880,000	135.

Series 1950C, Smith-Dillon

No.	Bank	Notes Printed	Unc
1260A	Boston	864,000	$135.
1260B	New York	2,448,000	125.
1260C	Philadelphia	576,000	135.
1260D	Cleveland	576,000	135.
1260E	Richmond	1,440,000	125.
1260F	Atlanta	1,296,000	125.
1260G	Chicago	1,584,000	125.
1260H	St. Louis	720,000	135.
1260G☆			275.
1260I	Minneapolis	288,000	150.
1260J	Kansas City	432,000	135.
1260K	Dallas	720,000	135.
1260K☆		not printed	
1260L	San Francisco	2,160,000	125.

Series 1950D, Granahan-Dillon

No.	Bank	Notes Printed	Unc
1261A	Boston	1,872,000	$125.
1261B	New York	7,632,000	125.
1261C	Philadelphia	1,872,000	125.
1261D	Cleveland	1,584,000	125.
1261D☆			375.
1261E	Richmond	2,880,000	125.
1261E☆			375.
1261F	Atlanta	1,872,000	125.
1261G	Chicago	4,608,000	125.
1261H	St. Louis	1,440,000	135.
1261I	Minneapolis	432,000	135.
1261J	Kansas City	864,000	135.
1261K	Dallas	1,728,000	125.
1261L	San Francisco	3,312,000	125.

Series 1963A, Granahan-Fowler

No.	Bank	Notes Printed	Unc
1263A	Boston	1,536,000	$135.
1263A☆		128,000	200.
1263B	New York	12,544,000	135.
1263B☆		1,536,000	175.
1263C	Philadelphia	1,440,000	135.
1263C☆		192,000	200.
1263D	Cleveland	2,304,000	135.
1263D☆	Chicago	192,000	135.
1263E	Richmond	2,816,000	135.
1263E☆		192,000	200.
1263F	Atlanta	1,280,000	135.
1263F☆		128,000	200.
1263G	Chicago	4,352,000	135.
1263G☆		512,000	175.
1263H	St. Louis	1,536,000	135.
1263H☆		256,000	200.
1263I	Minneapolis	512,000	150.
1263I☆		128,000	200.
1263J	Kansas City	1,024,000	135.
1263J☆		128,000	200.
1263K	Dallas	1,536,000	135.
1263K☆		192,000	175.
1263L	San Francisco	6,400,000	135.
1263L☆		832,000	135.

Series 1950E, Granahan-Fowler

No.	Bank	Notes Printed	Unc
1262B	New York	3,024,000	$125.
1262B☆			650.
1262G	Chicago	576,000	175.
1262L	San Francisco	2,736,000	135.
1262L☆		—	—

"IN GOD WE TRUST" added to the back
of 1963A and all subsequent notes.

Federal Reserve Notes/1969, 1969A, 1969C & 1974/Green Seal

Series 1969, Elston-Kennedy

No.	Bank	Notes Printed	Unc
1264A	Boston	2,048,000	$130.
1264A☆		128,000	185.
1264B	New York	11,520,000	130.
1264B☆		192,000	185.
1264C	Philadelphia	2,560,000	130.
1264C☆		128,000	185.
1264D	Cleveland	768,000	140.
1264D☆		64,000	200.
1264E	Richmond	2,560,000	130.
1264E☆		192,000	175.
1264F	Atlanta	2,304,000	130.
1264F☆		128,000	185.
1264G	Chicago	5,888,000	130.
1264G☆		256,000	185.
1264H	St. Louis	1,280,000	130.
1264H☆		64,000	225.
1264I	Minneapolis	512,000	140.
1264I☆		64,000	225.
1264J	Kansas City	1,792,000	130.
1264J☆		384,000	185.
1264K	Dallas	2,048,000	130.
1264K☆		1,048,000	185.
1264L	San Francisco	7,168,000	130.
1264L☆		320,000	185.

Series 1969A, Kabis-Connally

No.	Bank	Notes Printed	Unc
1265A	Boston	1,280,000	$130.
1265A☆		320,000	185.
1265B	New York	11,264,000	130.
1265B☆		640,000	175.
1265C	Philadelphia	2,048,000	130.
1265C☆		448,000	185.
1265D	Cleveland	1,280,000	130.
1265D☆		192,000	185.
1265E	Richmond	2,304,000	130.
1265E☆		192,000	185.
1265F	Atlanta	2,304,000	130.
1265F☆		649,000	175.
1265G	Chicago	5,376,000	130.
1265G☆		320,000	185.
1265H	St. Louis	1,024,000	130.
1265H☆		664,000	175.
1265I	Minneapolis	1,024,000	130.
1265I☆		not printed	—
1265J	Kansas City	512,000	140.
1265J☆		not printed	—
1265K	Dallas	3,328,000	130
1265K☆		128,000	225.
1265L	San Francisco	4,352,000	130.
1265L☆		576,000	185.

Series 1969B $20 notes were not printed.

Series 1969C, Banuelos-Shultz

No.	Bank	Notes Printed	Unc
1267A	Boston	2,048,000	$135.
1267A☆		64,000	275.
1267B	New York	15,616,000	125.
1267B☆		256,000	185.
1267C	Philadelphia	2,816,000	125.
1267C☆		64,000	275.
1267D	Cleveland	3,456,000	125.
1267D☆		64,000	275.
1267E	Richmond	7,296,000	125.
1267E☆		128,000	225.
1267F	Atlanta	2,432,000	135.
1267F☆		64,000	275.
1267G	Chicago	6,016,000	125.
1267G☆		320,000	185.
1267H	St. Louis	5,376,000	125.
1267H☆		64,000	275.
1267I	Minneapolis	512,000	150.
1267I☆		64,000	275.
1267J	Kansas City	4,736,000	125.
1267J☆		192,000	185.
1267K	Dallas	2,944,000	125.
1267K☆		64,000	275.
1267L	San Francisco	10,240,000	125.
1267L☆		512,000	185.

Series 1974, Neff-Simon

No.	Bank	Notes Printed	Unc
1268A	Boston	19,200,000	$120.
1268A☆		320,000	185.
1268B	New York	166,400,000	120.
1268B☆		1,664,000	140.
1268C	Philadelphia	5,120,000	120.
1268C☆		128,000	275.
1268D	Cleveland	16,640,000	120.
1268D☆		192,000	185.
1268E	Richmond	24,320,000	120.
1268E☆		384,000	185.
1268F	Atlanta	3,840,000	120.
1268F☆		704,000	185.
1268G	Chicago	39,680,000	120.
1268G☆		704,000	150.
1268H	St. Louis	15,120,000	120.
1268H☆		448,000	185.
1268I	Minneapolis	5,120,000	120.
1268I☆		192,000	185.
1268J	Kansas City	20,480,000	120.
1268J☆		640,000	185.
1268K	Dallas	38,400,000	120.
1268K☆		640,000	185.
1268L	San Francisco	39,680,000	120.
1268L☆		448,000	150.

Federal Reserve Notes/1977, 1981, 1981A & 1985/Green Seal

Series 1977, Morton-Blumenthal

No.	Bank	Notes Printed	Unc
1269A	Boston	19,200,000	$120.
1269A☆		320,000	145.
1269B	New York	166,400,000	120.
1269B☆		1,664,000	135.
1269C	Philadelphia	5,120,000	120.
1269C☆		128,000	145.
1269D	Cleveland	16,640,000	120.
1269D☆		192,000	135.
1269E	Richmond	24,320,000	120.
1269E☆		384,000	135.
1269F	Atlanta	3,840,000	120.
1269F☆		64,000	175.
1269G	Chicago	39,680,000	120.
1269G☆		704,000	135.
1269H	St. Louis	15,120,000	120.
1269H☆		448,000	135.
1269I	Minneapolis	5,120,000	120.
1269I☆		192,000	145.
1269J	Kansas City	20,480,000	120.
1269J☆		640,000	135.
1269K	Dallas	38,400,000	120.
1269K☆		640,000	135.
1269L	San Francisco	39,680,000	120.
1269L☆		448,000	130.

Series 1981, Buchanan-Regan

No.	Bank	Notes Printed	Unc
1270A	Boston	8,560,000	$120.
1270A☆		not printed	—
1270B	New York	95,600,000	—
1270B☆		not printed	—
1270C	Philadelphia	12,800,000	120.
1270C☆		not printed	—
1270D	Cleveland	8,960,000	120.
1270D☆		not printed	—
1270E	Richmond	23,680,000	120.
1270E☆		1,280,000	115.
1270F	Atlanta	640,000	120.
1270F☆		not printed	—
1270G	Chicago	33,280,000	120.
1270G☆		not printed	—
1270H	St. Louis	5,760,000	120.
1270H☆		not printed	—
1270I	Minneapolis	3,200,000	120.
1270I☆		not printed	—
1270J	Kansas City	23,680,000	120.
1270J☆		640,000	150.
1270K	Dallas	23,680,000	120.
1270K☆		not printed	—
1270L	San Francisco	24,960,000	120.
1270L☆		not printed	—

Series 1981A, Ortega-Regan

No.	Bank	Notes Printed	Unc
1271A	Boston	16,000,000	$120.
1271A☆		not printed	—
1271B	New York	64,000,000	120.
1271B☆		not printed	—
1271C	Philadelphia	3,200,000	120.
1271C☆		not printed	—
1271D	Cleveland	6,400,000	120.
1271D☆		not printed	—
1271E	Richmond	12,800,000	120.
1271E☆		not printed	—
1271F	Atlanta	12,800,000	120.
1271F☆		not printed	—
1271G	Chicago	22,400,000	120.
1271G☆		not printed	—
1271H	St. Louis	12,800,000	120.
1271H☆		not printed	—
1271I	Minneapolis	3,200,000	120.
1271I☆		not printed	—
1271J	Kansas City	not printed	—
1271J☆		not printed	—
1271K	Dallas	3,200,000	120.
1271K☆		not printed	—
1271L	San Francisco	19,200,000	120.
1271L☆		640,000	135.

Series 1985 Ortega-Baker

No.	Bank	Notes Printed	Unc
1272A	Boston	3,200,000	$120.
1272A☆		not printed	—
1272B	New York	369,200,000	120.
1272B☆		not printed	—
1272C	Philadelphia	19,200,000	120.
1272C☆		not printed	—
1272D	Cleveland	28,800,000	120.
1272D☆		3,200,000	135.
1272E	Richmond	54,400,000	120.
1272E☆		not printed	—
1272F	Atlanta	16,000,000	120.
1272F☆		not printed	—
1272G	Chicago	64,000,000	120.
1272G☆		not printed	—
1272H	St. Louis	12,800,000	120.
1272H☆		not printed	—
1272I	Minneapolis	12,800,000	120.
1272I☆		not printed	—
1272J	Kansas City	12,800,000	120.
1272J☆		3,200,000	135.
1272K	Dallas	48,000,000	120.
1272K☆		3,200,000	135.
1272L	San Francisco	38,400,000	120.
1272L☆		not printed	—

Federal Reserve Notes/1988, 1990, 1993 & 1996/Green Seal

Series 1988, Ortega-Brady

No.	Bank	Notes Printed	Unc
1273A	Boston	9,600,000	$120.
1273A☆		not printed	—
1273B	New York	505,600,000	120.
1273B☆		4,480,000	135.
1273C	Philadelphia	9,600,000	120.
1273C☆		not printed	—
1273D	Cleveland	35,200,000	120.
1273D☆		not printed	—
1273E	Richmond	19,200,000	120.
1273E☆		not printed	—
1273F	Atlanta	not printed	—
1273F☆		not printed	—
1273G	Chicago	51,200,000	120.
1273G☆		not printed	—
1273H	St. Louis	not printed	120.
1273H☆		not printed	—
1273I	Minneapolis	not printed	—
1273I☆		not printed	—
1273J	Kansas City	9,600,000	120.
1273J☆		not printed	—
1273K	Dallas	not printed	—
1273K☆		not printed	—
1273L	San Francisco	19,200,000	120.
1273L☆		not printed	—

Series 1990 Villalpando-Brady

No.	Bank	Notes Printed	Unc
1274A	Boston	167,000,000	$115.
1274A☆		not printed	—
1274B	New York	595,200,000	—
1274B☆		9,600,000	135.
1274C	Philadelphia	112,000,000	—
1274C☆		3,200,000	135.
1274D	Cleveland	115,200,000	—
1274D☆		not printed	—
1274E	Richmond	108,800,000	115.
1274E☆		not printed	—
1274F	Atlanta	163,200,000	115.
1274F☆		not printed	—
1274G	Chicago	134,400,000	115.
1274G☆		3,200,000	135.
1274H	St. Louis	121,600,000	115.
1274H☆		not printed	—
1274I	Minneapolis	147,200,000	115.
1274I☆		not printed	—
1274J	Kansas City	166,400,000	115.
1274J☆		3,200,000	135.
1274K	Dallas	166,400,000	115.
1274K☆		3,200,000	135.
1274L	San Francisco	147,200,000	115.
1274L☆		3,200,000	135.

Series 1993, Withrow-Bentsen

No.	Bank	Notes Printed	Unc
1275A	Boston	83,200,000	$ —
1275A☆		not printed	—
1275B	New York	224,000,000	—
1275B☆		40,000	125.
1275C	Philadelphia	41,600,000	—
1275C☆		1,280,000	115.
1275D	Cleveland	9,600,000	—
1275D☆		32,000	150.
1275E	Richmond	64,000,000	—
		not printed	—
1275F	Atlanta	150,400,000	—
1275F☆		not printed	—
1275G	Chicago	44,800,000	—
1275G☆		not printed	—
1275H	St. Louis	60,000,000	—
1275H☆		20,000	175.
1275I	Minneapolis	9,600,000	—
1275I☆		not printed	—
1275J	Kansas City	9,600,000	—
1275J☆		not printed	—
1275K	Dallas	48,000,000	—
1273K☆		not printed	—
1275L	San Francisco	16,200,000	—
1275L☆		not printed	

Series 1996, Withrow-Rubin

No.	Bank	Notes Printed	Unc
1276A	Boston	52,200,000	$ —
1276A☆		2,560,000	115.
1276B	New York	560,000,000	—
1276B☆		6,400,000	115.
1276C	Philadelphia	16,000,000	—
1276C☆			—
1276D	Cleveland	128,000,000	—
1276D☆		160,000	—
1276E	Richmond	131,200,000	—
1276E☆			—
1276F	Atlanta	32,000,000	—
1276F☆			—
1276G	Chicago	70,400,000	—
1276G☆			—
1276H	St. Louis	28,000,000	—
1276H☆			—
1276I	Minneapolis	9,600,000	—
1276I☆			—
1276J	Kansas City	19,200,000	—
1276J☆			—
1276K	Dallas	25,600,000	—
1276K☆			—
1276L	San Francisco	297,600,000	—
1276L☆		2,560,000	115.

Figures for Series 1996 are incomplete.

Federal Reserve Notes/1996/Green Seal

A security strip made is appearance with Series 1990. Microprinting, which cannot be reproduced on a photocopier, surrounds the portrait.

Series 1996

The second letter of the serial number identifies the Federal Reserve district. (See page for complete data.) Production for 1996 should total 1.2 billion $100 notes.

The Joseph Siffred Duplesis portrait of Benjamin Franklin was engraved by Thomas Hipschen. This note was then photoengraved under the supervision of William Baechler.

T. Hipschen and W. Baechler also created the image of Independence Hall. Jack Ruther designed both face and back.

Gold Certificate/Series 1928, 1928A & 1934

The portrait of Benjamin Franklin was engraved by Joseph Eissler. Other engravers were E.M. Hall and F. Lamasure.

The back design is similar to No. 1248.

No.	Series	Signatures	Notes Printed	VFine	Unc
1319	1928	Woods-Mellon	3,240,000	$200.	$ 750.
1319☆			11,566	400.	2250.
1319A	1928A	Woods-Mills	120,000	not issued	
1319Aa	1934	Woods-Mills	120,000	not issued	

United States Notes/Series 1862 & 1863/Red Seal

Albert Gallatin was elected to the U.S. Senate from Pennsylvania in 1793, 13 years after he arrived in America from Switzerland, where he was born in 1761. He served as Secretary of the Treasury and Minister to England and France. From 1832–1839 Gallatin was president of the National Bank of New York. This portrait was altered by Alfred Jones.

Signatures of Chittenden-Spinner

No.	Series	Obligation	Notes Printed	Notes Issued	Notes Outstanding	Known
1320	1862	First				2
1320a	1862	Second				0
1321	1863	Second	118,072	117,972	451	3
1321a	1863	Second				1

Remarks: The following serial numbers have been recorded: for No. 1320, 23956; No. 1321, 42223, 42227, 49519, and 64984. No. 1321a has duplicate serial numbers. A. Gallatin is one of five Americans of foreign birth to appear on U.S. paper money. The others are A. Hamilton, E.D. Baker (No. 1441), R. Morris (No. 578) and G.G. Meade (No. 1425).

United States Notes/Series 1869

Charles Burt engraved the portrait of John Quincy Adams (1735–1826), sixth president of the U.S. Adams was appointed Minister to Holland in 1794, Berlin in 1809, and England in 1815. Following his presidency he was elected to Congress. Adams assembled a nice collection of coins. *Justice* was engraved by S.A. Schoff.

No.	Series	Signatures	Seal	Notes Printed	Issued	Notes Outstanding	Known
1322	1869	Allison-Spinner	lg. red	89,360	87,980	499	6

Enlargement of the center of the back.

Remarks: These notes were withdrawn due to deceptive counterfeits. Martin Gengerke reports that one of the known notes, N32610, is questionable. The serial numbers of other recorded notes are: N16035, N16051, N31963, and N48792.

United States Notes/Series 1874–1880

Joseph King Mansfield (1803–1862), a West Point graduate, was born in New Haven Connecticut. Early in the Civil War he was made a brigadier general and was killed at the Battle of Antietam. His portrait and the figure of *Victory* were engraved by Charles Burt.

No.	Series	Signatures	Seal	Notes Printed	Known
		Nos. 1123A-1125 have large "D" twice, and red seals.			
1323	1874	Allison-Spinner	rays	56,000	4
1324	1875	Allison-New	rays	32,000	1
1325	1875	Allison-Wyman	rays	24,000	1
1326	1878	Allison-Gilfillan	rays	24,000	6
		All but Nos. 1327, 1328 & 1332 have red seals.			
1327	1880	Scofield-Gilfillan	brown	—	0
1328	1880	Bruce-Wyman	brown	12,000	2
1329	1880	Rosecrans-Jordan	large	8,000	0
1330	1880	Rosecrans-Hyatt	plain	20,000	0
1331	1880	Rosecrans-Huston	lg. spikes	—	3
1332	1880	Rosecrans-Nebeker	brown	16,000	2
1333	1880	Tillman-Morgan	scallops	20,000	6
1334	1880	Bruce-Roberts	scallops	8,000	5
1335	1880	Lyons-Roberts	scallops	12,000	5
1336	1880	Napier-McClung	scallops	existence doubtful	

Remarks: In 1983 No. 1323 (Z5381) sold for $44,500; No. 1326 (A4026) sold for $55,000. In 1996 No. 1335 (A85034) sold for $46,200. All were in EFine condition.

Compound Interest Treasury Notes/6%/Act of March 3, 1863

The Standard Bearer was engraved by George D. Baldwin. James Smillie engraved *New Ironsides.*

The back design includes an interest table.

Act of March 3, 1863

No.	Signatures	Printed	Notes Issued	Notes Outstanding	Known
1337	Chittenden-Spinner	June 10, 1864	—	16,468	1	1
1338	Colby-Spinner	June 10, 1864	—	0	0	0

Act of June 30, 1864

No.	Signatures	Printed	Notes Issued	Notes Outstanding	Known
1339	Chittenden-Spinner	July 15, 1864	84,612	76,000	22	1
1339a	Colby-Spinner	Oct. 1, 1865	included in above	included in above

Interest-bearing Notes/6%/Act of March 2, 1861

In addition to the portrait of George Washington there are two vignettes titled *Prosperity*, probably engraved by George W. Hatch, and *E Pluribus Unum*. (ABNCo)

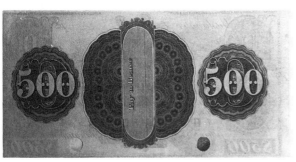

As the back shows this note was payable to bearer.

		Notes Issued		
No.	Term	Old Plates	New Plates	Known
1340	60 days	Unknown	18,254	1

Act of March 3, 1863 5%

1340a	One year	(Similar to No. 1339, unknown in any collection)		

Two-year Notes/6%/Act of March 2, 1861

The portrait of General Winfield Scott was engraved by Joseph P. Ourdan. The *Man With a Scythe* was engraved by Frederick Girsch; *The Traveler* cannot be attributed. (NBNCo)

Back design is on following page.

		Notes issued	
No.	Old Plates	New Plates	Known
1340b	4,291	44,157	1

Interest-bearing Notes/6%/Act of March 2, 1861 *(continued)*

Back design for No. 1340b is brown.

Interest-bearing Notes/5%/Act of March 3, 1863

Liberty and Union was engraved by Charles Burt. *The Eagle's Nest*, also used on Nos. 1446–1460, was engraved by Louis Delnoce.

The back design includes an anti-counterfeiting clause.

No.		Coupons	Notes Issued	Notes Outstanding
1341	Chittenden-Spinner	0	0	0
1342	Chittenden-Spinner	3	80,604	3

Remarks: In addition to the illustrated specimen of No. 1340b, which sold for $7,000 in 1982, there is a uniface plate proof that bears plate position "C" in a private collection. No circulated notes are known. At least 46,709 notes from new plates were printed. Additional notes could have been issued and printed. "For the" was probably written on notes from old plates by clerks who were authorized to sign for U.S. Treasury officials. Notes from new plates probably had "For the" engraved in the plate.

Interest-bearing Notes/7.3%/Act of July 17, 1861

This unique note, with *Justice*, G. Washington and *Transportation*, was prepared by ABNCo.

Uniface face and back are mounted as a complete note.

No.	Signatures for	Dated	Serial Numbers	Notes Issued	Notes Outstanding
1343	Chittenden-Spinner	Aug. 19, 1861	red	24,200	6
1344	Chittenden-Spinner	Oct. 1, 1861	red	46,391	8
1345	Chittenden-Spinner	Oct. 1, 1861	blue	1,117	0

Remarks: No. 1343 with serial number 1 is canceled at the Bureau of the Public Debt. Nos. 1344, 1345 and perhaps 1343 were signed "for" the two officials. Serial number 15502 is known for No. 1344.

Interest-bearing Three-year Notes/7.3%

Mortar Firing was engraved by James Smillie. The portraits of Alexander Hamilton and G. Washington (see No. 1140) were engraved by Owen G. Hanks. (Courtesy of the Coin and Currency Institute, Inc.)

The back design is similar to No. 1342; a "pay to bearer" clause replaces the counterfeit warning.

Act of June 30, 1864

No.	Dated	Notes Printed	Notes Issued	Notes Outstanding
1346	Aug. 15, 1864	154,250	171,668	17
1347	Mar. 3, 1865	45,887	included in above	

Act of March 3, 1865

No.	Dated	Notes Printed	Notes Issued	Notes Outstanding
1348	June 15, 1865	181,813	175,682	28
1349	July 15, 1865	115,000	108,654	12

Remarks: All notes had the signatures of Colby-Spinner. In addition to the illustrated example of No. 1346, serial number 7811 is recorded for No. 1348.

National Bank Notes/First Charter Period/Red Seal

James D. Smillie engraved *Civilization. The Arrival of the Sirius, 1838* is on the right.

John Trumbull's *Surrender of General Burgoyne to General Gates at Saratoga* was engraved by Frederick Girsch. Lettering on the face and back was engraved by W.D. Nichols and G.W. Thurber.

No.	Series	Signatures	Notes		Outstanding
			Printed	Issued	
1350	orig.	Chittenden-Spinner	21,645	19,523	
1350a	orig.	Colby-Spinner	included in above		
1350b	1875	Allison-Spinner			
1350c	1875	Allison-New			
1350d	1875	Allison-Wyman	6,368	4,371	173
1350e	1875	Scofield-Gilfillan			
1350f	1875	Bruce-Gilfillan			
1350g	1875	Bruce-Wyman			

The number of $500 national bank notes issued in each state:

State	Orig.	1875	State	Orig.	1875
Alabama	0	292	Massachusetts	10,031	842
Louisiana	720	0	New York	5,767	2,843
Maine	560	9	Pennsylvania	1,175	230
Maryland	860	50	Rhode Island	410	105

Remarks: Catalog numbers have been changed in this edition. The original series has no series date on the face. Known for Nos. 1350a–2; 1350c–1. The number of $50 national bank notes issued in each state was compiled by Peter Huntoon. See "The United States $50 & $1,000 National Bank Notes," *PAPER MONEY*, Vol. XXVII, No. 4, p. 103.

National Gold Bank Notes/Red Seal

The face design is similar to the preceding note.

The back design is similar to other national gold bank note denominations.

No.	Date	Issuing Bank	City	Issued
1351	1870	First National Gold Bank	San Francisco	300
1351a	1872	National Gold Bank & Trust Co.	San Francisco	250
1351b	1872	National Gold Bank of D.O. Mills & Co.	Sacramento	60

Remarks: A total of four notes are outstanding. Catalog numbers have been changed in this edition.

Silver Certificates/Series 1878 & 1880

Bostonian Charles Sumner (1811–1874) graduated from Harvard Law School in 1834. In 1852 he was elected to the U.S. Senate by a margin of one vote. This portrait, based on a photograph by Allen and Rowell, was engraved by Charles Burt.

No.	Series	Countersigned by	Payable at	Issued	Known
1352	1878	W.G. White*	New York	⎫	1
1352a	1878	J.C. Hopper*	New York	400	0
1352b	1878	T. Hillhouse*	New York	⎭ 0	0
1353	1878	R.M. Anthony	San Francisco	4,900	0
1354	1878	A.U. Wyman	Washington, DC	4,000	1
1354a	1878	A.U. Wyman	Washington, DC	included in above	0
		Signatures	**Seal**		
1355	1880	Scofield-Gilfillan	brown	0	0
1356	1880	Bruce-Gilfillan	brown	16,000	5
1357	1880	Bruce-Wyman	brown	8,000	2

Remarks: The (*) indicates autographed countersignatures. Nos. 1352–1354a have signatures of Scofield-Gilfillan and red seals.

Gold Certificates/Series 1863–1875

The portrait of Abraham Lincoln was engraved by Charles Burt.

Only the first issue has this back design.

No.	Issue	Series	Signatures	Payable at	Printed	Issued	Out	Known
1358	First	1863	Colby-Spinner	New York	18,00	15,000	0	0
1359	Second	1870	Allison-Spinner	New York	40,00	36,000	11	1
1360	Third	1875	Allison-New	New York	11,28	11,628	0	0

Remarks: No. 1359, a uniface note with serial number A25770, is at the Bureau of the Public Debt.

Treasury or Coin Notes/Series 1891

The portrait of General William Tecumseh Sherman (1820–1891) was engraved by Charles Schlecht. The date of this note suggests that it was intended to commemorate Gen. Sherman. See Hessler (1979) for illustration.

No.	Signatures	Printed	Issued
1360d	Rosecrans-Nebeker		
1360e	Tillman-Morgan	16,000	0
1360f	Bruce-Roberts		

Gold Certificates/Series 1882 & 1922

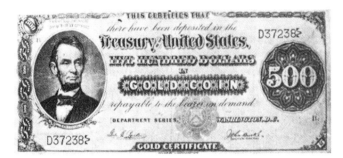

The portrait of Abraham Lincoln, based on a photograph by Matthew Brady, was engraved by Charles Burt.

The *Eagle with Flag* was originally engraved for the Baldwin Bank Note Co.

No.	Date	Signatures	Seal	Notes Printed	Known
1361	1882	Bruce-Gilfillan	brown	20,000	0
		Department Series, payable at Washington			
1362	1882	Bruce-Gilfillan	brown	8,000	0
1363	1882	Bruce-Wyman	brown	20,000	1
1364	1882	Rosecrans-Hyatt	lg. red	16,000	1
1365	1882	Lyons-Roberts	sm. red	128,000	23
1366	1882	Lyons-Treat*	—	—	0
1366a	1882	Napier-McClung*	—	—	0
1367	1882	Parker-Burke	sm. red	40,000	27
1368	1882	Teehee-Burke	sm. red	40,000	35
1369	1922	Speelman-White	sm. red	84,000	42

Remarks: The (*) indicates plate proofs at the Bureau of Engraving and Printing; there is no record of issue. No. 1361 has the autographed countersignature of Thomas C. Acton and is payable in New York. No. 1365, in VFine-EFine condition, was auctioned by Stack's in Oct. 1988 for $3,300.

Federal Reserve Notes/Series 1918/Blue Seal

The portrait of John Marshall, originally painted by Henry Inman, was engraved by Charles Schlecht.

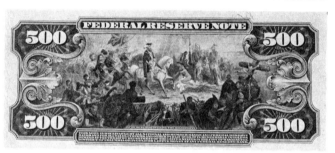

W.H. Powell's *DeSoto Discovering the Mississippi in 1541* was engraved by Frederick Girsch. The back is green.

No.	Bank	Signatures	Notes Printed	Issued	Known
1370A2	Boston	Burke-Glass	17,000	13,000	3
1370B2	New York	Burke-Glass	125,000	125,000	35
1370B4	New York	White-Mellon	125,000	125,000	2
1370C2	Philadelphia	Burke-Glass	24,000	6,000	4
1370D2	Cleveland	Burke-Glass	15,600	15,000	12
1370E	Richmond	unknown	23,200	4,000	—
1370F2	Atlanta	Burke-Glass	34,000	26,800	7
1370G1	Chicago	Burke-McAdoo	38,000	30,000	—
1370G2	Chicago	Burke-Glass	included in above		24
1370H2	St. Louis	Burke-Glass	14,400	6,800	3
1370I	Minneapolis	unrecorded	7,200	4,000	1
1370J2	Kansas City	Burke-Glass	16,000	7,200	13
1370K2	Dallas	Burke-Glass	6,000	4,400	3
1370L2	San Francisco	Burke-Glass	24,000	20,400	15
1370L3	San Francisco	Burke-Houston	—	—	2

Remarks: Although the above figures include all signature combinations, only those that have actually been observed are listed. Four consecutively-numbered pieces of No. 1370F exist in uncirculated condition. In 1991 No. 1370F2 sold for $10,000; in 1979 No. 1370K2 sold for $8,250; both were uncirculated. In the Oct. 1995 CAA sale, No. 1370B2, in fine condition, sold for $1,567.

Federal Reserve Notes/1928 & 1934/Green Seal

The portrait of William McKinley was engraved by John Eissler.

The back was engraved by F. Lamasure and L.S. Schofield.

Series 1928, Woods-Mellon

No.	Bank	Notes Printed	Unc
1371A	Boston	69,120	$800.
1371B	New York	299,400	700.
1371C	Philadelphia	135,120	800.
1371D	Cleveland	166,440	800.
1371E	Richmond	84,720	850.
1371F	Atlanta	69,360	850.
1371G	Chicago	573,600	750.
1371H	St. Louis	66,180	850.
1371I	Minneapolis	34,680	900.
1371J	Kansas City	510,720	750.
1371K	Dallas	70,560	850.
1371L	San Francisco	64,080	850.

Catalog Nos. 1371–1376a have been changed since the previous edition.

Series 1934, Julian-Morgenthau

No.	Bank	Notes Printed	Unc
1372A	Boston	56,628	$750.
1372B	New York	288,000	700.
1372B☆			—
1372C	Philadelphia	31,200	750.
1372D	Cleveland	39,000	750.
1372E	Richmond	40,000	750.
1372F	Atlanta	46,200	750.
1372F☆			950.
1372G	Chicago	212,000	700.
1372G☆			850.
1372H	St. Louis	24,000	800.
1372H☆			—
1372I	Minneapolis	24,000	800.
1372J	Kansas City	40,800	750.
1372J☆			1200.
1372K	Dallas	31,200	800.
1372K☆			—
1372L	San Francisco	63,400	750.
1372L☆			950.

Federal Reserve Notes/Series 1934A, 1934B & 1934C/Green Seal

Series 1934A, Julian-Morgenthau

No.	Bank	Notes Printed	Unc
1373A	Boston	276,000	$750.
1373B	New York	45,300	700.
1373C	Philadelphia	28,800	750.
1373D	Cleveland	36,000	750.
1373E	Richmond	36,000	750.
1373F	Atlanta	46,200	750.
1373G	Chicago	214,800	700.
1373G☆			850.
1373H	St. Louis	57,600	800.
1373I	Minneapoli	14,400	800.
1373J	Kansas City	55,200	750.
1373J☆		40,800	1250.
1373K	Dallas	34,800	800.
1373L	San Francisco	93,000	750.
1373L☆ 1000.			

Series 1934B, Julian-Vinson

No.	Bank	Notes Printed	Unc
1374	Atlanta	2,472	$3250.

Series 1934C, Julian-Snyder

No.	Bank	Notes Printed	Unc
1375A	Boston	1,440	3250.
1375B	New York	204	3500.

Gold Certificate/Series 1928

The portrait of William McKinley was engraved by John Eissler.

The back design is similar to the preceding note.

No.	Signatures	Notes Printed	Unc
1376	Woods-Mellon	420,000	$3500.

United States Notes/1862 & 1863/Red Seal

Charles Schlecht engraved the portrait of Robert Morris, patriot, U.S. Senator and our first Superintendent of Finance.

The back bears the second obligation.

Signatures of Chittenden-Spinner

No.	Date	Obligation	Printed	Notes Outstanding	Known
1376a	1862	first			0
1377	1862	second			0
1378	1863	second, one serial number, "American Bank Note Co." at right "National Bank Note Co." at left	155,928	201	1
1378a	1863	second, one serial number, "American Bank Note Co." at right			2
1378b	1863	second, two serial numbers, "American Bank Note Co." at right			1

Remarks: An example dated 1863 sold for $90,000 in 1995.

United States Notes/Series 1869/Red Seal

DeWitt Clinton (1769–1828) graduated from Columbia U. at age 17. He served as a U.S. Senator and as mayor and governor of New York. His portrait, based on a painting by C.C. Ingham, was engraved by Charles Burt. *Columbus in His Study* was engraved by Henry Gugler.

No.	Series	Signatures	Seal	Notes Issued	Outstanding	Known
1379	1869	Allison-Spinner	lg. red	87,100	499	2

An enlargement of the central portion of the back

Remarks: The official number printed is 74,400; reissued notes probably account for the above figure.

United States Notes/Series 1878 & 1880

The face design is similar to the preceding note.

No.	Series	Signatures	Seals	Notes Printed	Known
		All have red seals except for Nos. 1381 & 1385.			
1380	1878	Allison-Gilfillan	rays	24,000	2
1381	1880	Bruce-Wyman	brown	12,000	2
1382	1880	Rosecrans-Jordan	large	24,800	1
1383	1880	Rosecrans-Hyatt	plain	12,000	1
1384	1880	Rosecrans-Huston	lg. spike	—	1
1385	1880	Rosecrans-Nebeker	brown	28,000	1
1386	1880	Tillman-Morgan	scallops	56,000	2
1387	1880	Tillman-Roberts	scallops	—	1
1388	1880	Bruce-Roberts	scallops	24,000	1
1389	1880	Lyons-Roberts	scallops	32,000	13
1390	1880	Vernon-Treat	scallops	20,000	4
1391	1880	Napier-McClung	scallops	existence doubtful	

Remarks: An example in VF condition sold for $19,800 in 1995.

Compound Interest Treasury Notes/6%

Three-year Notes—Act of June 30, 1864

No.	Signatures	Dated	Notes Printed	Notes Issued	Notes Outstanding
1392	Chittenden-Spinner	July 15, 1864	24,000	20,000	
1392a	Colby-Spinner	Aug. 15, 1865	39,200	37,400	} 4
1392b	Colby-Spinner	Sep. 15, 1865	included in above		

Interest-bearing Notes/6%

Act of March 2, 1861

No.	Term	Notes Printed		Issued
		old plates	new plates	
1393	60 days	Unknown	9,333	8,597

Act of March 3, 1863—5%

The subjects are entitled *Justice, Eagle with Shield,* and *the Standard Bearer.* The back design for this uniface proof is unknown.

No.	Term	Dated	Known
1393a	One-year	Oct. 1, 1863	1

Remarks: At least 9,333 notes from new plates were printed for No. 1393. Printed and issued figures are approximate. Notes from old plates probably had "For the" written by the signers who signed for the Treasury officials. "For the" was probably engraved on new plates.

Interest-bearing Notes/Two-year/6%

Act of March 2, 1861

George Washington, *America*, and the *U.S. Treasury Building* adorn this note. *America* is the central figure in *The Progress of Civilization* by Thomas Crawford, the pediment above the Senate Wing of the U.S. Capitol. The green overprint was accidentally inverted on this specimen.

The color of the back is rust.

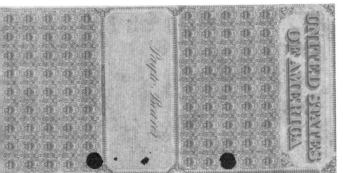

| No. | Signatures | Notes Issued | | Known |
		Old plates	New plates	
1393b	Chittenden-Spinner	3,068	24,509	2

Remarks: "For the" was probably written by the clerks who signed for the U.S. Treasury officials on notes from old plates. The National Bank Note Co., who also printed the first Confederate issue, used the same version of *Columbia* on the $1,000 note dated 6 May 1861.

In addition to the illustrated specimen, there is one plate proof, position "A," known in a private collection; no circulating notes are known. There is no example of this note at the Bureau of Engraving and Printing.

Interest-bearing Notes/Two-year/5%   Act of March 3, 1863

The *Naval Engagement Between the Guerriere and the Constitution,* and the *Discovery of the Mississippi by De Soto* appear on this unknown note. At least some of No. 1395 were prepared by the ContBNCo.

No.	Signatures	Coupons	Notes Issued	Outstanding
1394	Chittenden-Spinner	0	not issued	—
1395	Chittenden-Spinner	3	89,308	19

Three-year Notes—7.3%   Act of July 17, 1861

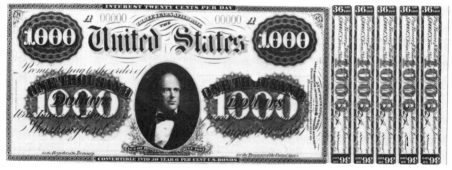

The portrait of Salmon P. Chase was engraved by Alfred Sealey.

No.	Signatures	Dated	Serial Nos.	Printed	Notes Issued	Outstanding
1396	Chittenden-Spinner	Aug. 19, 1861	red	—	22,922	3
1397	Chittenden-Spinner	Oct. 1, 1861	red	—	37,998	3
1398	Chittenden-Spinner	Oct. 1, 1861	blue	—	1,380	0
		Act of June 30, 1864				
1399	Colby-Spinner	Aug. 15, 1864		114,540	118,528	5
1400	Colby-Spinner	Mar. 3, 1865		43,460	—	—

Interest-bearing Notes

Justice with Shield, engraved by Charles Burt, occupies the center of this note; the five coupons are not shown.

These notes were payable to bearer as the back indicates.

Act of March 3, 1865—7.3%

No.	Signatures	Dated	Notes Printed	Issued	Outstanding
1401	Colby-Spinner	June 15, 1865	189,200	179,965	4
1402	Colby-Spinner	July 15, 1865	81,000	71,879	8

Remarks: The Bureau of the Public Debt has two canceled notes, No. 1401 serial number 102997 (with four coupons) and No. 1402, serial number 999999 (with five coupons). William E. "Long Bill" Brockway (Col. W.E. Spencer) was the brains behind the counterfeiting of this note. The admitted counterfeiter was Charles H. Smith (*Underwood's Counterfeit Detector*, March 1881). Counterfeit notes reported by 12 October 1867 had plates A or B.

"The Government reserves the right of paying in COIN, the interest on this Note at the rate of six percent per annum." This overprint suggests that some of these notes were reissued at a lower rate of interest. Or, some of the notes were issued at the reduced interest rate after the three-year redemption period.

National Bank Notes/First Charter Period/Red Seal

General Scott's Entrance into Mexico, by John Trumbull, was engraved by Alfred Jones and James Smillie; the latter also engraved the *U.S. Capitol.*

Washington Resigning his Commission, another mural by Trumbull, was engraved by Louis Delnoce and Frederick Girsch. Lettering on face and back was engraved by W.D. Nichols and G.W. Thurber.

No.	Date	Signatures	Notes Printed	Issued
1403	orig.	Chittenden-Spinner	5,888	5,743
1404	orig.	Colby-Spinner	included in above	
1404a	1875	Allison-Spinner		
1404b	1875	Allison-Wyman	2,402	1,636
1404c	1875	Scofield-Gilfillan		
1404d	1875	Bruce-Gilfillan		

The number of $1,000 national bank notes issued in each state:

State	Orig.	1875
Maryland	142	0
Massachusetts	1332	160
New York	3902	1465
Pennsylvania	237	11
Rhode Island	130	0

Remarks: The original series has no series date on the notes. A total of 21 notes are outstanding. The number of $1,000 national bank notes issued in each state was compiled by Peter Huntoon. (See "The United States $500 & $1,000 National Bank Notes," *PAPER MONEY*, Vol. XXVII, No. 4, p. 103.)

Silver Certificates/Series 1878 & 1880

The portrait of William L. Marcy (1786–1857) was engraved by Charles Schlecht. Following his graduation from Brown University, Marcy held numerous political positions; the most notable was Secretary of State.

No.	Series	Countersigned by	Seal	Payable at	Issued
1405	1878	T. Hillhouse	red	New York	90
1406	1878	R.M. Anthony	red	San Francisco	10,400
1407	1878	A.U. Wyman	red	Washington, DC	2,000
1407a	1878	A.U. Wyman*	red	Washington, DC	2,000

No.	Series	Signatures	Seal	Issued	Known
1408	1880	Scofield-Gilfillan	brown	doubtful	0
1409	1880	Bruce-Gilfillan	brown	8,000	0
1410	1880	Bruce-Wyman	brown	8,000	5

Remarks: The (*) indicates autographed countersignatures. Nos. 1405–1407a were all redeemed or destroyed. A portion of No. 1406 could have autographed countersignatures. The number issued for No. 1407 is based on conjecture. No. 1407a has the signatures of Scofield-Gilfillan. See "Series 1878 silver certificates…" by W. Breen, *Numismatic News*, May 24, 1975.) Three additional recorded notes for No. 1410 are B11437, B12623, and B12638.

Silver Certificates/Series 1891

The face and back of this note were designed by Thomas F. Morris. Non-portrait engravers were D.M. Cooper, J. Kennedy, S.B. Many, W. Ponickau and G.U. Rose, Jr.

The back was engraved by D.M. Cooper, E.M. Hall, W.F. Lutz, R. Ponickau and G.U. Rose, Jr.

No.	Series	Signatures	Notes Printed	Issued	Known
1411	1891	Tillman-Morgan	8,000	5,600	2

Remarks: A total of nine notes are outstanding for Nos. 1405–1411. The following appeared in the July 29, 1894 edition of *The New York Times*: "According to U.S. Treasury gossip, the female portrait was taken from a photograph of Josie Mansfield" (the mistress of James Fisk). In 1877 Charles Burt engraved an image of *Liberty* that was used on a $1,000 bond (X170D, Hessler 1988). It seems that G.F.C. Smillie re-engraved the image as it appears on No. 1411.

Gold Certificates/Series 1863–1875

E Pluribus Unum was engraved by Charles Skinner. The complete figure of *Justice* can be seen on No. 1393a.

The first issue has this back design, one of the first plates produced at the Bureau of Engraving and Printing.

Nos. 1413 and 1414, uniface, have portraits of Alexander Hamilton engraved by Charles Burt.

No.	Issue	Date	Signatures	Payable at	Printed	Issued	Out	Known
1412	First	1863	Colby-Spinner	New York	117,000	60,000	7	1
1413	Second	1870	Allison-Spinner	New York	50,000	47,500	16	1
1414	Third	1875	Allison-New	New York	14,371	14,371	0	0

Remarks: No. 1412, with serial number 19683, and No. 1413, with serial number A38887, are at the Bureau of the Public Debt. Nos. 1413 and 1414 are uniface.

Gold Certificates/Series 1882

The portrait of Alexander Hamilton is at the right.

The back design is yellow.

No.	Series	Signatures	Seal	Notes Printed	Known
1415	1882	Bruce-Gilfillan	brown	12,000	2
		Department Series, payable at Washington			
1416	1882	Bruce-Gilfillan	brown	8,000	1
1417	1882	Bruce-Wyman	brown	20,000	1
1418	1882	Rosecrans-Hyatt	lg. red	16,000	1
1419	1882	Rosecrans-Huston	lg. brn	8,000	3
1420	1882	Rosecrans-Nebeker	lg. red	8,000	3
1421	1882	Lyons-Roberts	sm. red	96,000	7
1422	1882	Lyons-Treat	sm. red	16,000	4

Remarks: Number 1415 has the autographed countersignature of Thomas C. Acton, and is payable at New York. No. 1421, in fine condition, with serial number C58223, was auctioned by NASCA in November 1979 for $6,600. In 1991 the same note was sold by Stack's for $9,500. The following notes are at the Smithsonian: No. 1416, A10199; No, 1417, A18818; No. 1418, C6477; No. 1419, C22708, C23727, C23847; No. 1420, C24623, C24675, C29156; No. 1422, D15131. In addition, Martin Gengerke has recorded the following notes: Nos. 1419, C22708; No. 1421, C58223, C63993, C68128, C74741, C83210, C100258, and C119261; No. 1422, D969, D10213, D14752 and D15131.

Gold Certificates/Series 1907 & 1922

The C.L. Ransom portrait of Alexander Hamilton was engraved by G.F.C. Smillie.

The *Great Seal of the U.S.* on the gold back was engraved by R. Ponickau. Additional engravers were E.M. Hall, G.U. Rose, Jr. and R.H. Warren.

No.	Series	Signatures	Notes Printed	Known
1423	1907	Vernon-Treat	32,000	6
1423a	1907	Vernon-McClung	12,000	0
1423b	1907	Napier-McClung	12,000	1
1423c	1907	Napier Burke	12,000	4
1423d	1907	Parker-Burke	48,000	7
1423e	1907	Teehee-Burke	112,000	28
1424	1922	Speelman-White	80,000	29

Remarks: These notes have been renumbered. In 1988 No. 1423e (D142760), in uncirculated condition, sold for $13,750. No. 1424 (E22477), in VG-F condition, sold for $3,750 in CAA Oct. 1995 sale. In addition to the illustrated note the following notes have been recorded. No. 1423: A9050, A2258, A13296, A26707 & A31075; No. 1423b: B19908; No. 1423c: D2626, D3953, D5936, D8776; No. 1423d: D40834, D40835, D40885, D40886, D44933, D45587 & D46670.

Treasury or Coin Notes/Series 1890 & 1891

George Gordon Meade (1815–1872) was born in Cadiz, Spain of American parents. After serving in the Union army during the Civil War, he rose to major-general. His portrait was engraved by Charles Burt.

The green back design was engraved by W.H. Dougal, E.M. Hall, G.U. Rose, Jr. and D.M. Russell.

No.	Series	Signatures	Seal	Notes Printed	Known
1425	1890	Rosecrans-Huston	brown	16,000	6
1426	1890	Rosecrans-Nebeker	red	12,000	2
1427	1891	Rosecrans-Nebeker	red	8,000	0
1428	1891	Tillman-Morgan	red	24,000	2

Series 1891

The face design is similar to the preceding note. The back was engraved by D. M. Cooper, W.H. Dougal, E.M. Hall, A.L. Helm and G.U. Rose, Jr.

Remarks: G.G. Meade is one of five Americans of foreign birth to appear on U.S. paper money. The others are Alexander Hamilton, Robert Morris (Nos. 578 & 1376), A. Gallatin (No. 1320) and E.D. Baker (No. 1441). The 1890 note is often called the grand watermelon note due to the shape and color of the zeros on the back (see No. 1242).

Federal Reserve Notes/Series 1918/Blue Seal

The C.L. Ransom portrait of Alexander Hamilton was engraved by G.F.C. Smillie.

The *Eagle*, on the back, was engraved by Marcus W. Baldwin.

No.	Bank	Signatures	Notes Printed	Notes Issued	Known
1429A2	Boston	Burke-Glass	39,600	20,800	2
1429B2	New York	Burke-Glass	} 124,800	124,800	13
1429B3	New York	Burke-Houston			4
1429B4	New York	White-Mellon			0
1429C2	Philadelphia	White-Mellon	16,400	12,800	11
1429D2	Cleveland	Burke-Glass	8,800	8,800	7
1429E2	Richmond	Burke-Glass	17,600	8,400	0
1429F2	Atlanta	Burke-Glass	43,200	43,200	3
1429F4	Atlanta	White-Mellon	included in above		4
1429G2	Chicago	Burke-Glass	23,600	19,600	17
1429H2	St. Louis	Burke-Glass	8,400	4,400	7
1429I2	Minneapolis	Burke-Glass	7,600	2,800	2
1429J2	Kansas City	Burke-Glass	15,200	4,400	4
1429K2	Dallas	Burke-Glass	6,000	4,400	3
1429L2	San Francisco	Burke-Glass	22,400	22,000	46
1429L4	San Francisco	White-Mellon	included in above		4

Remarks: Although the above figures include all signature combinations, only those that have actually been observed thus far are listed. The figures for No. 1429H2 might be incomplete. No. 1492D2 (D7853A), in gem unc condition, sold for $11,000 and No. 1429G2 (G16464A) in fine condition sold for $2,365 in the CAA Oct. 1995 sale. No. 1429L4 (L19268), in uncirculated condition, sold for $8,800 in 1988.

Federal Reserve Notes/Series 1928/Green Seal

The portrait of Grover Cleveland was engraved by John Eissler.

The back was engraved by H.S. Nutter, L.S. Schofield and W.H. Hall.

Series 1928, Woods-Mellon

No.	Bank	Notes Printed	EFine
1430A	Boston	58,320	$1250.
1430B	New York	139,200	1200.
1430C	Philadelphia	96,708	1200.
1430D	Cleveland	79,680	1250.
1430D☆			1500.
1430E	Richmond	66,840	1250.
1430F	Atlanta	47,400	1250.
1430G	Chicago	355,800	1200.
1430G☆			1500.

Series 1928, Woods-Mellon

No.	Bank	Notes Printed	EFine
1430H	St. Louis	60,000	$1250.
1430I	Minneapolis	26,640	1350.
1430J	Kansas City	62,172	1250.
1430K	Dallas	42,960	1250.
1430L	San Francisco	67,920	1250.
1430L☆			1500.

Federal Reserve Notes/Series 1934, 1934A & 1934C/Green Seal

Series 1934, Julian-Morgenthau

No.	Bank	Notes Printed	EFine
1431A	Boston	46,200	$1200.
1431B	New York	332,784	1150.
1431C	Philadelphia	33,000	1200.
1431C☆			1500.
1431D	Cleveland	35,400	1200.
1431E	Richmond	19,560	1250.
1431F	Atlanta	67,800	1200.
1431G	Chicago	167,040	1150.
1431G☆			1350.
1431H	St. Louis	22,440	1200.
1431I	Minneapolis	12,000	1250.
1431J	Kansas City	51,840	1200.
1431K	Dallas	46,800	1200.
1431L	San Francisco	90,600	1200.
1431L☆			1400.

Series 1934A, Julian-Morgenthau

No.	Bank	Notes Printed	EFine
1432A	Boston	30,000	$1200.
1432B	New York	174,348	1150.
1432C	Philadelphia	78,000	1200.
1432D	Cleveland	28,800	1200.
1432E	Richmond	16,800	1250.
1432F	Atlanta	80,964	1200.
1432G	Chicago	134,400	1150.
1432G☆			1400.
1432H	St. Louis	39,600	1200.
1432I	Minneapolis	4,800	1350.
1432J	Kansas City	21,600	1200.
1432K	Dallas		not printed
1432L	San Francisco	36,600	1200.

Series 1934C, Julian-Snyder

No.	Bank	Notes Printed	EFine
1433A	Boston	1,200	$2500
1433B	New York	168	3000.

Gold Certificates/Series 1928 & 1934

In addition to John Eissler, who engraved the portrait of Grover Cleveland, engravers were O. Benzing and W.B. Wells. Series 1928 lacks the large "1000" to the right of the portrait.

The back design is the same as No. 1430.

No.	Series	Signatures	Notes Printed	Unc
1434	1928	Woods-Mellon	288,000	6750.
1434a	1934	Julian-Morgenthau	84,000	—

United States Notes

The portrait of James Madison was engraved by Alfred Sealey. "Specimen Furnished the Chinese Government By the United States Treasury Department," at lower right, identifies this as an example of specimens sent to foreign governments for comparison purposes.

The *Eagle* was engraved by William Chorlton.

No.	Series	Signatures	Seal	Notes Printed	Outstanding
1435	1878	Scofield-Gilfillan	lg. brown	4,000	0

Interest-bearing Notes/6%

60–Day Notes/Act of March 2, 1861

		Notes Issued		
No.	Term	Old plates	New plates	Known
1435a	60–days	Unknown	1,466	0

The face design of this unknown note bears the *Altar of Liberty*. The designer was T.A. Liebler. The back design included a vignette entitled *Eagle and Stars*.

One-Year Notes/5%/Act of March 3, 1863

No.	Signatures	
1435b	Chittenden-Spinner	No data available on this unknown note.

Remarks: Additional notes could have been printed and issued for No. 1435a. Notes from old plates probably had "For the" written in by authorized clerks who signed for U.S. Treasury officials. "For the" was probably engraved in new plates.

Interest-Bearing, Three-Year Notes/7.3%

Justice, by T.A. Liebler, on the left, was engraved by Louis Delnoce; *America* was engraved by Charles Burt.

Act of July 17, 1861

No.	Signatures	Dated	Printed	Issued
1436	Chittenden-Spinner	Aug. 19, 1861	—	1,089
1437	Chittenden-Spinner	Oct. 1, 1861	—	1,871
		Act of June 30, 1864		
1438	Colby-Spinner	Aug. 15, 1864	6,145	4,166
1439	Colby-Spinner	Mar. 3, 1865	1,020	incl. in above
		Act of March 3, 1865		
1440	Colby-Spinner	June 15, 1865	4,430	4,045
1440a	Colby-Spinner	July 15, 1865	2,800	1,684

Remarks: All notes have been redeemed.

Currency Certificates of Deposit/Act of June 8, 1872

Five years after his birth in London, England, E.D. Baker (1811–1861) came to the U.S. He studied and practiced law in Springfield, Illinois, served as state senator in 1840 and was elected to Congress in 1844. This portrait was engraved by Charles Burt.

No.	Series	Signatures	Seal	Notes Printed
1441	1872	Allison-Spinner	red	8,000
1442	1875	Various	red	10,002

Remarks: Two additional sheets of three subjects each were prepared in 1889, one each for the Chinese and Japanese governments. Baker is one of five Americans of foreign birth to appear on U.S. paper money. The others are Alexander Hamilton, A. Gallatin (No. 1320), G.G. Meade (No. 1425) and R. Morris (Nos. 578 & 1376).

Gold Certificates/Series 1863–1875

E Pluribus Unum was engraved by Charles Skinner. The complete figure of *Victory* can be seen on No. 726.

The first issue had this back design, one of the first plates produced at the Bureau of Engraving and Printing.

Nos. 1444–1445 are uniface and have portraits of James Madison engraved by Alfred Sealey. The illustrated proof, the only example known, is at the Bureau of Engraving and Printing. The back design is similar to Nos. 1446–1451 .

No.	Issue	Date	Signatures	Payable at	Printed	Issued
1443	First	1863	Colby-Spinner	New York	94,600	64,600
1444	Second	1870	Allison-Spinner	New York	40,000	21,000
1444a	Second	1870	Allison-Gilfillan	(There is a proof at the BEP.)		
1445	Third	1875	Allison-New	New York	5,977	5,977

Remarks: No. 1443 with serial number 42023, is at the Bureau of the Public Debt. Three notes are outstanding for No. 1444. No other notes are known. Nos. 1444 and 1445 are uniface.

Gold Certificates/Series 1882

The portrait of James Madison was engraved by Alfred Sealey.

The Eagle's Nest is based on a painting by Gilbert Stuart.

No.	Signatures	Seal	Notes Printed	
1446	Bruce-Gilfillan	brown	4,000	
	Department Series, payable at Washington			
1447	Bruce-Gilfillan	brown	500	
1448	Bruce-Wyman	brown	3,500	
1449	Rosecrans-Hyatt	lg. red	4,000	
1450	Rosecrans-Nebeker	sm. red	4,000	
1451	Lyons-Roberts	sm. red	16,000	
1451a	Lyons-Treat*	sm. red	—	
1452	Vernon-Treat	sm. red	4,000	
1453	Vernon-McClung	sm. red	26,500	(estimate)
1453a	Napier-McClung	sm. red	included in above	
1453b	Napier-Thompson*	sm. red	—	
1453c	Parker-Burke	sm. red	—	
1453d	Teehee-Burke	sm. red	2 known	

Remarks: The (*) indicates a plate proof at the Bureau of Engraving and Printing; there is no record of issue. No. 1446 has the autographed countersignature of Thomas C. Acton and is payable at New York. Ten pieces are outstanding for Nos. 1446–1453d.

Gold Certificates/Series of 1888

This proof note bears a portrait of James Madison engraved by Alfred Sealey.

No.	Payable at	Notes Issued	Notes Printed	Outstanding
1454	Baltimore	512		
1455	Chicago	974		
1456	New York	6,388		
1457	Philadelphia	1,600	9,000	0
1458	St. Louis	48		
1459	San Francisco	1,736		
1460	Washington, DC	75		

Remarks: Signatures of Rosecrans-Hyatt appeared on 6,000 notes, and Rosecrans-Nebeker on 3,000. These official figures are from *Final Receipts for Notes and Certificates of the Bureau of Engraving and Printing*. Nevertheless, the issued figures supplied by Walter Breen total 11,333. Some notes could have been reissued.

Federal Reserve Notes/Series 1918/Green Seal

James Barton Longacre's portrait of James Madison was engraved by Alfred Sealey. John Trumbull's *Washington Resigning his Commission* was engraved by Frederick Girsch and Louis Delnoce.

No.	Bank	Printed	Issued	Known
1461A	Boston	2,800	800	0
1461B	New York	5,200	1,600	2
1461C	Philadelphia	2,000	none	0
1461D	Cleveland	800	400	1
1461E	Richmond	1,600	400	0
1461F	Atlanta	400	none	0
1461G	Chicago	2,800	400	1
1461H	St. Louis	1,200	400	0
1461I	Minneapolis	none	—	—
1461J	Kansas City	none	—	—
1461K	Dallas	1,200	none	—
1461L	San Francisco	3,600	2,800	1

Remarks: Only 13 notes are outstanding. Five notes are known: two at the Smithsonian and one each at the Federal Reserve Banks of Chicago and San Francisco. The issued figures for Chicago and St. Louis might prove to be incomplete.

Federal Reserve Notes/Series 1928, 1934, 1934A & 1934B/Green Seal

The portrait of James Madison was engraved by Alfred Sealey in 1869.

The back was engraved by F. Lamasure, C.F. Wittenauer and E.M. Hall.

Series 1928, Woods-Mellon

No.	Bank	Notes Printed
1462A	Boston	1,320
1462B	New York	2,640
1462C	Philadelphia	not printed
1462D	Cleveland	3,000
1462E	Richmond	3,984
1462F	Atlanta	1,440
1462G	Chicago	3,480
1462H	St. Louis	not printed
1462I	Minneapolis	not printed
1462J	Kansas City	720
1462K	Dallas	360
1462L	San Francisco	1,300

Series 1934, Julian-Morgenthau

No.	Bank	Notes Printed
1463A	Boston	9,480
1463B	New York	11,520
1463C	Philadelphia	3,000
1463D	Cleveland	1,680
1463E	Richmond	2,400
1463F	Atlanta	3,600
1463G	Chicago	6,600
1463H	St. Louis	2,400
1463I	Minneapolis	not printed
1463J	Kansas City	2,400
1463K	Dallas	2,400
1463L	San Francisco	6,000

Series 1934A, Julian-Morgenthau

No.	Bank	Notes Printed
1463aH	St. Louis	1,440

Series 1934B, Julian-Vinson

No.	Bank	Notes Printed
1463bA	Boston	1,200
1463bB	New York	12

Gold Certificate/Series 1928

The face and back designs are similar to No. 1463 except for the seal and obligation.

No.	Series	Signatures	Notes Printed
1464	1928	Woods-Mellon	24,000

United States Notes/Brown Seal

The Thomas Sully portrait of Andrew Jackson was engraved by Alfred Sealey.

No.	Series	Signatures	Notes Printed	Outstanding
1465	1878	Scofield-Gilfillan	4,000	0

The portrait enlarged.

Gold Certificates/Series 1863–1875

The portrait of Andrew Jackson, on No. 1468, was engraved by Alfred Sealey. This canceled note at the Bureau of the Public Debt is the only example known. No. 1466 probably resembled Nos. 1412 and 1443.

The first issue had this back design, one of the first plates produced at the Bureau of Engraving and Printing.

No.	Issue	Date	Signatures	Payable at	Printed & Issued
1466	First	1863	Colby-Spinner	New York	2,500
1467	Second	1870	Allison-New	New York	20,000
1468	Third	1875	Allison-New	New York	8,933

Remarks: Nos. 1467 and 1468 are uniface. All notes have been redeemed.

Gold Certificates/Series of 1882

The portrait of Andrew Jackson was engraved by Alfred Sealey.

The *Eagle of the Capitol* was engraved by James Bannister.

No.	Signatures	Seal	Notes Printed
1470	Bruce-Gilfillan	brown	8,000
	Department Series, payable at Washington		
1471	Bruce-Gilfillan	brown	500
1472	Bruce-Wyman	brown	4,000
1473	Rosecrans-Hyatt	lg. red	4,000
1474	Rosecrans-Nebeker	lg. brown	4,000
1475	Lyons-Roberts	sm. red	7,000
1475a	Lyons-Treat*	sm. red	—
1476	Vernon-Treat	sm. red	4,000
1476a	Vernon-McClung	sm. red	4,000
1476b	Napier-Burke	sm. red	4,000
1476c	Parker-Burke	sm. red	12,000
1477	Teehee-Burke	sm. red	108,000

Remarks: The (*) indicates a plate proof at the Bureau of Engraving and Printing; there is no record of issue. No. 1470 has the autographed countersignature of Thomas C. Acton and is payable at New York. A total of eight pieces are outstanding for Nos. 1470–1477; two notes are known for 1477. Nos. 1476b–1476d have been renumbered since the previous edition.

Gold Certificates/Series of 1888

The portrait of Andrew Jackson was engraved by Alfred Sealey.

No.	Payable at	Notes Issued	Notes Printed	Outstanding
1478	Baltimore	523		
1479	Chicago	952		
1480	New York	6,592		
1481	Philadelphia	2,665	9,000	0
1482	St. Louis	320		
1483	San Francisco	1,700		
1484	Washington, DC	149		

Remarks: Signatures of Rosecrans-Hyatt appeared on 6,000 notes and Rosecrans- Nebeker on 3,000. These official figures are from *Final Receipts for Notes and Certificates of the Bureau of Engraving and Printing*. Nevertheless, the issued figures supplied by Walter Breen total 13,304. No. 1482 bore the signatures of Lyons-Roberts; the illustrated proof shows signatures of Napier-McClung. Notes with other signatures may have been issued.

Gold Certificates/Series of 1900

The portrait of Andrew Jackson was engraved by Alfred Sealey. The cancellation on the left reads "Payable to the Treasurer of the U.S. or a Federal Reserve Bank."

No.	Payable to order in	Notes Issued
1485	Baltimore	17,265
1485a	Boston	9,803
1486	Chicago	9,916
1487	Cincinnati	2,790
1488	New Orleans	986
1489	New York	73,701
1490	Philadelphia	67,397
1491	St. Louis	7,097
1492	San Francisco	12,714
1492a	Washington, DC	75,581

Remarks: A total of 363,000 notes were printed. Notes still outstanding from the above came from the December 13, 1935 fire at the U.S. Post Office at 12th and Pennsylvania Avenue in Washington, DC. In a fruitless attempt to keep the fire from gutting the fire-proof building, file cabinets full of paper, including $1,142,000 in these uniface notes were thrown out of the windows. Paper included some canceled $10,000 notes that were carried by the wind to the hands of surprised passers-by. Even though these canceled notes are not redeemable, they have been considered illegal to hold. Nevertheless, more than 100 uncirculated notes entered the marketplace in 1995 with no repercussions, so far. Three notes, No. 1489 (H355361), in AU, and 1492a (M59727 & M143598), in choice Unc and AU respectively, sold for $797, $1,100 and $880 in CAA Oct. 1995 sale. John Isted has recorded the following number of signature combinations for the above:

Lyons-Roberts	36,000	Napier-McClung	18,000
Lyons-Treat	6,000	Napier-Burke	6,000
Vernon-Treat	36,000	Parker-Burke	30,000
Vernon-McClung	18,000	Teehee-Burke	213,000

Currency Certificates of Deposit/Act of June 8, 1872

Stephen A. Douglas (1813–1861), son of a cabinet-maker, was elected to Congress at age 21. He was the Democratic nominee for President of the U.S. in 1860. This portrait was engraved by Charles Burt.

No.	Series	Signatures	Seal	Notes Printed
1492b	1872	Allison-Spinner	red	20,000
1492c	1875	Various	red	114,000

Remarks: Two additional three-subject sheets were prepared in 1889, one each for the Chinese and Japanese governments.

Federal Reserve Notes/Series 1918/Green Seal

Salmon P. Chase, Secretary of the Treasury (1861–1864).

The *Embarkation of the Pilgrims* (see Nos. 953–964).

No.	Bank	Notes Printed	Issued	No.	Bank	Notes Printed	Issued
1493A	Boston	2,000	800	**1493G**	Chicago	1,200	none
1493B	New York	5,600	1,600	**1493H**	St. Louis	1,200	400
1493C	Philadelphia	2,400	none	**1493I**	Minneapolis	none	none
1493D	Cleveland	800	400	**1493J**	Kansas City	none	none
1493E	Richmond	800	400	**1493K**	Dallas	1,200	none
1493F	Atlanta	400	none	**1493L**	San Francisco	2,800	2,000

Remarks: Although ten notes are outstanding, the illustrated note is the only example known outside the Smithsonian Institution, where serial numbers B1A and D1A are located. The number listed as issued for St. Louis could prove incomplete. Known for Nos. 1493B—2; 1493D—1; 1493L—2.

Federal Reserve Notes/Series 1928, 1934, 1934A & 1934B/Green Seal

Salmon P. Chase,
Secretary of the Treasury
(1861–1864).

The back was engraved by
F. Lamasure, E.H.
Helmuth and E.J. Hein.

Series 1928, Woods-Mellon

No.	Bank	Notes Printed
1494A	Boston	1,320
1494B	New York	4,680
1494C	Philadelphia	not printed
1494D	Cleveland	960
1494E	Richmond	3,024
1494F	Atlanta	1,440
1494G	Chicago	1,880
1494H	St. Louis	480
1494I	Minneapolis	480
1494J	Kansas City	480
1494K	Dallas	360
1494L	San Francisco	1,824

Series 1934, Julian-Morgenthau

No.	Bank	Notes Printed
1495A	Boston	8,720
1495B	New York	11,520
1495C	Philadelphia	6,000
1495D	Cleveland	1,480
1495E	Richmond	1,200
1495F	Atlanta	2,400
1495G	Chicago	3,840
1495H	St. Louis	2,040
1495I	Minneapolis	not printed
1495J	Kansas City	1,200
1495K	Dallas	1,200
1495L	San Francisco	3,600

Series 1934A, Julian-Morgenthau

No.	Bank	Notes Printed
1495aG	Chicago	1,560

Series 1934B, Julian-Vinson

No.	Bank	Notes Printed
1495bB	New York	24

Gold Certificates/Series of 1928 & 1934

The face and back designs are similar to No. 1494 except for the seal and *obligation.*

No.	Series	Signatures	Notes Printed
1496	1928	Woods-Mellon	48,000
1497	1934	Julian-Morgenthau	36,000

G.F.C. Smillie engraved the portrait of Woodrow Wilson, the twenty-eighth president of the U.S. The remainder of the face and back of this note were engraved by O. Benzing, W.B. Wells and F. Pauling, D.R. McLeod, M. Fenton, R.L. Vallette, W.O. Marks, A.R Gould and J. Eissler.

No.	Series	Signatures	Notes Issued
1498	1934	Julian-Morgenthau	42,000

Remarks: This is the highest denomination bank note to be printed by the Bureau of Engraving and Printing. It was not meant for general circulation but was to be used in transactions between Federal Reserve Banks.

At one time a limited number of patterns, essay, and trial pieces were struck before a new coin design was accepted. The recipients were usually government officials who would give an opinion or vote on these proposed designs. These pieces sometimes found their way into the numismatic marketplace. Unissued paper money designs, to the contrary, rarely left the Treasury Department. During the last century, designers and engravers were occasionally permitted to keep a few examples of their work, often in the form of die proofs in various stages of completion. Some of these designs have since found their way into private collections. The syngraphist is left to wonder what the remaining essays and rejected designs looked like.

Just as the final manuscript for the first edition of this catalog was approaching completion, 12 paper money essays were observed at the Bureau of Engraving and Printing; they were illustrated in that edition. After five more years of research, additional essays and information about them were presented in *U.S. Essay Proof and Specimen Notes*. Some of the designs from this book are illustrated on the following pages.

The Acts of July 17 and August 5, 1861 authorized 3.65% interest-bearing treasury notes in denominations of $5, $10 and $20. After ABNCo prepared designs for each, the company was instructed to alter these designs so they could be issued as $1, $2 and $3 United States (legal tender) notes.

This illustration demonstrates how the engraved plate for the $20 note was altered. Nevertheless, none of these notes were issued. *Army and Navy*, by Henry Herrick, was engraved by Louis Delnoce. This subject was used on at least two state-issued notes: the Mt. Holly Bank, New Jersey $1.50; and the Harrisburg Bank, Pennsylvania $3.

In 1873 there was a plan to issue national circulating notes that would replace worn and mutilated national bank notes. Engraved plates were made for most denominations. There are $10 proof impressions for thirteen different national banks at the Bureau of Engraving and Printing. In 1875 the Secretary of the Treasury announced that new notes would not be issued. Instead, original national bank notes would have the date 1875 added to the original designs. The portrait of William H. Seward was engraved by Charles Schlecht.

Along with the $1, $2 and $5 1896 silver certificates, a $10 design was to be included. Although these notes continue to be considered exquisite designs, they were not accepted, primarily by bankers. The plates for all four denominations were altered to "simplify" the notes; the altered designs had the date of 1897. Nevertheless, none were issued with the latter date; the $10 note was issued with either date.

The 1901 $10 note (No. 483) was originally prepared as a silver certificate with this image of the battleship *Massachusetts* engraved by Marcus W. Baldwin. The portraits of William Bainbridge and Stephen Decatur were engraved by G.F.C. Smillie.

Series of 1928 small-size silver certificates were issued in denominations of $1 and $5 only. However, as this illustration demonstrates, a $2 note was considered. The portrait of Thomas Jefferson was engraved by Charles Burt.

Series of 1934 small-size silver certificates were issued in denominations of $1, $5 and $10 only. This illustration indicates that a $20 note was planned. The portrait of Andrew Jackson was engraved by Alfred Sealey.

This $100 silver certificate series of 1934 was not issued. The portrait of Benjamin Franklin was engraved by John Eissler.

There is a relationship between the U.S. Postal Service and the Treasury that is not generally known. Until 1829 the U.S. Postal Service was part of the U.S. Treasury. Thirty years later there was a symbolic relationship.

As the Civil War got under way, the value of essential metals began to rise rapidly. The intrinsic value of coinage soon exceeded the face value of the coins. The coins in circulation began to disappear, either into the hoarder's chest or into the melting pot. Commerce was handicapped because ordinary daily transactions were impeded by the lack of small denomination coins. Change for a sale was often taken in merchandise. Merchants were forced to issue tokens and scrip in denominations less than one dollar in value, and these would be redeemed only by the issuing firm. Many state and privately issued bank notes were discounted with the hope of putting some of the coins back into circulation.

On July 17, 1862, at the suggestion of Salmon P. Chase, President Abraham Lincoln signed into law a bill authorizing the acceptance of stamps as currency. Post office supplies of regular stamps were exhausted before special stamps without gum could be prepared.

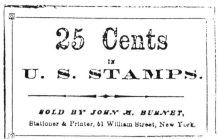

In a few of the larger northern cities merchants quickly had stationers print small envelopes with the merchant's name and address. These envelopes were meant to hold a specified number of postage stamps. Approximately 100 different types of these collectible envelopes from a possible 500 have been recorded. With the exception of a few pieces from Albany, Brooklyn, Boston Cincinnati, Jersey City and Philadelphia, the majority of recorded envelopes originated in New York City. Everyone did not have access to, nor did they take advantage of, these containers. Almost immediately the Treasury Department had a sticky problem on its hands the redemption of millions of soiled stamps, many of which had adhered to other stamps.

The Treasury Department began to issue small notes with designs that resembled postage stamps, but these had no legal backing because the law of July 17 applied only to genuine postage stamps. This defect in the law was corrected by the Act of March 3, 1863, which clearly stated that the government would issue fractional currency notes. At the request of the federal government, four private bank note companies printed notes for 3, 5, 10, 15, 25 and 50 cents.

There were five issues of fractional currency in these denominations. As the normal metal coinage slowly returned to circulation, Acts of Congress of January 14, 1875 and April 17, 1876 allowed for coin redemption of all these notes.

A total of $368,720,000 in these small notes was issued between 1862 and 1876; $2,000,000 worth are still unredeemed, many of which are in the hands of collectors.

The American Bank Note Company and the National Bank Note Company printed notes for the first and fourth issue while the Columbian Bank Note Company and Joseph R. Carpenter printed the backs of the fifth issue. The Bureau of Engraving and Printing printed the second and third issues, but only the face of the fifth issue.

Issue	Denominations	Periods of Circulation
First*	– 5, 10, – 25 and 50 cents	August 21, 1862–May 27, 1863
Second	– 5, 10 – 25 and 50 cents	October 10, 1863–February 23, 1867
Third	3, 5, 10, – 25 and 50 cents	December 5, 1864–August 16, 1869
Fourth	– – 10, 15, 25 and 50 cents	July 14, 1869–February 16, 1875
Fifth	– – 10, – 25 and 50 cents	February 26, 1874–February 15, 1876

* The first issue is usually referred to as postage currency because of the stamp facsimile designs.

Listing of Postage Stamp Envelopes

This list was compiled by Milton Friedberg with additions by the author. These envelopes often carry additionl messages for other advertisers; often there are varieties of each. All these pieces are rare with no more than six known of any one type. It is unlikely that more than a total of 500 pieces have survived. The average price is $300. Not listed are envelopes with no identifiable user or advertiser.

ms=manuscript, na=no amount, nc=no city, (NYC)=probable location

ARMSTRONG, H., 140 Sixth Ave., NYC 25¢
ARTHUR, GREGORY & Co. Stationers
  29 Nassau St., NYC 25¢ & 50¢
BENNETT & REAY Envelopes
  5 & 7 Spruce St. (nc) 25¢ & 50¢
BERGEN & TRIPP, 114 Nassau St., NYC 25¢
  & 50¢
BERLIN & JONES, Stationer
  134 William St., NYC 25¢
BRAISTED, P.D., Billiard Hall,
  14 & 16 Fourth Ave., NYC 25¢
BROWN, C.G., Lafarge House Segar Store
  669 Broadway, NYC 50¢

BROWN & RUSSELL, 162 Nassau St.,NYC 25¢
BRYAN, JOSEPH, Clothing,
  214 Fulton St., NYC 15¢
BROWNING & LONG, Salem, MA 25¢
BURNET, JOHN M., Stationer & Printer
  51 William St., NYC 25¢ & 50¢
CHICKHAUS, CHAS. T., Havana Segars
  176 Broadway, NYC 25¢ & 50¢
CLARRY & REILLEY, Stationer
  12–14 Spruce St., NYC (na)
COFREN, J.W., Apothecary, Augusta, ME 25¢
CORLIES, B.F. & MACY Stationers
  33 Nassau St., NYC 25¢ & 50¢

CROOK & DUFF Bar, Lunch/and Dining Room
    39 & 40 Park Row and 147 & 149 Nassau St.,
    (NYC) 25 & 30¢
CUTTER TOWER & CO. Stationer
    128 Nassau St., NYC (na)
DAWLEY, T.R. , Printer, New York, NY 50¢
DAWLEY, T.R., 104 Fulton St., NYC 25¢
DAWLEY, T.R. , Stationer & Printer
    28, 30 & 32 Centre DSt., NYC 25¢ & 50¢
DAWSON, E.S. & Co., Syracuse, NY 50¢
DOUBET, MAD. A., Importer
    697 Broadway, (NYC) 25¢ (ms)
DUFFY, FRANCIS, Oysters & Dining
    239–241 8th Ave., NYC 25¢
DUNTON & NINESTEEL Dealers in Ribbons, Flowers,
    Laces, Silks
    17 N. Second St., (Philadelphia, PA) (na)
EMBREE Stationer, 130 Grand St., (NYC) 25¢
EXCELSIOR ENVELOPE MANUFACTORY
    51 Ann St., NYC 25¢
FELT, WILLARD & Co. Stationers
    14 Maiden Lane, NYC 25¢
FORCE, JNO. C. (nc) 50¢
FOX'S OLD BOWERY THEATRE, (nc) 25¢
GERMAN OPERA, 485 Broadway, NYC (na)
GIRARD HOUSE
    Cor. W. Broadway Chambers St., (NYC) 25¢
GOULDS DINING ROOMS
    35 Nassau St., NYC 75¢
HALLENBECK'S Family Restaurant
    87 East 27th St., (NYC) 25¢
HARLEM & N.Y. NAV. Co. Stamps & Envelopes
    (NYC) 25¢
HARPEL, Printers, Cincinnati, OH 5¢ & 20¢
JAMES Hatter, (NYC) 25¢
HOVEY, S.F. & Co., Boston, MA 25¢ (ms)
HUDSON AND NEW POWER, (NYC) 50¢
IRVING HOUSE on the European Plan, (NYC) 10¢
HAMILTON JOHNSTON Card & Envelope Printer
    (NYC) ....$....Cts.
JONES, C.O., 76 Cedar St. (NYC) 25¢
KAVANAGH & FREEMAN Billiard Saloon
    Cor. Tenth St. & Broadway (NYC) 25¢
LEACH, J., Writing Paper, Envelopes and Blank Books
    86 Nassau St., NYC 15, 20, 25, 30, 50 & 75¢
LEE, D.W., Stationer, 82 Nassau St., NYC (na)
LETSON, R., Mercantile Dining Room
    256 Broadway, NYC (na)
LINCOLN, HENRY W., Apothecary
    Chestnut and Charles, Boston, MA 30¢
LINGARD, J.W., New Bowery Theatre, (NYC) 25¢
LITHO OF C. KNICKERBOCKER, Albany, NY 50¢
MACOVY & HERWIG Stationers and Printers
    112 & 114 Broadway, (NYC) 25¢
MAILLARD'S, HY, Confectionary and Saloon
    621 Broadway, (NYC) 20, 25 & 50¢
MASSASOIT HOUSE
    Springfield, MA 10, 25 & 50¢
McELROY, FRANK, 113 Nassau St., (NYC) 25¢
METROPOLITAN HOTEL, (NYC) 10¢
MILLER & GRANT Importers
    703 Broadway, NYC 25¢

MORRIS BROTHERS Minstrels
    Trowbridge, MA (na)
MOSER, ANDREW A., Stationer
    22 William St., (NYC) 25¢
MURPHY, Wm. (Printer), 438 Canal St., NYC 25¢
MURPHY, W.H., Stationer
    372 PEARL St., (NYC) 50¢
NATIONAL EXPRESS COMPANY
    74 Broadway, NYC 25¢
NEW BOWERY THEATRE, NYC 25¢
N.Y. CONSOLIDATED STAGE CO., (NYC) 50¢
N.Y.C.R.R., NYC 20¢
N.Y. CENTRAL R.R. CO., NYC 10, 25 & 50¢
NIBLO'S GARDEN, WM. WHEATLEY, (NYC) 50¢
NIXON'S CREMORNE GARDENS,
    (NYC) 10, 25 & 50¢
O'NEILL'S, CHRIS
    Hudson Av. & Prospect St. Brooklyn 25¢
OYSTER BAR HOUSE, 553 Broadway (NYC) 25¢
OYSTER HOUSE, 604 Broadway, NYC 25¢
OYSTER AND DINING SALOON, Wm. Van Name's
    216 Broadway, NYC 25¢
PAULDING'S EXPRESS, (NYC) 25¢ (ms)
PETTIT & CROOKS, (NYC) (na) ¢
POMROY'S, 699 Broadway, NYC 50¢
POWER, BOGARDUS & CO. Steamship Line
    Pier 34, N. River, NYC
RAYNOR, S. Envelope Mfgr.
    118 William St., NYC 25 & 50¢
REEVE'S, CAPT. TOM,
    214 Broadway, NYC 10 & 25¢
REVERE HOUSE
    604, 606 & 608 Broadway, NYC 25¢
RICE, W.B. & CO., 201 Hanover St., Boston, MA 25¢
RICHARDSON, THOMAS, AGT.
    66 Maiden Lane, NYC 25¢
RIGGIN, E.M.
    336 Delaware Ave. and Pine St. Wharf, Phila., PA
    50¢
ROBINS, WM., 49 & 51 Ann St., NYC 25¢
SCOVEL, REUBEN, 26 Nassau St., (NYC) 25 & 50¢
SHELLEY, C.C., 68 Barclay St., (NYC) 25¢
SMITH, H.
    137 William St., NY 10, 12, 13, 15, 20, 24, 25 &
    50¢
SNOW & HAPGOOD, 22 Court St., Boston, MA
    (na) cents, 10, 15, 25, 50 & 75¢
SONNEBORN Stationer & Printer
    130 Nassau St. NYC 25¢
TAYLOR'S HOTEL,
    Exchange Pl., Jersey City, NJ 25 & 50¢
THOMAS, DION, Stationer,
    142 Nassau St., NYC (na)
THOMPSON, R.D.
    152 William St., NYC 10 & 25¢
TICKNOR & FIELDS PUBLISHERS
    135 Washington St., Boston, MA 50¢
TURNEY, G.W. & S., 77Chatham St., NYC 25¢
WILEY, JAMES, Wines & Liquors
    307 Broadway, NYC 25 & 50¢

Three-Cent Notes/Third Issue

Portrait of George Washington

Back

No.	Description	Notes Issued	Fine	EFine	Unc
1500	portrait has light background	20,064,130	$15.	$25.	$60.
1501	portrait has dark background	included in above	15.	30.	85.

Remarks: There were 20,175,000 pieces printed for No. 1500.

Five-Cent Notes/First Issue

Face: brown. The portrait of Thomas Jefferson is on the 5-cent stamp of 1861 (Scott 75). The design was prepared under the direction of James MacDonough; the lettering is probably the work of William D. Nichols. The portrait was engraved by W. Marshall.

Back: black. The design was prepared under the direction of James P. Major and Nathaniel Jocelyn.

No.	Descriptions	Notes Printed	Fine	EFine	Unc
1502	perforated edges; "ABC" on back.	44,857,780	$15.	$30.	$110.
1503	perforated edges; without "ABC"		15.	35.	150.
1504	straight edges; "ABC" on back	included in above	12.	20.	50.
1505	straight edges; without "ABC"		15.	35.	165.

Remarks: Lot 406 of the Julian S. Marks collection, sold in 1971, was a canceled cover with No. 1504 used as postage. "ABC" stands for American Bank Note Co.

Five-Cent Notes/Second Issue

Face: brown. The portrait of George Washington, within the bronze oval, was engraved by J.P. Ourdan; the background was engraved by James Duthie.

Back: brown. George W. Casilear is the designer. The large "5" is bronze.

No.	Description	Notes Printed	Fine	EFine	Une
1506	without surcharge on back		$10.	$20.	$40.
1507	surcharge "18 63" on back	55,250,097	10.	20.	50.
1508	surcharge "S" and "18 63"		12.	30.	70.
1509	surcharge "R 1" and "18 63"	296,425	30.	75.	225.

Five-Cent Notes/Third Issue

Placement of letter "a."

Face: black. Spencer M. Clark was Superintendent of the National Currency Bureau under Abraham Lincoln. Clark was responsible for designing the U.S. Treasury seal, a variation of which is still used. When this note appeared, Congress immediately moved to ban the portrait of a living person on bank notes and other obligations (Act of April 7, 1866, Chap. XXVIII, Sec. 1, and Act of March 3, 1873, Chap. CCLXVIII, Sec. 3576).

No.	Description	Notes Issued	Fine	EFine	Une
1510	green back		$12.	$20.	$ 75.
1511	"a" on face, green back	13,400,000	15.	25.	100.
1512	red back		15.	30.	125.
1513	"a" on face, red back		20.	35.	150.

Ten-Cent Notes/First Issue

Face: green. The portrait of George Washington, as seen on the 10–cent stamp of 1861 (Scott 68) was engraved by W. Marshall; it was based on the painting by Gilbert Stuart.

Back: black. The design was prepared under the direction of James P. Major and Nathaniel Jocelyn.

No.	Description	Notes Printed	Fine	EFine	Unc
1514	perforated edges; "ABC" on back		$20.	$35.	$115.
1515	perforated edges; without "ABC"	41,153,780	20.	40.	150.
1516	plain edges; "ABC" on back		15.	25.	55.
1517	plain edges; without "ABC"		20.	70.	225.

Remarks: The monogram "ABC" stands for American Bank Note Co.

Ten-Cent Notes/Second Issue

Face: slate-gray. The portrait of George Washington, within the bronze oval, was engraved by J.P. Ourdan; the background was engraved by James Duthie.

Back: green.

No.	Descriptions	Notes Issued	Fine	EFine	Unc
1518	no surcharge on back		$ 15.	$ 30.	$ 60.
1519	surcharge "18 63" on back		15.	30.	65.
1520	surcharge "S" and "18 63" on back	61,803,393	20.	40.	75.
1521	surcharge "1" and "18 63" on back		20.	65.	200.
1522	surcharge "0" and "63" on back		375.	1100.	2250.
1523	surcharge "T1" and "18 63" on back	427,450	20.	35.	225.

Ten-Cent Notes/Third Issue

Face: black. Portrait of George Washington

Placement of "1".

Back: green or red

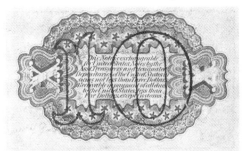

No.	Description	Notes Issued	Fine	EFine	Unc
1524	printed signatures of Colby-Spinner; green back		$15.	$25.	$ 50.
1525	as above with "1" near left margin on face		15.	30.	70.
1526	printed signatures of Colby-Spinner; red back		15.	35.	100.
1527	as above with "1" near left margin on face	169,761,345	20.	40.	125.
1528	autographed signatures of Colby-Spinner; red back		25.	50.	150.
1528a	autographed signatures of Colby-Spinner; green back		-----------	2 known	-----------
1529	autographed signatures of Jeffries-Spinner; red back		30.	60.	275.

Remarks: Although "cents" did not appear on these notes, they circulated, as intended, as 10–cent pieces. Of the 169,761,345 pieces issued, 18,000 have red backs.

Ten-Cent Notes/Fourth Issue

Face: black. The model for the bust of *Liberty* is said to have been Mary Hull. It was designed by Charles Burt and engraved by Frederick Girsch.

Back: green. The printer was the National Bank Note Co.

No.	Description	Seal	Notes Issued	Fine	EFine	Unc
1530	watermarked paper	lg. red		$10.	$15.	$55.
1531	pink fibers in paper	lg. red		10.	20.	60.
1532	pink fibers/blue ends	lg. red	179,097,600	10.	15.	40.
1533	previous listing inaccurate			—	—	—
1534	pink fibers/blue ends	sm. red		10.	25.	60.

Remarks: The large seal is 40 mm in diameter; the small seal is 38 mm.

Ten-Cent Notes/Fifth Issue

Face: black. The portrait of William Meredith, Secretary of the Treasury (1849–1850), is by Thomas Knollwood; it was engraved by Charles Burt.

Back: green. The printer was the Columbian Bank Note Co.

No.	Description	Notes Issued	Fine	EFine	Unc
1535	long thin key in green seal ⎫		$10.	$20.	$60.
1536	long thin key in red seal ⎬	199,899,000	10.	15.	25.
1537	short thick key in red seal ⎭		10.	15.	25.

Fifteen-Cent Notes/Fourth Issue

 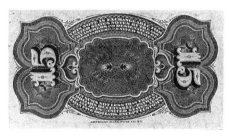

Face: black. The bust of *Columbia* is by designer C. Romerson; it was engraved by Charles Burt. The National Bank Note Co. prepared the plates.

Back: green. American Bank Note Co. prepared the plates. The letter engraving on both the face and back is by W.D. Nichols.

No.	Description	Seal	Notes Issued	Fine	EFine	Unc
1539	watermarked paper; pink fibers	lg. red ⎫		$25.	$40.	$115.
1540	plain paper; pink fibers	lg. red ⎬	27,240,040	35.	65.	200.
1541	violet fibers; blue ends	lg. red ⎭		30.	60.	165.
1542	as above	sm. red	8,121,400	25.	50.	150.

Twenty-Five Cent Notes/First Issue

Face: brown. The portrait of Thomas Jefferson was engraved by W. Marshall.

Back: black. The monogram "ABC" stands for American Bank Note Co.

No.	Description	Notes Issued	Fine	EFine	Unc
1548	perforated edges; "ABC" on back		$22.	$50.	$175.
1549	perforated edges; without "ABC"	20,902,768	25.	65.	275.
1550	plain edges; "ABC" on back		15.	25.	85.
1551	plain edges; without "ABC"		30.	70.	325.

Twenty-Five Cent Notes/Second Issue

Face: slate-gray. The portrait of George Washington, in the bronze oval was engraved by J.P. Ourdan; the background is by James Duthie. George W. Casilear is the designer.

Back: purple.

No.	Description	Notes Issued	Fine	EFine	Unc
1552	value only on back		$15.	$30.	$100.
1552a	surcharge "18 63" on back		15.	50.	150.
1553	surcharge "A" and "18 63" on back	29,299,585	15.	40.	135.
1554	surcharge "2" and "63" on back		20.	50.	150.
1555	surcharge "S" and "18 63" on back		20.	40.	135.
1556	surcharge "T-1" and "18 63" on back; fiber paper		30.	80.	250.
1557	surcharge "T-2" and "18 63," fiber paper	1,173,780	30.	60.	200.
1558	previous listing inaccurate		—	—	—

Twenty-Five-Cent/Third Issue

Face: black. Charles Skinner engraved the portrait of William P. Fessenden, Secretary of the Treasury in 1864.

Back: Nos. 1559–1560a red; Nos. 1561–1567 green.

Normal position of "a".

Large "a" on No. 1567.

No.	Description	Notes Issued	Fine	EFine	Unc
1559	red back		$ 25.	$ 45.	$ 125.
1560	"a" lower left; minor	16,000			
	variations in size of "a"		90.	150.	275.
1561	solid bronze on fiber				
	paper; "M 2 6 5" surcharge		300.	600.	1500.
1562	as above; small "a"		500.	900.	3000.
1563	outline bronze on fiber				
	paper; "M 2 6 5" surcharge	124,566,755	60.	100.	200.
1564	as above with "a"		75.	150.	300.
1565	outline bronze; no surcharge		20.	40.	100.
1566	as above; size of "a" varies		25.	50.	125.
1567	as above; large "a"		500.	800.	1600.

Remarks: The 7,107 notes issued on March 22, 1865 probably account for No. 1564. This issue violated the ban against portraits of living persons on U.S. currency (see Nos. 1510–1513).

Twenty-Five-Cent Notes/Fourth Issue

Face: black. Printed by the National Bank Note Co., the face was designed by Douglas C. Romerson and engraved by Frederick Girsch.

Back: green. Printed by American Bank Note Co.

No.	Description	Seal	Notes Issued	Fine	EFine	Unc
1568	watermarked paper	lg. red		$15.	$25.	$ 75.
1569	plain white paper	lg. red		15.	25.	60.
1570	pink fibers, blue ends in paper	lg. red	235,689,024	15.	25.	100.
1571	violet fibers, blue ends	sm. red		20.	40.	100.
1572	as above	lg. brn		20.	40.	100.

Remarks: The large seal is 40 mm in diameter, the small is 39 mm. For No. 1571 32,516,256 were issued.

Twenty-Five-Cent Notes/Fifth Issue

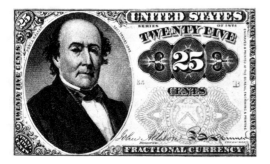

Face: black. The portrait of Robert Walker, Secretary of the Treasury (1845–1849), was engraved by Charles Burt.

Back: green. Printed by the Columbian Bank Note Co.

No.	Description	Notes Issued	Fine	EFine	Unc
1573	long thin key in red seal	144,368,000	$10.	$20.	$35.
1574	short thick key in red seal	included in above	10.	20.	35.

Remarks: The ink from the red seal occasionally bled through, giving the face a pink color.

Fifty-Cent Notes/First Issue

Face: green. The portrait of George Washington as it appears on the ten-cent stamp, Scott A27.

Back: black. Printed by American Bank Note Co.

No.	Description	Notes Issued	Fine	EFine	Une
1575	12 perforations per 20 mm; "ABC" on back		$35.	$ 60.	$250.
1575a	14 perforations per 20 mm; "ABC" on back	17,263,344		12–15 known	
1576	perforated; without "ABC"		75.	125.	400.
1577	plain edges; "ABC" on back		25.	50.	100.
1578	plain edges; without "ABC" on back		75.	135.	425.

Fifty-Cent Notes/Second Issue

Face: slate-gray. The portrait of George Washington, within the bronze oval, was engraved by J.P. Ourdan; the background was engraved by James Duthie.

Back: red.

No.	Description	Notes Issued	Fine	EFine	Une
1579	no surcharge on back		no authentic examples known		
1580	surcharge "18 63" on back		$30.	$ 75.	$250.
1581	"Λ" and "18 63" on back	11,844,464	35.	60.	150.
1582	"1" and "18 63" on back		35.	60.	175.
1583	"0–1" & "18 63" on back; fiber paper		60.	100.	300.
1584	"R-2" & "18 63" on back; fiber paper	1,246,000	60.	100.	300.
1585	"T-1" & "18 63" on back; fiber paper		50.	75.	225.

Fifty-Cent Notes/Third Issue

Face: black. The vignette is entitled *Justice with Scales*. See Nos. 1609–1619a for back design. Nos. 1586 through 1596 have red backs; the surcharge is "A-2–6–5."

No.	Description	Fine	EFine	Une
1586	no design figure on face; no surcharge	$ 35.	$ 75.	$ 250.
1586a	as above with "A-2-6-5" surcharge on back	35.	75.	250.
1587	"1" and "a" on face; no surcharge	125.	300.	900.
1587a	as above with "A-2-6-5" surcharge on back	125.	300.	900.
1588	"1" only on face; no surcharge	50.	90.	325.
1588a	as above with "A-2-6-5" surcharge on back	50.	90.	325.
1589	"a" only on face; no surcharge	60.	100.	350.
1589a	as above with "A-2-6-5" surcharge on back	50.	90.	325.
	The following have autographed signatures of Colby-Spinner and red backs.			
1590	no design features on face; no surcharge	—	100.	250.
1591	with surcharge	—	125.	300.
1592	with surcharge "S-2–6–4", fiber paper	100.	200.	400.
	The following have printed signatures on fiber paper and a "S-2–6–4" surcharge.			
1593	no design figures on face	3000.	6000.	12500.
1594	"1" and "a" on face	------------- 2 known ------------		
1595	"1" only on face, 5 known	4000.	7500.	15000.
1596	"a" only on face, 6 known, none better than EFine	4500.	8500.	17500.
	The following have green backs with no surcharge.			
1597	no design figures on face	30.	75.	200.
1598	"1" and "a" on face	75.	175.	750.
1599	"1" only on face	50.	125.	225.
1600	"a" only on face	50.	125.	250.
	The following have wide or narrow "A-2–6–5" surcharges.			
1601	no design figures on face; narrow surcharge	30.	75.	200.
1601a	no design figures on face; wide surcharge	40.	85.	300.
1602	"1" and "a" on face; narrow surcharge	75.	175.	750.
1602a	as preceding; wide surcharge	350.	750.	2250.
1603	"1" only on face; narrow surcharge	50.	125.	250.
1603a	as preceding; wide surcharge	65.	150.	400.
1604	no design figures on face	60.	125.	350.
1604a	as preceding; wide surcharge	70.	175.	500.
	The following, with green backs, have a "A-2-6-5" surcharge on fiber paper.			
1605	no design figures on face	60.	125.	350.
1606	"1" and "a" on face	300.	700.	2250.
1607	"1" only on face	75.	200.	500.
1608	"a" only on face	85.	225.	600.
1608a	surcharge "S-2–6–4" 8 known	—	20000.	—

Fifty-Cent Notes/Third Issue

Face: black. F.E. Spinner, U.S. Treasurer (1861–1875). This issue appeared during the lifetime of F.E. Spinner (see Nos. 1510–1513).

Back: green or red.

Position of "a" and "1" on face.

No.	Description	Fine	EFine	Unc
	Red backs; "A-2–6–5" surcharge			
1609	no design figures on face	$ 35.	$ 75.	$ 175.
1610	"1" and "a" on face	125.	250.	750.
1611	"1" only on face	60.	100.	250.
1612	"a" only on face	75.	125.	275.
1613	autographed signatures of Colby-Spinner	50.	100.	300.
1614	autographed signatures of Allison-Spinner	60.	125.	350.
1615	autographed signatures of Allison-New	1500.	2000.	3500.
	Green backs; "A-2–6–5" surcharge			
1616	no design figures on face; no surcharge	30.	60.	175.
1616a	as preceding with "A-2-6-5" surcharge on back	50.	100.	250.
1617	"1" and "a" on face; no surcharge	50.	100.	300.
1617a	as preceding with "A-2-6-5" surcharge on back	200.	500.	1500.
1618	"1" only on face; no surcharge	50.	100.	350.
1618a	as preceding with "A-2-6-5" surcharge on back	75.	150.	450.
1619	"a" only on face; no surcharge	60.	120.	400.
1619a	as preceding with "A-2-6-5" surcharge on back	85.	175.	500.

Remarks: One sheet of No. 1615 remained unsigned during the term of F.E. Spinner, and was signed by John Allison in 1869 or later; in 1875 or 1876 John C. New added his signature. (Walter Breen, "New look at old notes," Numismatic News, August 15, 1971, p. 28.) Based on reconstructed figures, 52,866,690 notes were issued for Nos. 1609–1619a; this figure is part of the third issue total of 73,471,853.

Fifty-Cent Notes/Third Issue

Back: green. The face design is similar to No. 1619.

No.	Description	Notes Issued	Fine	EFine	Unc
1620	no design figure on face		$40.	$ 90.	$ 255.
1621	"1" and "a" on face	10,868,028	100.	250.	850.
1622	"1" only on face		65.	125.	400.
1623	"a" only on face		75.	150.	450.

Remarks. The reconstructed figure above is part of the third issue total of 73,471,853.

Fifty-Cent Notes/Fourth Issue

Face: black. The portrait of Abraham Lincoln, based on a photograph by Anthony Berger, was engraved by Charles Burt; it was printed by American Bank Note Co.

The green back was printed by the National Bank Note Co.

No.	Description	Seal	VFine	EFine	Unc
1624	watermarked paper; pink fibers	lg. red	$65.	$90.	$125.
1625	previously listing inaccurate	—	—	—	—

Fifty-Cent Notes/Fourth Issue

Face: black. George W. Casilear is the probable designer of this note, which bears a bust of E.M. Stanton, Lincoln's Secretary of War. Charles Burt received $600 for this engraved portrait. This note was issued in January 1870; Stanton died on Dec. 24, 1869. Apparently the note was in production while Stanton was alive. See Nos. 1510–1513 for the restriction of images of living people on U.S. currency.

The green back was printed by American Bank Note Co.

No.	Description	Seal	Notes Issued	VFine	EFine	Unc
1626	violet fibers with blue ends	sm. red	86,048,000	$25.	$70.	$125.
1627	violet fibers with blue ends	sm. brn	incl. in above	25.	70.	125.

Face: black. George W. Casilear is the probable designer of this note, which bears a bust of Samuel Dexter, Secretary of War and the Treasury (1800–1802). Charles Burt engraved this portrait.

The green back was printed by the National Bank Note Co.

No.	Description	Seal	Notes Issued	VFine	EFine	Unc
1628	violet fibers, blue ends,	green	49,599,200	$25.	$75.	$125.

Fifty-Cent Notes/Fifth Issue/Red Seal

Face: black. The bust of William H. Crawford, originally painted by John W. Jarvis, was engraved by Charles Burt.

The green back was printed by Joseph R. Carpenter.

No.	Description	Notes Issued	VFine	EFine	Unc
1629	pink paper, pink fibers	13,160,000	$20.	$30.	$90.
1630	white paper, violet fibers, blue ends	incl. in above	20.	30.	90.

President Andrew Johnson selected members of the cabinet and certain legislators as the recipients of the first proof and specimen notes. Soon thereafter similar uniface notes, printed with both wide and narrow margins, were sold to the public. Some specimen notes were also used to make up fractional currency shields. By soaking, some of these notes were later removed by collectors.

Most specimen and proof notes were printed from adopted designs. Only wide margin examples and types not adopted will be illustrated here. The numbering system is the same as for regular issues with the addition of an "S".

On April 27, 1862 Union vessels seized the *Bermuda*, a ship returning from England with a cargo destined for the Confederate coast. Part of the cargo included bank note paper prepared for the Confederate States of America. This paper watermarked "CSA" was later purchased by the United States Treasury Department and used for proof and specimen fractional currency. Three separate purchases were made; the average price was about $2 per ream. The third purchase included 35 reams of foolscap at $6 per ream.

The dimensions of the shield are 20 × 25 inches.

Fractional currency shields, probably the idea of U.S. Treasurer Francis E. Spinner as illustrated here, were prepared before the release of the fourth and fifth issues. Each of the 4,500 shields produced consisted of 39 uniface specimen notes. Banks and merchants could purchase a shield for $4.50 for the purpose of comparison if a note was thought to be counterfeit. The demand for the shields did not meet the expectations of the Treasury Department. In 1869 the remaining shields were dismantled; the uniface specimen notes were sold to collectors. Some shields were probably destroyed.

No.	Description	Degree of Rarity
1633	shield with grey background	rare
1634	shield with pink background	very rare
1635	shield with green background	extremely rare

Three-Cent Notes

No.	Description	Pieces Issued	Narrow Margin	Wide Margin
1500S	Face, portrait has light background	7,000	$100.	2 known
	Back	7,000	25.	$150.
1501S	Face, portrait has dark background	7,000	40.	200.
	Back	7,000	25.	150.

Proof and Specimen Five Cent Notes

No.	Description	Pieces Issued	Narrow Margin	Wide Margin
1505S	Face with plain edges	5,445	$35.	$150.
	Back	5,445	35.	150.
1506S	Face	3,058	35.	100.
	Back; no surcharge	3,058	35.	100.
1510S	Face	10,500	35.	125.
	Back	10,500	35.	100.
1512S	Face	10,500	35.	125.
	Back; red	10,500	35.	100.

Remarks: The figures for No. 1506 are probably for wide margin pairs issued as of October 31, 1867; additional pairs could have been issued later.

Ten Cent Notes

No.	Description	Pieces Issued	Narrow Margin	Wide Margin
1517S	Face with plain edges	33,780	$40.	$150.
	Back	incl in above	40.	150.
1518S	Face	—	40.	125.
	Back; no surcharges	—	35.	125.
1524S	Back; green		40.	100.
1526S	Face; printed signatures of Colby-Spinner		35.	150.
1528S	Face; written signatures of Colby-Spinner	54,250	50.	125.
	Back; red		40.	100.
1529S	Face; written signatures of Jeffries-Spinner	—	200.	ex. rare
	Back; red	10,000	40.	100.

Fifteen Cent Notes

Portraits of Gen. W.T. Sherman and U.S. Grant.

No.	Description	Pieces Issued	Narrow Margin	Wide Margin
1543S	Face; printed signatures of Colby-Spinner		$ 100.	$200.
	Back; green		75.	175.
1544S	Face; written signatures of Colby Spinner		1000.	unknown
	Back; red		75.	175.
1545S	Face; written signatures of Jeffries-Spinner	9,016	150.	300.
	Back; red		75.	175.
1546S	Face; written signatures of Allison-Spinner		175.	450.
	Back; red		60.	125.
1547S	Face without signatures		2 known	unknown
	Back; red	10,000	75.	175.

Remarks: Of the 9,016 pieces issued for No. 1543S, 3,513 were outstanding in 1884.

Twenty-five Cent Notes

No.	Description	Pieces Issued	Narrow Margin	Wide Margin
1551S	Face with plain edges	15,672	$50.	$150.
	Back without "ABC"	included in above	40.	125.
1552S	Face	—	50.	150.
	Back; no surcharges	—	40.	150.
1559S	Face	8,600	40.	175.
	Back; red, no surcharges	8,600	40.	125.
1563S	Face	8,600	40.	175.
1565S	Back; green	8,600	40.	150.

Fifty-Cent Notes

No.	Description	Pieces Issued	Narrow Margin	Wide Margin
1578S	Face with plain edges	10,872	$75.	$175.
	Back	10,872	65.	165.
1579S	Face	6,385	60.	200.
	Back without "ABC" or surcharges	6,365	50.	150.

Enlargement of face portion

Fifty-Cent Notes

No.	Description	Pieces Issued	Narrow Margin	Wide Margin
1586S	Face; printed signatures of Colby-Spinner		$ 75.	$ 225.
	Back		50.	150.
1590S	Face; written signatures of Colby-Spinner		100.	275.
	Back; no surcharges		50.	150.
1592S	Face; written signatures of Jeffries-Spinner		200.	rare
	Back; no surcharges		75.	175.
1593S	Back; green, no surcharges		2000.	7500.

Remarks: No. 1592 is known only as a specimen.

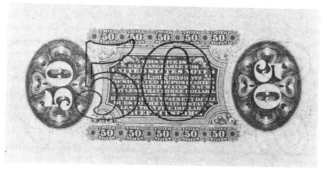

Fifty-Cent Notes

No.	Description	Pieces Issued	Narrow Margin	Wide Margin
1609S	Face; printed signatures of Colby-Spinner		$ 80.	$ 175.
1613S	Face; written signatures of Colby-Spinner		125.	225.
1614S	Face; written signatures of Allison-Spinner		7,000.	10,000.
1615S	Face; written signatures of Jeffries-Spinner		200.	rare
	Back; red, no surcharges		60.	165.
1616S	Back; green, no surcharges		60.	165.
1620S	Back; green, no surcharges		60.	165.

Remarks: No. 1615 is known in specimen form only. This note bears the Jeffries-Spinner signatures, not Allison-New. A total of 50,584 notes were printed for Nos. 1586S through 1620S. Specimens of these issues were printed but not sold to the public. A few were presented to VIPs; all examples are rare.

Inverted Printing

Second issued.

Third issue.

There are many examples of printing irregularities throughout the issuing period of fractional currency. The most common is an inverted printing. These range from the inversion of the entire back to pieces that have only a portion of the surcharge inverted. Advanced fractional currency collectors have demonstrated a substantial interest in these error printings. Inversions that have been observed or reported are summarized here.

INVERTED BACK

No.	Entire Back	Surcharge	Engraving	Other
1500	observed	—	—	—
1501	observed	—	—	—
1502	reported	—	—	—
1503	observed	—	—	without vertical perforations
1504	observed	—	—	—
1505	observed	—	—	—
1506	reported	observed	reported	with back of 1580, reported
1506	—	—	—	with back of 1583, observed
1507	reported	observed	—	—
1510	observed	—	—	—
1511	observed	—	—	—
1515	observed	—	—	—
1516	observed	—	—	—
1517	observed	—	—	—
1518	observed	—	—	—
1519	—	observed	—	—
1520	—	reported	observed	—
1521	—	observed	—	—
1523	—	reported	—	—
1524	—	reported	—	face & back s'chg inv. observed; face design inverted reported.
1524S	—	—	—	back has denom s'chg inv observed.
1525	—	—	—	face & back s'chg inv. observed without vertical perforations
1549	reported	—	—	—
1550	observed	—	—	—
1551	reported	—	—	—
1552	—	observed	—	back with surcharge of 1552 and engraved design of 1579 observed
1552a	reported	—	—	—
1554a	—	reported	—	—
1555	—	reported	reported	"S" of back s'chg. inv. observed
1556	—	reported	—	—
1557	—	reported	—	—
1559	—	—	reported	—
1565	—	—	—	—
1566	reported	observed	reported	—
1567	—	—	observed	—
1575	reported	—	—	—
1576	observed	—	—	—
1577	observed	—	—	—
1578	reported	—	—	—
1579S	—	—	—	back has denom. surcharge inverted to the engraving, observed
1580	reported	—	reported	—
1581	—	observed	reported	—
1582	—	observed	observed	—
1584	reported	—	—	—
1585	—	observed	—	—
1592	—	—	observed	—
1601	—	reported	—	—
1602	—	reported	—	—
1603	—	observed	observed	—
1603a	—	—	—	—
1604	observed	—	—	—
1605	—	—	—	—
1606	reported	—	—	—
1608	—	—	—	—
1616	reported	—	—	—
1616S	—	—	—	back has denomination surcharge inverted, observed
1616a	—	observed	—	—
1617	—	observed	—	—
1620	observed	—	—	—
1623	—	observed	—	—

Philately, or stamp collecting, and syngraphics share a group of collectible pieces encased postage. As stated in the preceding section on fractional currency, coins became scarce during the Civil War and substitutes were created; postage stamps were just one of many.

The U.S. Treasury estimated that about $27 million in silver coins was in circulation in January 1862. As a result of suspension of specie payment in December 1861, coins of all types, but especially silver coins, began to disappear from circulation in early 1862.

As you probably know from experience, a stamp, when exposed to moisture, can become a messy item, especially when handed from one person to another. Some New York firms adopted Horace Greeley's suggestion and pasted postage stamps on a piece of paper, the bottom of which was folded over to protect the stamps.

On August 12, 1862 Mr. J. Gault solved the problem by patenting a small brass disc with a mica window that covered an encased stamp. In that year the Scovill Button Works in Waterbury, Connecticut began a massive production of Mr. Gault's invention. These cases served as much of the nation's small change. Not only did the cases keep the stamp intact, but the brass backings soon became a convenient medium for advertising.

The stamps of 1861 were issued in denominations of 1 (*Scott* 63), 2 (not a regular issue), 3 (*S*65), 5 (*S*75), 10 (*S*68), 12 (*S*69), 24 (*S*70), 30 (*S*71) and 90 cents (*S*72). For about one year the public accepted postage currency in windowed discs. However the beleaguered federal government never issued enough of the postage stamps to satisfy the need. Notwithstanding, by the summer of 1863 U.S. fractional currency proved to be the better solution.

These encased postage stamps are not only of special interest to collectors of stamps and paper money, but collectors of coins as well. Do encased postage stamps belong to the field of numismatics, philately or syngraphics? They belong to all three and are unique in collecting history.

Most often surviving pieces are in VFine condition. The mica covering is expected to be clear, without any cracks or breaks. One should make certain there is no sign of tampering with the lip of the enclosure. For a thorough coverage of this subject see *Civil War Encased Stamps* by Fred Reed and the *Standard Catalog of Encased Postage* Stamps by Michael J. Hodder and Q. David Bowers.

One-cent Stamps: portrait of Benjamin Franklin

No.	Issuer	VFine	EFine
1637	Aerated Bread Co., New York	$1200.	$1725.
1638	Ayer's Cathartic Pills [Lowell, MA] (short arrows)	250.	375.
1638a	as preceding (long arrows)	rare	
1639	"Take Ayer's Pills" [Lowell, MA]	200.	425.
1640	Ayer's Sarsaparilla [Lowell, MA] (small "AYER'S")	350.	475.

No.	Issuer	VFine	EFine
1641	as preceding (medium "AYER'S")	250.	375.
1642	Bailey & Co., Philadelphia	800.	975.
1643	Joseph L. Bates, "FANCY GOODS," Boston	400.	650.
1644	as preceding, "FANCYGOODS" as one word	800.	975.
1645	Brown's Bronchial Troches [Boston]	700.	975.
1646	F. Buhl & Co., Detroit	750.	1200.
1647	Burnett's Cocoaine Kalliston [Boston]	500.	675.
1648	Burnett's Standard Cooking Extracts [Boston]	450.	675.
1649	Arthur M. Claflin, Hopkinton [Massachusetts]	6000.	9000.
1650	Dougan, New York	800.	1100.
1651	Drake's Plantation Bitters [New York City]	225.	325.
1652	Ellis, McAlpin & Co., Cincinnati	issue uncertain	
1653	G.G. Evans, Philadelphia	750.	975.
1654	Gage Brothers & Drake, Tremont House [Chicago]	750.	950.
1655	J. Gault [Boston and New York] (plain frame)	500.	875.
1656	as preceding (ribbed frame)	rare	
1657	L.C. Hopkins & Co., Cincinnati	unique	
1658	Hunt & Nash, Irving House [New York City] (plain frame)	2 known	
1658a	as preceding (ribbed frame)	rare	
1659	Kirkpatrick & Gault, New York	rare	
1660	Lord & Taylor, New York	rare	
1661	Mendum's Family Wine Emporium, New York City	400.	575.
1662	B.F. Miles, Peoria	2 known	
1663	John W. Norris, Chicago	1250.	1750.
1664	North American Life Insurance Company, New York ("INSURANCE" straight)	400.	575.
1665	as preceding ("INSURANCE" curved)	650.	950.
1666	Pearce Tolle & Holton, Cincinnati	unique	
1667	Schapker & Bussing, Evansville, Indiana	rare	
1668	John Shillito & Co., Cincinnati	rare	
1669	S. Steinfeld, New York	1250.	1600.
1670	N. & G. Taylor, Philadelphia	850.	1450.
1671	Weir & Larminie, Montreal	rare	
1672	White the Hatter, New York	1250.	1700.

Two-cent stamps, portrait of Andrew Jackson

No.	Issuer	VFine	EFine
1673	J. Gault (not a regular issue)	3 known	

Three-cent stamps, portrait of George Washington

No.	Issuer	VFine	EFine
1674	Ayer's Cathartic Pills [Lowell, MA] (short arrows)	$ 200.	$ 425.
1675	as preceding (long arrows)	200.	425.
1676	"Take Ayer's Pills" [Lowell, MA]	175.	325.
1677	Ayer's Sarsaparilla [Lowell, MA] (small "AYER'S")	175.	375.
1678	as preceding (medium "AYER'S")	175.	325.
1679	as preceding (ribbed frame)	rare	
1680	Ayer's Sarsaparilla (large "AYER'S" in plain frame)	250.	350.

No.	Issuer	VFine	EFine
1681	Bailey & Co., Philadelphia	500.	825.
1682	Joseph L. Bates, "FANCY GOODS," Boston	550.	800.
1683	as preceding, "FANCYGOODS" as one word	rare	
1684	Brown's Bronchial Troches [Boston]	400.	700.

No.	Issuer	VFine	EFine
1685	F. Buhl & Co., Detroit	rare	
1686	Burnett's Cocoaine Kalliston [Boston]	400.	700.
1687	Burnett's Standard Cooking Extracts [Boston]	400.	650.
1688	Arthur M. Claflin, Hopkinton [Massachusetts]	unique	
1689	Dougan, New York	800.	1100.
1690	Drake's Plantation Bitters [New York City]	150.	300.
1691	Ellis, McAlpin & Co., Cincinnati	rare	
1692	G.G. Evans, Philadelphia	800.	1100.
1693	Gage Brother & Drake, Tremont House [Chicago]	rare	
1694	J. Gault [Boston and New York] (plain frame)	600.	850.
1695	as preceding (ribbed frame)	rare	
1696	L.C. Hopkins & Co., Cincinnati	rare	
1697	Hunt & Nash, Irving House [New York City] (plain frame)	rare	
1698	as preceding (ribbed frame)	2 known	
1699	Kirkpatrick & Gault, New York	rare	
1700	Lord & Taylor, New York	500.	750.
1701	Mendum's Family Wine Emporium, New York City	rare	
1702	John W. Norris, Chicago	rare	
1703	North American Life Insurance Company, New York ("INSURANCE" straight)	550.	700.
1704	as preceding ("INSURANCE" curved)	rare	
1705	Pearce Tolle & Holton, Cincinnati	1100.	1,800.
1706	Schapker & Bussing, Evansville, Indiana	575.	750.
1707	John Shillito & Co., Cincinnati	475.	750.
1708	N. & G. Taylor, Philadelphia	1125.	1500.
1709	Weir & Larminie, Montreal	2 known	
1710	White the Hatter, New York	1275.	1800.

Five-cent stamps, portrait of Thomas Jefferson

No.	Issuer	VFine	EFine
1711	Ayer's Cathartic Pills [Lowell, MA] (short arrows)	$ 400.	$ 800.
1712	as preceding (long arrows)	700.	900.
1713	"Take Ayer's Pills" [Lowell, MA] (plain frame)	450.	800.
1714	as preceding (ribbed frame)	rare	
1715	Ayer's Sarsaparilla [Lowell, MA] (large "AYER'S")	rare	
1716	as preceding (medium "AYER'S")	400.	700
1717	Bailey & Co., Philadelphia	800.	1100.
1718	Joseph L. Bates, "FANCY GOODS," Boston	ex. rare	
1719	as preceding, "FANCYGOODS" as one word	2 known	
1720	as preceding, "FANCYGOODS" in ribbed frame	2 known	
1721	Brown's Bronchial Troches [Boston]	350.	500.
1722	F. Buhl & Co., Detroit	rare	
1723	Burnett's Cocoaine Kalliston [Boston]	400.	650.
1724	Burnett's Standard Cooking Extracts [Boston]	300.	425.
1725	Arthur M. Claflin, Hopkinton [Massachusetts]	4 known	
1726	H.A. Cook, Evansville, Indiana	850.	1350.
1727	Dougan, New York	rare	
1728	Drake's Plantation Bitters [New York City]	325.	450.
1729	as above (ribbed frame)	rare	
1730	Ellis, McAlpin & Co., Cincinnati	900.	1400.
1731	G.G. Evans, Philadelphia	2 known	
1732	Gage Brothers & Drake, Tremont House [Chicago]	200.	350.
1733	J. Gault [Boston and New York] (plain frame)	200.	375.
1734	as preceding (ribbed frame)	350.	575.
1735	L.C. Hopkins & Co., Cincinnati	1250.	1800.
1736	Hunt & Nash, Irving House [New York City] (plain frame)	650.	975.
1737	as preceding (ribbed frame)	400.	650.
1738	Kirkpatrick & Gault, New York	325.	425.
1739	Lord & Taylor, New York	500.	800.
1740	Mendum's Family Wine Emporium, New York City	450.	675.
1741	B.F. Miles, Peoria	6 known	
1742	John W. Norris, Chicago	rare	
1743	North American Life Insurance Company, New York ("INSURANCE" straight)	rare	
1743a	as preceding ("INSURANCE" curved)	doubtful	
1743b	as preceding ("INSURANCE" straight; ribbed frame)	rare	
1744	Pearce Tolle & Holton, Cincinnati	1250.	1800.
1745	Sand's Ale [Milwaukee]	rare	
1746	Schapker & Bussing, Evansville, Indiana	650.	1,000.
1747	John Shillito & Co., Cincinnati	350.	575.
1748	S. Steinfeld, New York	unique	
1749	N. & G. Taylor, Philadelphia	3 known	
1750	Weir & Larminie, Montreal	unique	
1751	White the Hatter, New York	2–4 known	

Nine-cent (three, three-cent) stamps, portrait of George Washington

No.	Issuer	VFine	EFine
1752	Feuchtwanger back (a fantasy piece in a rectangular frame)	—	—

Ten-cent stamps, portrait of George Washington

No.	Issuer	VFine	EFine
1753	Ayer's Cathartic Pills [Lowell, MA] (short arrows)	$ 350.	$ 650.
1754	as preceding (long arrows)	650.	1150.
1755	"Take Ayer's Pills" [Lowell, MA] (plain frame)	350.	650.
1755a	as preceding (ribbed frame)	unique	
1756	Ayer's Sarsaparilla [Lowell, MA] (small "AYER'S")	600.	800.
1717	as preceding (medium "AYER'S")	350.	650.
1718	as preceding (ribbed frame)	unique	
1719	as preceding (large "AYER'S" in plain frame)	rare	
1760	Bailey & Co., Philadelphia	825.	1100.
1761	Joseph L. Bates, "FANCY GOODS," Boston	600.	850.
1762	as preceding, "FANCYGOODS" as one word	2–3 known	
1763	as preceding, "FANCYGOODS" in ribbed frame	rare	
1764	Brown's Bronchial Troches [Boston]	600.	725.
1765	F. Buhl & Co., Detroit	850.	1300.
1766	Burnett's Cocoaine Kalliston [Boston]	325.	575.
1767	Burnett's Standard Cooking Extracts [Boston]	300.	475.
1768	as preceding (ribbed frame)	rare	
1769	Arthur M. Claflin, Hopkinton [Massachusetts]	2 known	
1770	H.A. Cook, Evansville, Indiana	1000.	1400.
1771	Dougan, New York	2–3 known	
1772	Drake's Plantation Bitters [New York City]	350.	500.
1773	as above (ribbed frame)	2–3 known	
1774	Ellis, McAlpin & Co., Cincinnati	700.	1000.
1775	G.G. Evans, Philadelphia	2 known	
1776	Gage Brothers & Drake, Tremont House [Chicago]	200.	350.
1777	as preceding (ribbed frame)	2 known	
1778	J. Gault [Boston and New York] (plain frame)	150.	350.
1779	as preceding (ribbed frame)	500.	650.
1780	L.C. Hopkins & Co., Cincinnati	rare	
1781	Hunt & Nash, Irving House [New York City] (plain frame)	625.	800.
1782	as preceding (ribbed frame)	500.	700.
1783	Kirkpatrick & Gault, New York	300.	450.
1784	Lord & Taylor, New York	550.	850.
1785	Mendum's Family Wine Emporium, New York City	750.	1100.
1786	as preceding (ribbed frame)	rare	
1787	John W. Norris, Chicago	1250.	1800.
1788	North American Life Insurance Company, New York ("INSURANCE" straight)	800.	1100.
1789	as preceding ("INSURANCE" curved)	rare	
1790	as preceding ("INSURANCE" straight; ribbed frame)	rare	

No.	Issuer	VFine	EFine
1790a	as preceding ("INSURANCE" curved; ribbed frame)	rare	
1791	Pearce Tolle & Holton, Cincinnati	2 known	
1792	Sand's Ale [Milwaukee]	2–3 known	
1793	Schapker & Bussing, Evansville, Indiana	400.	600.
1794	John Shillito & Co., Cincinnati	900.	1400.
1795	S. Steinfeld, New York	unique	
1796	N. & G. Taylor, Philadelphia	2 known	
1797	Weir & Larminie, Montreal	700.	1000.
1798	White the Hatter, New York	2–3 known	

Twelve-cent stamps, portrait of George Washington

No.	Issuer	VFine	EFine
1799	Ayer's Cathartic Pills [Lowell, MA] (short arrows)	$700.	$1000.
1800	as preceding (long arrows)	rare	
1801	"Take Ayer's Pills" [Lowell, MA]	500.	900.
1802	Ayer's Sarsaparilla [Lowell, MA] (small "AYER'S")	rare	
1803	as preceding (medium "AYER'S")	500.	800.
1803a	as preceding (large "AYER'S")	ex. rare	
1804	Bailey & Co., Philadelphia	2 known	
1805	Joseph L. Bates, "FANCY GOODS," Boston	rare	
1806	Brown's Bronchial Troches [Boston]	rare	
1807	F. Buhl & Co., Detroit	rare	
1808	Burnett's Cocoaine Kalliston [Boston]	725.	850.
1809	Burnett's Standard Cooking Extracts [Boston]	725.	850.
1810	Arthur M. Claflin, Hopkinton [Massachusetts]	2 known	
1811	Drake's Plantation Bitters [New York City]	850.	1350.
1812	Ellis, McAlpin & Co., Cincinnati	rare	
1813	Gage Brothers & Drake, Tremont House [Chicago]	2 known.	
1814	J. Gault [Boston and New York] (plain frame)	500.	900.
1815	as preceding (ribbed frame)	2–4 known	
1816	Hunt & Nash, Irving House [New York City] (plain frame)	rare	
1817	as preceding (ribbed frame)	rare	
1818	Kirkpatrick & Gault, New York	650.	900.
1819	Lord & Taylor, New York	rare	
1820	Mendum's Family Wine Emporium, New York City	900.	1200.
1821	North American Life Insurance Company, New York ("INSURANCE" straight)	2 known	
1821a	as preceding ("INSURANCE" curved)	uncertain	
1822	Pearce Tolle & Holton, Cincinnati	unique	
1823	Sand's Ale [Milwaukee]	issue uncertain	
1824	Schapker & Bussing, Evansville, Indiana	2 known	
1825	John Shillito & Co., Cincinnati	2 known	
1826	S. Steinfeld, New York	unique	
1827	N. & G. Taylor, Philadelphia	unique	

Twenty-four-cent stamps, portrait of George Washington

No.	Issuer	VFine	EFine
1828	Ayer's Cathartic Pills [Lowell, MA] (short arrows)	8 rare	
1828a	as preceding (long arrows)	unique	
1828b	"Take Ayer's Pills" [Lowell, MA]	unique	

No.	Issuer	VFine	EFine
1829	Joseph L. Bates, "FANCY GOODS," Boston	unique	
1830	Brown's Bronchial Troches	issue uncertain	
1831	F. Buhl & Co., Detroit	rare	
1832	Burnett's Cocoaine Kalliston [Boston]	2 known	
1833	Burnett's Standard Cooking Extracts [Boston]	2–3 known	
1834	Drake's Plantation Bitters [New York City]	2–3 known	
1835	Ellis, McAlpin & Co., Cincinnati	1600.	2600.
1836	J. Gault [Boston and New York] (plain frame)	700.	950.
1837	as preceding (ribbed frame)	2 known	
1838	Hunt & Nash, Irving House [New York City] (plain frame)	rare	
1839	as preceding (ribbed frame)	2 known	
1840	Kirkpatrick & Gault, New York	800.	1,250.
1841	Lord & Taylor, New York	rare	
1842	Pearce Tolle & Holton, Cincinnati	issue uncertain	

Thirty-cent stamps, portrait of Benjamin Franklin

No.	Issuer	VFine	EFine
1843	Ayer's Cathartic Pills [Lowell, MA] (short arrows)	unique	
1844	as preceding (long arrows)	rare	
1844a	"Take Ayer's Pills" [Lowell, MA]	unique	
1844b	Ayer's Sarsaparilla [Lowell, MA] (medium "AYER'S")	rare	
1845	Brown's Bronchial Troches	issue uncertain	
1846	Burnett's Cocoaine Kalliston [Boston]	2–3 known	
1847	Burnett's Standard Cooking Extracts [Boston]	2–3 known	
1848	Drake's Plantation Bitters [New York City]	3 known	
1849	J. Gault [Boston and New York] (plain frame)	1375.	1950.
1850	as preceding (ribbed frame)	2 known	
1851	Hunt & Nash, Irving House [New York City] (plain frame)	unique	
1852	Kirkpatrick & Gault, New York	1400.	1850.
1853	Lord & Taylor, New York	rare	
1854	Sand's Ale [Milwaukee]	rare	

Ninety-cent stamps, portrait of George Washington

No.	Issuer	VFine	EFine
1855	"Take Ayer's Pills" [Lowell, MA]	2 known	
1855a	Ayer's Sarsaparilla [Lowell, MA] (medium "AYER'S)	3 known	
1856	Joseph L. Bates, "FANCY GOODS" Boston	issue uncertain	
1857	Burnett's Cocoaine Kalliston [Boston]	unique	
1857a	Burnett's Standard Cooking Extracts [Boston]	unique	
1858	Drake's Plantation Bitters [New York City]	rare	
1859	J. Gault [Boston and New York] (plain frame)	$3500.	$6000.
1859a	as preceding (ribbed frame)	rare	
1860	Kirkpatrick & Gault, New York	rare	
1861	Lord & Taylor, New York	rare	

United States postal notes were a creation that descended from and filled the void after fractional currency was withdrawn in the mid-1870s after the need for low denomination notes had passed.

In addition to the need for small-change notes in daily use during the post-Civil War crisis, fractional currency was also convenient for sending small amounts through the mail. And, although there was a risk of postal theft, fractional notes were often inserted in a folded letter and usually went undetected. Postal notes were created from the public demand for a replacement.

Then, as now, the wheels of government moved slowly. Awakened by the American Express Co., which initiated a money order system in 1882, the U.S. Congress passed H.R. 5661 and introduced postal notes for a fee of 3 cents—2 cents less than that charged by American Express.

Postal notes were to be issued by post offices in sums less than $5; they were to be issued without notification to the paying office; they would be payable at a specific city; they were to be printed on thin bank note-like paper from engraved plates.

Issuance was restricted to the largest 63,000 post offices that would have sufficient funds to cash these notes. More notes were issued in the highest populated ares, i.e., New England, the mid-Atlantic and mid-Western states.

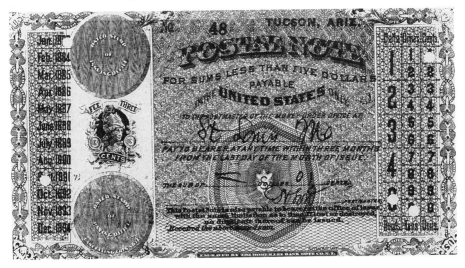

Type I

The first four-year contract (1883–1887) to design, engrave and print U.S. postal notes was awarded to the Homer Lee Bank Note Co. in New York City. The first notes, significantly larger than later ones, were printed on yellow paper. On the left portion of these notes was the date and fee shield; the notes were payable in a designated city only.

Type II

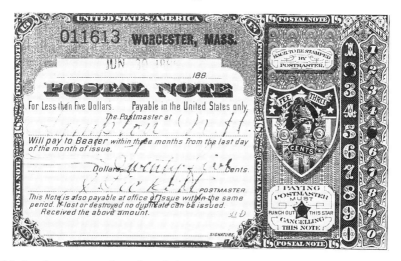

In 1884 the design was altered and the notes were printed on ivory-white paper.

Type II-A. To simplify cashing the notes, in early 1887 postal notes were individually rubber-stamped so they were payable at "ANY MONEY ORDER OFFICE."

Type III

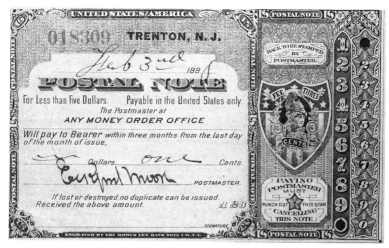

Toward the end of the contract with Homer Lee, postal notes were printed with "ANY MONEY ORDER OFFICE" engraved into the plates; this is the scarcest type.

Type IV

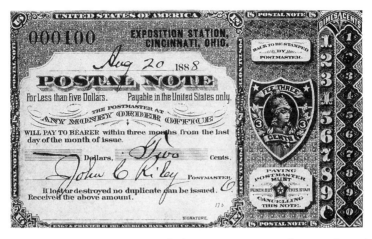

In 1887 the new contract was awarded to American Bank Note Co. Thomas F. Morris, Chief Designer at ABNCo, followed the basic Homer Lee format. The most noticeable design change was the style and placement of "ANY MONEY ORDER OFFICE."

The illustrated note, with serial number 100, was issued during the 100–day Centennial Exposition of the Ohio Valley and Central States in 1888. This note, issued at a mobile office, is the only known surviving note from the Centennial.

Type V. In September 1891 the final contract was awarded to Dunlap & Clarke in Philadelphia. This company merely produced a plate with the same design and added their name in the lower border. There are minor differences in the portrait.

Identification Guide by Type*

Type	Company	Identifying Characteristics
I	Homer Lee	yellow paper
II	Homer Lee	white paper and handwritten paying city
IIA	Homer Lee	rubber-stamped "ANY MONEY ORDER OFFICE"
III	Homer Lee	"ANY MONEY ORDER OFFICE" engraved in straight line
IV	ABNCo	American Bank Note Co. in lower face border
V	Dunlap & Clarke	Dunlap & Clarke in lower face border

Members of the American Numismatic Association (ANA) may borrow a postal note slide set and transcript from the ANA. This material, provided by U.S. postal note specialists Charles Surasky and Nicholas Bruyer, serves as an educational tool.

Remarks: A total of 70.8 million notes were issued; the total face value exceeded $126 million; the average postal note was issued for less than $2.

* *Identifying the Postal Notes of 1883 to 1894*, Charles Surasky, published by the author in 1985.

Current Federal Reserve notes are printed on 32–subject sheets. Most often, large-size notes were printed on 4–subject sheets.

Since the 1830s U.S. security paper has been printed from intaglio-engraved plates. With the exception of fractional currency, other circulating notes issued during the Civil War were printed from 4–subject sheets; some interest-bearing notes were printed from 3–subject plates. In 1918, 8–subject plates were put into use. Prior to 1898 only single-plate hand presses were in use, which yielded one sheet per impression. Steam presses were able to accommodate up to four plates simultaneously.

The reduction of size of U.S. paper money in 1928, and the need for more circulating money, brought printing improvements to the Bureau of Engraving and Printing. One such improvement in productivity involved the use of presses that would accommodate large engraved plates and print more subjects per sheet.

Among the notes produced by the older methods, some of the most interesting are the national bank notes. Large-size national bank notes were usually printed on sheets of 4 subjects, although some plates were prepared with only 2–subjects. For some $500 and $1,000 national bank notes, 1–subject plates were prepared. Surviving sheets represent only a small fraction of known subject combinations: ten sheets of the first charter period, each sheet comprised of $1–1–1–2; two sheets of $5–5–5–5; one sheet of $10–10–10–20. As for brown backs there are at least 20 sheets of $5–5–5–5; nine sheets of $10–10–10–20; one sheet of $10–10–10–10; one sheet of $50–$100.

There are four sheets of $5 subjects, all with second charter date backs and two sheets of $10–10–10–20. Only one sheet each with denomination backs is known for sheets with $5–5–5–5, the other with $10–10–10–20. There are dozens of third charter sheets; the vast majority are sheets of $5–5–5–5 with blue seals. Combinations such as $50–50–50–100 and $10–10–20–50 were made, but none have been preserved. Thus it is not always possible to determine the combination of the sheet from which any given national bank note was cut.

Uncut fractional currency sheets were shipped to post offices and banks and sold directly to the public. National bank notes were also shipped uncut to the issuing banks and were occasionally saved as souvenirs. Other sheets—with few exceptions—were separated and trimmed into single notes at the Bureau; the exceptions were a few sheets of 1896 silver certificates, several $1, $2 and $5 silver certificates of 1899, and two sheets of $5 United States notes of 1907, all of which appear to have been presented uncut to VIPs. A.A. Grinnell also had a pair of uncut Chicago 1915 Federal Reserve Bank note sheets in denominations of $10 and $20. Five $5 sheets are known - all from Atlanta. Even some of the presentation sheets were separated, as were their small-size counterparts dated 1928–1934.

Small-size notes, first printed in 12–subject sheets on August 6, 1928, were sold in sheet form to the general public beginning in 1935. The 1928–1934 sheets were presentation items; from six to a few dozen were made. When the 18–subject sheets of $1 notes were introduced in 1952, followed by higher denominations in

May 1953, a few hundred sheets of each were distributed uncut. The Treasury Department then discontinued the practice. No 32–subject sheets were issued to the public until 1981, though presentation pieces cannot be ruled out. It is possible that many 18–subject sheets were subsequently separated, since they are more scarce than the 12–subject sheets.

Small-size national bank notes, like their big brothers, were shipped uncut to 6,994 issuing banks in panels of six. They were printed in 12–subject sheets, as were all other small-size notes, Series 1928 through 1953. The national bank notes were printed minus the bank information and then were stored and overprinted with logotypes as orders arrived from individual banks. At present over 850 such sheets have been recorded, the vast majority with serial number 1 (Type I) or 1–6 (Type II). Over half are $5 notes. Among the rest, $10 notes outnumber $20s by 3 to 1; the $50 and $100 sheets are exceedingly rare.

Uncut sheets are usually collected by states. Texas, Michigan and New York are the most common. The rarities are the sheets from Delaware, Washington, DC, Arizona, Idaho and Wyoming. Sheets are not known for Alaska or Hawaii.

SUMMARY OF SMALL-SIZE CURRENCY SHEET SUBJECTS

	Denomination	12 Subjects	18 Subjects	32 Subjects
United States Notes	1	1928	none	none
	2	1928–1928G	1953–1953C	1963–1963A
	5	1928–1928F	1953–1953C	1963
	100	none	none	1966–1966A
Silver Certificates	1	1928–1935D	1935D-1935H	1957–1957B
	5	1934–1934D	1953–1953C	none
	10	1933–1934D	1953–1953B	none
Federal Reserve Notes	1	none	none	1963–
	2	none	none	1976
	5, 10, 20	1928–1950	1950A-1950E	1963–
	50, 100	1928–1950	1950A-1950E	1963–

Gold certificates, national bank notes, Federal Reserve Bank notes and Federal Reserve notes above $100 were all printed in sheets of 12 subjects.

United States Notes/Series 1880–1917/Sheets of Four

No.	Denomination	Series	Signatures	Value
26	$1	1917	Elliott-White	$ —
47	$1	1899	Lyons-Roberts	—
169	$2	1917	Elliott-White	—
187	$2	1899	Lyons-Roberts	—
263	$5	1880	Lyons-Roberts	—
271	$5	1907	Elliott-White	—
490	$10	1901	Elliott-White	—
491	$10	1901	Speelman-White	Unique
723	$20	1880	Elliott-White	—

Remarks: There has been no recent sales of the above.

Silver Certificates/Series 1896 & 1899/Sheets of Four

No.		Series	Signatures	Value	No.		Series	Signatures	Value
45	$1	1896	Tillman-Morgan	3 known	**187**	$2	1899	Lyons-Roberts	$ —
46	$1	1896	Bruce-Roberts	Unique	**190**	$2	1899	Vernon-McClung	Unique
48	$1	1899	Lyons-Roberts	$3500.	**193**	$2	1899	Parker-Burke	—
51	$1	1899	Vernon-McClung	3750.	**196**	$2	1899	Speelman-White	—
54	$1	1899	Parker-Burke	3750.	**359**	$5	1896	Bruce-Roberts	—
57	$1	1899	Elliott-White	3250.	**360**	$5	1896	Lyons-Roberts	3500.
185	$2	1896	Tillman-Morgan	3 known	**367**	$5	1899	Parker-Burke	—
186	$2	1896	Bruce-Roberts	—	**371**	$5	1899	Speelman-White	Unique

Treasury (or Coin) Notes/One Dollar/Sheets of Four

No.	Denomination	Series	Signatures	Value
62	$1	1890	Rosecrans-Huston	Unique
63	$1	1891	Tillman-Morgan	Unique

Remarks: This sheet bears the following inscription on the bottom margin: "This sheet of four $1 Treasury Notes, being the designer, as a courtesy and at my request, were delivered to me through the Treasurer of the United States, by paying $4.00 without separation. Geor. W. Casilear, Chief Engraver."

National Bank Notes/Sheets of Four

No.	Denomination	Signatures	Value
		Series 1865	
29&171	$1–1–1–2	Colby-Spinner	$ —
31&173	$1–1–1–2	Allison-Spinner	7,500.
33&175	$1–1–1–2	Allison-Wyman	—
34&176	$1–1–1–2	Allison-Gilfillan	7,500.
		Series 1875	
282	$5–5–5–5	Bruce-Gilfillan	—
501&732	$10–10–10–20	Allison-New	14,000.
		Series 1882–First Issue	
288	$5–5–5–5	Bruce-Wyman	—
291	$5–5–5–5	Rosecrans-Hyatt	—
292	$5–5–5–5	Rosecrans-Huston	—
293	$5–5–5–5	Rosecrans-Nebeker	—
298	$5–5–5–5	Lyons-Roberts	—
512&744	$10–10–10–20	Rosecrans-Jordan	—
514&746	$10–10–10–20	Rosecrans-Huston	—
515&747	$10–10–10–20	Rosecrans-Nebeker	—
520&752	$10–10–10–20	Lyons-Roberts	—

National Bank Notes/Second Charter Period/Sheets of Four

No.	Denomination	Signatures	Value
		Series 1882–Second Issue	
303	$5–5–5–5	Tillman-Morgan	$ —
524&756	$10–10–10–20	Rosecrans-Nebeker	—
527&759	$10–10–10–20	Tillman-Roberts	—
		Series 1882–Third Issue	
311	$5–5–5–5	Lyons-Roberts	—
536&767	$10–10–10–20	Lyons-Roberts	—

National Bank Notes/Third Charter Period/Series 1902/Sheets of Four

No.	Denomination	Signatures	Value
	Except for No. 542, all are $5 notes.		
		First Issue	
316		Lyons-Roberts	$ —
317		Lyons-Treat	—
318		Vernon-Treat	—
542&775	$10–10–10–20	Vernon-Treat	2200.
		Second Issue	
319		Lyons-Roberts	2000.
321		Vernon-Treat	2000.
322		Vernon-McClung	2000.
		Third Issue	
328		Lyons-Roberts	2000.
331		Vernon-McClung	2000.
332		Napier-McClung	2150.
333		Napier-Thompson	2250.
335		Parker-Burke	2000.
336		Teehee-Burke	2000.
337		Elliott-Burke	2000.
338		Elliott-White	2000.
339		Speelman-White	2000.
341		Woods-Tate	2250.

National Bank Notes/Third Charter Period/Sheets of Four

Series 1902–Third Issue
$10–10–10–20

No.		Signatures	Value
552&**785**		Lyons-Roberts	$2500.
554	($10–10–10–10)	Vernon- Treat	2500.
554&**787**		Vernon-Treat	2500.
555&**788**		Vernon-McClung	2500.
556&**789**		Napier-McClung	2500.
558&**791**		Napier-Burke	2500.
559&**792**		Parker-Burke	2500.
560&**793**		Teehee-Burke	2500.
561&**794**		Elliott-Burke	2500.
563&**796**		Speelman-White	2500.
565&**798**		Woods-Tate	3000.

Federal Reserve Bank Notes/Series 1915/Sheets of Four

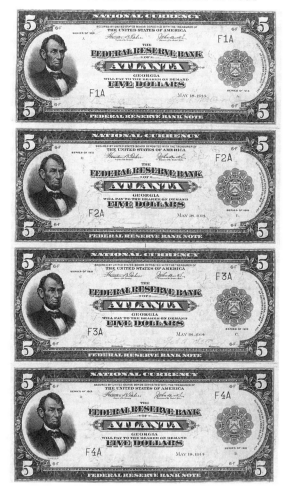

No.	Bank	Denomination	Signatures	Known
382F2	Atlanta	$5	T-B, Pike-McCord	5
620G1	Chicago	$10	T-B, McLallen-McDougal	Unique
850G	Chicago	$20	T-B, McLallen-McDougal	Unique

Remarks: Nos. 620G1 and 850G were included in the Grinnell sale in 1945 & 1946. Five sheets of No. 382F2 were sold by Christie's in September 1991, the first public sale of this denomination. The sheet numbered F1A to F4A sold for $9,350.

United States Notes/One Dollar/Series 1928/Sheets of Twelve

No.	Signatures	Delivered	Known	Value
69	Woods-Woodin	11	8	$7500.

Remarks: A sheet presented to James W. Wade, now in the Aubrey and Adeline Bebee Collection, has the autograph of W.H. Woodin on each note.

United States Notes

Two Dollar—Sheets of Twelve

No.	Series	Signatures	Delivered	Known	Value
204	1928	Tate-Mellon	no record	2	$7500.
204A	1928A	Woods-Mellon	no record	0	—
204B	1928B	Woods-Mills	no record	0	—
204C	1928C	Julian-Morgenthau	25	25	1200.
204D	1928D	Julian-Morgenthau	50	9	2000.
204E	1928E	Julian-Vinson	50	26	1200.
204F	1928F	Julian-Snyder	100	23	1200.
204G	1928G	Clark-Snyder	100	28	1200.

Two Dollar—Sheets of Eighteen

205	1953	Priest-Humphrey	100	26	1250.

Remarks: One sheet of No. 204C was autographed by Julian and Morgenthau.

United States Notes/Five Dollars/Series 1928–1953

Five Dollar—Sheets of Twelve

No.	Series	Signatures	Delivered	Known	Value
383	1928	Woods-Mellon	5	1	$ —
383A	1928A	Woods-Mills	no record	0	—
383B	1928B	Julian-Morgenthau	no record	0	—
383C	1928C	Julian-Morgenthau	no record	0	—
383D	1928D	Julian-Vinson	25	13	1750.
383E	1928E	Julian-Snyder	100	18	1200.
383F	1928F	Clark-Snyder	no record	0	—

Five Dollar—Sheets of Eighteen

No.	Series	Signatures	Delivered	Known	Value
384	1953	Priest-Humphrey	100	13	1750.

Remarks: The delivered figure for No. 383D is an estimate.

Silver Certificates/One Dollar/Series 1928–1935D/Sheets of Twelve

No.	Series	Signatures	Delivered	Known	Value
70	1928	Tate-Mellon	no record	14	$ 2,000.
71	1928A	Woods-Mellon	no record	0	—
72	1928B	Woods-Mills	6	0	—
73	1928C	Woods-Woodin	11	7	7,500.
74	1928D	Julian-Woodin	60	23	3,000.
75	1928E	Julian-Morgenthau	25	8	17,500.
76	1934	Julian-Morgenthau	25	10	3,000.
77	1935	Julian-Morgenthau	100	28	2,000.
78	1935A	Julian-Morgenthau	100	20	1,500.
79	1935A	Julian-Morgenthau (HAWAII)	25	20	3,000.
80	1935A	Julian-Morgenthau (N. Africa)	25	14	3,250.
83	1935B	Julian-Vinson	100	28	1,500.
84	1935C	Julian-Snyder	100	28	1,250.
85	1935D	Clark-Snyder	300	50	1,000.

Remarks: At least one sheet of Nos. 75 & 85 was autographed by the signers.

Silver Certificates/One Dollar/Series 1935D & 1935E

Sheets of Eighteen

No.	Series	Signatures	Delivered	Known	Value
86	1935D	Clark-Snyder	102	33	$1250.
87	1935E	Priest-Humphrey	400	53	1000.

Silver Certificates/Series 1934–1953

Five Dollar—Sheets of Twelve

No.	Series	Signatures	Delivered	Known	Value
386	1934	Julian-Morgenthau	25	12	$2000.
386A	1934A	Julian-Morgenthau	no record	0	—
386B	1934B	Julian-Vinson	no record	10	2000.
386C	1934C	Julian-Snyder	100	10	2000.
386D	1934D	Clark-Snyder	100	26	1500.

Five Dollar—Sheets of Eighteen

388	1953	Priest-Humphrey	100	21	2500.

Ten Dollar—Sheets of Twelve

621	1933	Julian-Woodin	1	0	—
621A	1933A	Julian-Morgenthau	1	0	—
622	1934	Julian-Morgenthau	10	7	3000.

Ten Dollar—Sheets of Eighteen

625	1953	Priest-Humphrey	100	10	3000.

Federal Reserve Notes/Series 1928

No.	Bank	Denomination	Signatures	Delivered	Known
391A	Boston	$5	Tate-Mellon	10	0
		$10	Tate-Mellon	10	0
		$20	Tate-Mellon	10	1
		$50	no record	no record	1
391B	New York	$5	Tate-Mellon	12	0
		$10	Tate-Mellon	12	0
		$20	Woods-Mellon	12	0
		$20	Tate-Mellon	no record	1
		$50	no record	1	0

Federal Reserve Notes/Series 1928

No.	Bank	Denom.	Signatures	Delivered	Known
391C	Philadelphia	$5	Tate-Mellon	5	1
		$10	Tate-Mellon	5	2
		$20	Tate-Mellon	5	2
		$50	Woods-Mellon	5	0
391D	Cleveland	$5	Tate or Woods-Mellon	2	0
		$10	Tate or Woods-Mellon	2	2
		$20	Woods-Mellon	2	0
		$50	Woods-Mellon	2	0
391E	Richmond	$5	Tate or Woods-Mellon	1	0
		$10	Tate or Woods-Mellon	1	0
		$20	Woods-Mellon	1	0
		$50	Woods-Mellon	1	0
391G	Chicago	$5	Tate-Mellon	5	1
		$10	Tate-Mellon	5	1
		$20	Tate-Mellon	5	1
391I	Minneapolis	$5	Tate-Mellon	5	0
		$5	Woods-Mellon	—	1
		$10	Woods-Mellon	5	2
		$20	Tate-Mellon	1	0
391J	Kansas City	$5	Tate or Woods-Mellon	5	0
		$10	Tate or Woods-Mellon	5	0
		$20	Tate or Woods-Mellon	5	0
391K	Dallas	$5	Woods-Mellon & Tate-Mellon	5	2
		$10	Woods-Mellon & Tate-Mellon	5	1
391L	San Francisco	$5	Tate-Mellon	2	0
		$10	Tate-Mellon	2	0
		$50	Woods-Mellon	2	0

Remarks: The No. 391G delivered figures are estimates. No. 391G $5 notes and No. 391I $10 notes were sold at the 1977 American Numismatic Association auction. The No. 391I $5 note (Woods-Mellon, Series 1928B) was in the 1945 & 1946 Grinnell sale. Nos. 391C sold for $6,655 and 391G sold for $6,350 in the CAA Oct. 1995 sale.

National Bank Notes/Series 1929/Sheets of Six

No.	Denomination	Rarity 1 & 2	Rarity 3 & 4	Rarity 5	Rarity 6	Rarity 7	Rarity 8
390	$5	$ 700.	$ 800.	—	—	—	—
627	$10	735.	875.	—	—	—	—
852	$20	825.	950.	—	—	—	—
1048	$50	4000.	5000.	—	—	—	—
1249	$100	5250.	6000.	—	—	—	—

Remarks: The above figures are for Type I notes; Type II notes command additional premiums, as much as twice the amount. See rarity table in chapter two. All small-size national bank notes and Federal Reserve Bank notes were printed in sheets of twelve, cut in half and delivered to the issuing banks in sheets of six.

Federal Reserve Bank Notes/Sheets of 12

Series 1929

No.	Bank	Denomination	Signatures	Known
626B	New York	$10	Jones-Woods	2
851C	Philadelphia	$20	Jones-Woods	2
851G	Chicago	$20	Jones-Woods	1
851I	Minneapolis	$20	Jones-Woods	1

Federal Reserve Notes/Series 1976–1990

Commencing with Series 1981, uncut sheets of $1 notes have been made available to collectors. Each series was offered in sheets of 32, 16 and 4. Sheets were not prepared for all 12 Federal Reserve Districts. Uncut sheets of $2 notes, Series of 1976, are also available. To purchase $2 sheets and current $1 sheets, write to the Bureau of Engraving and Printing, Public Sales Program, Room 602–11A, 14th and C Streets, SW, Washington, DC 20228.

No.	Denomination	Series	Signatures
106	$1	1981	Buchanan-Regan
107	$1	1981A	Ortega-Regan
108	$1	1985	Ortega-Baker
109	$1	1988	Ortega-Brady
110	$1	1988A	Villalpando-Brady
111	$1	1993	Withrow-Bentsen
112	$1	1995	Withrow-Rubin
207☆	$2	1976☆	Neff-Simon

Remarks: A sheet of No. 626B sold for $14,520 in 1995.

There are numerous avenues one can follow to assemble a collection of paper money. One can collect all the signature combinations or all denominations within a particular series. One of the most popular methods of collecting is to acquire one example of each type of note design; this is usually limited to one denomination. Notes executed by a particular engraver is another collecting possibility.

A fascinating path to follow is that of seeking unusual notes. On the following pages a few notes are illustrated that any collector would consider to be of special interest. There are many more.

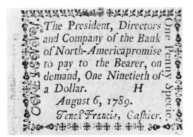

When this note circulated in the American Colonies, the Spanish Milled Dollar, exchangeable at 7 shillings 6 pence, or 90 pence, was the standard unit of currency.

The Bank of North America, chartered by the Continental Congress on December 31, 1781, was the only national bank to receive the privilege of deleting the word "national" from its title. The man responsible for the charter was Robert Morris, the first Superintendent of Finance. The bank's charter was allowed to expire in 1811. A second Bank of North America was later formed and became nationalized on December 4, 1864. The members of Congress at that time thought it fitting that the only bank to be chartered by the Continental Congress should retain its original title.

The Bank of North America was liquidated on February 28, 1923, and therefore issued only large-size notes. All are scarce and of great historical interest.

Forbidden Titles

National bank notes that used "United States," "Federal," or "Reserve" as part of their title were discouraged by the passage of the Federal Reserve Act of 1913. Titles that included these words were forbidden altogether by an the Act of May 24, 1926. Nevertheless 33 banks were chartered with "United States" in their titles between 1863 and 1926; 19 issued notes. Six banks used "Federal," and four used "Federal Reserve" in their titles. All notes with forbidden titles are extremely desirable and very scarce.

Racketeer Note

The National Bank of the Republic of New York had 1000 as its charter number. The first notes issued by this bank under its second charter, with "1000" on the back, were sought after by swindlers, who tried to pass them to illiterate people as $1000 bills.

This $5 note from the historic city of the Alamo is a popular one.

The Wells Fargo Nevada National Bank in San Francisco reminds us of stagecoach days.

This note was issued in the colorful location of California, Missouri.

Jackson's Disappearing Fingers

Andrew Jackson made his first appearance on U.S. federal paper money on the $5 United States note, series 1869. The portrait was engraved by Alfred Sealey.

A $10 note, series 1923, bears a modified portrait of Jackson. The oval in which the portrait is framed is smaller and therefore covers part of the hand.

Prior to the printing of $20 notes, series 1950E in 1957, wet paper had been used on flatbed presses. A certain amount of shrinkage took place as the mill-wet paper dried after being impressed with the printing plate, which were somewhat larger than the plates currently in use. To allow for this shrinkage, a new engraving of a larger portrait was prepared.

In order to retain the necessary size of Jackson's portrait on bills printed on dry paper, a retouched portrait was prepared. The most obvious change is the missing fingers.

Tombstone, Arizona, the town too tough to die, was the scene of the gunfight at the O.K. Corral where Wyatt Earp and "Doc" Holiday fought the Clantons.

This note bears what is probably the longest title for any national bank note. For some notes with interesting serial numbers see the following numbers in this catalog: 1, 47, 68, 202 and 483.

The entire production process of modern United States paper money at the Bureau of Engraving and Printing is automated, including an electronic scanning system that checks for errors. In addition there is a visual inspection for errors, nevertheless, some escape into circulation.

To understand how an error develops, one must possess at least a rudimentary knowledge of the sequence of paper money production. The incised plates are covered with ink and then wiped of excess ink. Under tremendous pressure, stacks of sheets, that receive 32 subjects, are imprinted with the image that has been incised into the plate. The backs are printed first, then about 24 hours later the face designs are printed. The third (over) print consists of the green serial numbers and the treasury and Federal Reserve seals.

At least 26 major types of paper money errors have been identified (Bart 1994). Errors differ in value from one variety to another, and also in the degree of severity of a specific type. Common errors, e.g. ink smudges, command smaller premiums than do more dramtic errors, e.g. double denominations.

Spurious and altered notes occasionally enter the market place. Notes with blue or yellow backs are a result of of direct or airborne contact with acidic or alkali solutions or vapors. Aside from a minuscule quantity of Series 1990 Federal Reserve notes printed with green, instead of black, district seals, no other genuine off-color notes are known.

Beware of cutting errors with serial numbers above 99840000. Some owners of the sheets sold by the Bureau can, with a scissors, cut notes to simulate spectacular errors. Consequently, know the dealer who offers error notes, or submit the serial number to the Bureau for authentication.

Values shown on the following pages represent estimates only for the error illustrated and may not be representative of values for similar errors.

Many of the illustrations in this section were provided by Harry Jones, a paper money dealer who specializes in error notes.

Ink and Solvent Smudge

This consecutive pair was smeared with excess solvent, which blurred the image.

Error Type	EFine	Unc
Solvent smear	$40.	$65.
Ink smear	30.	45.

The inked plate was not properly wiped; the result is a smudge across the portrait.

Insufficient and Missing Ink

This printing plate was not sufficiently inked; the result was a ghostlike image of George Washington.

Error Type	EFine	Unc
Insufficient ink	65.	125.

Offset Prints

The press probably started without the paper in position. The impression roller touched the entire engraved plate, and the sheet that followed received the full face impression of the back in retrograde. Subsequent printings will bear less and less of this error, and after a few impressions it will disappear.

This note received only a portion of the face offset onto the back.

This face design received only a portion of the back offset onto the face.

Error Type	VFine	EFine	Unc
Offset prints (total)	$100.	$150.	$200.
Offset prints (partial)	65.	90.	150.

Interior or Gutter Folds

These notes, with folds in place, went through the printing operation undetected. Only after the notes entered circulation did the paper unfold.

Error Type	VFine	EFine	Unc
Fold (single)	$35.	$60.	$115.
Fold (multiple)	50.	90.	190.

Cutting Errors

Faulty alignment during the cutting operation produced these errors. Notes are always cut and trimmed with the face showing. Nevertheless, the $1 is the most common off-center note to be found.

Error Type	EFine	Unc
Off-center, 10%	$ 50.	$125.
Off-center, 20%	85.	175.
Off-center, 30%	125.	250.

Cutting Error

These photographs show the note as it received the initial printing and after the corner was unfolded. Normally the plate number on the outer edge is trimmed away. This type of error would probably be found only in uncirculated condition. The premium would be about $100.

$1.50 Origami Note

This unique error was discovered in a pack of new notes as it appears in the first photograph; there are three distinct folds.

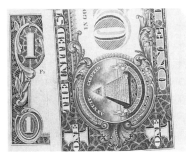

As the fold is undone, a partial face and portions of two backs are revealed.

As the note is unfolded further, three-fourths of one face and one-half of a second is visible. The second illustration shows the back.

Although technically classified as a cutting error, this example occured prior to lthe cutting process when the uncut sheet folded several times and remained folded during contact with the cutting blade. When totally unfolded, one-and-a-half notes are the result. The approximate value in uncirculated condition is about $750.

Overprint on Folded Note

The sheet from which this note came was folded when it was fed into the press for the overprint of seals and serial numbers. The second and third photographs show the note when unfolded. Value in uncirculated condition $750.

Paper Fold on Torn Sheet

Following normal face and back printing, the sheet from which this $20 note came developed a tear. The tear continued through the "W" in "TWENTY on the face. The torn sheet became folded and received the overprinting of seal and serial numbers. Following the overprinting, the sheet straightened out and was properly cut. It entered circulation in two pieces. The note was found taped together.

Overprint only

This note completely lacks the initial, intaglio face printing. Two sheets probably adhered to one another but became separated before the overprinting of seals, serial numbers and Federal Reserve District number. This same error has been observed from other districts.

Error Type	Unc
Paper fold on torn sheet	$750.
Overprint only	300.

Double Denominations

After the backs were printed, sheets of one denomination were inadvertently placed with those of another denomination for the face printing.

Error Type	EFine	Unc
Double denomination	$4,500.	$6,500.

Obstructed Print on Retained Fragment

Prior to 1957, when notes were wet-printed, paper dividers and tickets were inserted in counted stacks of paper destined for the Bureau of Engraving and Printing. Occasionally these tickets or another loose piece of paper would go unnoticed and adhere to the paper, sometimes throughout the entire printing and cutting operations. Only the adhering paper on the $1 note became separated.

Error Type	EFine	Unc
Obstructed print	$600.	$750.

Obstructed Print

Immediately after this note received the serial number imprint and just before the overprint of the Federal Reserve seal was made, a tear-off section of a Band-Aid found its way onto the sheet, or was carefully placed there. This note entered circulation and most certainly is unique. Value about $1,000.

Mismatched Serial Numbers

This star note was meant to replace an error note, yet it also bears an error, a mismatched serial number.

The "A" and "Q" prefix suggest a serious malfunction with the numbering cylinder.

This error was noticed and marked with the correct number. Nevertheless, it entered circulation.

Error Type	VFine	EFine	Unc
Mismatched prefix or suffix	$50.	$75.	$200.
Mismatched replacement number	85.	150.	375.

Turned and Stuck Digits

This group of notes demonstrates the sequence of turned and stuck digits.

Error Type	Unc
Partially turned digit	20.
Stuck digit	40.

Faulty Overprints

Misaligned Overprint

The overprint of seals and serial numbers are too far to the right.

Inverted Overprint

Both seal and serial number have been inverted.

Missing Overprint

The entire overprint is missing on this silver certificate.

Error Type	VFine	EFine	Une
Misaligned overprint	$ 50.	$ 75.	$100.
Inverted overprint	75.	125.	175.
Missing overprint	50.	100.	175.

Modern-day souvenir cards usually commemorate an event, and most often are issued at a numismatic or philatelic meeting or convention; here we are concerned only with the former. There are forerunner cards, those issued prior to 1960. Nevertheless, it was at this time that cards specifically intended for collectors were created.

In the United States, "official" souvenir cards are issued regularly by the Bureau of Engraving and Printing. The bank note designs on these cards are printed from the original, intaglio-engraved plates. They are often the only way one can obtain notes that are either uncollectible or extremely rare. "Semi-official" cards are offered irregularly by American Bank Note Company (ABNCo) and the unions and guilds that make up the artisans who are employed by the Bureau and ABNCo. Due to the subject matter in this catalog only the official cards that portray U.S. paper money subjects are listed. The one exception to this is the 1981 International Plate Printers, Die Stampers and Engravers Union of North America card that features the unissued $2 design for the 1861 U.S. note.

Souvenir cards prepared and issued by ABNCo are no less beautiful, but the notes they portray are U.S. obsolete notes or those originally printed for foreign governments and banks. All official and semi-official cards are listed in *The Souvenir Card Collectors Society Numbering System*.

Souvenir cards, usually lithographed, are offered by the host organization to raise money or cover expenses incurred by a local numismatic club. These cards should never be compared to those prepared by the aforementioned sources.

A brisk secondary market has been established for all engraved official and semi-official souvenir cards, the earliest of which originally sold for only a few dollars. The Souvenir Card Collector Society (SCCC), established in 1981, issues a quarterly journal devoted to all types of souvenir cards. The secretary of the society is Dana M. Marr, who can be reached at P.O. Box 4155, Tulsa, OK 74159-0155. Annual dues are $20.

The numbering system used here is the one adopted by the SCCC and is used with the society's permission. The number in parenthesis is the one that relates to that design in this catalog; the number in italics represents a back design.

B114 (1470)

No.		Printed	Sold	Current $ Value	No.		Printed	Sold	Current $ Value
F1981B	(953)	unknown		40.	B116	(203)	10,000	unknown	12.
PS1	(274)	unknown	10,391	300.	B119	(620)	10,000	unknown	10.
B2	(951)	12,400	12,347	75.	B121	(1043)	10,000	unknown	10.
B7	(collage)	12,017	12,013	95.	B124	(1435)	10,000	unknown	10.
B12	(45)	54,721	54,694	5.	B125	(1461)	unknown		12.
B18	(185)	74,172	69,078	5.	B126	(269)	unknown		10.
B24	(358)	49,544	49,530	7.	B129	(1411)	unknown		15.
B29	(SE21*)	72,000	41,591	10.	B130	(1151)	unknown		45.
B31	(36)	28,039	28,022	22.	B132	(SB103)	unknown		12.
B32	(45)	54,981	45,593	10.	B133	(SE19*)	5,800	5,800	10.
B35	(1246)	55,380	50,000	10.	B135	(82)	5,800	5,800	10.
B38	(185)	unknown	38,636	8.	B136	(SE3*)	5,800	5,800	10.
B41	(361)	69,556	57,806	5.	B139	(612)	9,500	unknown	10.
B44	(497)	53,615	28,004	5.	B140	(1411)	unknown		12.
B46	(358)	25,638	21,933	18.	B143	(197)	unknown		12.
B47	(483)	35,792	30,907	12.	B144	(929)	8,500	unknown	15.
B53	(834)	22,000	19,482	15.	B145	(704)	8,500	unknown	12.
B54	(349)	26,100	19,417	10.	B146	(243)	3,000	unknown	35.
B56	(1163)	26,300	10,385	10.	B147	(167)	8,500	unknown	10.
B57	(90)	20,690	9,195	15.	B148	(843)	8,500	unknown	10.
B59	(1242)	28,900	8,521	20.	B149	(1435)	8,500	unknown	15.
B61	(850)	unknown	9,072	18.	B150	(243)	3,000	unknown	35.
B64	(15)	unknown	6,874	20.	B153	(LE5*)	3,000	unknown	10.
B69	(1465)	unknown	15,446	20.	B154	(5)	unknown		10.
B71	(1361)	unknown	10,580	10.	B155	(1380)	unknown		12.
B75	(827a)	unknown	6,024	12.	B157	(243)	3,000	unknown	35.
B77	(987)	unknown	6,447	12.	B158	(380)	unknown		10.
B79	(1044)	unknown	5,551	12.	B159	(274)	8,500	8237	10.
B81	(1465)	unknown	7,465	15.	B160	(243)	3,000	unknown	35.
B82	(1361)	unknown	8,749	10.	B165	(1425)	8,500	6926	10.
B84	(533)	unknown	6,723	10.	B167	(155)	8,500	6312	10.
B87	(1242)	unknown	6,791	10.	B169	(1184)	8,500	6386	10.
B88	(483)	unknown	6,557	10.	B170	(1380)	8,500	6406	10.
B93	(316)	unknown	7,264	10.	B171	(1370)	8,500	7407	10.
B94	(1506)	unknown	5,187	10.	B173	(1244)	8,500	6601	10.
B98	(605)	unknown	7,537	12.	B179	essai*	8,500	9662	10.
B99	(1628)	unknown	6,460	10.	B182	essai*	8,500	7088	10.
B100	(1493)	unknown	7,278	15.	B183	essai*	8,500	7388	10.
B102	(5)	unknown	7,654	12.	B184	essai*	8,500	5773	10.
B103	(TN)	unknown	10,454	12.	B187	essai*	8,500	6011	10.
B104	(316)	unknown	7,409	15.	B192	essai*	8,500	8065	10.
B105	(842)	unknown	7,259	10.	B195	(27)	8,500	6094	10.
B106	(178)	unknown	8,069	10.	B196	(62)	8,500	6837	10.
B108	(605)	7,500	5,309	10.	B199	(68)	8,500	5600	10.
B109	(seals)	2,500	2,365	10.	B201	(28)	8,500	4878	10.
B111	(372)	7,500	5,317	15.	B203	(1355)	8,500	7860	10.
B112	(1629)	7,500	unknown	10.	B205	(1352)	8,500	7214	10.
B114	(1470)	10,000	unknown	10.	B206	(1423)	8,500	5385	10.
B115	(361)	10,000	unknown	10.					

Remarks: No. B103 is a $500,000,000 treasury note. No. B132 has an engraving of *Chief Hollow Horn Bear* as seen on the $10 military payment certificate Series 692. Nos. B150, B157 & B160 bear the image of *Freedom*; each is printed in a different color.

* This is illustrated in Hessler (1979).

PAPER MONEY THAT CIRCULATED OUTSIDE THE
CONTINENTAL UNITED STATES

Numerous paper money issues have circulated in territories and possessions of the United States. The territories and possessions and the paper money that circulated there are all important to the history of the United States.

ALASKA

"Seward's Folly" was the name given to the $7.2 million purchase of Alaska from the Imperial Russian Government in 1867. William H. Seward, who negotiated the purchase as Secretary of State, took much abuse for his "icebox," but he has since been vindicated a thousand times over. Alaska became the 49th state of the Union in 1958.

Alaska and its outlying islands were surveyed by explorers James Cook, George Vancouver, Alexander MacKenzie and Vitus Bering under the auspices of the Czar's Imperial Russian government. In 1790 a joint venture was formed by royal charter, called the Russian-American Company, to exploit the natural resources of Alaska. Trading in furs, skins and ivory was brisk. The company issued an unusual currency printed on walrus skin between 1818 and 1825. The notes, called seal skin notes, were in denominations of 10, 25 and 50 kopecks as well as 1 and 25 rubles.

Before 1938 privately issued tokens and scrip circulated in Alaska in addition to regular U.S. currency. Large- and small-size national bank notes for Alaska are extremely scarce and in great demand.

No. 316

No. 390.

HAWAII

Today, tourists who visit Hawaii are welcomed with a lei, a wreath of friendship. Captain James Cook, who sailed to the Hawaiian Islands in 1778, received a shower of spears as a welcome; his death site is marked by a monument.

Christian missionaries arrived in Hawaii in large enough numbers to discourage such a hostile reception. In 1840 the missionaries persuaded King Kamehameha III to declare his kingdom a constitutional monarchy. In 1893, with the deposition of Queen, a provisional government was formed under American control. In 1898 Hawaii was annexed to the United States. It became a territory in 1900 and a state in 1959.

The first paper money to be issued by American authority for Hawaii was the second charter national bank notes. A few large- and small-size national currency notes are scarce, but most are extremely rare. Bank notes that bore a "HAWAII" overprint were used during World War II, to insure identification should they fall into enemy hands. These notes are listed under $1 silver certificates and $5, $10 and $20 Federal Reserve notes.

No. 561

No. 627

THE PHILIPPINES

As a spoil of the 1898 Spanish-American War, the United States took control of Spanish possessions in the Caribbean and the Pacific. The war ended with the destruction of the Spanish battleships in Manila Harbor. By 1901 the American government had successfully replaced Spanish rule. On July 4, 1946 the Philippine Islands gained their independence when they became the Republic of the Philippines.

Spanish-Philippine currency is dated as early as 1852. In 1903 the first bank notes under American rule were issued. Four types of notes circulated from 1903 until independence: silver certificates, Philippine National Bank circulating notes and Bank of the Philippine Islands notes. All four were printed by the United States Bureau of Engraving and Printing.

Fearful that new Philippine silver certificates would be confused with those of the United States (two Philippine pesos equalled a U.S. dollar), notes smaller in size were prepared. The size of current U.S. currency grew out of this concept. However it took 25 years to be put into effect. For more information on all Philippine issues see *A Guide Book of Philippine Paper Money* by Neil Shafer.

Silver Certificates (1903-1918)

In 1906 the redemption clause was changed, whereby silver certificates were redeemable "in silver pesos or in gold coin of the United States of equivalent value." Originally these notes were redeemable only in silver pesos.

Series	Peso Notes Issued	Series	Peso Notes Issued
1903	2, 5 and 10	**1910**	5
1905	20, 50, 100 and 500	**1912**	10
1906	2 and 500	**1916**	50 and 100
1908	20		

THE PHILIPPINES

Silver Certificates

Series 1903 with a portrait of William McKinley.

Series 1905. This specimen note bears the portrait of General Henry W. Lawton engraved by G.F.C. Smillie.

Series 1906. The illustrated specimen note bears the G.F.C. Smillie portrait engraving of the first Spanish Colonial Governor, Miguel Lopez de Legazpi.

Back for the preceding.

THE PHILIPPINES

Treasury Certificates

Treasury certificates replaced silver certificates on August 1, 1918. The 1936 notes reflected the Commonwealth status, which had come in 1935. "Philippines" replaced the legend "Philippine Islands" on earlier notes; a new seal was also introduced. The 1944 issue was overprinted "VICTORY" for General MacArthur's return.

Series	Peso Notes Issued	Series	Peso Notes Issued
1918	1, 2, 5, 10, 20, 50, 100 & 500	1936	1, 2, 5, 10, 20, 50, 100 & 500
1924	1, 2, 5, 10 & 100	1941	1, 2, 5, 10 & 20
1929	1, 2, 5, 10, 20, 50, 100 & 500	1944	1, 2, 5, 10, 20, 50, 100 & 500

Series 1929. The portrait of José Rizal was engraved by G.F.C. Smillie.

Series 66 (1944). C.A. Huston designed this note; John Eissler engraved the Washington portrait.

Back for the preceding.

THE PHILIPPINES

Philippine National Bank Circulating Notes

The Philippine National Bank came into existence through the effort of William A. Jones, whose portrait appears on the 20 peso note. Charles Conant, the man who was instrumental in setting up the Philippine currency system is depicted on the 1 peso note. These national bank circulating notes were used until they were withdrawn on June 1, 1948. They were redeemable for one additional year.

Series	Peso Notes Issued	Series	Peso Notes Issued
1916	2, 5 & 10	**1920**	50 & 100
1917＊	10, 20 & 50 centavos, & 1 peso	**1921**	1, 2, 5, 10 & 20
1918	1	**1924**	1
1919	20	**1937**	5, 10 & 20

＊ These emergency notes were printed in the Philippines.

Series 1918. The portrait of C.A. Conant was engraved by M.W. Baldwin.

Back for the preceding.

Series 1920. The portrait of Henry W. Lawton was engraved by G.F.C. Smillie

THE PHILIPPINES

Philippine National Bank Circulating Notes

Series 1921 with a portrait of George Washington.

Back for the preceding.

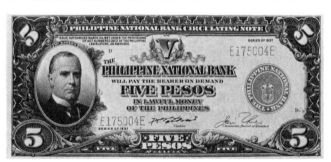

Series 1937 with a portrait of William McKinley.

Back for the preceding.

THE PHILIPPINES

Bank of the Philippine Islands

In 1852 the Banco Español-Filipino was established; in 1908 the Spanish title was changed to the Bank of the Philippine Islands. When World War II began these notes were withdrawn from circulation.

Series	Peso Notes Issued	Series	Peso Notes Issued
1908*	5, 10, 20, 50, 100 & 200	1928	5, 10, 20, 50, 100 & 200
1912	5, 10, 20, 50, 100 & 200	1933	5, 10 & 20
1920	5, 10 & 20		

* This issue bears the original Spanish title.

Series 1908.

The back for the preceding.

Series 1903.

PUERTO RICO

Puerto Rico, the "rich port" of the West Indies, was claimed as a territory of the United States after the Spanish-American War in 1898. The tropical island had become a province of the Spanish Empire after Columbus landed there in 1493. In 1590 Juan Ponce de León became Puerto Rico's first governor.

Paper money was issued by the Spanish authorities in Puerto Rico as early as 1813. In 1900, after Puerto Rico had become an American possession by the terms of the Treaty of Paris, notes with that date were overprinted as "MONEDA AMER-ICANA." These overprinted notes are sometimes collected along with the special notes issued by the United States for the territory. National bank notes were printed for use in "Porto Rico," but these large-size notes are extremely rare.

Beginning on January 1, 1899, United States coins and currency became the official money of Puerto Rico. The Spanish 25 peseta and French 20 franc gold pieces had been the only money acceptable for customs, taxes and postage. The native Puerto Rican coinage, which closely resembled that of Spain, was gradually withdrawn and melted. Today, the Territory of Puerto Rico uses U.S. coins and currency.

The 5 peso note dated 1900, overprinted "MONEDA AMERICANA," was printed by American Bank Note Co.

Back for the preceding.
(Courtesy of David Tang)

PUERTO RICO

Moneta, the goddess of money, appears on this 1904 issue printed by American Bank Note Co.

The Versailles portrait of Christopher Columbus appears on this 1909 issue printed by American Bank Note Co.

U.S. national bank notes issued in "Porto Rico" are extremely rare. (See No. 773)

THE UNITED STATES VIRGIN ISLANDS

On his second voyage to the New World in 1493, Christopher Columbus sailed to a group of islands that he named after the Virgin Mary. The Virgin Islands group consists of Saint Thomas, Saint John and Saint Croix, plus a number of smaller islands.

In 1671 the Danish West India Company claimed the islands in the midst of Spanish possessions. After the close of the Civil War, the United States realized the need for a strategic base in the West Indies. Negotiations for the purchase of the islands began in 1867 and ended in 1917. When World War I had begun and the concern about German submarines and raiders made the need for a naval base even more necessary.

The National Bank of the Danish West Indies had been in existence since 1905. Under the new American rule, the bank was granted permission to continue to issue 5, 10 20 and 100 franc gold certificates; all were withdrawn in 1934. These notes are especially desirable to some collectors. They are printed in two languages (Danish and English), bear the portrait of a foreign monarch (King Christian IX of Denmark) and were legal tender in the United States.

The portrait of King Christian IX of Denmark appears on all 1905 gold certificates printed by Bradbury Wilkinson & Co. Ltd.

A new world of collecting was opened to the syngraphist after World War II. The victorious United States found itself occupying large areas of countries whose economies were in a state of collapse. At that time United States overseas military personnel were being paid in local currencies, which could later be changed into American dollars. This system resulted in the conversion to dollars of vast amounts of francs and marks. Some U.S. servicemen added to their supply of convertible currency by doing a brisk business in cigarettes, silk stockings, candy bars, etc.

The need for new currency was fulfilled by United States military payment certificates, valid only in specified areas under the complete control of the occupying military authority. These certificates were issued to American military and civilian personnel. The first issue, Series 461, was released on September 16, 1946.

These new notes differed from regular United States bills in that they were not printed by engraved plates at the Bureau of Engraving and Printing. Instead, they were lithographed by private printing firms on a paper different from that used for regular currency from plates prepared at the BEP. The paper was imbedded with planchettes of small, colored discs rather than with colored threads. Thus, there is a similarity to the first printing of the federal greenbacks, in that both the military payment certificates and the first greenbacks were printed by private firms rather than by the government itself. Tudor Press,Inc. of Boston printed Series 461, 471, 472 and 541; Forbes Lithographic Co., also located in Boston, printed Series 481, 521 and 591. Series 611, issued on January 6, 1964, and those that followed, were printed by the Bureau of Engraving and Printing.

As with regular United States paper money, certain notes are prepared to replace defective ones. Military payment certificate replacement notes have a separate numbering sequence and are easily identified since the suffix letter is deleted.

It was periocically necessary to recall all circulating military payment certificates and issue a new series. Change-over, or C-Day, was quietly put into operation and completed within a 24–hour period. Counterfeiters, black market operators, and unauthorized holders of these military certificates were thereby caught off guard. Although two Series, 691 and 701, have been printed and are in storage for a time of need, military payment certificates are no longer in circulation anywhere in the world.

Size of Certificates

5¢ through 50¢: 110×55 mm.

$1: 112×66 mm.

$5, Series 461 through 481: 156×66 mm.

$5, Series 521 and subsequent issues: 136×66 mm.

$10 and $20: 156×66 mm.

Series 461, issued September 16, 1946, withdrawn March 10, 1947.

Face: grey, aqua and black.

Back: reddish-tan.

S-B No.	Denomination	Certificates Printed	VFine	EFine	Unc
11	.05	7,616,000	$ 4.	$ 10.	$ 60.
11☆		16 reported	75.	175.	300.
12	.10	8,064,000	4.	10.	60.
12☆		16 reported	75.	175.	300.
13	.25	4,704,000	6.	15.	80.
13☆		4 reported	250.	—	—
14	.50	4,032,000	4.	15.	100.
14☆		5 reported	250.	—	—
15	1.00	14,566,000	5.	12.	85.
15☆		12 reported	90.	300.	—
16	5.00	5,400,000	20.	40.	160.
16☆		7 reported	300.	650.	—
17	10.00	40,800,000	20.	40.	155.
17☆		8 reported	300.	650.	—

Series 471, issued March 10, 1947, withdrawn March 22, 1948.

Face: aqua and red.

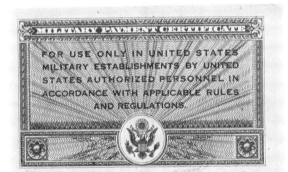

Back: blue and red.

S-B No.	Denomination	Certificates Printed	VFine	EFine	Une
18	.05	8,288,000	$ 4.	$ 12.	$ 65.
18☆		3 reported	450.	—	—
19	.10	7,616,000	4.	30.	65.
19☆		8 reported	350.	—	—
20	.25	4,480,000	8.	35.	160.
20☆		4 reported	550.	—	—
21	.50	4,032,000	8.	35.	160.
21☆		2 reported	750.	—	—
22	1.00	41,560,000	8.	40.	10.
22☆		7 reported	350.	—	—
23	5.00	5,400,000	350.	1,500.	3,000.
23☆		2 reported	1200.	—	—
24	10.00	13,600,000	175.	400.	1,500.
24☆		2 reported	—	—	—

Series 472, issued March 22, 1948, withdrawn June 20, 1951.

Face: aqua and black.

Back: violet and brown.

S-B No.	Denomination	Certificates Printed	VFine	EFine	Unc
25	.05	7,968,000	$ 1.	$ 2.	$ 5.
25☆		26 reported	35.	100.	185.
26	.10	7,960,000	1.	6.	40.
26☆		21 reported	35.	110.	—
27	.25	4,824,000	3.	12.	80.
27☆		none reported	—	—	—
28	.50	4,232,000	4.	15.	120.
28☆		6 reported	175.	350.	—
29	1.00	11,760,000	4.	25.	150.
29☆		14 reported	—	—	—
30	5.00	4,200,000	50.	200.	1,000.
30☆		1 reported	—	—	—
31	10.00	11,600,000	30	100.	950.
31☆		3 reported	—	—	—

Series 481, issued June 20, 1951, withdrawn May 25, 1954.

Face 50¢: aqua and black. *Commerce* was engraved by Marcus W. Baldwin.

Back: purple and blue.

Face $1: pale blue-green and brown. The allegorical figures of *Composition and Reflection* by Bela Lyon Pratt can be seen on the Tradition Door of the Library of Congress.

Back: deep blue and purple

Series 481 *(continued)*

Face, $5, Series 481: pale
blue-green and brown.
(See No. 987.) The back is
blue and violet.

S-B No.	Denomination	Certificates Printed	VFine	EFine	Unc
32	.05	23,968,000	$ 3.	$ 5.	$ 20.
32☆		18 reported	35.	85.	250.
33	.10	23,064,000	3.	5.	22.
33☆		25 reported	65.	85.	250.
34	.25	14,776,000	3.	8.	40.
34☆		15 reported	—	50.	175.
35	.50	10,032,000	5.	20.	100.
35☆		1 reported	—	—	—
36	1.00	25,480,000	9.	25.	175.
36☆		8 reported	200.	495.	—
37	5.00	8,600,000	65.	200.	1,000.
37☆		none reported	—	—	—
38	10.00	24,800,000	35.	175.	750.
38☆		4 reported	—	550.	—

Series 521, issued May 25, 1954, withdrawn May 27, 1958.

Face 25¢: green and tan.

Back: green and tan. The female head was engraved by A.L. Wasserback.

Remarks: The designs are the same for the 5¢, 10¢ and 50¢ notes. The colors are: 5¢ face, yellow and green with blue print, back, yellow with blue print; 10¢ face, blue and green with violet print, back, pale blue with violet print; 50¢, violet with pale green print for face and back.

Series 521 *(continued)*

Face $1: orange, pale blue and brown. *Liberty* was engraved by G.F.C. Smillie.

Back: pale blue and brown. The female profile was engraved by John Eissler.

Face $5: violet, green and blue. *Flowers of the South* was engraved by L.S. Schofield and D.S. Ronaldson.

Back: violet and blue. The female head was engraved by G.F.C. Smillie.

Series 521 *(continued)*

Face $10: gold, pale blue and reddish-tan. *Ceres*, based on *Antique Poesy* by J. Lefebvre, was engraved by G.F.C. Smillie.

Back: reddish-tan and blue. *Justice* was engraved by Marcus W. Baldwin.

S-B No.	Denomination	Certificates Printed	VFine	EFine	Unc
39	.05	27,216,000	$ 2.	$ 5.	$ 20.
39☆		20 reported	65.	150.	—
40	.10	26,880,000	3.	6.	22.
40☆		12 reported	75.	165.	—
41	.25	14,448,000	5.	10.	40.
41☆		10 reported	125.	225.	—
42	.50	11.088,000	4.	15.	80.
42☆		7 reported	165.	250.	—
43	1.00	28,000,000	3.	18.	80.
43☆		8 reported	135.	225.	—
44	5.00	6,400,000	100.	300.	1,300.
44☆		7 reported	350.	750.	—
45	10.00	24,400,000	75.	300.	1,200.
45☆		3 reported	350.	750.	—

Series 541, issued May, 1958, withdrawn May 26, 1961.

Face 5¢: green and violet. Back: pale green and violet.

Face 10¢: orange and green. The female portrait was engraved by A.L. Wasser-back.

Series 541 *(continued)*

Back 10¢: orange and green.

Face $1: gold, green and blue. The female was engraved by E.J. Hein.

Back: gold and blue. The *Female with Fasces* was engraved by G.F.C. Smillie.

Face $5: yellow, green and red.

Remarks: The designs are the same for the 5¢, 25¢ and 50¢ notes. The colors are: 5¢ face, green with violet print, back, pale green with violet print; 25¢ face, green and pink with blue print, back, pink with blue print; 50¢ face, green and yellow with red print, back, yellow with red print.

Series 541 *(continued)*

Back $5: pale green and red. The female was engraved by J.C. Benzing.

Face $10: aqua and brown. The female was engraved by G.F.C. Smillie.

Back: aqua and brown.

S-B No.	Denomination	Certificates Printed	VFine	EFine	Unc
46	.05	18,816,000	$ —	$ 1.	$ 4.
46☆		40 reported	40.	75.	200.
47	.10	18,816,000	1.	3.	15.
47☆		61 reported	40.	75.	200.
48	.25	12.096,000	3.	7.	20.
48☆		19 reported	90.	180.	300.
49	.50	8,064,000	3.	10.	50.
49☆		75 reported	20.	45.	150.
50	1.00	20,160,000	6.	40.	250.
50☆		13 reported	90.	200.	—
51	5.00	6,000,000	300.	900.	2,750.
51☆		none reported	—	—	—
52	10.00	21,200,000	150.	750.	1,750.
52☆		8 reported	600.	950.	—

Series 591, issued May 26, 1961, withdrawn Jan. 6, 1964 (Jan. 13 in Europe).

Face 50¢: blue and green with brown print. *Liberty*, also seen on a U.S. 17¢ stamp, was engraved by M. Fenton.

Back: pale blue with brown print.

Face $1: purple and blue with reddish-blue print. The female profile was engraved by R. Bower.

Back: purple with reddish-orange print.

Remarks: The designs are the same for the 5¢, 10¢ and 25¢ notes. The colors are: 5¢ face, yellow and green with red print, back, yellow with red print; 10¢ face, pink and green with blue print, back, pink with blue print; 25¢ face, blue and purple with green print, back, purple with green print.

Series 591 *(continued)*

Face $5: violet and green with blue print. The female portrait is based on the Gilbert Stuart painting of *Miss Ann Izard*; it was engraved by C. Brooks.

Back: violet with blue print.

Face $10: red and green.

Back: red and green

Series 591 *(continued)*

S-B No.	Denomination	Certificates Printed	VFine	EFine	Unc
53	.05	7,392,000	$ 2.	$ 6.	$ 50.
53☆		24 reported	50.	200.	—
54	.10	8,400,000	3.	7.	65.
54☆		4 reported	150.	—	—
55	.25	4,704,000	15.	30.	110.
55☆		none reported	—	—	—
56	.50	3,696,000	15.	45.	200.
56☆		3 reported	—	—	—
57	1.00	10,080,000	20.	45.	180.
57☆		6 reported	250.	—	—
58	5.00	2,400,000	200.	350.	1,950.
58☆		1 reported	—	—	—
59	10.00	6,800,000	90.	275.	1,200.
59☆		4 reported	—	—	—

Series 611, issued Jan. 6, 1964 (Jan. 13 in Europe), withdrawn April 28, 1969.

Face 10¢: aqua with green print. *Liberty*, by C. R. Chickering, was engraved by Arthur Dintaman.

Back: aqua, violet and green.

Face $1: vivid orange with aqua print. *Tiara* was painted by C.R. Chickering and engraved by M. Fenton.

Remarks: The designs are the same for the 5¢, 25¢ and 50¢ notes. The colors are: 5¢ face, violet and green with blue print, back, the same colors; 25¢ face, aqua with pale brown print, back, pale blue with brown print; 50¢ face, yellow and green with red print, back, yellow with red print.

Series 611 *(continued)*

Back $1: vivid orange with aqua print.

Face $5: pale blue and violet with vivid orange print. The female head by C.R. Chickering, was engraved by C. Brooks.

Back: violet with blue print.

Face $10: pale blue and violet with blue print. The female profile, by C.R. Chickering, was engraved by M. Fenton.

Series 611 *(continued)*

Back $20: violet with blue print. The engravers were J. Eissler and R. Bower.

S-B No.	Denomination	Certificates Printed	VFine	EFine	Unc
60	.05	9,408,000	$ 1.	$ 2	$ 8.
60☆		123 reported	20.	30.	75.
61	.10	10,080,000	1.	3.	17.
61☆		145 reported	20.	30.	75.
62	.25	5,376,000	4.	8.	25.
62☆		5 reported	200.	300.	—
63	.50	4,704,000	8.	22.	45.
63☆		none reported	—	—	—
64	1.00	10,640,000	8.	12.	45.
64☆		156 reported	35.	65.	150.
65	5.00	2,800,000	60.	140.	400.
65☆		10 reported	95.	350.	950.
66	10.00	8,400,000	50.	110.	330.
66☆		19 reported	175.	300.	750.

Series 641, issued August 31, 1965, withdrawn October 21, 1968.

Face 5¢: pale blue and purple with dark blue numerals. The female was engraved by R. Bower.

Back: pale blue and purple.

Remarks: The designs are the same for the 10¢, 25¢ and 50¢ notes. The colors are: 10¢ face, aqua and red, red numerals with green print, back, aqua and red with green print; 25¢ face and back, aqua with deep green numerals and red print; 50¢ face and back, aqua with brown numerals and orange print.

Series 641 *(continued)*

Face $1: yellow and green with red print. The female profile was engraved by E.J. Hein.

Back: yellow and red (See $1 note, No. 28 for same border design.)

Face $5: red and aqua. The female, *Laura*, was engraved by R. Bower. (See Nos. 361-371 for the same border design.)

Back: similar to face. *Europe* was engraved by A. Dintaman. The source for this profile is *Architectural Armaments in Berlin*, printed by Rommeler & Jonas in Dresden. (See Nos. 361-371 for the same border design.)

Series 641 *(continued)*

Face $10: aqua, orange and brown. The female profile was originally engraved by Marcus W. Baldwin (See *Commerce* on No. 186.)

Back: orange and brown. *Liberty* was engraved by R. Bower.

S-B No.	Denomination	Certificates Printed	VFine	EFine	Unc
67	.05	22,848,000	$ —	$ 1.	$ 5.
67☆		38 reported	30.	45.	125.
68	.10	23,520,000	—	2.	7.
68☆		20 reported	30.	45.	125.
69	.25	12,096,000	2.	4.	10.
69☆		22 reported	40.	50.	150.
70	.50	11,424,000	2.	10.	18.
70☆		10 reported	40.	50.	400.
71	1.00	33,040,000	4.	10.	20.
71☆		12 reported	75.	150.	400.
72	5.00	6,800,000	25.	50.	125.
72☆		7 reported	200.	400.	800.
73	10.00	20,400,000	20.	50.	160.
73☆		20 reported	100.	175.	—

Series 651, issued April 28, 1969, withdrawn May 19, 1969 (Japan), June 11, 1969 (Libya), November 19, 1973 (Korea).

Face $1: aqua, deep red and green.
Back: red and green.

Face $5: aqua, red and brown.
Back: same as face.

Face $10: aqua, brown and purple.
Back: brown and purple.

Remarks: An adaptation of the *Minute Man* statue by Daniel Chester French was used on the $1, $2 and $5 certificates, and on the 1941, U.S. Defense Postal Savings Stamps.

S-B No.	Denomination	Certificates Printed	VFine	EFine	Une
74	.05	4,032,000			$3500.
74☆			—	—	—
75	.10	7,960,000			3500.
75☆			—	—	—
76	.25	2,688,000			3500.
76☆			—	—	—
77	.50	2.016,000			3000.
77☆			—	—	—
78	1.00	6,720,000	$ 5.	$ 10.	30.
78☆		1 reported	—	—	—
79	5.00	1,600,000	45.	60.	130.
79☆			—	—	—
80	10.00	3,600,000	45.	60.	175.
80☆		5 reported	900.	1800.	3000.
			—	—	—

Series 661, issued October 21, 1968, withdrawn August 11, 1969.

Face 10¢: violet, aqua and blue with blue numerals. The female profile was engraved by John Eissler.

Back: blue and violet.

Face $1: purple, aqua and blue. The female was engraved by A.L. Wasserback.

Remarks: The designs are the same for the 5¢, 25¢ and 50¢ notes. The colors are as follows: 5¢ face, red, aqua and green, back, green and red; 25¢ face, orange, aqua and brown, back, orange and brown; 50¢ face, aqua and pale reddish orange, orange-red numerals, back, orange-red and aqua.

Series 661 *(continued)*

Back $1: blue, purple and pale blue. *Mt. Ranier and Mirror Lake* are also seen on the U.S. 1934, 3¢ postage stamp.

Face $5: red, aqua and brown. *Meditation* was engraved by G.F.C. Smillie.

Back: red and brown. The head was engraved by Marcus W. Baldwin.

Face $10: aqua, orange and red. *Union and Civilization* was engraved by G.F.C. Smillie. (See No. 773)

Series 661 *(continued)*

Back $10: orange and red. *Ceres*, based on *Antique Poesy* by J. Lefebvre, was engraved by G.F.C. Smillie.

Face $20: aqua, tan and grey. The female was engraved by F.T. Howe, Jr.

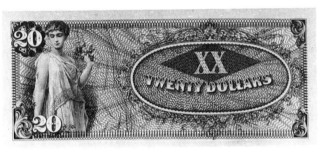

Back: grey and tan. *The Bouquet* was engraved by E. Felver.

S-B No.	Denomination	Certificates Printed	VFine	EFine	Unc
81	.05	23,520,000	$ —	$ 1.	$ 3.
81☆		12 reported	35.	50.	110.
82	.10	23,520,000	—	1.	3.
82☆		50 reported	35.	50.	110.
83	.25	13,440,000	1.	2.	6.
83☆		13 reported	55.	85.	200.
84	.50	10,080,000	1	3.	6.
84☆		4 reported	350.	450.	—
85	1.00	33,040,000	1.	2.	8.
85☆		56 reported	35.	50.	110.
86	5.00	7,200,000	2.	5.	10.
86☆		13 reported	110.	175.	300.
87	10.00	4,800,000	100.	300.	900.
87☆		7 reported	—	650.	1500.
88	20.00	8,000,000	75.	225.	400.
88☆		10 reported	250.	550.	—

Series 681, issued August 11, 1968, withdrawn October 7, 1970.

Face $20: aqua, blue, brown and pink. The *Soldier* was engraved by A. Dintaman.

Back: brown and red. The *B52A Bomber* was engraved by E. Felver.

5¢ Face: aqua, blue and green. The *Submarine Thomas A. Edison* and the *Astronaut* were engraved by E. Felver. Back: blue and green The same designs appear on the 10¢, 25¢ & 50¢ notes.

25¢ Face: aqua, blue, green and red. Back: blue and red.

$1 Face: aqua, red and purple. The *Pilot* was engraved by C. Brooks. Back: violet and orange.

10¢ Face: aqua, blue and purple. Back: blue and purple.

50¢ Face: aqua, blue and brown. Back: blue and brown.

$5 Face: aqua, pale green and purple. The *Sailor* was engraved by J. Creamer. Back: yellow and purple.

$10 Face: aqua, pale red and blue. The *Tank* was engraved by A. Dintaman. Back: blue and brown

S-B No.	Denomination	Certificates Printed	VFine	EFine	Unc
89	.05	14,112,000	$ 1.	$ 2.	$ 5.
89☆		30 reported	25.	40.	85.
90	.10	14,112,000	1	2.	6.
90☆		15 reported	25.	40.	90.
91	.25	8,736,000	1.	3.	8.
91☆		5 reported	—	200.	350.
92	.50	6,720,000	3.	7.	15.
92☆		31 reported	25.	40.	110.
93	1.00	22,400,000	2.	5.	10.
93☆		26 reported	30.	45.	115.
94	5.00	4,800,000	5.	13.	25.
94☆		9 reported	85.	125.	450.
95	10.00	3,200,000	20.	45.	125.
95☆		15 reported	70.	100.	400.
96	20.00	6,400,000	25.	40.	110.
96☆		40 reported	100.	175.	325.

Series 692, issued October 7, 1970, withdrawn March 15, 1973 (fractional notes June 1, 1971).

Face 25¢: yellow, blue and grey.

Back: grey and blue.

Face $1: violet, grey-blue, green and reddish-brown.

Back: grey-blue. The *Bison* design was also used on U.S. 30¢ postage stamps in 1923 and on No. 483 in this catalog.

Face 5¢: tan, pink and reddish-brown. The sculpture *Guardianship*, by James Earl Fraser, guards the entrance to the National Archives. Back: same colors.

10¢ Face: aqua, orange, blue and green Back: aqua, blue and green.

50¢ Face: gold, pink and purple. Back: brown and purple.

Series 692 *(continued)*

Face $5: blue, brown and orange The female portrait of *Eve* was engraved by E. Felver.

Back: brown and tan.

Face $10: blue, purple, pink and red. *Chief Hollow Horn Bear*, of the Brule Sioux, is also seen on U.S. 14¢ postage stamps of 1923 and 1931. The portrait, based on a photograph by DeLancey Gill, was engraved by L.S. Schofield.

Back: blue and purple. The *Eagle*, by W.A. Roach, was engraved by C. Brooks.

Series 692 *(continued)*

Face $20: purple, deep orange and pale red. The portrait of *Chief Ouray* was engraved by F.H. Noyes.

Back: purple and blue.

S-B No.	Denomination	Certificates Printed	VFine	EFine	Une
97	.05	14,112,000	$ 1.	$ 3.	$ 6.
97☆		72 reported	30.	50.	100.
98	.10	14,112,000	2.	4.	8.
98☆		62 reported	30.	50.	100.
99	.25	8,736,000	3.	7.	10.
99☆		19 reported	50.	110.	—
100	.50	6,720,000	5.	10.	20.
100☆		16 reported	75.	150.	275.
101	1.00	22,400,000	4.	8.	25.
101☆		28 reported	17.	30.	65.
102	5.00	4,800,000	50.	75.	135.
102☆		2 reported	—	—	—
103	10.00	3,200,000	90.	150.	350.
103☆		3 reported	—	—	—
104	20.00	6,400,000	75.	150.	340.
104☆		19 reported	400.	800.	1,200.

Remarks: Although Series 691 was never issued, an example of the $1 is in a private collection. The $10 denomination was displayed by the Bureau of Engraving and Printing at the 1978 convention of the American Numismatic Association. Both denominations are similar to the respective notes in Series 541.

SELECT BIOGRAPHIES OF BANK NOTE DESIGNERS AND ENGRAVERS

There is increasing interest in the artists who designed and engraved the subjects on U.S. currency. Presented here are a few brief biographies of designers and engravers extracted from *The Engraver's Line, An Encyclopedia of Paper Money and Postae Stamp Art*, by this author.

The numbers at the end of each biography refer to those in this catalog.

MARCUS W. BALDWIN. b. Irvington, NJ 31 March 1853, d. NYC 15 July 1925. He served his apprenticeship at American Bank Note Co. (ABNCo) under Louis Delnoce and Alfred Jones. Baldwin was employed by both ABNCo and the National Bank Note Co. (NBNCo). In 1880 he formed Baldwin, Gleason & Co. Baldwin engraved privately until 1891 when he joined the Bureau of Engraving and Printing (BEP).

See Nos. 483, 618, 620, 850 & 1429. In addition see military payment certificates Series 481, 50¢; Series 661, $5; Series 521, $10.

JOACHIM C. BENZING. b. Ellicott City, MD 19 Nov. 1880. At 14 he studied clay modeling with George Morgan, medalist at the U.S. Mint. Benzing learned engraving under James Blakie and in 1895 was apprenticed at E.A. Wright Co. in Philadelphia. In 1900 he was with ABNCo and in 1905 with the BEP.

Benzing engraved the portrait of Thomas Jefferson on all small-size $2 notes and the Lincoln Memorial on the back of all small-size $5 notes.

CHARLES BROOKS. b. Washington, DC 26 April 1905. He was educated in Philadelphia and was apprenticed at E.A. Wright Co. where he engraved from October 1920 to February 1925. After working as a self-employed engraver Mr. Brooks joined the BEP on 23 March 1938 and remained until 29 August 1947. After working at the Security Bank Note Co. he returned to the BEP; Mr. Brooks retired in December 1966.

See military payment certificates: Series 591, $5; Series 611, $5; Series 681, $1 and Series 692, $10.

WILLIAM CHORLTON. b. Manchester, England 20 March 1847, d. 1874. He came to the U.S. about 1852. At 16 Mr. Chorlton was engraving for the NBNCo under Alfred and James Smillie. He joined the BEP about 1872.

See Nos. 154, 618, 619, 620 & 1435.

LUIGI DELNOCE. b. Italy 1822, d. Melrose (Bronx), NY 1880. He studied engraving with John W. Casilear. From 1855 until 1860 Delnoce worked as a book illustrator. He engraved for six bank note companies and the BEP.

See Nos. 153, 171, 274, 728, 799, 953, 1013, 1122, 1151, 1207, 1212, 1403 & 1461.

FREDERICK GIRSCH. b. Beidingen, near Darmstadt, Germany 31 March 1821, d. Mt. Vernon, NY 18 December 1895. He supported his mother and four sisters by painting. After study at the Royal Academy, Girsch engraved for G.G. Lange in Darmstadt. In 1848 he went to Paris. The following year he arrived in NYC where he initially engraved book illustrations. As a bank note engraver Girsch worked for Danforth, Wright & Co., ABNCo and the NBNCo.
   See Nos. 207, 463, 464, 497, 1151, 1350, 1370, 1530, 1539 & 1568.

HENRY GUGLER. b. Germany 1816, d. 1880. He came to the U.S. in 1853 and almost immediately began to engrave for bank note companies. On 15 January 1863, Gugler was employed as one of the first engravers at the National Currency Bureau (BEP).
   See Nos. 245, 466, 724, 727 & 1379.

ALFRED JONES. b. Liverpool, England 7 April 1819, d. NYC 28 April 1900. By 1834 he was serving as an apprentice with Rawdon, Wright, Hatch & Edson in Albany, NY. Jones studied at the National Academy of Design in NYC. After a trip to Europe for more study he returned to the U.S. and engraved for bank note companies. In 1866 Jones became the president of the United States Bank Note Co. He became the superintendent of the Picture Department at ABNCo.
   See Nos. 509, 567, 700, 703, 1014 & 1404.

THEODORE A. LIEBLER. b. Constanz (Baden), Germany 22 February 1830, d. Brooklyn, NY 10 August 1890. He came to the U.S. in 1848. It is possible that he designed the eagle trademark for ABNCo.
   See Nos. 29, 497 & 567.

CHARLES SCHLECHT. b. Stuttgart, Germany 1843, d. NYC 1932. He came to the U.S. in 1852. Schlecht was apprenticed at ABNCo in 1859; additional instruction came from Charles Burt and Alfred Jones. In 1864 he joined the Western Bank Note Co. but returned to ABNCo. In 1893 he joined the BEP where he remained until 1900.
   See Nos. 45, 178, 590, 808, 843, 1014, 1242, 1370, 1376 & 1405.

WALTER SHIRLAW. b. Paisley, Scotland 6 August 1838, d. Spain 26 December 1908. Born to American parents, the family returned to the U.S. in 1841. At age 12 Shirlaw was apprenticed at Rawdon, Wright, Hatch & Edson; he attended school in the evenings. He was employed at Western Bank Note Co. as a designer and engraver from 1865-1870. He returned from a European trip in 1877. Shirlaw did illustrations for *Harper's Monthly*. He helped to found the Chicago Institute of Art and a few other art organizations.
   See Nos. 274; 358; 540.

CHAPTER FOUR

Care and Preservation
of Paper Money

ALTHOUGH much information some good and some bad has appeared on the care and preservation of coins has appeared in print, the same for paper money is noteworthy for its paucity. This may be due to the relatively recent growth in interest in the field of syngraphics but, at any rate, the serious collector should evince a high degree of concern for this facet of the hobby. Therefore, the question of how best to preserve our notes from future deterioration must be addressed. To get at answers to these queries, we must first consider the material with which we are dealing.

United States bank notes are in all instances made from cellulose from one or more natural sources and in varying degrees of basic quality. For the most part, the quality of the paper made from cellulosic raw material is very high which means that it is essentially pure cellulose with no significant inclusion of process chemicals or fillers other than very small quantities of uniquely identifiable materials used for anticounterfeiting purposes. The devices printed on the paper substrate are normally derived from mineral type pigments but, in some cases, the colors may be organic in nature. In the former case the stability of the pigments to outside influences will generally be greater than in the latter case, despite the fact that the organic dyes used will be the most stable types available.

We can conveniently divide the discussion of the care and preservation into two parts, viz., measures related to the paper itself and considerations regarding the pigments of the printed devices.

Cellulose has a certain affinity for water vapor and, as a result, there will always be small amounts of moisture incorporated into the molecular structure. The proportion will depend on the relative humidity and temperature of the storage area. Too little moisture may cause a certain degree of embrittlement of the paper with consequent increased susceptibility of damage on handling. Too great an amount of moisture can enhance deterioration of the cellulose by a small amount of acid or alkali inadvertently present from some undefined former exposure either in the manufacturing process or from environmental pollution. In addition, fungus growth be induced. Therefore, it is best to store notes in an enclosure wherein the relative humidity is about 45% and the ambient temperature is not above 20°C (68°F). The presence of excessive acid or alkaline in the note can be ascertained with the aid of a small drop of distilled water and a piece of pH paper (obtainable from drug stores or local scientific supply houses).

Place the drop of water on the note at the edge or other non-critical location. Do not contaminate the paper with moisture from the fingers! The pH indication should be between 6 and 7. If it is outside this range, soak the note for 5-10 minutes in a solution made from one fourth teaspoon of baking soda in one cup distilled water, blot dry with a clean cotton towel and rinse with distilled water three times by one minute soaks, followed by blotting with the towel.

Circulated notes often have dirty surfaces or disfigurements from pencil or pen streaking. To avoid possible damage to the printed devices, it is usually best to leave such extraneous material undisturbed. However, if one is irresistibly tempted to effect some sort of cleaning, it is best to judiciously use a soft gum eraser, on the unprinted portions of the note only. Always remember that erasers contain abrasive filler to a greater or lesser extent, depending on the purpose for which the eraser was designed. Soft gum erasers have minimum content of such fillers which can quickly remove printing ink along with the dirt, particularly if the filler is coarse and present to a high degree as in pencil erasers.

HOUSING OF PAPER MONEY

The question of suitable storage containers for bank notes is an important one since the wrong choice can lead to eventual irreparable damage to the paper itself or to the legends and devices. Paper envelopes of all types are to be avoided since the paper contains residues of the chemicals used in the papermaking process and these can be ultimately harmful. There are several types of plastic materials that can be used as holders. If chosen properly, they have the advantage of transparency that permits display of the note without actual handling. The following list is arranged in decreasing order of desirability.

1. Mylar a polyester terephthalate has no added chemicals such as plasticizers or ultraviolet light stabilizers, is mechanically strong in the biaxially oriented condition and offers excellent clarity. It is heat sealable at 425-450 F.

2. Biaxially oriented crystal polystyrene film has excellent clarity, good strength but may contain small amounts of ultraviolet light stabilizers. If the film is a grade approved for food packaging they are not likely to be harmful to bank notes. The film is heat sealable at 250-350 F.

3. Uncoated propylene homopolymer or randomly polymerized propylene-ethylene copolymer films are mechanically strong in the biaxially oriented state, have good clarity and contain small quantities of ultraviolet light stabilizers that

are likely to be harmful. They are generally somewhat more limp than Mylar films of the same thickness and are heat sealable at 300-320 F.

4. Cellulose triacete is a cast type film used for photographic film substrate and contains no plastizers or ultraviolet light stabilizers. It has good clarity and strength but is not heat sealable.

5. Cellophane is regenerated cellulose, has good strength and clarity and is heat sealable at 180-350 F due to residual acetate moeities. It has no plasticizer nor stabilizer.

Irrespective of the type of film chosen for security paper storage, it must be remembered by the collector that exposure of the notes to ultraviolet light from any source should be minimized since, in the inevitable presence of oxygen and small amounts of moisture, slow deterioration of the inks and even the cellulose itself can occur.

BEWARE OF "RESTORED" PAPER MONEY

Before you attempt to clean a bank note with the intention of reclassifying it as a better condition note, reconsider one could easily become a victim of the practice.

First, bleaching agents such as Chlorox are so strong and so alkaline that the paper itself, as well as some of the inks used in the device printing, may be harmed, particularly if the bleach is not removed completely by thorough washing. Residue of chemicals can cause slow deterioration over extended periods of time. Second, common solvents such as rubbing alcohol, cleaning fluid and carbona are effective in dissolving only oily material and this will not generally remove significant amounts of dirt from the note. In addition, they are likely to leave traces of impurities that they themselves contain, and they may dissolve portions of some of the printing inks from the devices. Third, strong laundry-type detergents are usually quite alkaline in nature and, as a consequence, may damage the cellulose substrate, particularly if they are not thoroughly removed by washing or neutralized with baking soda as noted earlier.

Drying a note after washing can result in scorching if a hot iron is used. A steam iron can leave obvious blisters. Beware of notes that seem sticky and too thick. This is usually the result of starching the paper in an effort to restore body. Toning may have been done by applying coffee to cover bleached areas. Be especially careful with the 1929 series, which has numerals, names and signatures overprinted in black ink on dry paper, all of which are easily damaged or removed by washing and drying; know that the wet-printed notes issued prior to the 1957 silver certificate series in uncirculated condition should have minor ripples and creases because they were allowed to dry in the pack and should have these features to be virginal.

After the bath and the dryer, beware of the eraser and the scissors. Soft erasers may sometimes be ethically used to remove a minor pencil mark. However, extensive erasures can be detected by the loss of surface sheen and mottled scarring. The use of scissors to trim the edge of a bill is the worst offense. Check the edges and the size of the bill if there is any doubt.

In order to protect your hobby, learn to detect the signs of fraud.

The preceding was extracted from Peter Huntoon's four-part series in *Coin World*, March 7, 14 and April 4 and 11, 1973.

CARE OF YOUR COLLECTION

Captain Kidd was primarily a coin collector, but the James boys were more interested in paper money. Things have not changed much, and the syngraphist should give some thought to the security of his collection before, rather than after, a tragedy happens.

Fortunately, paper money is light in weight and can be kept in a variety of containers in the home or in a bank safe deposit box. However, based on news stories that seem to be a regular part of hobby publication coverage, the latter place is the safer of the two.

Insurance can be obtained in most areas for collections, even though art, jewels and other items of value are certain targets for burglars. Regions usually differ in premiums and requirements for insurance, but the American Numismatic Association now has a group plan for members in this organization. Additional information may be obtained by writing to the association at 818 North Cascade Avenue, Colorado Springs, CO 80903-3279.

A record of identification is of prime importance. No recovery is possible without complete proof of ownership. Syngraphists have an advantage over the coin or stamp collector since bank notes, with very few exceptions, have identifying serial numbers. An accurate record of all the notes in your collection can be made with little effort.

A record of ownership, as well as a complete record of the price paid for each item, is necessary for resale or auction. We all must go some day, and when we do we should leave our heirs a record that will not complicate their lives and require them to pay unnecessary taxes. For instance, if you purchased a $20 note for $200 and it later sells for $250, only $50 is taxable.

It is advisable to designate at least one person in your family to be familiar with your collection, where it is kept and the records of purchase. It would also be a good idea to suggest the names of a few dealers or friends who could assist if disposition of the collection is considered.

For the most part the rarity of a national bank note is based on the number of such banks recorded for a particular state. However, there are other criteria that will affect the availability of particular notes, i.e., the size of the community or city where the bank was located, denominations issued, the length of time the bank operated and the desirability created by odd or interesting names.

Notes issued by the Alamo National Bank of San Antonio, TX, the Old Colony National Bank in Plymouth, MA, and the Lincoln National Bank of Lincoln, NE are just a few of these interesting names. Notes from interesting locales, e.g., Dry Run, PA, Painted Post, NY, and Buzzards Bay, MA are among many that are sought by collectors. More than $64 million in large- and small-size national bank notes remain outstanding.

National Bank Note State and Type Rarity Table

State	Large size	Small	State	Large size	Small
Alabama	R4	R3	Montana	R4	R6
Alaska	R9	R9	Nebraska	R4	R3
Arizona	R8	R8	Nevada	R8	R8
Arkansas	R6	R5	New Jersey	R2	R2
California	R1	R1	New Mexico	R8	R7
Colorado	R5	R4	New York	R1	R1
Connecticut	R4	R2	North Carolina	R4	R3
Delaware	R7	R7	Ohio	R6	R2
District of Columbia	R5	R3	Oklahoma	R6	R4
Florida	R6	R4	Oregon	R6	R4
Georgia	R6	R3	Pennsylvania	R1	R1
Hawaii	R5	R4	Puerto Rico	R9	—
Idaho	R8	R7	Rhode Island	R7	R4
Illinois	R1	R1	South Carolina	R5	R4
Indiana	R1	R1	South Dakota	R5	R6
Iowa	R2	R1	Tennessee	R4	R3
Kansas	R3	R2	Texas	R3	R1
Kentucky	R3	R2	Utah	R7	R6
Louisiana	R5	R4	Vermont	R6	R4
Maine	R6	R4	Virginia	R4	R2
Maryland	R4	R3	Washington	R5	R3
Massachusetts	R2	R2	West Virginia	R5	R2
Michigan	R2	R2	Wisconsin	R3	R1
Minnesota	R3	R2	Wyoming	R7	R7
Mississippi	R7	R6	Territories		R8

Between January 11, 1902 and February 26, 1924 a letter was printed near the bank charter number. This letter helped with the sorting of the notes geographically. The letters and their meaning are as follows:

N —	New England States	M —	Middle States
E —	Eastern States	W —	Western States
S —	Southern States	P —	Pacific States

National Bank Note Charter Numbers

On June 20, 1863 the First National Bank of Philadelphia received charter number 1. Nevertheless, the first notes released to the public were from The First National Bank of Washington, DC, Charter 26. Charter numbers were granted through 14,348 which was received by the Roodhouse Bank of Roodhouse, IL. However, some of the banks with higher numbers did not issue national bank notes for any of several reasons. The highest charter number to appear on a national bank note is 14,320 for the National Bank and Trust Company of Louisville, KY.

Charter Numbers	Year Granted	Charter Numbers	Year Granted	Charter Numbers	Year Granted
1-179	1863	3833-3954	1888	10120-10305	1912
180-682	1864	3955-4190	1889	10306-10472	1913
683-1626	1865	4191-4494	1890	10473-19672	1914
1627-1665	1866	4495-4673	1891	10673-10810	1915
1666-1675	1867	4674-4832	1892	10811-10932	1916
1676-1688	1868	4833-4934	1893	10933-11126	1917
1689-1696	1869	4935-4983	1894	11127-11282	1918
1697-1759	1870	4984-5029	1895	11283-11570	1919
1760-1912	1871	5030-5054	1896	11571-11903	1920
1913-2073	1872	5055-5108	1897	11904-12082	1921
2074-2131	1873	5109-5165	1898	12083-12287	1922
2132-2214	1874	5166-5240	1899	12288-12481	1923
2215-2315	1875	5241-5662	1900	12482-12615	1924
2316-2344	1876	5663-6074	1901	12616-12866	1925
2345-2375	1877	6075-6566	1902	12867-13022	1926
2376-2405	1878	6567-7081	1903	13023-13159	1927
2406-2445	1879	7082-7451	1904	13160-13269	1928
2446-2498	1880	7452-8027	1905	13270-13412	1929
2499-2606	1881	8028-8489	1906	13413-13516	1930
2607-2849	1882	8490-8979	1907	13517-13586	1931
2850-3101	1883	8980-9302	1908	13587-13654	1932
3102-3281	1884	9303-9622	1909	13655-13920	1933
3282-3427	1885	9623-9913	1910	13921-14217	1934
3428-3612	1886	9914-10119	1911	14218-14348	1935
3613-3832	1887				

National Bank Notes Outstanding by State*

State	Number of banks through 1935	In Circulation June 29, 1929**	In Circulation Dec. 31, 1934***
Alabama	170	$13,638,000.00	$11,191,000.00
Alaska	5	58,000.00	171,000.00
Arizona	31	1,025,000.00	857,000.00
Arkansas	141	3,883,000.00	3,466,000.00
California	509	34,984,000.00	92,979,000.00
Colorado	216	4,403,000.00	6,628,000.000
Connecticut	120	9,754,000.00	9,159,000.00
Delaware	30	1,008,000.00	1,203,000.00
District of Columbia	31	4,891,000.00	2,402,000.00
Florida	132	4,791,000.00	8,016,000.00
Georgia	181	7,750,000.00	5,224,000.00
Hawaii	6	450,000.00	3,350,000.00
Idaho	109	1,389,000.00	1,301,000.00
Illinois	813	35,949,000.00	19,750,000.00
Indiana	430	21,834,000.00	13,965,000.00
Iowa	542	14,121,000.00	6,375,000.00
Kansas	445	9,565,000.00	8,374,000.00
Kentucky	245	15,248,000.00	10,306,000.00
Louisiana	101	6,207,000.00	8,659,000.00
Maine	127	4,848,000.00	3,986,000.00
Maryland	140	7,399,000.00	4,952,000.00
Massachusetts	370	19,157,000.00	16,483,000.00
Michigan	310	16,119,000.00	9,330,000.00
Minnesota	484	14,404,000.00	20,316,000.00
Mississippi	76	3,006,000.00	2,385,000.00
Montana	193	2,311,000.00	1,886,000.00
Nebraka		4,848,000.00	3,986,000.00
Maryland	140	7,399,000.00	4,952,000.00
Massachusetts	370	19,157,000.00	16,483,000.00
Michigan	310	16,119,000.00	9,330,000.00
Minnesota	484	14,404,000.00	20,316,000.00
Mississippi	76	3,006,000.00	2,385,000.00
Montana	193	2,311,000.00	1,886,000.00
Nebraska	401	6,068,000.00	6,700,000.00
Nevada	16	1,194,000.00	407,000.00
New Jersey	414	22,835,000.00	25,314,000.00
New Mexico	82	1,253,000.00	1,155,000.00
New York	990	67,138,000.00	52,081,000.00
North Carolina	147	8,142,000.00	3,174,000.00
Ohio	689	35,963,000.00	34,367,000.00
Oklahoma	736	6,673,000.00	9,286,000.00
Oregon	147	5,222,000.00	7,599,000.00
Pennsylvania	1,274	82,256,000.00	95,243,000.00
Puerto Rico	1	—	—
Rhode Island	67	3,799,000.00	5,753,000.00
South Carolina	118	5,811,000.00	2,422,000.00
South Dakota	219	1,885,000.00	1,508,000.00
Tennessee	205	14,738,000.00	16,047,000.00
Texas	1,151	44,136,000.00	12,210,000.00
Utah	38	2,233,000.00	2,471,000.00
Vermont	85	4,304,000.00	3,941,000.00
Virginia	248	19,679,000.00	18,120,000.00
Virgin Islands	1	—	—
Washington	220	11,453,000.00	16,023,000.00
West Virginia	188	10,323,000.00	9,136,000.00
Wisconsin	269	15,991,000.00	12,812,000.00
Wyoming	58	1,485,000.00	1,355,000.00
Totals	14,348	$649,542,000.00	$654,456,000.00

* Van Belkum, pp. 15-16   ** Large-size notes   *** Small-size notes

Some might be surprised to know that a considerable number of women signed paper money in the early 19th century. The positions they held are abbreviated as follows: AC=Assistant Cashier; C=Cashier; P=President; VP=Vice President. Note type abbreviations are: BB=Brown Back; DB=Date Back; PB=Plain Back; RS=Red Seal; T1=Type I and T2=Type 2, both small-size notes.

City	State	Charter	Series	Type	Bank Officer's Name	Title
Gentry	AR	12340	1902	PB	Sadie Monroe	C
Marked Tree	AR	11122	1902	PB	Rubie Hastings	AC
Mena	AR	7163	1902	PB	Naomi Pryor	AC
Tombstone	AZ	6439	1902	PB	Ruth C. Costello	VP
Tombstone	AZ	6439	1902	PB	Ruth C. Costello	C
Tombstone	AZ	6439	1902	PB	Ruth C. Costello	P
Ducor	CA	10301	1929	T1	Rhoda Perkins	C
Hermosa Beach	CA	12271	1902	PB	Anne Meuret	AC
Akron	CO	10901	1902	PB	Edna B. Clark	C
Carterville	IL	7889	1902	PB	Mabel Hatfield	AC
Casey	IL	6026	1929	T1	Rose Turner	C
Cuba	IL	11144	1929	T1	Marie C. Harrison	C
Fairmount	IL	11443	1929	T1	Shirley T. Catlett	C
Freeburg	IL	7941	1929	T1	Susie M. Wolf	C
Gilman	IL	5856	1902	PB	Marie W. Hausmann	AC
Greenville	IL	9734	1902	PB	Myrtle T. Bradford	P
Lawrenceville	IL	5385	1929	T1	Edna E. Thorn	C
Marion	IL	4502	1929	T1	Shannon Holland	P
Princeton	IL	2165	1882	DB	Pearl Lafferty	C
Columbus	IN	1066	1929	T1	Elizabeth Lucas	P
Green Fork	IN	7124	1929	T1	Elizabeth J. Ward	C
La Grange	IN	4972	1882	BB	Katherine R. Williams	VP
Diagonal	IA	9125	1902	PB	Bessie D. Ferris	AC
Fontanelle	IA	7061	1902	PB	L. Bess Currie	AC
Lyndon	KS	7222	1902	PB	Ada Niehart	C
Morgan City	KY	7891	1929	T1	Bertha J. Leslie	C
Belfast	ME	7586	1902	PB	Alberta Farnham	AC
Fort Kent	ME	11403	1902	PB	Irene Cyr	C
Limerick	ME	2785	1902	PB	Mildred B. Johnston	C
Limerick	ME	2785	1929	T1	Mildred B. Johnston	C
Medomak	ME	1108	1929	T2	Frances D. Storer	C
Van Buren	ME	10628	1902	PB	Alexis A. Ceyr	C
Van Buren	ME	10628	1929	T1	Alexis A. Ceyr	C
York Village	ME	4844	1902	PB	Elizabeth Davidson	P
Albany	MO	7205	1929	T1	Mrs. R.L. Whaley	P
Joplin	MO	8947	1902	RS	Mrs. V.F. Church	C
Joplin	MO	8947	1902	DB	Tillie Muller Ade	C
Perryville	MO	11402	1929	T2	Mary C. Frioux	C
Stewartville	MO	4160	1902	PB	Nell Snow	AC
Stewartville	MO	4160	1929	T1	Nell Snow	C
Stewartville	MO	4160	1929	T2	Nell Snow	C
Versailles	MO	13367	1929	T1	Beatrice Sherril	C
Fairfax	MN	9771	1929	T1	Gertrude O. Fiss	C
Mabel	MN	9031	1929	T1	Betsy Tollefson	P
Grass Range	MT	10939	1902	PB	W. Louise Davis	C

City	State	Charter	Series	Type	Bank Officer's Name	Title
Elgin	NB	5440	1902	PB	Carrie McBride	P
Elgin	NB	5440	1929	T1	Carrie McBride	P
Humphrey	NB	5337	1882	BB	Bey Martin	P
Lexington	NB	3292	1882	DB	Henrietta R. Temple	P
Lexington	NB	3292	1902	DB	Jennie M. Temple	P
McCook	NB	9436	1902	PB	Mrs. V. Franklin	P
Minatare	NB	13316	1929	T2	Helen M. Littlejohn	C
Minden	NB	9400	1929	T1	Clara S. Hines	C
Minden	NB	9400	1929	T1	Clara H. McQuinllan	C
Minden	NB	9400	1929	T2	Clara H. McQuinllan	C
Naper	NB	9665	1902	DB	Vera F. Erickson	C
Naper	NB	9665	1902	PB	Vera F. Erickson	C
Plattsmouth	NB	1914	1902	PB	Anna Wanga	AC
Trenton	NB	8218	1902	RS	Ethyl Hall	C
Framington	NM	6183	1929	T2	H.B. Sammons (Harriet)	P
Hagerman	NM	7503	1902	PB	Ruth Lathrop	AC
Lake Arthur	NM Terr	8584	1902	DB	Ida Hammond	AC
Nara Vista	NM	8663	1902	DB	Ruth Burns	C
Argyle	NY	13521	1929	T1	Lillian J. Johnson	C
Argyle	NY	13521	1929	T2	Lillian J. Johnson	C
Cherry Creek	NY	10481	1902	DB	N.B. Lake	C
Cherry Creek	NY	10481	1929	T1	Nora B. Lake	C
Mexico	NY	5293	1929	T1	Alice K. Halligan	C
Mexico	NY	5293	1929	T2	Alice K. Halligan	C
Montour Falls	NY	13583	1929	T1	Belle P. Cornell	C
North Rose	NY	10016	1902	PB	Martha A. Peck	C
North Rose	NY	10016	1929	T1	Martha A. Peck	C
Roslyn	NY	13326	1929	T1	Helen A. Wood	C
Roslyn	NY	13326	1929	T2	Helen A. Wood	C
Westfield	NY	12476	1929	T1	Lucille Lichtenwalter	C
Canfield	OH	3654	1902	Pb	Ethel L. Fowler	AC
Cleves	OH	13774	1929	T2	Ruth Firth	C
Altus	OK	6113	1929	T1	Mrs. J.A. Henry	P
Beggs	OK	6868	1902	PB	Iva M. Reading	C
Coyle	OK	12148	1902	PB	Nora M. Fruin	C
Coyle	OK	12148	1929	T1	Nora M. Fruin	C
Foraker	OK	10356	1902	PB	Selma J. Codding	C
Luther	OK	8563	1929	T2	Gladys Bednar Hickok	C
Pond Creek	OK Terr	6655	1902	RS	Naomi Wheatley	AC
Atglen	PA	7056	1929	T1	Louise L. Hastings	C
Atglen	PA	7056	1929	T2	Louise L. Hastings	C
Mechanicsburg	PA	326	1902	PB	Ruth M. Heffelfinger	AC
New Alexandria	PA	6580	1902	DB	Doty Guthrie	P
New Alexandria	PA	6580	1929	T1	Nora J. Dornon	C
Williamsburg	PA	6971	1929	T1	Alice F. Dietrick	C
Providence	RI	1007	1929	T1	Shirley Harrington	C
Deport	TX	6430	1902	PB	Mrs. J.H. Moore	P
Deport	TX	6430	1929	T1	Mrs. J.H. Moore	P
Haskell	TX	14149	1929	T2	Mrs. M.S. Pierson	P
Jacksboro	TX	7814	1902	DB	Ellie Mither	C
Marlin	TX	5606	1929	T1	Mrs. Emma Reed	P
Winnsboro	TX	5674	1902	PB	Pearl James	AC

City	State	Charter	Series	Type	Bank Officer's Name	Title
Poultney	VT	2545	1902	PB	Adeline L. Nieframe	AC
Woodstock	VT	1133	1929	T1	Helen H. Saul	C
Woodstock	VT	1133	1929	T2	Helen H. Saul	C
Meeteetse	WY	6340	1902	PB	Sarah L. Hogg	VP

The preceding list, by Frank Clark, originally appeared in the December 1994 issue of the *Bank Note Reporter*. It appears here throught the courtesy of Krause Publications.

Blocks

The term block refers to the prefix and suffix letters, or star, combination of the serial number. Some collectors collect all or specific blocks, i.e., A-A, A-B, A-C etc.

Mules

Between 1938 and 1953, face and back plates with micro (0.6 mm high) and macro (1 mm high) numbers were combined at random. Mules appear on all denominations, $1 to $10,000. The following list of mules appeared in the *Standard Guide to Small-Size U.S. Paper Money* by Dean Oakes and John Schwartz, and is reprinted here through the courtesy of the publisher, Krause Publications.

Denomination	Class	Series	Face	Back
$1	Sil. Cert	1935	micro	macro
		1935A	macro	micro
$2	U.S. note	1928C	micro	macro
		1928D	micro	macro
		1934A	macro	micro
		1934C	macro	micro
	U.S. note	1928B	micro	macro
		1928C	macro	micro
		1928D	macro	micro
	FR note	1934 dark green seal	micro	macro
		1934 Hawaii	micro	macro
		1934A dark green seal	macro	micro
		1934B	micro	micro
		1934B NY 212 unreported	intermediate	micro
		1934C	macro	micro
$10	Sil. Cert	1934	micro	macro
		1934 North Africa	micro	macro
		1934A	macro	micro
	FR note	1934 light green seal	micro	macro
		1934 dark green seal micro	macro	
		1934A light green seal	macro	micro
		1934A dark green seal	macro	micro
$20	FR note	1934 dark green seal	micro	macro
		1934 Hawaii	micro	macro
		1934A light green seal*	macro	micro
		1934A dark green seal	macro	micro
		1934A Hawaii	macro	micro
$50	FR note	1934 dark green seal	micro	macro
		1934A dark green seal	macro	micro
		1934B	macro	micro
		1934C	macro	micro
		1934D	macro	micro
		1950	macro	micro
$100	FR note	1934 dark green seal	micro	macro

Denomination	Class	Series	Face	Back
		1934A dark green seal	macro	micro
		1934B	macro	micro
		1934C	macro	micro
		1934D	macro	micro
		1950	macro	micro
$500, $1000, $5000 and $10,000		1934 possible mules		

* Chicago Federal Reserve notes might have been printed

Attractive Serial Numbers

Collectors often seek specific combinations among the eight-digit serial numbers. The most desirable is a note with one digit repeated, e.g., 99999999. Sequential or ladder notes, e.g., 12345678; radar notes e.g., 12344321; and numbers that repeat, e.g., 78787878 are also popular.

CATALOG NUMBER CROSS REFERENCE OF TYPE NOTES
Large-Size Notes

Type	$1	$2	$5	$10	$20	$50	$100
Federal Reserve Bank Notes	95–111	204–206	274–286	628–655	853–878	1047–1073	1250–1273
Demand Notes	—	—	242	463	700	—	—
United States Notes	1–28	153–170	243–273	464–492	701–723	926–941	1120–1136
National Bank Notes							
First Charter Period	29–35	171–177	274–286	497–508	728–740	53–964	1151–1162
Second Charter Period	—	—	287–315	509–539	741–772	965–986	1163–1183
Third Charter Period	—	—	316–342	540–566	773–798	987–1012	1184–1206
National Gold Bank Notes	—	—	343–348	567–577	799–807	1013–1014f	1207–1211
Compound Interest Treasury Notes	—	—	—	493–495	724–726	942–944	1137–1139d
Interest-Bearing Notes	—	—	—	496	727	945–952	1139g–1150
Silver Certificates	36–61	178–196	349–372	578–602	808–827	1014g–1028	1212–1221
Treasury (Coin) Notes	62–67	197–202	373–379	612–617	843–847	1043	1242–1243
Refunding Certificates	—	—	—	603–604	—	—	—
Gold Certificates	—	—	—	605–611	828–842	1029–1042	1222–1241
Federal Reserve Notes	—	—	380–381	618–619	848–849	1044–1045	1244–1245
Federal Reserve Bank Notes	68	203	382	620	850	1046	—

Small-Size Notes

Type	$1	$2	$5	$10	$20	$50	$100
United States Notes	69	204–206	383–385	—	—	—	—
Silver Certificates	70–94	—	386–388	621–625	—	—	—
Federal Reserve Notes	95–111	207	391–420	628–655	853–878	1047–1073	1250–1273
Gold Certificates	—	—	—	699	925	1119	1319
Federal Reserve Bank Notes	—	—	389	626	851	1047	1248
National Bank Notes	—	—	390	627	852	1048	1249

Cross-Reference for Large-Size Notes Found in
Paper Money of the United States by R. **F**(riedberg) and this catalog by
Gene **H**(essler)

AR=all redeemed   NL= not listed   NP=not printed

F	H	F	H	F	H	F	H
1	242B	32	19	73	253	115	484
1a	242B	33	20	NL	254	116	485
2	242C	34	21	74	255	117	486
2a	242C	35	22	75	256	118	487
3	242A	36	23	76	257	119	488
3a	242A	37	24	77	258	120	489
4	242D	37a	25	78	259	121	490
4a	242D	38	26	79	260	122	491
5	242H	39	27	80	261	123	492
5a	242H	40	28	81	262	124	701
6	463B	41	153A	82	263	125	701a
6a	463B	41a	153	83	264	126	701b
7	463C	42	154	84	265	126a	701c
7a	463C	43	155	85	266	126b	702
8	463A	44	156	86	267	127	703
9	463D	45	155A	87	268	128	704
10	463H	46	155B	88	269	129	705
10a	463H	47	157	89	270	130	706
11	700B	48	158	90	271	131	707
11a	700B	49	159	91	272	132	708
12	700C	50	160	92	273	133	709
12a	700C	51	161	93	464	134	710
13	700A	52	162	94	465	135	711
13a	700A	53	163	95	465a	136	712
14	700D	54	164	95a	465b	137	713
14a	700D	55	165	95b	465c	138	714
15	700E	56	166	96	466	139	715
16	1	57	167	97	467	140	716
16a	2	58	168	98	467A	141	717
17	3	59	169	99	468	142	718
17a	4	60	170	100	469	143	719
18	5	61	243	101	470	144	720
19	6	61a	243a	102	471	145	721
20	12	62	243b	103	472	146	722
21	7	63	244a	104	473	147	723
22	8	63a	244b	105	474	148	926
23	9	64	245	106	475	149	926a
24	10	65	247	107	476	NL	926b
25	11	66	246A	108	477	150	927a
26	13	67	246B	109	478	150a	927
27	14	68	248	110	479	151	928
28	15	69	249	111	480	152	929
29	16	70	250	112	481	153	930
30	17	71	251	113	482	154	931
31	18	72	252	114	483	155	932

AR=all redeemed   NL= not listed   NP=not printed

F	H	F	H	F	H	F	H
156	933	186a	1376a	193b	1139d	212a	1148
157	934	186b	1377	194	1337	212b	1346
158	935	186c	1378	NL	1338	212b	1347
159	936	186d	1378a	194a	1339	212c	1399
160	937	186e	1378b	194b	1339a	212c	1400
161	938	186f	1379	195	1392	212d	951
162	939	187a	1380	195a	1392a	212d	952
163	940	187b	1381	195a	1392b	212e	1149
164	941	187c	1382	195b	945	212e	1150
165	1120	187d	1383	195c	1139g	212f	1348
165a	1120a	187e	1384	195d	1340	212f	1349
166	1120b	187f	1385	196	496	212g	1401
167	1121	187g	1386	196a	496	212g	1402
167a	1121a	187h	1387	197	727	213	603
167b	1121b	187i	1388	197a	727	214	604
168	1122	187j	1389	198	945a	215	36
169	1123	187k	1390	199	1140	216	37
170	1124	187l-l	1391	200	1340a	217	38
171	1125	188	1435	NL	1394	218	39
172	1126	189	1465	201	1395	219	40
173	1127	190	493	NL	1435a	220	41
174	1128	190a	494	202	1435b	221	42
175	1129	190b	495	202a	945b	222	43
176	1130	190b	495a	202b	1141	223	44
177	1131	190b	495b	202c	1340b	224	45
178	1132	NL	724	202d	1393b	225	46
179	1133	191	725	203	945c	226	47
180	1134	NL	725a	NL	945d	226a	48
181	1135	191a	726	204	1142	227	49
182	1136	191a	726a	NL	1143	228	50
183a	1320	191a	726b	205	1341	229	51
183b	1320a	191a	726c	NL	1342	230	52
183c	1321	191a	726d	206	1394	231	53
183d	1321a	191a	726e	NL	1395	232	54
184	1322	191a	726f	207	946	233	55
185a	1323	192	942	207	947	234	56
185b	1324	NL	943	207	948	235	57
185c	1325	NL	943a	208	1144	236	58
185d	1326	192a	944	208	1145	237	59
185e	1327	192b	944a	208	1146	238	60
185f	1328	192b	944c	209	1343	239	61
185g	1329	192b	944d	209	1344	240	178
185h	1330	192b	944e	209	1345	241	179
185i	1331	193	1137	210	1396	242	180
185j	1332	193a	1138	210	1397	243	181
185k	1333	193b	1139	210	1398	244	182
185l	1334	193b	1139a	212	949	245	183
185m	1335	193b	1139b	212	950	246	184
185n	1336	193b	1139c	212a	1147	247	185

CROSS REFERENCE FOR LARGE-SIZE NOTES

AR=all redeemed   NL= not listed   NP=not printed

F	H	F	H	F	H	F	H
248	186	292	591	334	1027	364	378
249	187	293	592	335	1028	365	379
250	188	294	593	336	1212	366	612
251	189	295	594	336a	1212a	367	613
252	190	296	595	336a	1212b	368	614
253	191	297	596	337	1213	369	615
254	192	298	597	337a	1214	370	616
255	193	299	598	337b	1214a	371	617
256	194	300	599	338	1215	372	843
257	195	301	600	339	1216	373	844
258	196	302	601	340	1217	374	845
259	349	303	601a	341	1218	375	846
260	350	304	602	342	1219	375a	847
261	351	NL	808	343	1220	376	1043
262	352	305	809	344	1221	377	1242
263	353	306	809a	345a	1352	378	1243
264	354	306a	810	345a	1352a	NL	1360d
265	355	306b	811	345a	1352b	NL	1360e
266	356	307	812	345a	1353	379	1360f
267	357	308	813	345a	1354	379a	1425
268	358	309	814	345a	1354a	379b	1426
269	359	310	815	345b	1355	379c	1427
270	360	311	816	345c	1356	379d	1428
271	361	312	817	345d	1357	380	29
272	362	313	818	346a	1405	381	30
273	363	314	819	346a	1406	382	31
274	364	315	820	346a	1407	383	32
275	365	316	821	346a	1407a	384	33
276	366	317	822	346b	1408	385	34
277	367	318	823	346c	1409	386	35
278	368	319	824	346d	1410	387	171
279	369	320	825	346e	1411	388	172
280	370	321	826	347	62	389	173
281	371	322	827	348	63	390	174
282	372	323	1014g	349	64	391	175
283	578	323	1014h	350	65	392	176
284	579	324	1015	351	66	393	177
284a	580	324a	1016	352	67	394	274
284b	581	324b	1017	353	197	397	275
284c	582	324c	1017a	354	198	398	276
285	583	325	1018	355	199	399	277
285a	583a	326	1019	356	200	401	278
286	584	327	1020	357	201	402	279
286a	585	328	1021	358	202	403	280
287	586	329	1022	359	373	404	281
288	587	330	1023	360	374	405	282
289	588	331	1024	361	375	406	283
290	589	332	1025	362	376	406a	284
291	590	333	1026	363	377	407	285

AR=all redeemed   NL= not listed   NP=not printed

F	H	F	H	F	H	F	H
408	286	461	1159	496	744	541	525
408a	286a	462	1160	497	745	542	526
NL	286b	462a	1161	498	746	543	527
409	497	463	1162	499	747	544	528
412	498	NL	1350	500	748	545	529
413	499	464	1350a	501	749	546	530
414	500	NL	1350b	502	750	547	531
416	501	464a	1350c	503	751	548	532
417	502	NL	1350d	504	752	548a	532a
418	503	NL	1350e	505	753	549	755
419	504	NL	1350f	506	754	550	756
420	505	NL	1350g	507	965	551	757
421	506	465	1403	508	966	552	758
422	507	465	1404	509	967	553	759
423	508	465	1404a	510	968	554	760
423a	508a	465	1404b	511	969	555	761
424	728	465	1404c	512	970	556	762
427	729	465	1404d	513	971	556a	762a
428	730	466	287	514	972	557	763
429	731	467	288	515	973	558	978
431	732	468	289	516	974	559	979
432	733	469	290	517	975	560	980
433	734	470	291	518	976	561	981
434	735	471	292	518a	977	562	982
435	736	472	293	519	1163	563	983
436	737	473	294	520	1164	564	984
437	738	474	295	521	1165	565	985
438	739	475	296	522	1166	566	1175
439	740	476	297	523	1167	567	1176
440	953	477	298	524	1168	568	1177
442	954	477a	298a	525	1169	569	1178
443	955	478	299	526	1170	570	1179
444	956	479	509	527	1171	571	1180
444a	957	480	510	528	1172	572	1181
445	958	481	511	529	1173	572a	1182
446	959	482	512	530	1174	573	309
447	960	483	513	531	1174a	573a	310
448	961	484	514	532	300	574	312
449	962	485	515	533	301	574a	311
450	963	486	516	533a	302	574b	311a
451	964	487	517	534	303	575	313
452	1151	488	518	535	304	575a	314
454	1152	489	519	536	305	575b	315
455	1153	490	520	537	306	576	533
456	1154	491	521	538	307	576a	534
457	1155	492	522	538a	NL	576b	535
458	1156	493	741	538b	308	577	536
459	1157	494	742	539	523	577a	536a
460	1158	495	743	540	524	578	537

AR=all redeemed   NL= not listed   NP=not printed

F	H	F	H	F	H	F	H
579	538	621	548	667	990	709	68A2
579a	538a	622	549	668	991	710	68A3
579b	539	623	550	669	992	711	68B1
580	764	623a	551	670	993	712	68B2
580a	765	624	552	671	994	713	68B3
580b	766	625	553	672	995	714	68C1
581	767	626	554	673	996	715	68C2
582	768	627	555	674	997	716	68C3
583	769	628	556	674a	998	717	68C4
584	770	629	557	675	999	718	68D1
584a	771	630	558	676	1000	719	68D2
585	772	631	559	677	1001	720	68D3
586	986	632	560	678	1002	721	68E1
586a	1183	633	561	679	1003	722	68E2
587	316	634	562	679a	1004	723	68F1
588	317	635	563	680	1005	724	68F2
589	318	636	564	681	1006	725	68F3
590	319	637	565	682	1007	726	68F4
591	320	638	566	683	1008	727	68G1
592	321	639	773	684	1009	728	68G2
593	322	640	774	685	1010	729	68G3
594	323	641	775	685a	1011	730	68H1
595	324	642	776	NL	1012	731	68H2
596	325	643	777	686	1184	732	68H3
597	326	644	778	687	1185	733	68H4
597a	327	645	779	688	1186	734	68I1
598	328	646	780	689	1187	735	68I2
599	329	647	781	690	1188	736	68I3
600	330	648	782	691	1189	737	68J1
601	331	649	783	692	1190	738	68J2
602	332	649a	784	693	1191	739	68J3
603	333	650	785	694	1192	740	68K1
604	334	651	786	695	1193	741	68K2
605	335	652	787	696	1194	742	68K3
606	336	653	788	697	1195	743	68L1
607	337	654	789	698	1196	744	68L2
608	338	655	790	699	1197	745	68L3
609	339	656	791	700	1198	746	68L4
610	340	657	792	701	1199	747	203A1
611	341	658	793	702	1200	748	203A2
612	342	659	794	702a	1201	749	203A3
613	540	660	795	702b	1201a	750	203B1
614	541	661	796	703	1202	751	203B2
615	542	662	797	704	1203	752	203B3
616	543	663	798	705	1204	753	203C1
617	544	663a	798a	706	1205	754	203C2
618	545	664	987	707	1206	755	203C3
619	546	665	988	707a	1206a	756	203C4
620	547	666	989	708	68A1	757	203D1

AR=all redeemed   NL= not listed   NP=not printed

F	H	F	H	F	H	F	H
758	203D2	801a	382J2	843	380L	892	618A
759	203D3	802	382J3	844	381A1	893	618B
760	203E1	802a	382J3	845	381A2	894	618C
761	203E2	803	382J4	846	381A3	895	618D
762	203F1	804	382J5	847	381A4	896	618E
763	203F2	805	382K1	848	381B1	897	618F
NL	203F3	806	382K2	849	381B2	898	618G
764	203F4	807	382K3	850	381B3	899	618H
765	203G1	808	382L1	851	381B4	900	618I
766	203G2	809	382L2	852	381C1	901	618J
767	203G3	809a	382L3	853	381C2	902	618K
768	203H1	NL	382L4	854	381C3	903	618L
769	203H2	810	620B	855	381C4	904	619A1
770	203H3	811	620F1	856	381D1	905	619A2
771	203H4	812	620F2	857	381D2	906	619A3
772	203I1	813	620G1	859	381D3	907	619A4
773	203I2	814	620G2	860	381D4	908	619B1
774	203J1	815	620H	861	381E1	909	619B2
775	203J2	816	620J1	862	381E2	910	619B3
NL	203J3	817	620J2a	862	381E3	911	619B4
776	203K1	817a	620J2b	863	381E4	912	619C1
777	203K2	818	620J4	864	381F1	913	619C2
NL	203K3	819	620K1	865	381F2	914	619C3
778	203L1	820	620K2	866	381F3	915	619C4
NL	203L2	821	620K3	867	381F4	916	619D1
779	203L3	822	850F1	868	381G1	917	619D2
780	203L4	822–1	850F1a	869	381G2	918	619D3
781	382A1	822a	850F3	870	381G3	919	619D4
782	382B1	823	850F4	871	381G4	920	619E1
783	382C1	824	850G1	872	381H1	921	619E2
784	382C2	825	850H1	873	381H2	922	619E3
785	382D1	826	850J1	874	381H3	923	619E4
786	382D2	827	850J2	875	381H4	924	619F1
787	382D3	NL	850J2a	876	381I1	925	619F2
788	382F1	828	850K1	877	381I2	926	619F3
789	382F2	829	850K2	878	381I3	927	619F4
790	382F3	830	850K3	879	381I4	928	619G1
791	382F4	831	1046	880	381J1	929	619G2
792	382F5	832	380A	881	381J2	930	619G3
793	382G1	833	380B	882	381J3	931	619G4
794	382G2	834	380C	883	381J4	932	619H1
795	382G3	835	380D	884	381K1	933	619H2
796	382H1	836	380E	885	381K2	934	619H3
797	382H2	837	380F	886	381K3	935	619H4
798	382H3	838	380G	887	381K4	936	619I1
799	382I1	839	380H	888	381L1	937	619I2
800	382J1	840	380I	889	381L2	938	619I3
800a	382J1	841	380J	890	381L3	939	619I4
801	382J2	842	380K	891	381L4	940	619J1

AR=all redeemed   NL= not listed   NP=not printed

F	H	F	H	F	H	F	H
941	619J2	990	849G3	1039	1045D4	1088	1245B1
942	619J3	991	849G4	1040	1045E1	1089	1245B2
943	619J4	992	849H1	1041	1045E2	1090	1245B3
944	619K1	993	849H2	1042	1045E3	1091	1245B4
945	619K2	994	849H3	1043	1045E4	1092	1245C1
946	619K3	995	849H4	1044	1045F1	1093	NP
947	619K4	996	849I1	1045	1045F2	1094	NP
948	619L1	997	849I2	1046	1045F3	1095	1245C4
949	619L2	998	849I3	1047	1045F4	1096	1245D1
950	619L3	999	849I4	1048	1045G1	1097	1245D2
951	619L4	1000	849J1	1049	1045G2	1098	1245D3
952	848A	1001	849J2	1050	1045G3	1099	1245D4
953	848B	1002	849J3	1051	1045G4	1100	1245E1
954	848C	1003	849J4	1052	1045H1	1101	1245E2
955	848D	1004	849K1	1053	1045H2	1102	NP
956	848E	1005	849K2	1054	1045H3	1103	1245E4
957	848F	1006	849K3	1055	1045H4	1104	1245F1
958	848G	1007	849K4	1056	1045I1	1105	NP
959	848H	1008	849L1	1057	1045I2	1106	1245F3
960	848I	1009	849L2	1058	1045I3	1107	1245F4
961	848J	1010	849L3	1059	1045I4	1108	1245G1
962	848K	1011	849L4	1060	1045J1	1109	NP
963	848L	1012	1044A	1061	1045J2	1110	1245G3
964	849A1	1013	1044B	1062	1045J3	1111	1245G4
965	849A2	1014	1044C	1063	1045J4	1112	1245H1
966	849A3	1015	1044D	1064	1045K1	1113	NP
967	849A4	1016	1044E	1065	1045K2	1114	NP
968	849B1	1017	1044F	1066	1045K3	1115	1245H4
969	849B2	1018	1044G	1067	1045K4	1116	1245I1
970	849B3	1019	1044H	1068	1045L1	1117	NP
971	849B4	1020	1044I	1069	1045L2	1118	NP
972	849C1	1021	1044J	1070	1045L3	1119	1245I4
973	849C2	1022	1044K	1071	1045L4	1120	1245J1
974	849C3	1023	1044L	1072	1244A	1121	NP
975	849C4	1024	1045A1	1073	1244B	1122	NP
976	849D1	1025	1045A2	1074	1244C	1123	1245J4
977	849D2	1026	1045A3	1075	1244D	1124	1245K1
978	849D3	1027	1045A4	1076	1244E	1125	NP
979	849D4	1028	1045B1	1077	1244F	1126	NP
980	849E1	1029	1045B2	1078	1244G	1127	1245K4
981	849E2	1030	1045B3	1079	1244H	1128	1245L1
982	849E3	1031	1045B4	1080	1244I	1129	NP
983	849E4	1032	1045C1	1081	1244J	1130	1245L3
984	849F1	1033	1045C2	1082	1244K	1131	1245L4
985	849F2	1034	1045C3	1083	1244L	1132	1370A2
986	849F3	1035	1045C4	1084	1245A1	1132	1370B2
987	849F4	1036	1045D1	1085	1245A2	1132b	1370B4
988	849G1	1037	1045D2	1086	NP	1132	1370C2
989	849G2	1038	1045D3	1087	1245A4	1132	1370D2

AR=all redeemed   NL= not listed   NP=not printed

F	H	F	H	F	H	F	H
1132	1370E	1135	1493I	1166	1211	1184	839
1132	1370F2	1135	1493J	1166–I	1211a	1185	840
1132	1370G1	1135	1493K	1166–II	1211b	1186	841
1132	1370G2	1135	1493L	1166–III	1211c	1187	842
1132	1370H2	1136	343	1166–IV	1211d	1188	1030
1132	1370I	1137	344	1166–a	1351	1189	1029
1132	1370J2	1138	345	1166–a	1351a	1189a	1031
1132	1370K2	1139	346	1166–a	1351b	1190	1032
1132	1370L2	1140	347	1166–b	827a	1191	1033
1132a	1370L3	1141	348	1166–b	827b	1192	1034
1133	1429A2	1142	567	1166–c	1222	NL	1034a
1133	1429B2	1143	568	1166–c	1222a	1193	1035
1133a	1429B3	1144	569	1166–d	1358	1194	1036
1133b	1429B4	1145	571	1166–e	1412	1195	1037
1133	1429A2	1146	570	1166–f	1443	1196	1038
1133	1429B2	1147	570a	1166–g	1466	1197	1038
1133	1429B3	1148	572	1166–h	1223	1198	1040
1133	1429B4	1149	573	1166–h	1224	1199	1041
1133b	1429C2	1150	574	1166–i	1359	1200	1042
1133	1429D2	NL	574a	1166–j	1413	1200	1042a
1133	1429E2	1151	575	1166–k	1444	1201	1228
1133	1429F2	1151a	576	1166–k	1444a	1202	1226
1133	1429F4	1152	799	1166–l	1467	1203	1227
1133	1429H2	1153	800	1166–m	1225	1204	1230
1133	1429I2	NL	800a	1166–m	1225a	1205	1231
1133	1429J2	1154	801	1166–n	1360	1206	1232
1133	1429K2	1155	802	1166–o	1414	1207	1233
1133	1429L2	1155a	802a	1166–q	1468	1208	1234
1133b	1429L4	1156	803	1167	605	1209	1235
1134	1461A	NL	804	1168	606	1210	1236
1134	1461B	1157	804a	1169	607	1211	1237
1134	1461C	NL	804b	1169a	607a	1212	1238
1134	1461D	1158	805	1170	608	1213	1239
1134	1461E	NL	805a	1170a	608a	1214	1240
1134	1461F	1159	806	1171	609	1215	1241
1134	1461G	1159a	807	1172	610	1215a	1362
1134	1461H	1160	1013	1173a	611	1215b	1361
1134	1461I	1160a	1013a	1173	611a	1215c	1363
1134	1461J	1161	1014	1174	828	1215d	1364
1134	1461K	1161a	1014a	1175	829	1216	1365
1134	1461L	1161b	1014b	1175a	830	NL	1366
1135	1493A	1161c	1014c	1176	831	NL	1366a
1135	1493B	1161d 1	014d	1177	832	1216a	1367
1135	1493C	1161e	1014e	1178	833	1216b	1368
1135	1493D	1161f	1014f	1179	834	1217	1369
1135	1493E	1162	1207	1180	835	1218	1416
1135	1493F	1163	1208	1181	836	1218a	1415
1135	1493G	1164	1209	1182	837	1218b	1417
1135	1493H	1165	1210	1183	838	1218c	1418

AR=all redeemed   NL= not listed   NP=not printed

F	H	F	H	F	H	F	H
1218d	1419	1221b	1448	1222b	AR	1223g	1477
1218e	1420	1221c	1449	1223	1471	1224	1478–
1218f	1421	1221d	1450	1223a	1470	1224a	1480–
1218g	1422	1221e	1451	1223b 1	472	1224b	1482
1219	1423	NL	1451a	1223c	1473	1225	1485–
1219a	1423a	1221f	1452	1223d	1474	1225	1492a
1219b	1423b	1221g	1452	NL	1475a	NL	1492b
1219c	1423c	1221h	1453a	1223e	1475	NL	1492c
1219d	1423d	NL	1453B	1223f	1476	NL	1441
1219e	1423e	1221i	1453c	NL	1476a	NL	1442
1220	1424	1221j	1453d	NL	1476b		
1221	1447	1222	AR	NL	1476c		
1221a	1446	1222a	AR	NL	1476d		

Bibliography

Annual Reports of the Director of the Bureau of Engraving and Printing, Government Printing Office, Washington, DC.

Appleton's Cyclopaedia of American History. D. Appleton & Co., New York, 1887.

Bart, Dr. Frederick J. *Comprehensive Catalog of United States Paper Money Errors.* BNR Press, Port Clinton, OH, 1994.

Bayley, Rafael A. *The National Loans of the United States of America from July 4, 1776 to June 20, 1880*, as prepared for the Tenth Census of the United States. Washington, DC, 1882.

Blake, George H. *United States Paper Money.* Published by the author, 1908.

Bowen, Harold L. *State Bank Notes of Michigan.* Havelt Advertising Service Inc., 1956.

Clain-Stefanelli, Elvira and Vladimir. *American Banking.* Acropolis Books, Ltd., Washington, DC, 1975.

Columbia Viking Desk Encyclopedia. Viking Press, New York, 1968.

Coudert, L.L. *The Romance of Intaglio Bank Notes.* American Bank Note Co., New York, 1925.

Dannen, F. And I. Silverman. "The Supernote," *The New Yorker*, October 23, 1995.

DeKnight, W.F. *History of the Currency of the Country and the Loans of the United States.* Government Printing Office, Washington, DC, 1897.

Dillistin, William H. *A Descriptive History of National Bank Notes.* Printed by the author, 1956.

Fielding, Mantle. *Dictionary of American Painters, Sculptors and Engravers.* James F. Carr, New York, 1965.

Friedman, M. & A.J. Schwartz. *A Monetary History of the United States 1867–1960.* Princeton University Press, Princeton, 1963.

Friedberg, Robert. *Paper Money of the United States.* Coin and Currency Institute, Inc., New York, 1989.

Gengerke, Martin. *United States Paper Money Records.* Published by the author, New York, 1995.

Gies, F. & J. *"Cathedral, Forge, and Waterwheel:* Technology and Invention in the Middle Ages." Harper Collins, New York, 1994.

Gould, Maurice. *Hawaiian Coins, Tokens and Paper Money.* Whitman Publishing Co., Racine, WI, 1960.

Gould, Maurice, and L.W. Higgie. *The Money of Puerto Rico.* Whitman Publishing Co., Racine, WI, 1962.

Griffiths, William H. *Story of American Bank Note Company.* American Bank Note Company, New York, 1959.

Groce, George C. and David H. Wallace. *New York Historical Society Dictionary of Artists in America, 1564-1860.* Yale University Press, New Haven, 1957.

Haxby, James. *Standard Catalog of United States Obsolete Bank Notes, 1782-1866*. Krause Publications, Iola, WI, 1988.

Hepburn, A. Barton. *A History of Currency in the United States*. MacMillan Co., New York, 1924.

Hessler, Gene. *An Illustrated History of U.S. Loans, 1775-1898*. BNR Press, Port Clinton, OH, 1988.

———. *The Engraver's Line*, BNR Press, Port Clinton, OH, 1993.

_____. *U.S. Essay, Proof and Specimen Notes*. BNR Press, Port Clinton, OH, 1979.

Hickman, John, and Dean Oakes. *Standard Catalog of National Bank Notes*. Krause Publications, Iola, WI, 1982.

History of the Bureau of Engraving and Printing 1862-1962. Treasury Department, Washington, DC, 1964.

Hodder, M.J. and Q.D. Bowers. *The Standard Catalogue of Encased Postage Stamps*. Bowers and Merena, Wolfeboro, NH, 1989.

Hunter, Dard. *Papermaking*. Dover Publications, New York, 1978.

Huntoon, P. "The United States $500 & $1,000 National Bank Notes." *PAPER MONEY*. Society of Paper Money Collectors. No. 136, July/Aug. 1988, pp. 103-121.

Huntoon, P. and L. Van Belkum. (ed. M.O. Warns). *The National Bank Note Issues 1929-1935*. The Society of Paper Money Collectors, 1970.

Isted, John. *U.S. Large-Size Currency*. Unpublished manuscript.

Knox, John Jay. *United States Notes*. T. Fisher Unwin, London, 1885.

Lehman-Haupt, H. *Gutenberg and the Master of the Playing Cards*. Yale University Press, New Haven & London, 1966.

Limpert, Frank Alvin. *United States Paper Money, Old Series 1861-1923 Inclusive*. Published by the author, 1948.

Morris, Thomas F., II. (ed. Barbara R. Mueller). *The Life and Works of Thomas F. Morris, 1852-1898*. Published by the author, 1968.

Murray, Douglas D. *Handbook of United States Large Size Star Notes*. Published by the author, Kalamazoo, MI, 1996.

Muscalus, John A. *Famous Paintings Reproduced on Paper Money of State Banks, 1806-1866*. Published by the author, 1969.

Newman, Eric P. *The Dollar Sign Its Written and Printed Origins*, Coinage of the Americas Conference American Numismatic Society, New York, 1995.

———. *The Early Paper Money of America*. Krause Publications, Iola, WI, 1990.

Oakes, Dean & John Schwartz. *Standard Guide to Small-Size U.S. Paper Money*. Krause Publications, Iola, WI, 1994.

O'Donnell, Chuck. *The Standard Handbook of Modern United States Paper Money*. Krause Publications, Iola, WI, 1982.

Radford, C., MD. *The Souvenir Card Collectors Society Number System*. Souvenir Card Collectors Society, Tulsa, OK, 1989.

Reed, Fred L. III, *Civil War Encased Stamps*, BNR Press, Port Clinton, OH 1995.

Schwan, Carlton F. *Military Payment Certificates*, BNR Press, Port Clinton, OH, 1981.

Schwan, Carlton F. and Joseph E. Boling. *World War II Remembered*. BNR Press, Port Clinton, OH, 1995.

Shafer, Neil. *A Guide of Modern United States Currency*. Western Publishing Co., Racine, WI, 1979.

_____. *A Guide Book of Philippine Paper Money*. Whitman Publishing Co., Racine, WI, 1964.

Schafrick, R.E. and S.E. Church, "Protecting the Greenback," *Scientific American*, July 1955.

Springs, Agnes Wright. *The First National Bank of Denver: the Formative Years 1860-1865*. Bradford-Robinson Printing Co., Denver, Colorado, undated.

Timberlake, Richard. *Gold, Greenbacks, and the Constitution*. The George Edward Durrell Foundation, Berryville, VA, 1991.

Van Buren, A.H., & S. Edmonds. "The Master of the Playing Cards," *The Ar Bulletin*. March 1974, pp. 12-30.

Williams, L.N. *Fundamentals of Philately*. American Philatelic Society, State College, PA 1990.

Publications:

Coin World
PAPER MONEY
Bank Note Reporter
The Essay-Proof Journal
The Numismatist

Auction catalogs and price lists:

Bebee's (James M. Wade Collection)
Bowers & Merena
Christie's
Currency Auctions of America (CAA)
William P. Donlon
Albert A. Grinnell (reprinted by W.T. Anton, Jr. and M. Perlmutter, 1971)
Hickman & Oakes
John Hickman (deceased)
Lyn F. Knight
Dean Oakes
Robert A. Siegal
R.M. Smythe
Stack's Superior Stamp & Coin Co.

Index

EXPERIENCE AND LONGEVITY
A COMMITMENT TO THE MARKETPLACE

Since 1985 we have been one of America's largest active buyers and sellers of historical bonds and shares and are recognized as one of the world's leading market makers for good quality American material. We have contributed in large part to the development of many of the finest collections of American material in the world today and understand the needs of both he casual and serious collector.

EXCITING MAIL AND PHONE BID CATALOGS

We conduct some of America's finest mail bid auctions offering a large selection of items in virtually every collecting category imaginable. Our fully illustrated and well researched catalog are an important permanent reference work for serious collectors and dealers alike.

PRIVATE TREATY SALES TO COLLECTORS, DEALERS, AND CORPORATIONS

We maintain a large and diversified inventory of items ranging in price from less than a dollar to in excess of $10,000. Some major categories found in our inventory—
autographs, automotive, aviation, banking, early finance, entertainment, insurance, mining, oil, railroad, shipping, telephone and telegraph, utilities

Scott J. Winslow Associates, Inc.

Post Office Box 10240
Bedford, New Hampshire 03110
(800) 255-6233 ~ (603) 472-7040
Fax (603) 472-8773, e-mail SWins82687@aol.com

Great paper money books!

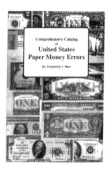

The Comprehensive Catalog of United Stares Paper Money Errors is the only complete reference book on one of the most popular categories of paper money collected today. Frederick J. Bart is a veteran collector of error notes. He has collected error notes, information, and photographs for the past fifteen years and brought them together in this new book which is likely to become a standard reference. It includes features which will be of interest to beginners and advanced collectors. More than 300 different notes are listed, described, illustrated and valued. All major types of U.S. paper money including fractional notes and even military payment certificates are covered. An innovative rarity scheme is presented for silver certificates and Federal Reserve notes. Bob Leuver, former director of the Bureau of Engraving and Printing, provides an insightful foreword for this interesting book. hardbound, $35.00; softbound, $25.00

Gene Hessler's masterpiece is now ready: *The Engraver's Line, an Encyclopedia of Paper Money and Postage Stamp Art.* This is the first major composite listing of designers and engravers of bank notes and postage stamps; there are over 500 pages and illustrations. Encyclopedias and histories of artists, sculptors and engravers rarely acknowledge most of the men and women listed here. Some of the most beautiful bank notes were designed or engraved by major American artists such as F. O. C. Darley, Asher B. Durand, Will Low, Walter Shirlaw and Kenyon Cox. But their paper money designs are seldom mentioned in art studies even though these designs were seen and handled by more people than all of those who saw their work in galleries and art museums. For the first time collectors and art lovers will have access to lists of bank notes (and postage stamps) by the artists included here.

The Engraver's Line, regular deluxe edition $85.00, philatelic deluxe $185.00

The leader in paper money books— ask for a free list

BNR Press
132 E. Second Street
Port Clinton, Ohio 43452-1115-04
order via voice or fax 800 793-0683
also (419) 732-NOTE (6683)
e-mail bnrpress@dcache.net

since 1977

Civil War Encased Stamps
by Fred Reed

D uring the Civil War, governments and merchants alike had to be creative in solving financial difficulties. Both sides experienced severe financial difficulties. Gold and silver coinage was hoarded and disappeared from circulation. Both sides then issued paper money. As amazing as that seems today, that was the first successful use of federal paper money. Fractional currency was created and huge quantities of tokens were issued.

Encased postage stamps were perhaps the most interesting and innovative money of them all. Postage stamps were encapsulated so that they could circulate without deteriorating. The denomination was visible to establish the value and the other side was available for advertising. This was the perfect free enterprise solution, but the introduction of fractional currency ended the need for encased stamps.

Fred Reed has studied Civil War encased stamps in a way that few issues have been studied. He has done the traditional things. He studied collections, auction catalogs, old price lists and the like. He has developed pedigrees and lists. Of course he has also cataloged and evaluated each piece and used computer technology to generate emission models for each issue.

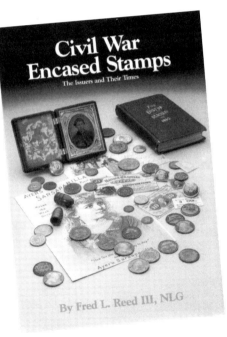

You would expect all of the above in a numismatic catalog. However, he went far beyond that. He researched each issuer in detail and in twenty years he had remarkable results. You will love the text and amazing graphics in this book.

Civil War Encased Stamps by Fred Reed is a monumental new reference. It has been TWENTY YEARS in the making: 558 pages, $65.

BNR Press
132 E. Second Street
Port Clinton, Ohio 43452-1115-04
order via voice or fax 800 793-0683
also (419) 732-NOTE (6683), e-mail bnrpress@dcache.net

Ian A. Marshall
World Paper Money

c/o Parkway Mall Box 62509
85 Ellesmere Rd. Scarborough
Ontario, Canada M1R 5G8

Phone & FAX 416-445-0286

Specialist in
Military payment certificates, Africa, Europe, German and French Notgeld, British Commonwealth & The Americas.
An Extensive Inventory from A to Z. Rarities and bulk modern uncirculated notes always required.

Retail & wholesale lists upon request
Wants lists actively solicited & worked.

Life member ANA
IBNS • CNA • SPMC • NI • CPMS

R. J. BALBATON.........

BUYS AND SELLS

- U. S. LARGE AND REGULAR SIZE NOTES
- CONFEDERATE STATES CURRENCY
- ENCASED POSTAGE STAMPS
- ALLIED MILITARY CURRENCY
- BOOKS ON VARIOUS AREAS OF NUMISMATICS
- COLONIAL AND CONTINENTAL CURRENCY
- EPHEMERA OF DIFFERENT TYPES
- INTERNATIONAL BANKNOTES
- MILITARY PAYMENT CERTIFICATES
- OBSOLETE BANKNOTES AND MERCHANTS SCRIP
- SELECTED WORLD COINS
- UNITED STATES COINS OF ALL TYPES

We respond best to priced offers. We'll buy one piece or a hoard of an item! Timely FREE price lists or catalogs issued in most of the above listed areas of interest.

We welcome your inquiry whether BUYING or SELLING, contact me now.
Member of: P.C.D.A., A.N.A., N.E.N.A., A.P.S., etc.
AUTHORIZED SUBMISSION CENTER FOR :
P.C.G.S., A.N.A.C.S.
*****more than 35 years of service to collectors*****

DORIC COINS & CURRENCY
POB 911
No. Attleboro, MA 02761-0911
508-699-2266 FAX: 508-643-1154

MPC

bought and sold

Now paying
$10,000

for the following uncirculated replacements:

$5 series 481, 541, 591, 651

also $5,000 or more for others.

Find me some great replacements!!

Fred Schwan

132 E. Second Street

Port Clinton, Ohio 43452-1115-04

voice or fax (419) 732-6683

Confederate and
obsolete notes,
CSA counterfeits
stocks and bonds
(especially automotive)
**obsolete notes,
error notes,
national bank notes,
U. S. paper money**

professional • prompt • reliable
service
Lawrence Falater

Colonel Grover Criswell

15001 NE 248th Ave. Road
Salt Springs, FL 32134
(352) 685-2287, 2358
fax (352) 685-1014

Available from the author directly…
Confederate and Southern States Currency, 1992, hardbound 420 page book covers all of the notes ates, Indian territories, the Florida Republic and Territory, and the Republic and independent government of Texas. If you need the information mentioned above, this 1992 work has 255 pages of information and you probably cannot afford to be without it. It is out of print, but we have a few copies, autographed at $75.

Confederate and Southern States Bonds, 380 pages, hardbound, published in 1979, lists all CSA bonds plus those issued by the southern states, the Territory of Florida and the Republic of Texas. This book has been long out of print, but again we have a few autographed copies available at $55.

Confederate and Southern States Currency by William W. Bradbeer, New York, 1915. This is a 1956 reprint by Aubrey Beebe. This book is itself a collector's item and is part of the lore of collecting Confederate money. It is seldom available for less than $100, special $75.

Many other rare and hard to find paper money and historical books are available. Send for our complete list of books…FREE

Our latest *Compendium Price List,* 432 page book listing paper money, autographs, slavery material, Army, Navy papers, documents, and etc. is available for $8 postpaid. Prices includes a refund slip good on a $25.00 order or free with any book offered above.

My 50th year in buying and selling paper money, stocks and bonds, autographs etc.

Great Lakes Bank Note Company
fine intaglio products
hand crafted souvenirs
souvenir cards
engraved business cards
custom engraving
Post Office Box 1146
Olney, MD 20832
(800) 793-0683

BNR Press is your source for paper money information. See our web page for up-to-the-minute information on all parts of the hobby including expanded Hot Contact List™

//http://www/dcache.net/~bnrpress

American Coins and Collectibles
Always Buying, Selling, Appraising

ACC President Richie Self has purchased over $3,000,000 annually in coins and currency from people just like you. *"We want your business!"*

- Competitive prices paid on all U. S., Confederate, and obsolete paper money, as well as a wide variety of U. S. coins.

- Over 100 years cumulative experience and a friendly sales staff.

- Financially secure with banking and trade references available on request.

American Coins and Collectibles is always buying and selling

- Confederate currency
- Obsolete currency
- Broken bank notes
- Southern states notes

- Fractional currency
- United States currency
- Historic newspapers
- Rare autographs

- Rare maps
- Civil War artifacts
- Confederate bonds
- Early Americana

ANA–R154522   SPMC–8978
Louisiana Professional Coin Dealers Association

American Coins and Collectibles, Inc.
855 Pierremont Rd., Suite 123 Shreveport, LA 71106 phone (318)-868-9077

1-800-865-3562

Hot Contact List™

Dealers and resources for collectors

Allens	(614) 882-3937
American Coins & Collectibles	(800) 865-3562
American Numismatic Association	(800) 367-9723
Dick Balbaton	(508) 699-2266
Fred Bart	(810) 979-3400
Keith Bauman	(810) 262-1514
BNR Press	(419) 732-6683, 734-6683
toll free	(800) 793-0683
fax	(419) 732-6683
fax	(800) 793-0683
e-mail	bnrpress@dcache.net
Ed Carn	(614) 882-3937
Currency Dealer Newsletter	(310) 515-7369
David Cieniewicz	(205) 852-7015
fax	(617) 357-8163
Coinage	(805) 644-3824
Coin Dealer Newsletter	(310) 515-7369
Coin World	(800) 253-4555
Grover Criswell	(352) 685-2287
fax	(352) 685-1014
Tom Denly	(617) 482-8477
fax	(617) 357-8163
Doric Coins & Currency	(508) 699-2266
fax	(508) 643-1154
Early American Numismatics	(619) 459-4159
fax	(619) 459-4373
Lawrence Falater	(517) 869-2541
fax	(517) 869-2994
Great Lakes Bank Note Company	(800) 793-0683
Dana Linet	(619) 459-4159
fax	(619) 459-4373
Lowell C. Horwedel	(317) 583-2748
fax	(317) 583-2763
Krause Pulications	(715) 445-2214
Ian Marshall also fax	(416) 445-0286
Memphis Coin Club	(901) 754-6118
Bob Merrill (Heritage)	(214) 528-3500
Stanley Morycz	(513) 898-0114
John Parker	(404) 351-7960
Bob Reed	(504) 361-5684
fax	(504) 361-1808
John Rowe	(214) 826-3036
fax	(214) 823-1923
Fred Schwan	(419) 732-6683
Richie Self	(318) 868-9077
Hugh Shull	(803) 432-8500
fax	(803) 432-9958
R. M. Smythe	(212) 943-1880
toll free	(800) 622-1880
fax	(212) 908-4047
Scott Winslow Associates	(603) 472-7040
fax	(603) 472-8773
e-mail	SWins82687@aol.com
Crutch Williams	(281) 334-3297
e-mail	crutch@prodigy.com

Auction companies

Early American Numismatics	(619) 459-4159
fax	(619) 459-4373
Heritage Rare Coins	(800) 872-6467
Scott Winslow Associates	(603) 472-7040
fax	(603) 472-8773
e-mail	SWins82687@aol.com

Publications

BNR Press	voice/fax (419) 732-6683
Coinage	(805) 644-3824
Coin World	(800) 253-4555
Currency Dealer Newsletter	(310) 515-7369
Krause Pulications	(715) 445-2214

Airline reservations

America West	(800) 235-9292
American	(800) 433-7300
Continental	(800) 525-0280
Delta	(800) 221-1212
Hawaiian	(800) 367-5320
Midwest Express	(800) 452-2022
Northwest	(800) 225-2525
Southwest	(800) 435-9792
TWA	(800) 221-2000
United	(800) 241-6522

Hotel reservations

Best Western	(800) 528-1234
Budgetel	(800) 428-3438
Clarion/Choice Hotels	(800) 221-2222
Courtyard by Marriott	(800) 321-2211
Days Inn	(800) 325-2525
Doubletree	(800) 528-0444
Drury Inns	(800) 325-8300
Embassy Suites	(800) 362-2779
Excell Inns	(800) 356-8013
Fairmont	(800) 527-4727
Fairfield by Marriott	(800) 228-2800
Hampton Inns	(800) 426-7866
Hilton	(800) 445-8667
Holiday Inn	(800) 465-4329
Hyatt	(800) 233-1234
Inter-Continental	(800) 327-0200
Lowes	(800) 235-6397
Marriott	(800) 228-9290
Motel 6	(800) 437-7486
Omni	(800) 843-6664
Outrigger Resorts	(800) 733-7777
Peabody	(800) 732-2639
Preferred Hotels	(800) 323-7500
Radisson	(800) 333-3333
Ramada	(800) 272-2632
Red Lion	(800) 547-8011
Red Roof	(800) 843-7663
Sheraton	(800) 325-3535
Super 8	(800) 800-8000
Sofitel	(800) 763-4835
Stouffer	(800) 468-3571
Westin	(800) 228-3000
Wyndham	(800) 822-4200